Risky Living

Where Eagles Soar

A Way Through the Wilderness

ISBN 0 85476 829 7

Published by
KINGSWAY PUBLICATIONS
Lottbridge Drove, Eastbourne, BN23 6NT, England.
E-mail: books@kingsway.co.uk

Designed and produced for the publishers by
Bookprint Creative Services, P.O. Box 827, BN21 3YJ, England.
Printed in Great Britain.

Reproduced from the original typesetting
of the single-volume editions.

RISKY LIVING

Keys to Inner Healing

Jamie Buckingham

KINGSWAY PUBLICATIONS
EASTBOURNE

Contents

Foreword

In a recent issue of *Reader's Digest* I ran across an article by the renowned architect, Peter Blake, who is also editor-in-chief of an international publication called *Architecture Plus*. In the opening paragraph of his article, Blake said:

> There exists a great temptation, in the life of an artist or scientist or modern architect like myself, to commit oneself to a dogma in one's youth and then to build one's entire work on that foundation. Unhappily for me and for some of my friends, the premises upon which we have almost literally built our world are crumbling.

As I read I realised Blake was not talking just about architecture and architects. He was talking about theology, about life. He was talking about me, about my wife, and about my friends. I read on.

> We have begun to discover that almost nothing that we were taught by our betters in or out of the architecture schools [and here I inserted, as I read, theological schools] of the mid-century has stood the test of time. Nothing – or almost nothing – turns out to have been entirely true (*RD*, May 1975, p. 163).

I let my mind drift back to that opening day on the campus of the Baptist seminary I attended in Ft Worth, Texas. Fresh from college, I was eager to get started on my theological training. Wandering about the campus, I discovered the cornerstone on the administration building. There, chiselled in granite, was a portion of the Scripture which was actually the motto of the seminary: 'As ye go, preach . . . ' (Matthew 10:7).

The Scripture verse, like everything else I had ever been taught, was incomplete. Unfinished. Where there should have been some kind of practical application, there was only an ellipsis, three dots signifying there was more, but that it wasn't important. Like all of us, the founding fathers were walking as best they could in the light they had. Their mistake came, perhaps, when they determined to chisel their theology – with all its incompleteness – in stone. As a result, a lot of us in that mid-century generation did the same as Peter Blake. We committed ourselves to a dogma in our youths which later turned out to be not entirely true. Like many of the others around me, I made the same commitment, only to find that when the rains came, my foundation crumbled beneath me. My theological house as well as my reputation and security – all fell.

Yet out of the ashes, like the fabled Phoenix, came a new being. It began with a dazzling experience I now recognise was the 'baptism in the Holy Spirit', and has continued ever since. Almost at once I became aware that there was more to that ancient command of Jesus to his disciples than to simply 'go preach'. It was as though blinkers had fallen from my eyes. I turned to the Bible and read with new understanding.

> As ye go, preach, saying, the kingdom of heaven is at hand. Heal the sick, cleanse the lepers, raise the dead, cast out devils; freely ye have received, freely give (Matthew 10:7, 8).

During those first years following my experience with the Holy Spirit, I mistakenly thought the 'more' that I had discovered was limited to the sensational miracles found in the latter part of that verse. I was enamoured with the 'gift ministries': healing the sick, raising the dead, casting out devils, et cetera.

Then gradually I began to realise that even more important than the command to heal the sick and raise the dead, was the message that 'the kingdom of heaven is at hand'.

There is more to Christianity than the experience of conversion, the experience of joining a church, the experience of the baptism in the Holy Spirit, the experience of deliverance from evil spirits. True, Jesus told His disciples that 'signs and wonders' would follow their ministry, but it took me several years before I realised that statement was given to the disciples as a graduation address – and then only after three years of intense training in discipleship.

I have finally realised that the deepest hunger in the hearts of men and women is not to see miracles, but to enter the kingdom of God. Of course it is here that miracles abound, but to try to build a superstructure before the foundation is laid, always leads to disaster.

Unfortunately, even among those who are 'walking in the Spirit', the commands of Jesus often go begging.

Love one another.
Be kind, tenderhearted, forgiving of one another.
Look not upon yourselves as better than others.
Walk the second mile.
Turn the other cheek.
Give with abandon.
Keep no score of wrongs done.
Lay down your life for the brethren.

Of such is the kingdom of Heaven.

Until we begin to walk in these simple commands, the real questions which plague us through life will go unanswered. Is it possible for me to be happy? Will I always scream at the children? Do I have to live with this lustful spirit forever? Why am I fat and miserable? Will I ever reach the place where I won't lose my temper with my wife? Why does my stomach get all knotted up when I think about that event in the past? Can I be healed so I won't withdraw in self-pity every time I hear the name of the mistress my husband used to keep?

The Holy Spirit came not only to comfort the afflicted, but to afflict the comfortable. Unfortunately, across the years many of us have become salt without savour, wine without ferment, rooted and rutted into our moulds of immaturity and selfishness. We have grown comfortable, finding it easier to wear a mask than to permit ourselves to be seen by living transparently – and run the risk of being seen for what we really are.

That's really what this book is all about. Transparency. Openness. God knows I'm not there yet. The day before I sat down to write the final draft of this book I found myself in an argument with my wife. And because she didn't want to do the rather brash thing I had suggested, I stormed out of the room calling her a 'stick in the mud'.

There was a time I would have called her something a lot worse than that. And there was a time I wouldn't have admitted that we argued. I'm different from what I used to be and I know that public confession of the truth about myself, and willingness to allow others to peer into my life and see my imperfections, are not only evidence of growth, but integral to the healing-growth process itself.

When the time arrived for me to type the final draft of this manuscript, Jackie and I agreed that the thing for me to do was get alone somewhere I could work undisturbed. So, picking up my typewriter, notes, dictionary, Bible, and a ream of clean paper, I drove south to a motel along the highway where I ensconced myself in a small, sterile room overlooking an orange grove – and began to write.

The last day, as I was finishing the final pages, I heard a familiar knock at the door. It was the same young maid who had come in every day at the same time to change the bed and bring fresh towels. Always before she had worked around me, being careful not to bother the growing stacks of paper on the unused bed or disturb the various piles of notes lying on the dresser and tables. This day, however, she began to ask questions. Maybe she had never seen a writer at work, or maybe she figured I was about to leave. Whatever it was, that morning she was serious.

Her name was Debbie. At twenty-four years of age she was in the process of getting a divorce, although she was four months pregnant and supporting two other children at home. 'My husband's hooked on drugs bad,' she said. 'He finally left me and the kids, so I had to get this job. You won't believe some of the stuff I have to take just to keep my job, but it's better than nothing.'

She asked if she could sit down for a minute and rest. 'It's hard to work when you're pregnant,' she said. Then, looking over at me she blurted out, 'You're a Christian, aren't you?'

I nodded.

'I thought so,' she said. 'I saw your Bible when I came in the other day, and I've been reading the stuff you've thrown in your wastepaper basket.' Then her eyes filled with tears and she asked, 'Do you think a person like me can ever be happy?'

So it's for Debbie, and all the others just like her, that this book is written. All those who are self-sufficient should stop here. The rest won't apply to you. But if you are needy, if your inner person is lonely, empty, and confused, then read on. Happiness *is* possible.

Remember, I'm talking about risky living. The kind that, if practised, will turn your entire world upside down. But, what's the use of living if you don't attempt the impossible – even if it kills you.

1

DIVINE MADNESS

The question that continually bothers me is: Why am I not able to hear from God directly? Why is my channel always clogged? I want to hear from God, but I continue to stumble through life, believing that God has a perfect plan for me to fulfil, yet never quite getting there. At times I sense there is a great wall between me and the perfect will of God. Like Paul, the things I want to do, I don't do. The things I don't want to do, I am constantly doing. So I keep asking, is it possible to really hear the voice of God? And if so, is it possible to follow his direction?

It's easy for me to rationalise this and say, 'The real problem in my life is my wife. If Jackie would hear clearly from God, then everything else would fall into place.' But I know that is not the case. As much as I want her to hear from God, my real problem is me.

Every time I start down some path, I invariably come to a fork in the road. It's at these forks of decision where I have my problems. I start, then I stop. I'm constantly backing up and starting over again, so that far more time is spent regrouping in confusion than marching forward in victory.

Now, after a number of years of going and coming, I have determined that the secret of hearing the voice of God is contained in Romans 8:5, 6. Here Paul says:

For they that are after the flesh do mind the things of

*the flesh; but they that are after the Spirit the things of the
Spirit. For to be carnally minded is death, but to be
spiritually minded is life and peace.*

A quick caution here. The word 'flesh' in the Bible does
not refer to your problem with overweight or lust. Those
kinds of thing only *result* from walking according to the flesh.
But Paul is talking about a kingdom in which we live, a
materialistic realm which puts wax in our ears and prevents
us from hearing the voice of God, because, in that kingdom,
we rule.

The Bible recognises another kind of kingdom. A kingdom
of the Spirit. In this kingdom God rules, and all who enter
become his servants. They hear his voice and walk in his
abundance.

Everybody who rules in his own kingdom is doomed to
die. In fact, Jesus says they are dead already.

> *He that believeth on him is not condemned; but he that
> believeth not is condemned already . . . (John 3:18).*

I vividly remember the afternoon a pretty, fifteen-year-old
girl came into my study. Her world had fallen apart. She was
pregnant. Rejected by her parents, she had taken the jagged
edge of a Band-Aid tin and had attempted suicide by
lacerating the arteries in her wrist. Happily she was unsuc-
cessful, but it was indicative of her hopelessness. I talked to
her, but I don't think she heard anything. She left, telling me
that sooner or later she would again attempt suicide. She
gave me a poem she had written. In four lines it collected the
thoughts of a million lonely kids. It said:

These are the ones on whose tombs they'll inscribe:
'Died at fifteen, buried at seventy-five.'
Out of the night we breath a sigh
For those who are dead, but cannot die.

To live in the dimension of the Spirit is life and peace. To
live in our own kingdoms is death.

Somewhere in this life, perhaps only in isolated areas, there are people who walk through this world exuding life and peace. They are surrounded by the problems of old age, poverty, sickness, grief, pain, hatred, and loneliness. Yet their spirit is a spirit of life and peace. No matter what comes at them, no matter what kind of catastrophe falls on their lives, inside they are filled with life and peace. They are like the rose petals which, when crushed, give forth beautiful perfume. Rare. Seldom seen. But they do exist.

God wants to bring us to that place. Yet we are wordlings. We are a people of reason and logic. We judge success by outward standards. We make our decisions on the basis of verifiable data: Is this course of action going to cost us money? Is it going to cost us reputation? Is it going to cost us popularity? As a result of our logical answers to these questions, we turn either right or left at the forks of our roads.

Last Christmas I had a long talk with our teenage son who was home from college for the holidays. Like many college students, he was always short of money. So, as fathers often do with children who handle money with reckless abandon, I called him aside for a conference. We sat on the side of the bed in an upstairs bedroom and our conversation went something like this:

'Bruce, you are spending too much money out there at college.'

'But, dad, what's money for? Isn't it to spend?'

'Well, yes, son. That's the purpose of money. But you also need to save some for tomorrow.'

'Is that what you're doing with the money you make?'

'Yes, we spend only as much as we need. The rest we save for the day when we won't have any earning power.'

He just sat there looking at me. And the more he looked the more uncomfortable I became. I had a feeling he had been listening to my sermons on the joy of giving – and taking them literally. I slowly began to realise that I was saying to

17

him, 'Son, the time may come when God won't provide for you, and you'll have to provide for yourself. The *wise* man is one who stores money away to meet this kind of emergency.' Yet even as I spoke, I realised I was giving him the wisdom of this world, rather than the word of God.

We talked long that afternoon, and I received as much insight into God's plan for money as he did. Perhaps even more, as I realised how much I was depending on myself rather than God.

Plato, the Greek philosopher and a disciple of Socrates, said that there are three valid sources of knowledge. The first source of knowledge, according to Plato, is the five senses. We share these with the animals. We taste, hear, see, feel, and smell.

The second source of knowledge, according to Plato, is reason. Reason is the thing that sets us above all the other creatures. It enables us to reach a logical conclusion. It is this process that enables me to sit down and deduce, 'Okay, I'm going to have fifteen more productive years during which I shall earn money. After that, my earning power will be greatly diminished.' Therefore, on the basis of this premise I should begin to lay aside money for the time when the productive years will be over. Then I will not have to live off my children, who might one day come to me and say, 'Daddy, you are spending too much money. You're going to have to cut down.' There's nothing wrong with this kind of reasoning, but it can take you only a limited distance.

That's why Plato saw a third concept of knowledge. He called it 'divine madness', referring to the entire world of spiritual communication. Here a man receives knowledge in a way which is neither through the senses nor through the mind. It comes from the Source of Power to our Spirit. Some might call it *intuition*, others, *inspiration*.

Later, Aristotle, who was Plato's disciple, eliminated this third, or supernatural, source. He thought the entire intuitive faculty was invalid. Unfortunately, much of what we experience in the Western world is based on Aristotle's philosophy.

We say if knowledge does not come through our senses or our reason, it is invalid. If we can't taste it, feel it, smell it, or if we can't deduce it, it is not real. Thus have we lost that vital balance which brings maturity to decisions based on knowledge received through the senses or by reason. In the Eastern and primitive cultures, references to the spiritual world abound. Dreams, visions, supernatural communication, talk of spiritual things – are common. Walk through the marketplace in Bangkok, Katmandu, or Manila, and everyone is talking about communication with the spiritual world. But for a man to use such language on the floor of the Stock Exchange, or in a board meeting at ICI, would be sheer madness. Here in the West we rule out all talk of God giving us divine knowledge as poppycock. Oh, we believe in God, but we are unwilling to believe he can, or will, communicate to us through any means other than the senses and reason.

I do not believe God intends to destroy our reasoning power. In fact, I believe he often uses it to communicate his purpose. In Isaiah 30, the prophet indicates that if a man is walking with God, he will basically walk by listening to his reason and following the five senses. However, if he steps off the path, or makes a wrong turn at the fork of the road, then he can expect to hear a gentle voice from within giving correction.

> And thine ears shall hear a word behind thee, saying, This is the way, walk ye in it, when ye turn to the right hand, and when ye turn to the left (Isaiah 30:21).

Now we, in our Western idiom, call that 'conscience'. We would be much more accurate if we called it the 'voice of God'. But our 'reason' forbids that. We know that if we stand in the marketplace and say, 'God told me . . . ' we'll be laughed at. Therefore we opt for a cultural cop-out. Instead of saying, 'No, I shall not do that because God forbids me,' we grin and say, 'My conscience would bother me.'

I was amazed, during a visit to Thailand last year, to hear the wife of a high government official say at a luncheon, 'The spirits commanded me to do a certain thing'. I looked around at the military and political leaders who were present and saw they were all nodding their heads. They understood. But here in America we are unwilling to acknowledge the presence of God – or evil spirits. Why? Because we are *reasonable* people.

Reason causes us to say we should not act until we have full understanding. Until all the facts are in. But the Bible says that if we dwell in the secret place of the Most High (that is, if we are living in the kingdom of God), we shall abide under the shadow of the Almighty (Psalm 91:1). In other words, the closer we get to God, the more we walk by faith and not by sight.

The more you walk by faith and not by sight, the less you need to understand him. Something else begins to happen. He takes over and directs your walk, your life, by divine intuition.

In Matthew 14 we read the story of Jesus walking on the water. When Simon Peter, the big fisherman, saw Jesus out there, he must have realised it was illogical. Peter had been raised on the water. He knew it was unreasonable for a man to walk on the surface. But when Jesus beckoned to Peter and said, 'Come!' Peter forgot about reason. In a moment of spiritual exuberance, he threw his legs over the side of the boat and started out on the water himself – walking towards Jesus. It was not until his reasoning faculty began to work again that he sank. He had moved from faith to sight, only to discover that while Aristotle had grasped a portion of the truth, he had missed the better part.

Some of you have been there before. You started out in faith, but the closer you got to God, the darker things became. Then you backed off, reaching for the safety of the boat. 'Boy, have I done a foolish thing,' you think, as you head back to 'safety'. But had you gone on, you would have come into the actual presence of the Lord himself.

In my little studio on the second floor of my house, I have an electric typewriter. If I were to come in one morning and flick the switch and not hear the familiar whirr, I would immediately look to see if my machine were plugged in. I wouldn't sit in my chair in front of the keyboard and wail, 'Oh, electricity, please come into my typewriter and make it work.' Nor would I bow my head in prayer and plead, 'God, in the name of Jesus, fill my typewriter with power.' No, I would simply plug the cord into the socket, which is the outlet for power, which in turn is connected with the source of power, and wait for the machine to begin to hum.

The entire universe is filled with the healing power of God. But in order to be healed, one has to come in contact with that power. God is the source of the power and the Holy Spirit is the outlet. Aristotle may call it invalid, and Plato may refer to it as 'divine madness', but the Bible calls it the anointing of the Holy Spirit. Without it we are powerless, ignorant, and left to our own devices.

God has made a world that is run by law – his laws. There are laws of nature, gravity, physics, chemistry, sound, and light. But there is another law – the law of love and grace – which supersedes all other laws. When God invokes this law, that is, when he intervenes in the affairs of men personally, we call it a miracle. But to God, such dealings are just as 'natural' as an apple falling downwards when it drops from a tree. Reason may say man cannot walk on water. But faith allows us to do the impossible.

Dr Alexis Carrel, physician and scientist, declared that he had seen skin cancer disappear at the command of faith. That is not breaking the laws of nature. It is the superimposition of a higher law. If we were to investigate such healings we would always find that somewhere, someone along the line had reached down and plugged themselves into the available power – the power of the Holy Spirit who transcends all man's reason and senses.

There are millions of Christians who have died of disease whom God longed to heal. Countless others live on in misery and defeat because they are unwilling to pay the price of inner healing. God has provided, in the person of his Holy Spirit, the healing agent. All we have to do is reach out and touch him.

When we are under the shadow of the Almighty, we are not walking by sight, but by faith. Yet it is here, in the shadowy place, that he covers us with his wings and gives his angels charge over us, to keep us in all our ways. It is here we find provision, protection, and joy – and healing. It cannot be reasoned out. It can only be accepted. By faith.

2

THE BLACK PIT

When you choose to follow Jesus, you voluntarily surrender the right to choose, or the power to vary, the consequences of that decision. From that time on, what happens to you is the responsibility of the one you voluntarily designated as the Lord of your life. It is his responsibility to direct the course of your life so you will eventually 'be conformed to the image of his Son' (Romans 8:29). Thus every circumstance is part of God's design to bring us to maturity.

In his great chapter on maturity, the Apostle Paul says God is never satisfied with us

> *Till we all come in the unity of the faith, and of the knowledge of the Son of God, unto a perfect man, unto the measure of the stature of the fulness of Christ: That we henceforth be no more children, tossed to and fro, and carried about with every wind of doctrine, by the sleight of men, and cunning craftiness, whereby they lie in wait to deceive; but speaking the truth in love, may grow up into him in all things, which is the head, even Christ . . ,* (*Ephesians 4:13-15*).

I spent a night with my good friends, Dick and Betty Schneider, in their home near Morristown, New Jersey. I first met Dick at a writers' workshop sponsored by *Guideposts* magazine in 1967. Later Dick joined the staff of *Guideposts* and eventually moved up to the position of senior editor before he joined some of his former associates from *Guideposts* in a new publishing company.

As I was preparing for bed Dick came into my room and said a dear old friend of his wanted to meet me before I returned to Florida the next day. Since I needed to catch an early plane, Dick had invited him for breakfast. He promised me I was in for a pleasant experience.

Like many good editors, Dick underplayed his expectations. When I came down the next morning, I was greeted by a man in his early seventies. His name was Seabury Oliver and his grey striped trousers and conservative black coat gave the appearance of a man of refined taste and deep cultural origins. This, coupled with his slight British accent, made me wonder if the Schneiders had not imported him directly from across the Atlantic!

Dick introduced Mr Oliver as a financial consultant who had offices both in New York and in New Jersey. A widower, he was now semi-retired and living alone.

As we talked over Betty's breakfast, I soon realised that his spiritual heritage was just as rich as his business knowledge. He was attending the services at the First Christian Assembly in Plainfield, New Jersey, where Dick and Betty often worshipped. It didn't take me long to realise there was much I could learn from him.

During the course of our conversation I asked him how he came to know the Lord in such a deep, personal way.

He lowered his cup of tea and with a slight twinkle in his eye answered me in one word.

'Trouble.'

Then he added, 'How does anyone come to know him?'

In one sentence he had summed up the heart of Paul's theology found in the eighth chapter of Romans.

> *And we know that all things work together for good to them that love God, to them who are the called according to his purpose (Romans 8:28).*

In the jargon of the professional writer there is a term which describes that place in life when all the lights go out, when all our crutches are snatched away, when we physically, emotionally, and spiritually 'hit bottom'. The term is 'the black pit'. When a Christian writer interviews someone, he automatically begins to probe around looking for the black pit. When he finds it, he knows he has a story, for it is here that God has the best opportunity to speak in words we all can understand.

In Jesus' parable of the Prodigal Son, he tells about a boy who had everything his heart could desire, but was restless because he had to live under the authority of his father. He wanted to run his own life. Demanding his inheritance, he left home and 'wasted his substance with riotous living.' It's an old, familiar tale – common to all of us. After he had spent all he had, he learned his security had been in the wrong things. His friends disappeared as quickly as his money, and when hard times came he hired himself out to feed pigs – dipping into the swill in order to stay alive. For a Jewish boy, feeding pigs and having to eat their slop must have been the blackest pit of all. But it was here, for the first time, he saw himself as he was. Realising how much better off he would be at home, he determined to go back to his father, admit his mistake, and offer himself as a hired servant. Leaving the pigsty he headed home, only to be welcomed by his father – not as a hired servant, but as a lost son who had been found.

Jesus told that story not just to illustrate the tender love of the heavenly Father for all those who decided to come home, but to point out a principle of life. No man ever comes to inner healing until he has had the outer surface stripped away so the light of reality can shine on the impurities in the dark recesses of his life.

We cannot serve Jesus Christ on our own terms. We cannot insist that, if we follow him, he must guarantee that certain kinds of things will never happen to us, or that certain other kinds of things must happen. Whatever method he chooses to shape our lives is his business, not ours.

25

I received some fresh insight into this when I attended a Camp Farthest Out (CFO) at Ardmore, Oklahoma. I was sharing the rostrum with a Methodist evangelist, Tommy Tyson, and a grand old Bible scholar, Estelle Carver. During one of the morning sessions Miss Carver, who was in her mid-eighties, was speaking about the gentle ways God uses to mould us until we begin to look like Jesus Christ. The more I listened, the more painful it became. It was as though God was attacking the canker sores in my inner nature with a sharp scalpel, scraping and cutting out the infection. On the verge of tears, I whispered to my wife that I had to leave the room. She reached over, squeezed my hand, then released me. She understood.

It was early April and the wind whipping off the water of Lake Murray was sharp and chilly. The little white clouds scudding through the sky seemed to match the frothing whitecaps which lashed the rocky shore. Wanting to be completely alone, I walked out on the long wooden dock and sat cross-legged, my back against a large piling which gave only partial protection from the biting wind. It was one of those incisive times when a man doesn't want warmth and security, but needs to expose himself to the elements as well as to the searching finger of God's Spirit – the *ruach* (or wind) which was the Old Testament word for the Holy Spirit.

Almost at once a Scripture verse came to mind.

Looking unto Jesus, the author and finisher of our faith (Hebrews 12:2).

I had read this verse many times and always envisioned the writer talking about the spiritual qualities of Jesus. 'Author and finisher' had always seemed synonymous with the first and the last, the alpha and the omega, the beginning and the end. But now I saw it with a fresh understanding. Jesus was a carpenter, and these were carpenter's terms. Author meant creator, architect, the one who drew the plans and nailed the thing together. Finisher was also a carpenter's term. The man who does the finishing work on a piece of furniture is the fellow who works with sandpaper, smoothing and polishing until the creation reflects the face of the creator.

That's what Jesus was doing to me. In fact, that's what he had been doing ever since that summer night back in 1953 when I turned my life over to him. As I reflected, I could see that everything that had happened to me since that time had been designed by God to finish me, to bring me to the place where I was conformed to the image of his Son.

In 1950, after having been members of churches for a number of years, after having raised their children in the best traditions of morality and ethics their humanistic backgrounds afforded, my mother and father had a dynamic conversion. Daddy was already in his sixties and was considered by the members of his church and his business associates to be a dedicated churchman – and thus a Christian. However, his Christianity was cultural rather than personal. It took a black pit experience for him to reach that place the Prodigal Son reached when he came to himself. His conversion, along with Mother's, was dramatic and life-changing. Almost at once they began to concentrate their efforts on their blacksheep son – me.

It took three years before I finally gave in and agreed to accompany them for a week during the summer to a place called Word of Life Camp on an island in Schroon Lake in the Adirondack Mountains of New York State. One night, during a campfire service, an invitation was given asking those present who had never made commitments to Jesus Christ to come forward. I was hesitant, shy. When the others stepped forward, I hung back. However, after all the others had returned to their rooms, I lay under the stars, watching the sparks from the fire drift heavenward, and surrendered my life to Christ. I did not want to be as one of those sparks which burned brightly and then died to fall back to earth as dead ash. I wanted to be like one of the stars which burned forever. I asked him to take my life.

I didn't know it then, but I had surrendered the right to

27

choose or the power to vary the consequences of my decision. In the fifth book of the law, Moses laid down an unerring principle concerning the nature of God. He always requires our vows of us.

> *When thou shalt vow a vow unto the Lord thy God, thou shalt not slack to pay it: for the Lord thy God will surely require it of thee; and it would be sin in thee (Deuteronomy 23:21).*

One of the reasons there are so many unhappy Christians is they have never understood this principle. They feel God should do them favours, heaping them with material rewards and benefits, rather than working as a carpenter to shape their lives back into his own image.

My own black pit came in the autumn of 1967. After a series of failures in the ministry, I was almost ready to give up on organised Christianity as irrelevant, a force without power, salt without taste. I had signed a contract to write my first book, *Run Baby Run*, the life of a young Brooklyn boy from Puerto Rico, Nicky Cruz, who had been converted under the street ministry of David Wilkerson of *The Cross and the Switchblade* fame. But even the excitement of becoming a professional writer did not ease the nagging feeling that there was something missing from my life. For several months I had been hearing stories of miracles happening in some corners of Christianity, but it all seemed so elusive, so far away from where I stood culturally. I knew Jesus and his followers laid hands on the sick, even the dead, and saw them restored. But I was unable to relate that to our modern, sophisticated type of Christianity which was confined to church buildings and church programmes. I was on the verge of giving up the whole thing as impossible when God broke through in a dramatic way.

In November of 1967 I met with Nicky Cruz to begin my research on the book. My publisher, Dan Malachuk, a New

Jersey businessman, had just established Logos International. *Run Baby Run* was his first major book, and he encouraged me to interview Nicky on his own turf – the streets of Brooklyn.

It was a cold, rainy afternoon when Nicky, Dan, and I came down the stairs in the old Teen Challenge building on Clinton Avenue in Brooklyn. In the vestibule we found our way blocked by a heroin addict, a 'junkie', who had dragged himself in out of the rain and lay retching and moaning on the stairway. As we stepped around and over his shivering body, Nicky reached out and laid his hand on the back of the man's head. I watched in silence. That anyone would touch such a miserable creature was a shattering experience, especially since his head was full of open, running sores. But it wasn't the fact that Nicky prayed for the man, it was how he prayed – in a strange, unknown tongue. It lasted only a few seconds, and then Nicky moved on.

I had never heard tongues before, always believing it was some kind of 'trance-talk'. How well I remembered the time when I was a seminary student in Ft Worth and the students and faculty were all a twitter about some of the people in a Baptist Church in nearby Handley, Texas, who were reportedly 'speaking in tongues'. The reaction ranged from 'tsk-tsk' to 'that's heresy'. But this wasn't heresy. It was power. Within seconds the junkie ceased his heaving, groaning, and shaking. Laying his head over on the steps, he simply went to sleep. Attendants from Teen Challenge helped him up the stairs to a bedroom. I learned later he had been completely delivered from dope in those few seconds.

But it was the few seconds that 'blew my mind'. Something had happened. Something spectacular. It was as though God had come down and surrounded us in the vestibule of that old building in Brooklyn.

Nicky and Dan walked on outside, laughing and talking, leaving me behind dumbfounded. Shaking myself loose, I finally caught up with them. We stood in the freezing rain on the pavement while I gasped breathlessly, 'Didn't you see what happened back there? That prayer was answered instantly!'

I was not accustomed to instant answers. Dan looked at me strangely and said, 'Don't you Baptists believe God answers prayer?'

It was not a fair question. Baptists do believe God answers prayer. And so did I. It was just that I had never seen it happen in such a dramatic fashion.

After we got in the car and headed back towards New Jersey where the Logos offices were situated, I recalled something J. B. Phillips had written in his Translator's Preface to *Letters to Young Churches*, his modern translation of the Epistles of Paul in the New Testament. Phillips said of those early Christians:

Perhaps if we believed what they believed, we might achieve what they achieved.

Was this so? Had I actually seen the 'works of Jesus' carried out by a Puerto Rican kid who could hardly speak English, or was it some kind of illusion I had manufactured because I wanted to believe it so badly?

The secret, Dan told me, was an experience called 'the baptism in the Holy Spirit'.

There followed three months of arguing with myself and with anyone who dared mention the subject of the supernatural power of God. I was afraid, I now realise, to completely turn my intellect and emotions over to God – afraid he might cause me to do something foolish. As long as I was in control, I wouldn't do anything foolish, but if God was in total control could I really be sure? Yet, it was this element of self-control that had brought me to the edge of despair, had thrust me into the black pit. In reality, I was far more out of control than I cared to admit.

Three months later I met Nicky again for our second interview. I flew to Washington, D.C., to attend a regional convention of the Full Gospel Business Men's Fellowship

International (FGBMFI). Nicky was to speak at the youth meetings and it was a good opportunity to spend some more time with him.

Something happened to me that week-end in Washington. It was the beginning of an entirely new life for me. It took me several months to evaluate adequately the experience, and even then I was still too awestruck to arrive at any firm conclusions. But one thing was certain. I was not the same man.

I returned from Washington on a Saturday, and on Sunday morning, February 25, 1968, I met with the small band of people who made up the little Baptist church I was patronising in Melbourne, Florida. All my life I had been afraid to go into the pulpit without first having written out every word I was going to say. But that morning, without notes, I stood before the people and shared from my heart. The following is a word-for-word transcript of what I said.

I am not sure how you will receive what I am about to share with you. It could be construed as the words of a man gone completely insane – or the words of one who has witnessed and experienced the power of God in an awesome way. I shall leave the evaluation up to you.

Last Monday night I attended a prayer meeting held in a school building in Arlington, Virginia. It was made up of businessmen from many churches in the Washington area. [Actually this was a group called 'New Adventures in Prayer' which met under the supervision of a businessman named Jack Zirkle. After more than ten years the meeting is still going with large numbers of people from the Washington area in regular attendance.] There were more than six hundred present. I was dumbfounded at their enthusiasm and freedom of worship. They sang with great intensity, and when they prayed many of them raised their hands. The service was punctuated with shouts of 'Praise God', 'Amen', and 'Thank you, Jesus'.

The next afternoon I went with Nicky and a local

businessman, Al Malachuk [Al is the brother of Dan Malachuk and has for many years been active in the Washington FGBMFI] to the U.S. Naval Academy at Annapolis where Nicky addressed a group of Christian midshipmen. I sat back in amazement as these young middies and their officers shared in the time of testimony. There was no timidity. They spoke boldly of the changing effect of Jesus Christ on their lives. Many of them testified of having been 'baptised in the Holy Spirit'. I was especially impressed with the testimony of a young naval aviator, Lt Commander Bob Wright, who was overflowing about the power of God in his life.

Wednesday night I had my first experience with the Full Gospel Business Men. Al Malachuk chaired the meeting which was held at the huge Shoreham Hotel. I was amazed that they had no formal order of service. They said they were 'following the leadership of the Spirit'.

I had reservations about my participation in the meeting, fearful those attending would be fanatical in nature. But they weren't. They came from all kinds of churches – Methodist, Presbyterian, Baptist, and Episcopal. I was especially interested in the large number of Roman Catholics present, many of them priests and nuns. Al introduced me at the meeting and I spoke for about five minutes, telling about the book and the testimony I felt the book would have. However, I was very ill at ease. The people seemed genuinely interested in what I was saying, and when I finished they clapped in approval.

I took a seat on the front row while the other guests were introduced. During the early part of the service, Al came down off the platform and whispered in my ear that he felt 'led by the Spirit' to ask me to sing a solo. I was dumbstruck. I enjoy singing, but this was a new experience to me. Al returned to the platform after telling me that as soon as the introductions were finished I should come forward. I had no music and my mind had gone blank. I couldn't even remember the words of the Doxology. I made my way around to the organist and asked if she had any music. She was playing by ear. Even the organ bench was empty. By this time Al was motioning for me to come to the microphone. About to panic, I frantically told the organist to begin playing 'How Great Thou Art'. I sang the first verse and the chorus and could remember no more. In desperation I asked the congregation to join me as we sang through the chorus again. They did. My, how they did! They came to their feet singing with more enthusiasm and joy than I had ever experienced in my life. They forgot all about me, and with arms raised towards the ceiling and tears running down their faces, they sang, 'How Great *Thou* Art'. I was deeply moved and almost staggered off the stage to my seat.

The next afternoon I attended a Bible study led by David duPlessis, a South African with a travelling ministry. There were more than 2,000 eager people present, most of them with Bibles and notebooks. I stood next to the wall of the crowded ballroom, carefully observing the people present.

My eyes were drawn to a beautiful young woman sitting on the end of a row. She looked like a fashion model. As we sang 'Amazing Grace', she raised her hand – just one delicately gloved hand – and there was a radiance on her face like I had never seen before.

Directly in front of her was a little, stooped man. He must have been ninety years old. He was bent and feeble, but as we sang, 'When we've been there ten thousand years', he raised his head and the same radiance was on his face. He held up both arms as far as they would go, not much past his chest, and with tears streaming down his face, sang about the glory of heaven. I was so overcome I could hardly breathe.

Something special was going on. Where did this freedom come from? Where did they receive the power to lose their earthly inhibitions? I had to find out.

After the meeting I cornered an Episcopal priest who

had been on the platform. I felt that I would be safer talking to a man with a clerical collar. He agreed to have dinner with me in the dining room prior to the evening service. I confessed I was afraid of these strange people who 'spoke in tongues', yet I needed some answers.

That night, at the dinner table, we openly discussed this experience known as the 'baptism in the Holy Spirit'. I had a growing feeling I was familiar with what he was describing, only I had always referred to it as 'total commitment' or 'surrender'. Yet as we talked, I realised this was not something you did – it was something you received.

'But didn't the Holy Spirit come into me when I accepted Jesus as my Saviour?' I asked.

'Yes, in fact, without him you could not have accepted Christ. Paul says: "No man can say that Jesus is the Lord, but by the Holy Ghost" (I Corinthians 12:3). However, there is more.'

The priest went on to illustrate his point. 'I own an ocean-going ship,' he said. 'Aboard this ship I have a twelve-man life raft. It is bulky, heavy, and contains a cartridge of compressed CO_2. If I throw it overboard in that condtion, however, it will sink. It *contains* the CO_2 (Spirit) but it is not *filled*. Only when the release is pulled does the gas fill the raft, blowing it out to the size and shape for which it was made. That's what the Holy Spirit wants to do to you. He's in you, now he wants to fill you.'

I was still having trouble. 'There's no such thing as a second experience,' I said, quoting some of my former professors.

Much to my embarrassment, he pushed back the dishes on the table, and while those around us looked on, he produced a huge black Bible. He opened it to Acts 9 and very deliberately read me the story of Saul's conversion on the road to Damascus. However, he added, three days later the Holy Spirit sent a man called Ananias to lay hands on Saul that he might 'be filled with the Holy

Ghost (Acts 9:17). I saw, but was afraid.

He asked me what I thought of Mark 16. I told him I simply ignored the last few verses as something I couldn't understand. He asked me if I believed the Bible was true. I said yes. Then he said, 'Why don't you believe these passages?' I had no answer. He asked if I believed that Peter, John, Philip, and the others actually performed miracles. I said yes. He said, 'Do you think God can still perform miracles through his people?' I recalled the experience on the steps of the Teen Challenge building in Brooklyn. Yes, I believed that also. Then he asked the clincher: 'Has he ever performed a miracle through you?' I had no answer.

After supper we hurried back to the main assembly hall. There were more than 3,000 people present. The meeting had already started and the only seat left for me was on the third row directly in front of the preacher.

The meeting began with a series of testimonies. Judge Kermit Bradford from Atlanta told of the amazing power of God which changed his life. A priest from Notre Dame told of receiving the Holy Spirit and later speaking in tongues. Several businessmen gave similar testimonies. All said this new 'infilling' allowed them to witness and praise God without restriction.

All around me people were smiling, clapping, and saying, 'Praise God,' right there in public.

Then the moderator said, 'Let's be quiet and listen for a word from God.' The assembly got unbelievably quiet. It had been noisy before, not bedlam, but a warm, friendly noisiness. Now it was still.

Suddenly from the far back I heard a voice. It was the most beautiful, melodious speaking voice I had ever heard. I knew it was an 'unknown' tongue. Yet it wasn't babble. It was ecstatic. It sounded like some American Indian dialect. The voice spoke in sentences with voice inflections which indicated punctuation. The speaker continued for about a minute and then stopped.

Immediately a man four seats down from me on the same row began to speak in the first person with the most authoritative voice I had ever heard. He said:

I have sent you and anointed you to preach. I shall never leave nor forsake you. I shall be with you always. You will be great in the kingdom of God because it is my Spirit that leads you. The task is great and many are lost, but in my Spirit you shall overcome.

I was overcome. As he spoke I stood trembling, choking back the tears. I had the awesome feeling that this was God's message to me – alone. That out of all these 3,000 people he was speaking to me, the sceptic.

We sat down and I felt that anything else that followed would be anti-climactic. I was embarrassed over my emotional condition, but no one else seemed to notice. The experience of having had a 'word from God' was so strong I could hardly contain it. I wanted to stand back up and shout, 'He spoke to me', but I didn't dare. I had the feeling that if I did, everyone in the room would have shouted, 'Praise God', or something like that.

They introduced the preacher. He was John Osteen, a Southern Baptist from Houston, Texas, a graduate of Baylor University and Southwestern Baptist Theological Seminary. It was, without doubt, the greatest sermon I had ever heard – yet all he did was share his testimony. I identified with everything he said. He told of how he had longed for additional power in his ministry. How he felt that God had intended him for greater things than a denominational box. How he recognised the superficiality and powerless of all his church activities. He told of seeking this power, yet being afraid to receive it. After he received this 'baptism in the Holy Spirit', he began preaching and ministering with new power. He told of one service in India when he put his hands on blind people and they literally received their sight. It was fantastic.

At the close of his message he gave an invitation for any who wanted to accept Christ to come forward. About fifteen did, and he prayed for them right there. Again I was impressed. Everything was definitely Christ-centred.

Then he called all those who wanted to be 'baptised in the Spirit' to come forward. Hundreds responded. I began to feel terribly uncomfortable and wanted to leave the room, but I couldn't get out. I was trapped in the mob of people milling around the front. Some of them were praying, some crying, some laughing, and others speaking in tongues. I kept reminding myself I was there as a writer, I wasn't supposed to get involved. But I was involved. I was right in the thick of the action and couldn't get away from my chair because of the crush of the crowd.

I decided to sit down and wait for things to thin out so I could leave. I put my head on the back of the chair in front of me and suddenly began to cry. I was crying so hard I could hardly catch my breath. It felt like all the dams inside had burst and I was being flooded from within.

I felt someone bump me as he sat down beside me. I tried to look up, but couldn't. I was blinded by the tears. Then I recognised the voice of the Episcopal priest with whom I had eaten dinner. I could sense he was praying for me. I tried to get him to stop, but he kept right on. I was sobbing, 'No, no, no, no.' I wanted to turn loose, but was afraid, still bound to this earth and its kingdoms.

Then I felt an arm go around me from the other side and heard another voice praying. He was asking God to baptise me in the Holy Spirit. I had never gone through such an intense emotional turmoil. I knew that if I turned loose God would take all the things I held precious, leaving me helpless, totally dependent on him. I struggled to hang on, but was crying so hard I could no longer object.

The priest moved around in front of me and put his hand on my head. When he did, something snapped loose inside of me, in the vicinity of my heart. For a split second I wondered if I was going to die. Then I didn't care any more. A great peace swept over me, as though God had taken his hand and wiped away the tears.

I looked up to see who was on the other side. It was Commander Wright, resplendent in his dress uniform, his chest full of ribbons. How he had spotted me in that mob of people I will never know. Here were the only two men in Washington I respected enough to have reached me – and God had put both of them beside me there in the black pit.

That was back in 1968. I closed the testimony that morning saying: 'Whether I'm mad or not, time will tell, but I have the feeling that something inside me has been healed. For the first time in my life I feel like a "whole" person.'

The lights had been turned on in my black pit.

3

LORD OF THE SUBCONSCIOUS

It was on a Sunday morning, almost four years after that remarkable experience with the Holy Spirit, that I became aware of the healing work which had been going on in my inner man – and the tremendous need I had for more. I awoke at my regular time that morning, then realising I could enjoy the luxury of a few minutes of extra sleep, deliberately turned over and buried my head in the pillow.

As I slept, I dreamed. It was a typical dream – inane, senseless, and composed, I think, of various people from my childhood parading back and forth engaging in foolish activity. It lasted only seconds and then was gone.

I awoke and realised I had been dreaming another of my nonsensical dreams. Most of my dreams are like this. One recurring dream has me slogging my way through a gooey swamp. I am up to my knees in thick mud. Each step is laborious and I am panting for breath. Behind me, almost ready to catch up with me, is some kind of monster that is gliding along the surface of the swamp with ease, ready to pounce on me. Fortunately I have always awakened just before he wrapped himself around me.

I seldom give any thought to my dreams, but this morning, standing in the bathroom shaving, I began to run a quick self-inventory.

'Why is it, Jamie, that you never dream of spiritual things?' This bothered me since some of my more spiritual friends were always talking about the great revelations that came to them while they were asleep. They dreamed about angels, cherubim, heavenly hosts, and even about Jesus himself, while my dreams were confined to faceless monsters chasing me through a swamp.

It bothered me, especially since I was beginning to have a deeper walk with God during my waking hours. Dreams, I knew, are the reflections of our real selves. They are, for the most part, the mirror of our souls – the conscious revelation of the subconscious part of our selves.

If the mind were pictured as a deep mountain lake, the consciousness would be the surface and the subconsciousness all that lies beneath the surface. The surface not only reflects all that is around it, but it acts as a receiving point for everything that enters. Except for the contour and capacity of the basin (heredity), everything that is in the lake has been put there (environment) through the conscious. Some of it stays on the surface where it can be seen, but the vast majority of all our experiences have sunk – or been pushed – into the depths of the subconscious.

Everything that has happened to us, from the moment we were conceived in our mothers' womb, is part of that vast reservoir called the subconscious. Most of the unpleasant experiences have been pushed under so we can maintain a relatively calm and pure surface appearance. Yet deep inside, often forgotten yet still very real, lie the painful traumatic experiences that make up a big part of our real selves.

As the conscious mind goes to sleep and relaxes, items from the subconscious – that great storehouse of suppressed material that involves the larger part of the mind – come floating to the surface – much as bubbles rise to the surface of a lake. Often they actually break out into the open, mixing with the conscious mind in sleep, causing us to dream.

The same process takes place when the conscious pain-sensitive mind is put to sleep by an anaesthetic. Sodium Pentothal (sometimes known as 'truth serum') is an anaesthetic used to put the conscious mind to sleep artificially, allowing the subconscious, under the direction of an authority figure or some stimulus, to respond to facts long stored beneath its surface.

When I was in my later years at school I dislocated my elbow during an afternoon football practice. My father and mother went with me to the emergency room of the local hospital where our family doctor, E. B. Hardee, tried to manipulate the arm back into its socket. It would not budge.

'I'm going to give you an injection,' Dr Hardee said. 'It will put you to sleep for a few minutes and while you're asleep, I'll adjust your elbow.'

'Uh, what kind of injection?' I asked.

'Sodium pentothal,' the doctor answered, preparing the needle. 'Now I want you to begin counting backwards from one hundred and . . . '

'Just a minute, doctor,' I said, trying to get up from the stretcher. 'Isn't that the stuff they call "truth serum"?'

He grinned and nodded his head. 'You've been reading too many detective thrillers,' he said.

'Won't that stuff make me say a lot of things I might not ordinarily say?' I asked. Like so many school football players, I had been exposed to some pretty bad language, and had engaged in some of it myself. Not only that, but I had a lot of other junk down inside I didn't want exposed, especially in the presence of my mother and father.

Dr Hardee approached me with the needle. 'Don't worry, son,' he said gently. 'You won't expose anything that's not already in your mind.'

I felt the sharp prick of the needle in my arm and remembered drifting off to sleep saying, 'That's what I was afraid of.'

My parents (bless them) never did say whether I revealed any deep, hidden secrets. They didn't have to. I knew I was capable of it just the same.

Back when I was sixteen it didn't seem very important that my lake was filled with refuse. But now, having made an open profession of faith in Jesus Christ, and having put on all the outward trappings of a Christian, I was concerned about my double life. On the surface I certainly looked like a Christian: I spoke the language of Zion, I controlled my tongue and actions. But down inside I knew I was a cesspool.

In the twelfth chapter of Luke, Jesus talks about the 'leaven of the Pharisees, which is hypocrisy'. He is actually describing each one of us who spends time cleaning off the surface of our lake, but is not willing to pay the price of dredging the refuse from the bottom.

As I stood looking in the mirror that Sunday morning I realised I had given considerable time and effort to keeping the surface of my lake clean. My conscious mind, to the best of my knowledge, was dedicated to God. Yet at the same time I realised that much of me was simply a reflection of those around me. In fact, rather than have someone ripple the surface of my lake and therefore reveal what might be lurking beneath the surface, I found myself often agreeing with everything other people said. That way my surface remained calm, peaceful. Yet all the while, inside, I was a cesspool of disagreement and impurity.

How easy it was to agree with the preacher in church. As I left I would shake his hand and say with a wide grin, 'Great preaching, brother!' This kept the surface of my lake un-ruffled.

But once in the car I would reveal my true self.

More and more, on the surface, my lips were speaking praises to God and my life was showing forth the image of Jesus simply because I willed it to be. But my subconscious, that vast reservoir of who I really was, that area revealed primarily through dreams and sudden disturbances of the surface, still seemed to be as un-Christlike as ever.

That same morning at church I had another vivid illustration of just how devoid of spiritual things most of my subconscious actually was. I was in the process of growing a beard, and it was just beginning to take on some kind of personality of its own, looking less and less each day like I had smeared peanut butter on my face and wrapped my jaws in briers. I was standing in the vestibule of the building, talking to one of the elders, when an old friend, Allen Reid, walked up and with a practical joker's look, reached out, grabbed a pinch of whisker under my chin – and yanked.

I reacted violently – with a clenched fist. He danced back, laughing and pointing to my fist, already up in a fighting position. 'Scratch the surface of the lamb and find a wolf,' he chuckled, much to my embarrassment.

I was chagrined, not that I had reacted (for a man will always react to pain), but that I had reacted with closed fists. Allen had broken the surface of my consciousness and revealed a Christless area where self reigned supreme.

I sat in the back of the room that morning, half-listening to the teaching and half-reflecting on how much my life was out of tune with God's perfect harmony. I remembered how I had reacted the day before in the car park of the grocery store. I had come out of the store with my arms loaded with shopping. A pretty girl had driven up in a sleek sports car and was wriggling out from under the steering wheel. As she did, her skirt slithered up beyond the point of propriety and suddenly I was suffused with lust. It was stupid. I had no intention of being immoral, especially not there in the grocery store car park. But the glands of my body were suddenly activated. On the surface I was God's man of faith and power. Underneath I was a dirty old man.

That afternoon, still smouldering from the revelation of my 'dead-men's-bones-character', I spent some time on the patio helping my teenage son, Bruce, build a wooden gate to fence off our dustbins. He was holding one end of a board while I nailed. During the process he accidentally moved the board just as I was bringing the hammer down. The result was catastrophic. The hammer glanced off the side of my thumb, peeling the flesh. This disturbed the surface of my lake, and roaring out of the muck and goo on the bottom of my subconscious came an expletive I hadn't used since those high school football days.

I looked up at Bruce and his eyes were wide with amaze-

43

ment. Never, not in all his seventeen years, had he heard his daddy say such a word. And with such vigour!'

I quickly regained my composure and apologised. 'I'm sorry, Bruce. I don't know *where* that word came from.'

But I did know. I knew when it had entered my life and who had put it there. I also knew that I had pushed it under the surface of my lake, hoping it would never reappear again. But it had. The stirring of the water with the head of a hammer had been just the right stimulus to bring it forth.

For the most part I had been able to keep my overt reactions under control. (One of the fruits of the Spirit is self-control.) But it bothered me that beneath the seemingly calm and tranquil surface of my life there lay that seething mass of self that was for the most part materialistic, animalistic, carnal, and only slightly flavoured with the Christ who had seeped down from the conscious surface into the dark, hidden areas of the subconscious.

In less than twenty-four hours I had seen evidence that even though my consciousness was under control, my subconscious was still quite capable of fleshy acts. It was not a pleasant revelation.

Not everything that lies beneath the surface of our conscious mind is so easily identifiable. Carol Mull, the wife of the county fire chief in our community and a deeply spiritual person, told me of an incident that illustrates the kind of problem that affects all of us. The Mull's daughter, Cindy, had married a young airman, Dave LeBeau. They were stationed at McDill Air Force Base in Tampa, Florida, and lived in an apartment building with several other couples.

Cindy was eight months pregnant when the apartment building caught on fire. Dave was at the base and she had been resting when she smelled smoke. She rushed out and found the flames already roaring down the hall. Since her father was a fireman, she knew the danger and went from apartment to apartment, frantically warning others and making sure all the children and animals were safe. Several fire engines answered the call and they finally pulled Cindy from the building, assuring her everyone was safe.

Everything they had was destroyed, and Dave and Cindy moved in with friends in the church. They stayed there until after the baby, a little girl named Michele, was born. However, it wasn't long before they began to realise that Michele seemed to have an inordinate fear of loud noises. Especially was she scared of sirens and would look wide-eyed with fright whenever she heard one. Fortunately, her parents knew something about the necessity of inner healing. They began, at an extremely early age, to lay hands on her and pray for her. As she grew older, Dave took her out to the base and showed her the fire engines. When they came to visit Cindy's parents, the Mulls would let her sit in the fire chief's car. Whenever they heard a siren they would love her, comfort her, and pray for her. She's two years old now, and even though she still has a vestige of fear of loud noises, she is rapidly being healed of that wound which scarred her life even before she was born.

Realising that we are a composite of all the experiences we've ever had, the Freudian psychoanalyst spends much of his time digging into our past, our subconscious. He may use drugs, hypnotism, or other forms of therapy to help bring the latent problems to the surface. However, once they have been exposed, the most the secular psychoanalyst can do is help us 'adjust' to our condition.

There is a vast difference, however, between adjusting to the wounds of the past and having them healed. I still remember the sensitive young man who belonged to a rival fraternity when I was in college. He had strong homosexual tendencies and on the advice of a counsellor, sought psychiatric help. After a number of sessions the doctor finally told him he would be a lot happier if he learned to adjust to his gay life. Three weeks later the boy shot himself.

The average man lives behind a mask. His smiles, his laughter, his piety, his shows of confidence are all part of the role he is playing. Seldom, if ever, does he let anyone know what he really is. Only in times of pain, fear, or perhaps when he has had too much to drink, does his mask come down and we see him as he really is.

For thirty-five years I wore a mask and was largely unaware of it. I didn't like myself, and was continually imitating someone who seemed successful (never dreaming that he, too, was probably wearing a mask). As a minister, if I heard of some programme or activity that was 'working' in some other church, I could hardly wait to get it started in mine. I tried to sound like Billy Graham when I preached, like Bev Shea when I sang, and like Cliff Barrows when I made 'announcements'. I wanted to be all things to all men that I might be thought 'winsome'.

Always, though, my mask was up. I dreaded the thought of someone peeking behind it, seeing the real me, and rejecting me. Afraid of growing bald, I considered a hairpiece. Afraid I would not be known as an 'effective' speaker, I memorised the sermons of several successful men of the cloth. I knew God wanted me to take off my mask. To be open, honest, and transparent. But the fear was too great. It was almost strangling me. What if people discovered I was nothing more than a shell, the lid on a dustbin? Would they still love me? Still respect me? I thought not. The things I had buried were, I knew unacceptable. I had rejected them. Why wouldn't others, if they discovered the awful truth?

A friend of mine says the best way to disarm your critics is to confess publicly ahead of time. This way no one can ever accuse you of something you have not already confessed. But what do you do when you have so much to confess – so much refuse in your lake?

I began to get some insight into who I really was when I realised that my life was, on the whole, a reaction to stimuli.

It had been several years since I had been to Ft Worth, Texas, where my wife and I spent the first four years of our married life. Flying to Dallas on a business trip, I decided to rent a car and drive over to Ft Worth on a nostalgia trip. With the construction of the new roads, the highways between Dallas and Ft Worth were unfamiliar. Coming into

Ft Worth, I found myself in one of those multi-level inter-changes called a 'mixmaster'. Knowing that if I got off on the wrong road I could be swept off towards Oklahoma, I slowed down, carefully studying my map and paying close attention to the big green highway signs that loomed over-head. Suddenly I was jolted by the blast of an air horn from behind. Looking up into my mirror, I saw a lumbering old lorry almost touching my rear bumper. The driver, snarling, was leaning on his horn. No doubt he had seen my out-of-state licence plate and was disgusted that some foreigner was blocking his Texas highway.

I reacted. Out of my lake came roaring all kinds of thoughts. My first thought was to slam on the brakes. I knew that rear-end accidents in Texas were always blamed on the following driver. That would teach him a lesson or two, even if it demolished my car. My next thought was even worse. I considered throwing my map out the window, hoping it would spread across his windshield, causing him to swerve off the road and crash on to the next level of high-ways, far below.

Fortunately, my conscious mind took control and pushed the thoughts of hatred and murder back into my sub-conscious. I motioned him by and turned off at the proper junction towards my destination. But it didn't end there. For the next ten miles I fumed. I enjoyed chewing the cud of what I could have done. I even half-heartedly wished another lorry would blow his horn at me. This time I had things all planned out.

You see, the driver of the lorry had suddenly taken charge of my life. My stomach was in knots, my lips dry, my breath-ing shallow. All because I had given in to a reaction, rather than responding positively in love

Moving from the area of reaction to the area of positive response is one of the most difficult of all spiritual tasks. In order to do so, the reservoir of the subconscious mind must be cleansed, dredged out. The Bible says we were made in the image of God. This is our true heredity. Yet our nature has a penchant to sin. And rather than dealing with our unhappy experiences as they have happened, we continue to push them beneath the surface of our lake. Thus when the surface is broken, instead of revealing the form of God the Father in whose image we are made, we reveal our wounded, angry selves.

We try, so bravely, to cover up. We stoically push the hurts deeper and deeper, or we cover them up with a nervous giggle or a smear of false piety. Yet deep inside we're still the same. Unredeemed. Real healing will always include a healing of these memories. This will allow us to begin to become transparent so that any rift in the surface will reveal, not ourselves – which is an accumulation of the old wounds, disappointments, and fears – but the heavenly Father.

Jesus was able to do this. Jesus was transparent. That is the reason he was able to say to Philip, 'He that hath seen me hath seen the Father.' Jesus never called men to look at him. He said he had come to reveal the Father. The way he did this was through perfect transparency. There was no muddy water in the subconscious mind of Jesus. He never blurred the image of the Father by reacting.

Unfortunately, we are not like this. When the surface of *our* lake is peeled back, we 'show ourselves' rather than revealing the Father.

Perhaps, though, we can at least understand what Jesus meant in the Sermon on the Mount when he said, 'Let your light so shine before men that they may see your good works, and glorify your Father which is in Heaven.'

For years I had been concerned about what I called the 'curse of ancestry'. Every medical examination called for a series of questions on my ancestry. Has anyone in your family died of cancer? Did your father have heart disease? Diabetes? Is there a history of insanity or epilepsy?

I have a godly father, a man who deeply loves the Lord. He has provided a heritage rich in culture and deep in the things of the Spirit. I am grateful. But he is still a man with human frailties and physical disabilities. And according to the Bible, I do not have to remain a slave to my ancestry. One of the most fascinating promises in the Scriptures tells me that through Christ I can actually die to my old ancestry and become an heir to God and a joint heir with Christ. No longer do I have to be in bondage to the fact that my father had diabetes, or my mother had high blood pressure. When I became a new creature in Christ, old things passed away, all things became new (2 Corinthians 5:17). This means I am now the inheritor, not of my earthly father's liabilities, but of the assets of my heavenly Father. John, talking about Jesus, said that 'as many as received him, to them gave he power to become the sons of God' (John 1:12), and Paul indicates that the whole creation is standing on tiptoe, waiting to see who will be the first to step forward as a 'manifested son of God'. That's exciting. But it will come only as we allow the Holy Spirit to permeate our entire being, claiming it for Christ.

Paul was talking of this when he wrote:

> For though we walk in the flesh, we do not war after the flesh: (For the weapons of our warfare are not carnal, but mighty through God to the pulling down of strong holds.) (2 Corinthians 10:3, 4).

Most of our warring, or battles with self and Satan, are on the conscious (or fleshly) level. The Bible commands us to be holy people. Therefore, to achieve holiness, we try to clean up the surface of our lake. We cut out smoking, try to lead chaste lives, stop gambling, cut our hair (if we're men) or don't cut our hair (if we're women), wipe off the facial makeup, lower our hemlines, raise our necklines, and go through a hundred different mechanical procedures trying to achieve holiness.

But Jesus didn't call this holiness. He called it hypocrisy, because the inner man was still polluted. Such battles, Paul says, are not to be fought on the surface level. Holiness is not attained by cleaning the surface of the lake. This battle must be waged on a spiritual level, which is the reason that any sincere study of inner healing needs to include a study of spiritual warfare.

Several months ago I spoke at a Full Gospel Business Men's meeting in Morristown, New Jersey. Before the meeting, a group of men asked if I would join them and pray for a young housewife named Elizabeth who had been brought to the meeting on a stretcher. Tumours in her hip bones had progressed to the point where she could not bend her body into a sitting position. She either had to stand up or lie down.

We prayed and, as is often the case, she experienced a dramatic healing. In fact, the very next day she was able to drive her car for the first time in many months.

Several months later I was back in the Morristown area and called her on the phone. She was discouraged. Although her body still showed evidence of the healing, she was coming under strong attack from some unlikely places.

When the minister of her church discovered she had been healed, he told her she could no longer take a responsible role in church activities. It was evident he feared she might testify of her healing. He was unprepared to handle this kind of 'fanaticism'. In fact, he told her, it would be far better if she just dropped out of church completely.

This wounded not only Elizabeth, but her husband, who was not a Christian and had a serious drinking problem.

'I don't want to feel bitter and resentful towards my minister,' she said over the phone. 'But I can't help it. What can I do?'

It was obvious to me that the battle was a spiritual battle. The minister, unfamiliar with the healing aspect of God's personality, was not striking out at her. He was striking out at the unfamiliar. He opposed anything that might threaten the security of his ministry. Unfortunately, in the process he had literally become the devil's advocate. Therefore it was extremely important that Elizabeth not give in to her natural feelings, but neither should she try to hide them. The battle was being fought in the heavenlies, as though it was being waged over her head. Satan had found a co-operative warrior in the form of the minister, but if she tried to battle Satan in her own strength she would surely lose. I told her about the archangel Michael who was the one God usually sent to do battle against Satan. And since he was the one who would do the actual fighting, all she had to do was keep herself transparent so the minister could see the image of God at the bottom of her lake.

When she saw this, she was greatly relieved. The attack was not against her. In fact, it was not even coming from the minister. The minister, in this case, was merely the devil's advocate. She, in turn, should be Christ's advocate. Thus all she had to do was reflect the character of Jesus and let the angels fight the battle for her. The last time I heard from her, she had done just that. In fact, she had grown stronger spiritually since she now realised it was not up to her to do the fighting.

In the same Corinthian passage Paul goes on to say that the way to come into complete inner healing is by

> *Casting down imaginations, and every high thing that exalteth itself against the knowledge of God, and bringing into captivity every thought to the obedience of Christ* (2 Corinthians 10:5).

Our reactions lurk beneath the surface of our lives, waiting for a chance to pop through. Our job is not to run busily over the surface of our lake making sure none appear, but to let them come, see ourselves as we really are, confess the sin, thank God for the cleansing and ask him to change our heart.

Impossible, you say. Yes, if we try to fight the battle on the surface of the lake. But if we let the Holy Spirit go to work with a sieve, not just pulling down the imaginations but dredging them up, then we can see that transparency is possible.

I determined that was what I wanted for myself. Not only to reflect Christ on the surface of my life, but deep down in the subconscious areas as well. I was tired of looking at the mushrooming pornography appearing all around us and being forced by my reactions to think lust. I knew that I could spend the rest of my life trying to fight that battle on the surface – with both blue laws and cold showers – and never win. I knew there had to be a place where I could enter so deeply into the kingdom that even when I was surrounded by pornography and vulgarity I would, instead of looking upon a woman to lust after her, see in that naked body the very image of God.

I was tired of being pinched and reacting with a closed fist, of feeling myself flare up when someone blew a horn at me, or biting back the curse of words when I hit my thumb with a hammer. I was tired of finding tender places in my life where the veneer was so thin that if I were scratched I revealed vast, unhealed areas of self-pity, prejudice, and resentment. I wanted to be Christ's to the core. I wanted him to be the Lord of my subconscious.

But how?

We were getting ready to build some upstairs rooms on our Florida house. Before we could actually start the construction, however, the builder wanted to test the soil around the base of the foundation to make sure it could take the additional weight. He didn't want to run the risk of having the house tilt or the floor crack as the earth settled.

One Monday afternoon a team of geological engineers came to the house. They had a clever kind of drill that punched a small hole in the earth, going down about twenty feet and coming back up with samples of the various layers of soil. They discovered that the surface sand was only about three feet deep. After that it changed to marl (which is a sandy type of clay), then shale, and finally bedrock. They concluded the soil could easily stand the additional weight of the second storey.

After they left I stood in the yard and looked at the soil samples they had dumped out on the grass, wondering what would happen if someone should take a similar boring of me.

Despairingly, I concluded that although they would find Jesus Christ in great abuandance on the surface, in the deep areas of my life they would find only me.

Yet my desire was that such a drilling would reveal Jesus Christ all the way down to the bottom. I wanted to be so pure that when I was cut, I would bleed Jesus. I thought of that story in the seventh chapter of Acts where Stephen was stoned. The Bible says the surface of two lakes were broken that afternoon. Stephen's words to the religious leaders cut them to their hearts. What was revealed? Hatred, bitterness, and murder. They reacted so violently they dragged Stephen through the city streets and stoned him to death. Yet as he was cut with the stone, Stephen, instead of reacting, responded with such positive love that eventually one of those involved in the stoning, a Pharisee named Saul, was converted.

I wanted to be like that. But how could it be? My lake, it seemed, could never be free from pollution. I was learning to handle the junk that was falling into it on a daily basis – but what could I do about the dregs which had long since settled below the surface and rose only in times of stress, anger, or temptation?

In other words, was it possible (as Paul commanded in Romans 12:2) for my mind to be actually transformed to prove what was that good, and acceptable, and perfect will of God? The Scriptures said that I was 'predestined to be conformed to the image of his Son' (Romans 8:29), but by what method was this to be accomplished? 'Walk in the Spirit, and you shall not fulfil the lust of the flesh,' Paul said to the Galatians (Galatians 5:16). A similar promise was made to the Ephesians 'That he would grant you, according to the riches of his glory, to be strengthened with might by his Spirit in the inner man; that Christ may dwell in your hearts by faith' (Ephesians 3:16, 17). Again he said, 'Put off concerning the former conversation the old man, which is corrupt according to the deceitful lusts; and be renewed in the spirit of your mind' (Ephesians 4:22, 23).

So what I desired was not an impossibility. In fact, it was to be the goal of every follower of Jesus Christ. Being made conformable to his image would not begin with an outward expression, however, but with the healing of the inner man (the subconscious). In other words, the best way to clean up the surface of the lake was not by skimming the top, but by purifying the source of the flow from the wellsprings at the bottom.

Still the question remained: How is this brought to pass? I saw several scriptural principles that applied.

First, the Christian must be committed to a walk of absolute obedience to Christ in his *conscious* life. He must stand guard at the doorpost of his mind to repel each evil thought by which Satan would gain entry. Also, he must hurl out those he finds already inside, in the name of Jesus. The Bible says the Lord will honour such obedience with a cleansing of the heart. But if the Holy Spirit is to have completely free access to minister to all corners of the subconscious, he must be invited in.

It was there I discovered the full meaning of Paul's phrase, 'pray in the Spirit'.

For years I had heard people talk of the benefit of 'praying in tongues'. In fact, I myself had a 'prayer language' which came as a result of being baptised in the Holy Spirit. But I had always used the prayer tongue simply because the Bible said I should. 'I would that ye all spake with tongues' (1 Corinthians 14:5). Now I began to understand there was a purpose for the prayer language other than simply obeying God.

In 1 Corinthians 14:4, Paul said, 'He that speaketh (prays) in an unknown tongue edifieth himself.' Now that's what I needed, to be edified – to be strengthened – in my spirit, in the deep areas of my subconscious. In that same chapter he said, 'If I pray in an unknown tongue, my spirit prayeth, but my understanding is unfruitful' (1 Corinthians 14:14). It was beginning to make sense.

About that time I made a visit to Peru to interview members of the Wycliffe Translators about their jungle aviation programme. The first man I came in contact with in Lima was a noted linguist with several Ph.D. degrees in linguistics. Before I could ask any questions concerning my mission, he said, 'Do you pray in tongues?'

I was taken aback, not expecting even to get into this subject. However, I quickly recovered and told him that I did use a prayer language in my private devotions. He was greatly excited. 'I've been wanting to talk to someone about this for a long time.'

He went ahead to say that, as a linguist, he was constantly having to filter words through his intellect before he could speak them. 'Every sound I make has to come through my mind,' he said. 'As a result, I am always polluting my prayer life with my thoughts. For a long time I have longed to be able to pray, to commune with the Father without having to think about the words – simply letting the Holy Spirit who is in me bypass my intellect and go directly to the Father who is in heaven. Is that what tongues is all about?'

I had never thought of it that way, but as I heard it from the lips of this distinguished linguist, I realised that was it – exactly. Not only that, but by praying in tongues I was actually inviting the Holy Spirit to come into my spirit, to enter my subconscious, and bring the purity of the heavenly Father with him. It was a tremendous revelation.

While I was in Peru I restudied this entire concept of inner healing, especially in the light of Romans 8. In verse 26 of that chapter I ran across the secret of how to bring into captivity every thought of the obedience of Jesus Christ. Here is what Paul says:

> *Likewise the Spirit also helpeth our infirmities; for we know not what we should pray for as we ought: but the Spirit itself maketh intercession for us with groanings which cannot be uttered.*

I had always viewed this verse as an explanation of intercessory prayer – the prayers we pray for someone else. But as I read it over again during my stay in South America, I came to a new understanding. Simply by changing the pronouns from plural to singular I understood.

Likewise the Spirit also helpeth *my* infirmities; for *I* know not what *I* should pray for as *I* ought; but the Spirit itself maketh intercession for *me* with groanings which cannot be uttered.

Paul was talking about praying in the Spirit, whether it was in tongues or by letting the Spirit make intercession with groanings which could not be uttered. In so doing I would invite the Spirit to abide in my subconscious. Even though the prayer would be meaningless to my understanding, I knew his presence would eventually bring my every thought into captivity to obedience to Jesus Christ. No wonder Paul said we should pray without ceasing. To cease would quench the Spirit and block our inner healing.

Now I can see where the sick areas of my mind, including the bad memories of the past, can actually be healed as the timeless Christ walks back through my past and touches with healing; or as he descends far beneath the conscious surface of my mind into the hell of my own creation and preaches the good news of deliverance to those thoughts so long held in captivity. As I pray in the Spirit (and for me that means using my prayer language), those areas of my subconscious where self has always sat on the throne are brought under subjection to the King of the mind, Jesus Christ, revealing even my subconscious to the One who 'searcheth the heart and knoweth what is the mind of the Spirit' (Romans 8:27).

I recalled an incident that began two days after I experienced the baptism in the Holy Spirit. I had returned from Washington, D.C. with a new honesty. It was an honesty that compelled me to confess – to my wife – events which I had for years pushed beneath the surface of my lake in a vain attempt to keep them hidden. Now came a desire to be transparent, and a knowledge that this could only transpire as I got things out in the open.

The following night, after this long confessional period, I began to dream. In my dreams I relived many of the carnal activities of prior years. People I had not thought of for years appeared in my dreams – people I had manipulated, despitefully used, lied to and hurt. Night after night they paraded through my dreams, helping me relive in vivid detail all the immorality and evil manipulations of the past.

I was mystified. Why, after I had just gone through this deep purification process, was I now having to suffer through this. The only other Spirit-baptised person I knew of in our community was a former minister with the Church of God, Anderson, Indiana. Elbert Jones had been dismissed from his church and was now ministering to a small interdenominational group meeting on Tuesday nights at the Women's Club building. Later he was to become one of my closest friends and would serve by my side as a fellow minister in the local body. However, at this time he was a virtual stranger.

Desperately needing help, though, I sought him out and asked if he could give me some kind of explanation for my bizarre dreams.

He smiled and said, 'The Holy Spirit is busy dredging up the junk in your subconscious, letting it float to the surface.'

'But what can I do with it?' I asked.

'Rebuke it,' he said matter-of-factly. 'It is floating to the surface because the Holy Spirit is now moving actively in the deep areas of your mind, stirring the waters, so to speak. When you rebuke these memories of the past you not only cast them out, but you close the door on the areas where they first came in.'

I followed his advice, and have continued to do so ever since. In about two weeks the dreams ceased, and even though I am aware that my lake is still polluted, I realise it is being purified by the fresh water that wells up from that free flowing fountain in my inner being. As a result, even my dreams are beginning to take on spiritual overtones – and, on occasion, I even hear from God while I am sleeping.

Thus the baptism of the Holy Spirit, rather than being a climax to the Christian experience, is simply the door through which the Holy Spirit entered my subconscious. Eventually he would 'fill' me. And when that happened, well, even before it happened, I would find the mirror of my soul, my dreams, beginning to reflect the condition of my subconscious. Eventually I would dream, not about monsters and swamps, but about Jesus.

4

PRAYING IN THE SPIRIT

The other morning, just at dawn, I was driving north along the deserted ocean highway between Vero Beach and my home in Melbourne, Florida. The highway follows a strip of sand and trees which separates the Indian River, which is actually a salt-water lagoon extending along the east coast of the state, from the Atlantic Ocean.

Suddenly my little Volkswagen was atop the high bridge over the Sebastian Inlet. On one side the blue of the Indian River shimmered towards the mainland, barely visible on the western horizon. On the other side was the magnificent sunrise, exploding out of the emerald green sea in a kaleidoscope of colour that was so awesome it literally took my breath away.

Early that morning I had read from the Living Bible. Now the words of David burst spontaneously from my lips: 'Hallelujah, yes, praise the Lord! Sing him a new song!'

I remembered the words of the grand old hymn I learned as a boy in the First Baptist Church of Vero Beach:

Holy, holy, holy, Lord God Almighty,
Early in the morning my song shall rise to thee.

But even this was not sufficient to express the explosion of adoration that came rushing from my soul as I longed to worship, to praise him in the 'womb of the morning'. My human vocabulary was too limited, too restrained.

I pulled off the highway, up a little sand road to the top of a dune overlooking the ocean, and cut off my engine. For long moments I sat in silence, feasting my soul on the miracle of God's new day. Then, from the very depths of my inner being, I heard the Holy Spirit himself begin to speak, praising the Father through my lips. I was speaking in the language of the angels.

It was an unforgettable moment. Sheer ecstasy. And long after the sun had risen like a great fireball, dragging behind it the heat and light of a new day, I sat in the front seat of my little car, looking out beyond the crashing surf, praising God in the Spirit.

Praying in tongues was not a new experience for me. Although it was not the 'initial' evidence of my baptism in the Holy Spirit, I do believe I received the gift at that time (even though it was more than two years before I appropriated it) and believe it is surely for all believers – regardless of whether their experience with the Holy Spirit is similar to mine or not. However, using tongues to praise God was new. Wonderfully new.

I remembered, shortly after experiencing the baptism of the Holy Spirit, that I shared my testimony before an inter-denominational group. A visiting pastor, angered by what I said, approached me after the meeting. 'Even if tongues are for today,' he snapped, 'what good are they?'

I was disturbed by his defensiveness, for although I did not speak in tongues at the time, I believed it was a valid gift of the Spirit. But I was equally disturbed that I could not answer him intelligently.

'All I know is that Paul says he spoke in tongues more than all the others,' I answered, 'so it must have been of some value to the Christian.'

He snorted and walked off, leaving me frustrated. I believed some things were to be accepted on faith alone. But I also agreed with my friend that there was a difference between toys and gifts. Toys are to be played with. Gifts used. I didn't believe God would give us 'gifts' unless he had a solid purpose for each one.

It was in the two years following my baptism that I began to discover his purposes. It started with a growing desire to appropriate this gift into my devotional life. Shortly after I received the baptism in the Holy Spirit, my wife, Jackie, wakened me in the middle of the night, walking through the house laughing, crying, reading her Bible, and praising God. A week later she made a special visit to the home of a local Baptist minister, Bob Johnson, to ask his wife, Woody, to pray with her about speaking in tongues. She knew the Johnsons had been 'praying in the Spirit' for some time and was eager to receive all God had for her too.

Woody later told me what happened that morning when Jackie came to the house. After they prayed, she said, they got up and began walking around the room, their hands raised as they praised God out loud. This was new for Jackie. Like myself, she had been raised in a Southern Baptist church, and of course for the last fifteen years I had been her pastor as well as her husband. According to Woody, the more they praised God, the more they were aware of his presence. They were experiencing the truth of David's psalm: 'O thou that inhabitest the praises of Israel' (Psalm 22:3).

Then, without warning, Jackie's language changed. Instead of walking around the room saying, 'Praise God, Hallelujah, I love you Lord,' she was simply saying 'La-la-la-la-la.' Again it was reminiscent of an Old Testament experience prophesied by Isaiah and later referred to by Paul in his letter to the Corinthians:

> *For with stammering lips and another tongue will he speak to this people (Isaiah 28:11).*

Jackie returned home that afternoon ecstatic with joy. I suspected she had spoken in tongues, but was reluctant to quiz her about it. Even though I had reached the place in my spiritual growth where I could give credence to the gift, I was still fearful. The scars of the past when I had formerly equated the 'tongue speakers' with the ignorant people of the community who couldn't control their emotions were still with me. Even though I saw the tremendous difference the exercise of the gift made in Jackie's devotional life, I was still too proud to reach out and appropriate it for myself.

My problem was aggravated one afternoon when two women came by the house. I had been working hard on the final draft of my first book for Kathryn Kuhlman, *God Can Do It Again*. Jackie was out of town and the children were in school when I answered the door. I knew the women. They had attended our church and some of the home meetings. One was a Pentecostal evangelist and the other the mother of one of the young couples in the church.

They immediately got to the point. 'God has sent us to pray for you to receive the baptism of the Holy Ghost.'

'But I had that experience last February,' I said.

'We've heard your testimony,' the evangelist said, 'and praise God for the wonderful change in your life. But you haven't received the baptism in the Holy Ghost, because that's always accompanied by speaking in tongues. You need the gift of tongues.'

I was open for anything the Lord had for me. Even though I was certain that God had touched me with his Spirit, revolutionising my life, I didn't want to quench his spirit. If these women had a 'word from God' I was ready to listen.

They wanted to go back to my study so we wouldn't be disturbed by the phone. After asking me to sit in a chair, they began marching around the little room praying loudly in tongues. The walls echoed, almost shuddered, with their prayers and praises. All this time I sat in the chair with my head bowed, beginning to feel a little uneasy, yet not wanting to miss a blessing if God had something special for me.

The praying turned to prophesying. Through the din I could hear first one woman, then the other, crying out, 'Thus saith the Lord'. They laid hands on my books. On my typewriter. They prophesied over the picture of an aeroplane hanging on the wall. They sang, chanted, laughed, and cried. But they never laid hands on me and, to my knowledge, never prayed for me specifically. This lasted for almost half an hour and finally, in exhaustion, the woman who was the mother of the young couple in our church said, 'We've done what we were supposed to do. It's time to go.'

I bid them good-bye and they left through the back door. I sat back down in the same chair, filled with wonderment. What in the world was that all about? They said they came to pray for me to receive the baptism of the Holy Spirit, yet they never did. Had God revealed something to them? Did they realise, as they prayed, that I had indeed been baptised in the Spirit? Or, did they discern something about me that was so filthy and unworthy that I was unqualified to receive any gift from God? I never did find out what happened that afternoon, but somehow it seemed to be related to the work of the Spirit in my life.

That summer Jackie, the children, and I spent a month in our little mountain cabin in North Carolina. We often spent our holidays there, enjoying the fresh mountain air and the unhurried atmosphere of rural life. Art Katz, a young Jewish Christian, had joined us the week before, and I was spending most of the daylight hours working with him on the manuscript of his book, *Ben Israel*. At night Art and his wife, Inger, were staying in the nearby village, leaving our family alone up on the mountain.

Combining what was supposed to be our holiday with my work had put considerable strain on our family relationships. One night, after we had gone to bed, Jackie and I had some kind of disagreement. I don't even remember what started the argument, but I have no trouble remembering how self-righteous I felt about it. This book had been ordained by God. It was critical we get it out as soon as possible. Jackie had no right to criticise me for taking time away from less important things (like being with the children) to work on the manuscript. On and on we went, neither of us stopping long enough to actually hear what the other was saying.

Frustrated, I finally threw back the covers in the dark bedroom and said, 'Maybe you'd just like me to leave.'

Jackie grew very quiet. She knew, after living with me for all those years, that I had reached the boiling point.

'Answer me!' I said through gritted teeth, not wanting to wake the children who were sleeping in another part of the house.

She said nothing, and in exasperation I stormed out of bed, grabbed my trousers, and pulled them on over my pyjamas. 'I can't stand this any more. Here I am trying to do the work of God, and all I get from you is criticism.'

I started out of the room but paused at the door, waiting in the darkened hall, hoping she would respond. In the darkness I could see the form of her body on the bed, still, motionless. Snorting, I walked through the living room, felt my way through the dark kitchen and out the back door into the chilly night air. I let the door close with an audible click and then waited outside the house, hoping that Jackie would follow me, entreating me to return to bed. But the house was silent. Suddenly I realised I had played the part of the fool.

I glanced around. It was past midnight and the grass and small rocks under my feet were wet with dew. I shivered in the cool air. The heavy woods behind the house were silent. Even the frogs and crickets had gone to sleep. And here was I, God's man of faith and power, sulking around in bare feet and pyjamas, hoping my wife would come outside and beg me to return to bed. I was mortified.

My pride was too great to let me go back inside immediately, so I turned and walked down the familiar path into the woods behind the house. I had walked that path every summer since I was eight years old. I knew every stump, the location of every poplar, white pine, hickory, and laurel bush. The woods were dark and deep, hushed. I reached a junction where the path goes down the hill to a small brook and paused, looking up through the towering trees at the stars overhead.

'I've made a fool of myself,' I told God out loud. 'Forgive me.'

There was no answer, but deep inside I remembered those strange ladies who came by the house, saying I needed to speak in tongues.

'Is that why you have me out here in the woods in the middle of the night?' I asked aloud. 'Do you want me to speak in tongues?'

Again no audible answer, but once more, deep inside, I heard an inner urging that said, 'Get down before me.'

'Is that what it is going to take?' I thought. But without hesitation, for I was learning then to be obedient to the still, small voice, I dropped to my knees on the moist leaves which carpeted the forest path. I fully expected to break forth in tongues, but there was nothing.

Again the inner voice said, 'Get down before me.' This time I started to protest. I did not relish the thought of prostrating myself on the ground. Even though the frogs and crickets had gone to sleep, I knew the little creatures that lived under the leaves were still very much awake – and crawling around. But the urging did not diminish. 'Get down before me.'

'If that's what it takes to speak in tongues, then I'm ready,' I said. Without further hesitation, I spread myself flat on the ground, face down, arms extended. I was as low as I could get. I waited, expecting a torrent of sounds to come tumbling from my lips. Nothing! I waited for a long time and gradually began to feel like a complete idiot. I rose, brushed myself off, and returned to the house. It never occurred to me that God had been talking about a condition of my soul – pride – rather than a physical position when he said, 'Get down before me.' That revelation would take a full nine months before it was ready to be born.

Slipping back into the house, I got as far as the living room, but my pride once again blocked the way. I simply could not go back into the bedroom, for to do so would mean admitting defeat. Jackie had won. Actually, she had

65

been right all along, and my explosion of childish anger was simply the shield I had thrown up to keep from being exposed. I eased myself on to the couch in the living room, resigned to spending the night there, covered with old newspapers and cushions to protect me from the chill of the mountain night, rather than in my warm bed.

As I got quiet I heard, coming faintly from the bedroom, the sound of Jackie praying in tongues. Her voice was soft and melodious. She knew I was out there, shivering, my teeth chattering, my pyjamas covered with wet leaves, too proud to come into the bedroom. And she was praying for me. It was almost more than I could take, and I turned my face to the wall and wept my way to sleep.

That seed, planted, unknown to me, by the Holy Spirit that night, grew slowly during the next nine months – much as a foetus grows in a mother's womb. I completed *Ben Israel* and started to work on a book for Pat Robertson, *Shout It From the Housetops*. My publisher encouraged me to visit Pat at the Christian Broadcasting Network offices in Portsmouth, Virginia, and later to drive up to Washington, D.C., to attend the regional convention of the Full Gospel Business Men's Fellowship International. Since my initial experience with the Holy Spirit had been at one of these conventions, I eagerly accepted his invitation.

The second afternoon of the convention was billed as a 'Miracle Service'. Kathryn Kuhlman was to minister and since I had grown to appreciate her, working closely with her on *God Can Do It Again*, I made plans to attend the meeting. I had been feeling dizzy that morning and skipped lunch. I didn't think much about it, but as the Kathryn Kuhlman meeting got underway I began feeling worse. I kidded with myself, saying I would probably be the first person in history to attend a healing service and fall ill. But get ill I did. In fact, I got so ill, feverish, and nauseated, that I finally staggered out of the ballroom in the Washington Hilton and made my way to the lift and up to my room.

I was too sick to undress and just fell across the bed. One

moment I was burning up with fever, the next I had pulled all the covers around me as I shivered in a bone-rattling chill. I was aware it had grown dark outside, but I was too ill to switch on a light. Sometime during the afternoon I kicked off my shoes, but I remained fully dressed, moaning under the covers.

About six o'clock I picked up the phone and asked the reception desk if there was a doctor on duty. The receptionist said the doctor had gone home for the day and would not be back until ten in the morning. I hung up, thinking it would be too late by then. I had never been so ill in all my life. In my delirium I faced the possibility that I might be dying. I was too ill to care.

Off and on, as the night dragged by, I heard myself praying. I begged God to 'do something'. I knew I could call my publisher who was staying in the same hotel, but I hated to disturb him in the middle of the night. I finally reached the place of saying, 'God, I've written a book on healing which tells all about your healing miracles. But I've doubted whether what I was writing was true or not – even though I have seen the evidence. Now I need to be healed. I've been too proud to ask you for anything, but I'm asking you, now, to teach me.'

Then, softly, coming up out of my subconscious, I remembered that night on the damp leaves of the forest floor in North Carolina. And I heard God saying, 'Now, you're down before me.'

I began to pray again, but this time, instead of English I heard different sounds coming from my lips. Strange sounds. They seemed almost oriental in nature, without the nasal inflections. I was praying in tongues.

Several weeks before I had attended a Don Basham teaching seminar on the Holy Spirit at the Eastminster Presbyterian Church in Melbourne. In his lesson on speaking in tongues, Don had suggested it might be a good idea to write down phonetically, the first sounds you spoke in tongues. As I prayed, his words came back to me. Still deathly sick, I crawled out of bed and, on my hands and knees, made my way across the carpet of the darkened hotel room to the coffee table in the middle of the room. There, on the small notepad, using only the light that filtered through the window blinds, I printed out, phonetically, the sounds that were coming from my mouth.

'Ya-she-ka-see-ma-tee-lay-moe-tuu-shan.'

Leaving the pad on the table, I crawled back into my bed. With some satisfaction I thought, 'Now, when they find my corpse in the morning, they will also find that pad. My Pentecostal friends will be satisfied. They will know I died speaking in tongues.'

But I didn't die. In fact, as the night wore on I began to feel better. I dozed, and each time I awoke I was speaking in tongues, saying those same words over and over with new joy and power.

Sometime, just before daylight, I had an encounter with Satan. 'You're just making that up,' he said. 'It's a product of your fever and delirium. Anyway, that's not tongues, that word you're saying is the name of your Japanese camera.'

I listened, and sure enough, the first word, the most predominant word I was speaking, did sound like *Yashica*. But the battle was already won, and Satan's tactics failed. I dozed off to sleep saying, 'Even if it is the name of my Japanese camera, I'll say it to the glory of God.'

When I awoke it was mid-morning. The sun was streaming through the windows. The little pad of paper was still on the table. The words were still tumbling from my lips when I prayed. And I was healed.

Had the language been the babbling sounds of a delirious mind? No, I believe it was the Holy Spirit praying through me, taking over uttering words which my delirious mind could not handle. I believe it was the kind of praying referred to in Romans 8:26:

Likewise the Spirit also helpeth our infirmities: for we know not what we should pray for as we ought: but the

Spirit itself maketh intercession for us with groanings which cannot be uttered.

Besides, if it had been simply delirious babbling, it would not have continued. Yet it has continued, for years, and its use has grown more precious and meaningful each day of my life.

It was another year before I discovered the value of praying in the Spirit for inner healing. Our family was sharing a holiday cottage on the outer banks of North Carolina with Judge Allen Harrell, his writer-wife Irene, and their six children. One morning after the women and children had taken off for the beach, the judge and I sat in the porch and talked. It was one of those special times when two men expose their souls to each other.

I had been intrigued with the concept of my subconscious being the composite of all my experiences, the mountain lake idea discussed in the last chapter. 'How do I purge my inner self of the refuse I have collected across the years?' I asked Allen.

In his eastern North Carolina drawl, the judge told me: 'I hold court in several cities. Each morning when I leave the house and drive out of town, I use the time in the car to pray or sing in the Spirit. And you know,' he chuckled, 'God is using this to cleanse me, to purify my soul.'

It was his testimony which led me to discover something of the tremendous purgative, cathartic purpose of praying in the Spirit. There is a deep healing that goes on in the subconscious as one prays in tongues. Down there, in the deep areas of the mind, as the Holy Spirit communes with the Father, old hurts are dredged up and healed, inherent character flaws are replaced with supernatural strength, and the carnal nature dies to take on the nature of Jesus. It is what Paul refers to in Romans 12:2 when he talks about the transformation that takes place by the 'renewing of your mind'. Once again I saw the beautiful practicality of this gift which edifies (builds up, strengthens) the believer.

Is the gift of tongues for the church today? Of course, just as much as are the gift of prophecy and the gift of healing. But as with any gift, it is to be administered under the authority of the church government and should at all times be for the building up of the entire body.

Is tongues the initial evidence of the baptism in the Holy Spirit? Not necessarily. In my own case it was more than two years after I received the baptism in the Holy Spirit before I spoke in tongues. There are several places in the New Testament where men received the baptism in the Holy Spirit and there is no evidence they immediately spoke in tongues. Such was the case with Paul in Acts 9. However, we later find Paul saying he speaks in tongues 'more than ye all'. Therefore I have to conclude that tongues is not the evidence, but the consequence of the baptism in the Holy Spirit.

Is it proper to seek the gift of tongues? From my own experience, and from a study of the Scripture, I have concluded that any time we seek anything less than the kingdom of God we are asking for too little. That is not to say God will not honour a person's sincere desire to receive a prayer language in order to praise and intercede with fullness. But when Paul outlines all the gifts of the Spirit in I Corinthians 12, he finishes the chapter by saying that all do not have the gifts of healing, all do not speak with tongues, and all do not interpret. These are gifts that God divides 'severally as he will' (1 Corinthians 12:11). However, Paul says, we should covet earnestly the best gifts.

What is the best gift? Some might say it is love. But love is not a gift, it is the *way* in which the gifts are to be manifested according to 1 Corinthians 13. The best gift is the person of the Holy Spirit himself. This leads me to the conviction that I am not to seek the gifts, but the Giver. Once I receive him into the inner places of my life, once he comes to transform me by the renewing of my mind, once he becomes the Lord of my subconscious as well as my conscious mind – then whether I speak in tongues is immaterial, for I shall speak whatever he wants.

70

Perhaps I can best illustrate this by telling you a couple of personal stories. Several years ago I flew to Colombia, South America, to begin my research for *Into the Glory*, the story of the pilots and mechanics of the Jungle Aviation and Radio Service, the flying arm of the Wycliffe Bible Translators.

My old friend, Tom Smoak, had flown me deep into the jungle to a small Indian village. We landed our single-engine plane on a tiny airstrip only to learn the chief of the tribe had been taken by canoe and river launch to a hospital in an upriver town.

The chief's old wife, fearing her husband was dying, was preparing to leave that day by canoe to see him. It would take her three days of paddling to reach the town. We could fly her there in twenty minutes, and offered to do it.

Tom helped her into the back seat of the plane and strapped her down. All the time she kept speaking in her language and gesturing outside the plane. She wanted her grandson, a half-naked nine-year-old, to come with her. He was standing outside the window of the plane, tears making little streaks in the dirt on his face.

Tom patiently explained that we were at maximum weight and any additional weight would mean the plane could not clear the towering trees on takeoff. The chief's wife understood, but the little boy, standing under the wing, continued to cry and beg to go along.

Something in me let me understand how he felt. His grandfather, the chief, had been taken away, maybe dying. Now his grandmother was strapped in the back of a strange silver plane that would roar off into the sky. Panic, terror, fear, and loneliness – I could read it all in his eyes as he huddled against the fuselage, wetting the window with his tears.

I stepped out of the cockpit and bent over, putting my arm around his bare shoulders. I heard myself praying softly in tongues. It lasted only seconds, but when I finished, the child turned and looked in my face, his eyes filled with wonder. Pulling away, he ran to the edge of the grass strip to join the other Indians who had come out of the village to watch the takeoff. We taxied to the end of the strip, gunned the engine, and released the brakes. As we roared into the air, I saw the little boy clutching the skirt of an Indian woman and waving at the plane – his face wreathed in smiles.

I have no idea what I said, or what the Holy Spirit prayed through me. I don't know whether my words were in a language he understood or whether God answered my prayer by speaking to the child directly and changing his fear to faith. I guess the explanation is immaterial. Whatever it was, it was a beautiful example of the supernatural power of a supernatural God who loves little Indian boys.

A year later I was back in South America, this time in Peru. The Wycliffe Bible Translators base in Peru is at a place called Yarinacocha, east of the towering Andes on the Ucayali River which joins the Maranon to form the Amazon River. The base is a mission compound, a sort of self-contained village in the heart of the dense Amazon jungle. Here the translators return from their remote Indian villages to work on the actual pen-to-paper translations.

The translators often bring several Indians out of the jungle with them to help with the translation work. These Indians prefer to live in small huts similar to those they have in the village, rather than in the larger homes occupied by the linguists and support personnel on the base. However, they are well accepted as part of the community.

One afternoon while I was taking a siesta in my small room on the river's edge, I had a visitor. Jim Daggett, an American linguist working with the Chayahuita tribe, was at the door. He had a concerned look on his face. It seemed his Indian helper, whom he had brought out of the jungle, a twenty-four-year-old tribesman named Miguel, was dying. He had not eaten for many days, and was too weak to stand up. Dr Doug Swanson, the base medical doctor, had examined him. Although he could not find anything physically wrong, he confirmed his condition was very grave. Miguel was begging to be returned to his parents in the tribe so he could die at home. However, before they took him back

Jim wanted me to come pray for him.

'What do you think is wrong?' I asked.

'He's possessed with demons,' Jim said soberly.

I had heard stories of Indians in the jungle who had even been killed by evil spirits, but had never had a firsthand encounter. On several occasions, back in the States, I had ministered to people who were under demonic influence, but never to anyone who was literally dying.

Jim went on to explain that when Miguel became a Christian the year before, the witch doctor put a curse on him. He told Miguel he would die unless he renounced Christ. Now, it seemed, the curse was coming to pass. Whether it was simply the power of suggestion or an actual demon who was strangling the life out of him was immaterial – Miguel was dying.

I felt totally inadequate. Yet how could I refuse this gentle request from this highly trained linguist who was giving his life to help these Indians. I agreed to go, although my faith was more than weak – it was nonexistent.

That evening several of us, including Jim and Dr Swanson, went to Miguel's little hut. We found him, a handsome, brown-skinned man, lying on a thatched mat under a mosquito net. He was so weak he could not even open his eyes.

Dr Swanson pointed out several vivid purple welts on Miguel's stomach.

'Suck marks,' he said softly. 'After the witch doctor cursed him, Miguel went to a second witch doctor and asked him to remove the curse by sucking. Those marks are blood blisters under the skin. They have been there six months.'

I felt my hands grow clammy. 'Why doesn't one of you pray for him?' I asked. 'You know him better than I.'

'We have,' Jim confessed.

'But we're new in the Spirit. We thought maybe you . . . '

'But I can't speak his language,' I objected. 'He won't understand what I am saying.'

Dr Swanson put his hand on my shoulder. 'We're not asking you to pray *to* him,' he said kindly. 'We want you to

73

pray *for* him, using your prayer language.'

I recalled many of my prayers for Americans back in the States. I would first analyse their situation, then tell God what needed to be done. 'Lord, my brother has deep-seated problems. I ask you to heal that resentment he has towards his wife which came in when his mother spanked him at the age of three.' Or, 'Lord, his lungs aren't functioning correctly. You know how hard he's tried to give up smoking. God give him new strength to stop, and while you're at it, Lord, he has a problem of biting his fingernails. You know how nervous he is because he lost his job and his son is smoking pot . . .'

How foolish all that now sounded in the light of this situation.

Apprehensively, I knelt beside Miguel's corpse-like form and pulled back the mosquito net. The little hut was quiet with only the jungle sounds filtering through the thatch: the chatter of the monkeys, the squawking of the parrots, and the hum of a billion insects.

I swallowed hard. I knew, as a child of God, I had the same authority that Jesus had to cast out evil spirits. But it seemed so strange since the one I was praying for didn't know what was happening.

Then it dawned on me. He didn't need to know. I was not going to speak to him, but to the demons.

'In the name of Jesus Christ,' I commanded, 'I order you evil spirits to depart from Miguel and be cast into the middle of the sea. I bind you there forever.'

I looked up. Miguel hadn't moved. His eyes were still closed, his face expressionless. I felt stupid. If only he could understand me. I could tell him to renounce the witch doctor. I could advise him to claim his deliverance. I could tell him that sometimes evil spirits come out by vomiting or coughing or screaming . . . But none of my psychological manipulations were operative here in the jungle. I could preach all I wanted, to no avail. Miguel just lay there. Inert. Seemingly lifeless. However, I had gone too far to back down. I reached out and put my hand on his chest.

'Father,' I prayed, 'please send your Holy Spirit to heal all the wounds caused by the demons, and prevent them from ever returning again.'

Then, suddenly, I was praying in my prayer language, using words only God could understand. Yet even as the Spirit prayed through me I was secretly hoping Miguel would understand the words, much like the little Indian boy in Colombia. But my 'tongue' was obviously not in the Chayahuita dialect. If it was, Jim would have understood. No, this battle was being fought on a far different level from the mind – it was in the Spirit.

I looked up again. Nothing. Miguel still had not moved. But I noticed something. From the corner of each eye a tear had appeared and was running down the side of his bronze face, making a tiny streak in the dust.

'Amazing,' Jim whispered reverently. Then, seeing my puzzled look, he continued. 'These Indians never cry. Something is happening.'

Two tears. That was all I had to rest my faith on. We replaced the mosquito net and left the hut. Miguel was still motionless on the rattan mat. I returned to my room feeling confused, almost defeated.

I was busy with my final interviews during the next few days and did not have time to go back and check on Miguel. In fact, I was afraid to ask about him and tried to put him out of my mind. From now on I would confine my prayers to people who understood English.

But the afternoon I was preparing to return to the States, Jim Daggett came by my room. I was just closing my suitcase.

'I wanted to tell you about Miguel before you left,' he grinned. 'The day after you prayed for him he got up and said he was hungry. I prepared him a big bowl of fish and rice and he ate enough to fill a horse. The next day he told me he wanted to stay here at the base and help with the translation.'

I was amazed. 'Did he understand what we did the other

night?' I asked. Maybe, I thought, he understood my prayer language after all.

'No, I had to tell him about it,' Jim confessed. 'But now he plans to call all the other Indians together to tell them what happened. He wants them to know that in Christ they have more authority than the witch doctor, that they no longer have to live in fear of demons, but in the name of Jesus can cast them out.'

Before I left that evening I walked over to Miguel's hut. He was healthy and smiling. There was something else. I noticed the purple suck marks on his stomach were almost gone. He had been healed – from the inside out.

How thickheaded I had been, trying to comprehend how this could happen unless there had been some kind of mental communication. It was difficult, but gradually I was beginning to understand: praying in the Spirit is the key that unlocks the door of the cupboard behind the place of the intellect, allowing the Holy Spirit to come into the deep level and bring to pass that which the conscious mind would reject if it tried to comprehend. One of the most important keys to inner healing is praying in the Spirit.

5

HANDLING YOUR AUGHTS AND ANYS

Nothing in the Christian life is more difficult, or more necessary for inner healing and spiritual wholeness, than forgiving those who have offended you or sinned against you. It was more than three years after I experienced the baptism in the Holy Spirit, though, before I began learning how necessary forgiveness is.

As a child, the summer week I dreaded most was the week our church set apart for Vacation Bible School. Not only was it an infringement on my holiday time, but I disliked being made a spectacle of when we were forced to march down the aisle of the church behind the flags singing 'God Bless America'. I hated having to make things out of pipe cleaners, saying a pledge of allegience to the Bible, and gluing ice-lolly sticks together to make a teapot stand for my mother.

I carried that same dislike for VBS into my ministry. Especially did I dread the opening day parade. The idea was to gather at the church early in the morning and decorate the cars with toilet paper and big poster signs that said, 'COME TO VBS'. The local fire department would send a truck and the cars, filled with screaming kids and driven by the women of the church, would line up to drive slowly through the sub-divisions – honking their horns and shouting at the children who ran into their gardens to see the cause of the commotion. The pastor was usually the only man present (except for the firemen on the truck) and was expected to lead the parade, right behind the big, red fire engine. All summer long I would try to forget what was to come, but as the time drew near I would begin to have stomach cramps. By the time of the parade I would be praying desperately for a flat tyre.

As our church began to break loose from some of the old traditions, we dropped a lot of these programmes. However, primarily because of our strong-willed Vacation Bible School superintendent, Inez Thompson, we continued to have VBS. Inez had cut her teeth on VBS back in Texas and Oklahoma. Even though she was a close personal friend – and a deeply spiritual person – she refused to listen when I suggested we should omit it from the church programme that summer.

'Call off the Sunday school if you please,' she said stubbornly, 'even stop taking the offering and put a bucket at the door. But we're going to have Vacation Bible School if I have to do all the work myself.'

Inez was a hard worker. Dedicated to the Lord, she had been with the growing church from the first day we opened the doors. But I found her stubbornness irritating, especially her insistence that I take part in the school.

'Every year you plan your schedule so you are away during Bible school week,' she said in the early spring. 'This year we're planning the school for the end of summer. I want you to promise me you'll be present. We need you.'

I agreed, reluctantly. I arranged my calendar, making sure I would be around that week. I owed it to Inez – and to the children.

We had a productive summer. I had accepted a job as a roving editor for *Guideposts* magazine and was enjoying the extra challenge of writing magazine articles, plus the close contact with some very dear friends on the magazine staff. The church was growing, moving more deeply into the life of the Holy Spirit. I was looking forward to the time when I no longer had to receive a salary from the church, but could support myself through my writing – pastoring the church as an avocation rather than a vocation.

As the summer drew to a close, Inez approached me weekly, reminding me of my commitment to be present for the VBS. Not only did she want me to lead the opening parade, but I was scheduled to lead a Bible study each morning at the joint worship service.

Then, on the Saturday night before the Bible school was to begin the following Monday – it was the second week of August 1971 – I received a long distance phone call from my friend John Sherrill. John was at that time the senior editor of *Guideposts* and the man who was most responsible for my entrance into the field of professional writing.

John's usually cheerful voice was serious. He was asking me to join a small group of friends of Len LeSourd, who was the executive editor of *Guideposts*, and his wife, Catherine Marshall LeSourd, for a prayer retreat on Cape Cod. The infant child of Peter John Marshall, Catherine's son, and his wife Edith had serious congenital defects. The doctors said there was no hope for three-week-old Amy Catherine, but John felt that a few of us who were close to the family should gather around them in prayer during this critical time. Fifteen others were flying in from all over the United States. John realised it was short notice, but asked if I could catch a plane the next day and join them, beginning Sunday night.

I knew I was supposed to go. Jackie agreed, but immediately reminded me of my promise to be present during the Vacation Bible School.

'Inez will have your head on a platter,' she said. 'You need to call her tonight and let her know.'

But I was too cowardly. As long as I could remember I had been intimidated by authoritative women. No, I would rather face her the next morning at church and then slip out and catch the afternoon plane to Boston. It would be easier that way than trying to make an explanation over the phone.

The next morning the first person I saw as I came through the door of the Tabernacle was Inez Thompson. She immediately suspected something. 'Don't tell me,' she said half sarcastically. 'You're leaving town during Bible school.'

I swallowed. Hard. 'I'm sorry, Inez. It's an emergency. I received a phone call last night and I have to fly to Boston . . . '

She didn't let me finish. I saw the fire flashing in her eyes. 'I knew it! I knew you'd find some way to weasel out of your responsibility! You never can be counted on for the really important things. You are constantly making promises and then backing down. Nobody can trust you! You're the most irresponsible person I've ever known!'

My cheeks were burning. I tried to interrupt and make an explanation, but she was in no mood to listen to my excuses. I finally turned and walked away, feeling her glaring at the back of my neck, which felt as if it were on fire from embarrassment.

I wasn't very effective in the pulpit that morning. However, I had promised John I would inform the brethren in Melbourne of the situation. I knew they would want to join me in prayer for Peter, John, Edith, Len and Catherine, and of course, little Amy. After I preached I asked if there were any present who would join me at the altar for a few moments of prayer before I left.

A number of people came forward and knelt with me at the altar rail. After most of them had returned to their seats, I felt someone kneel down beside me. Looking up, I saw Inez's tear-stained face.

'I'm sorry, Jamie,' she said gently. 'I was selfish in wanting you to stay when you are needed up there. Please forgive me for the way I acted.'

I reached out and took her hand. We prayed together and I told her I understood. We embraced and then I had to leave. It was time to catch the plane.

Friends met me at Logan International Airport in Boston and drove me out to Peter John's little Community Church at East Dennis, on Cape Cod. The quaint white-sided church building was packed with people. They, too, were praying for the infant daughter of their young pastor. The evening service had already begun when we arrived and I was amazed to find Peter and Edith present in the service, along with most of the others from the special group. Instead of the sombre atmosphere I expected, however, the group seemed filled with joy and victory. The service was one of great happiness as the people sang and praised God for His goodness.

I made my way through a side door and took the only seat available, in a side choir loft between Catherine Marshall and another dear friend, Virginia Lively. Like Catherine and myself, Virginia lives in Florida, and is well known among Episcopal circles for her ministry of counselling and healing. I slipped in between them, nodded to Peter who was leading the singing, and joined in the praise and worship.

It was almost heavenly. Never had I been in a service of such intense worship and joy. Even though little Amy Catherine was dying in Boston Children's Hospital, the people, including the parents and grandparents, were determined to praise God. I joined in, thanking him I could be a part of such a time of worship among friends.

Then, suddenly, without warning, I began to feel dizzy. The more we sang and praised the Lord, the more nauseated I became. My head felt like it was caught in a giant vice and the pain behind my eyes was so intense I thought I was going to faint.

I turned to Virginia and said, with some difficulty. 'Virginia, I've just become deathly sick. Please pray for me.'

Virginia is a gracious, yet sometimes very blunt woman. A widow for a number of years, her time of walking with the Lord has given her deep insight into the things of the Spirit. She turned her head and looked deep into my eyes. 'Jamie, is there someone in your life you haven't forgiven?'

That was all she said. She continued to stare for a moment and then turned back to rejoin the singing. I was aghast. I had asked for bread and it seemed she had given me a stone. I didn't want a sermon, I wanted prayer.

I started to object, but could say nothing. I closed my eyes and when I did, deep inside, in that secret place where God often makes me aware of his voice, I heard him say:

'What about Inez?'

I wanted to argue with the Lord. I had forgiven her. I had even said so that morning at the altar rail. But the more I argued, the more I knew I hadn't. In fact, I had been sitting there thinking how good it was to be in Massachusetts sitting between Virginia and Catherine, rather than being back in Florida decorating my car with toilet paper.

The more I thought of this, the more I began to see Inez's side of the question. She had given months of her life to plan the Vacation Bible School. She wasn't doing it for herself, but for the children. And she was right in her accusations. I was an irresponsible louse. I had pulled this trick a dozen times in the past – not only with her, but with others as well. I was constantly making promises and then backing out in order to do something else which seemed more important.

And then, just as suddenly as the headache and nausea had appeared, it was gone. Vanished. I opened my eyes and realised I could sing again. I had been healed – not through the laying on of hands or prayer, but by forgiving that one against whom I had harboured resentment and by seeing the truth about myself.

The week went by in a hurry. The retreat was spent at the Community of Jesus near Orleans. We prayed for one another and prayed for the baby. Even though Amy Catherine eventually died, all of us who attended the prayer retreat knew that God had done a special work of grace in our hearts. Catherine, writing about that week in her book, *Something More*, said, 'It was as if the tiny baby Amy became a divine catalyst, calling forth a concentration of God's power and love for others.'

She was right. I returned to Florida chastened and eager to discover more about the healing power of forgiveness.

The very next week I locked myself in my little writing studio, along with my Bible and a concordance, determined to learn all I could about the Biblical concepts of forgiveness. If forgiving Inez, whom I loved, could bring instant healing, what power there must be if I went the extra mile and forgave those I didn't love.

The first verse I came upon was the one I had often heard David du Plessis use in his talks on forgiveness.

And when ye stand praying, forgive, if ye have aught against any: that your Father also which is in heaven may forgive you your trespasses (Mark 11:25).

I sat for a long time looking at that verse. I slowly underlined it with my yellow felt marker. Surely this must be another of the keys to inner healing.

For some reason it never occurred to me that God's forgiveness of my sins (not his forgiveness of my sin, for that was taken care of at Calvary and is an unmerited gift) was conditioned on my forgiveness of others. According to Jesus' statement, God would not forgive me as long as I held 'aught' against anyone else. In my unforgiveness of others, I had blocked God's forgiveness for myself. No wonder I could get ill so suddenly. I had stepped out from under his protection.

I decided it was time to take stock of my relationships and see if there was anyone else I held aught against. Taking a note pad and pencil, I prayed, asking God to reveal anyone I had not forgiven. There was too much at stake – God's forgiveness of my own trespasses – not to do so.

As I prayed a man came to mind. It was the name of a young man who had been a part of our church in its early days when we were meeting in the lounge of an old hotel located on the Indian River in Melbourne. Steven was a young, energetic fellow with a small business and a large family. In 1967, just before Christmas, he had stopped at my home with a sad tale that he couldn't pay his rent, his children weren't going to have any Christmas, and his wife needed medicine. I believed him. After all, he was devoting as much time to the church as he was to his business – which was probably one of the reasons things were going so badly for him. I felt responsible to help, but when he told me it would take $400 to pull him out, I realised it was more than I had. Jackie was having to juggle our own housekeeping account each week, trying to meet the needs of a young family with five children.

Still, we did have a savings account we had opened for the children. And since I knew Steven would pay me back, I dipped into it and withdrew $400 – which was all the children had.

He insisted on signing a note with interest. 'On or before May 1, 1968, I agree . . . '

But long before May 1st rolled around, Steven and his family had rolled out of town, taking up residence in a small town on the Gulf Coast of Florida.

I should have known better than to lend money to a friend. Give it maybe; but lend it, never. How well I remembered my dad quoting Shakespeare's advice in *Hamlet* when Polonius says to Laertes,

> Neither a borrower nor a lender be; for loan oft loses both itself and friend.

That's exactly what happened. A year later I wrote Steven a letter and sent it to his new address. 'Forget the interest and just pay the principal,' I wrote.

He wrote back. Business was bad, but he was due to get a bonus at the end of the year and would pay me. In the future, he asked, would I send all correspondence to his office since matters like this upset his wife.

Another year went by and I heard nothing. 'Matters like this also upset *your* wife,' Jackie said. 'I'm going to get some action.' She picked up the phone and called his wife. She was extremely apologetic and a week later we got a cheque for $50 with a promise to pay the balance in monthly instalments.

Two more years passed and we heard nothing. Gradually the situation began to eat away inside me. Sometimes at night

I would lie awake thinking about how to get my money back, and my blood would boil. All kinds of thoughts came to my mind and once again I thought of Shakespeare. Only this time it was *The Merchant Of Venice*, as I identified with Shylock who, when he could not collect his debts, determined to collect a pound of flesh instead.

Now, sitting in my little studio with my Bible in my lap open to Mark 11:25, I realised that although the bad debt obviously wasn't affecting my friend, it had been tearing me all to pieces. Slowly I became aware of the spiritual damage it was doing as I stewed in my resentment and bitterness. Instead of feeling such seething reaction, I knew I should be praying for my nonpaying friend. But it was impossible. All I wanted to do was choke him until he coughed up the money. And not only that, I found myself wanting to choke a lot of other people who had wronged me.

I returned to the Bible and the list of Scriptures on forgiveness. Before me was that familiar passage from the Lord's prayer:

> *And forgive us our debts, as we forgive our debtors (Matthew 6:12).*

I had repeated those words thousands of times, but had never seen them in this light. I actually had been asking God to forgive me the same way I was forgiving – or not forgiving – Steven. I trembled. What if God had answered that prayer? Surely he didn't lie awake at night figuring out ways to get even with me – at least I hoped not.

Every place I turned I found evidence of the truth that God was going to forgive me only in proportion as I forgave others. In one place Jesus said I was to forgive not seven times, but seventy times seven (Matthew 18:22). That added up to four hundred and ninety times, and I couldn't even forgive once.

In another place he indicated even my gifts to God were unacceptable as long as I was unreconciled with my brother.

That meant that although I had been tithing my income these last four years, I had missed the greater blessing from God because of my unforgiving attitude towards Steven.

'Oh, oh,' I moaned, 'the good news has become bad news.'

But how could I forgive him? He owed me money and I still had the note to prove it. It didn't seem there could be true forgiveness until the debt was paid. It was then I discovered another verse which is surely one of the key verses to abundant living and inner healing.

> And be ye kind to one another, tenderhearted, forgiving one another, even as God for Christ's sake hath forgiven you (Ephesians 4:32).

I was to forgive Steven exactly the same way God had forgiven me – by paying the debt myself. Going to my file cabinet, I dug through the yellow manilla folders and pulled out the four-year-old note. I wrote across the bottom, 'Paid in full for Jesus Christ's sake. Ephesians 4:32.' and I dropped it in the postbox.

It was as though a heavy weight had lifted from my mind. Since Steven no longer owed me money, I could love him again – and my channel to love others was also unplugged. Returning from the post office, I could hardly wait to tell Jackie the good news. The debt was paid.

Jackie stood in the kitchen, stirring a big pot of vegetable soup, as I told her of my decision. Replacing the lid on the simmering cauldron, she turned and grinned.

'Great! When Steven gets that note it will really prick his conscience. I'll bet we have our money back in less than a week.'

I reached out and pulled her close. Putting my finger on her nose in one of those little private affection touches which most husbands and wives develop across the years, I said gently 'You don't understand. The note is paid. Now if he sends us the money, we'll have to send it back or give it away. It's not ours. He doesn't owe us anything.'

Jackie nodded. 'You mean like we can't repay God, because Jesus has already paid the price.'

'Exactly!'

Interestingly enough, Steven did try to repay the loan. And true to our commitment, we could not accept it. When he refused to take it back, saying it had weighed heavily on his conscience, we agreed to give it away. He did reluctantly accept our cheque when we returned the interest. The balance we sent to a Filipino pastor who is operating a struggling Bible school on the island of Mindanao. However, I am convinced the thing which set Steven free to pay the debt was my forgiveness. It was the perfect explanation of a verse of Scripture which had long been a mystery to me:

> *Verily I say unto you, whatsoever ye shall bind on earth shall be bound in heaven; and whatsoever ye shall loose on earth shall be loosed in heaven (Matthew 18:18).*

I had, in my spirit, bound Steven to the very conditions I wanted changed. By my unforgiveness I had stood between him and the Holy Spirit's work in convicting him of the debt he owed. By stepping out of the way through forgiveness, I had released him from judgement and opened him to hear from the Holy Spirit, and be convicted he should repay the money he owed. Not only that, but I had released myself to receive the forgiveness of God and step into a new dimension of abundant living.

Forgiving Steven was only the beginning. It was now painfully evident there were many other *anys* whom I held *aught* against. I needed to get busy.

The next one that came to mind was even more difficult, for I was sure the person had already died. In fact, he had been dead a long time and, besides, I didn't even know his name. Yet the aught had been swimming around in the lake of my subconscious for more than twenty years, causing untold problems.

In the spring of my final year in college I bought a car to

drive back to Macon. There were five of us, school chums, who lived in the little town of Vero Beach, Florida, and had gone off to college together at Mercer University in Macon, Georgia. The other boys were as glad to see me get the car as I was. Now they could ride back and forth to college without having to spend all day and part of the night on a Greyhound bus. The car's maiden trip from Vero Beach to Macon came after the spring holidays. However, as we crossed the Georgia state line, I noticed the engine was running sluggishly. I had filled the car with petrol in Waycross, and by the time we got to Hawkinsville it was empty. I pulled into a little roadside garage and asked the mechanic if he could take a look at it.

He nodded and opened the bonnet. After a few minutes he withdrew his head and looked us over. It was obvious we were college kids, and of course the car had a Florida licence tag. He pulled the stub of an unlit cigar from his mouth and wiped his greasy hands on a piece of red cloth which seemed dirtier than his hands.

'You boys just wander around town for a while,' he said. 'I think I can have this fixed in an hour or so.'

An hour later we were back in the garage. He handed me a grimy piece of paper and said, 'She needed a new carburettor. That old one was shot. You owe me thirty-five dollars.'

Thirty-five dollars! That was all the money I had, and I expected it to last me until the end of term. Still, my folks had warned me the car would be an expensive item and it certainly wouldn't work without a carburettor. I paid him in cash and we drove on north to Macon. It ran like a top and I concluded it was probably worth the money to get it fixed.

The next day I was showing off the car in the car park and asked one of my fellow students, who had a reputation as a mechanic, to look at the engine.

'I've just had a new carburettor put in,' I said, 'so I know that's in good shape.'

After looking under the bonnet he said, 'This isn't a new

carburettor. It's the same one that's been on the car all along.'

'But I paid that fellow thirty-five dollars for a new one.'

My friend gave me a wide smile and said, 'Old buddy, you bought yourself thirty-five dollars worth of screw adjustment.'

I was furious. In fact, I was so angry I threatened to round up a carload of ATOs and drive back down to Hawkinsville and get my money back. I didn't, of course. I seldom do all the horrible things I threaten to do. But the resentment stayed with me, and from that time on, every time I drove through Hawkinsville I shook my fist at the old garage alongside the road.

A few years later, Jackie and I returned to Mercer for a visit. Driving through Hawkinsville I saw the old garage. Again the old feelings came bubbling to the surface. Anger. Bitterness. Hatred.

A number of years later we had to detour off the interstate highway and found ourselves once again in the small Georgia town of Hawkinsville. This time my children were in the car with us, and I deliberately drove down Highway 129 so I could point out the dingy old garage where I had been cheated. Inwardly I justified my actions, saying I needed to teach the children about dishonest mechanics who prey on unsuspecting people. What I was actually doing however, was trying to get even by turning my children against my old enemy, the mechanic.

I didn't realise it at the time, but at that point I was treading on very thin ice. In reality I was usurping an authority that belongs only to God. God never allows his children the luxury of 'getting even'. In fact, he doesn't even allow us the pleasure of nursing hurt feelings. To do so is the basest sort of sin.

Dearly beloved, avenge not yourselves, but rather give place unto wrath: for it is written, 'Vengeance is mine, I will repay,' saith the Lord (Romans 12:19).

Inadvertently, I was committing the same sin that caused Lucifer, the anointed cherub of God, to be banned from heaven. In Isaiah 14 the prophet lists the seven 'I wills' of Satan (Lucifer) who determined to usurp the power and authority of God, setting himself above God's law, vowing to do the things that God had reserved for himself. If God threw one of his servants out of heaven for such arrogance, what would he do to me? Yet in my forgiveness I continued seeking vengeance, not realising it was causing far more harm to me than to the one I hated.

The last time we came through Hawkinsville, the old garage was gone. It had burned down, or perhaps been torn down. All that remained was an empty field outside of town, cover with weeds, rusted car parts, and decaying rubber tyres. Yet as we passed the field there was still something inside me that raised its ugly head and cursed the old mechanic, who surely after all these years was dead and buried.

As this incident came to mind, I found myself raising the question: How can I forgive when the garage is gone and the owner dead? It was then the Lord showed me the secret of the *healing of memories*.

In the kingdom of God there is no time limitation. God, who lives in an entirely different dimension from us, is just as much a part of the past as he is of the present. I thought of the old Gospel song we used to sing:

When the trumpet of the Lord shall sound
And time shall be no more ...

The Bible says Jesus Christ is the same yesterday, today, and forever. He is not a part of this earthly kingdom which is limited by calendars, watches, yesterdays, and tomorrows. It is just as easy for Jesus Christ to reach back into the past and bring forgiveness as it is for him to touch us today, this instant.

Thus one afternoon, sitting in my car in a Melbourne,

Florida filling station while the attendant checked under my bonnet, I determined it was time to take care of this old 'aught'. I let my mind flash back to that afternoon in Hawkinsville when the old mechanic, with grease under his fingernails and a cigar in his mouth, had cheated me. In my mind I relived the event, and as I did I saw something I had never seen before. The man was ignorant of his sin. Oh, he knew he was cheating me; it was a way of life for him. He felt no qualms about taking advantage of a car full of college students. But then I saw him through the eyes of Jesus, and I was suddenly filled with an enormous love. So much love, in fact, that my eyes drowned in tears as I thought of all the hatred I had spewed out against him over the years.

'Oh, God,' I said inwardly, 'forgive me. I didn't know what I was doing either.' And the task was done. I saw Jesus standing in the garage, watching the old man as he took my money. I saw him when the next car of college boys came through, and he cheated them also. Jesus had been there all along, saying to the Father, 'He doesn't know what he's doing.' Jesus was not condoning his sin, nor was he trying to hide it. He was just forgiving it the same way he forgave those men who drove the spikes through his hands.

There are some who suggest the way to healing of the memories is by pretending certain things didn't happen. But God is a God of truth. He says that in the end everything that is covered shall be uncovered. Healing does not come by pretending, nor by imagining things could have been different. It comes by looking at our fellow men through the eyes of Jesus – and forgiving as God, for Christ's sake, forgives us.

There were many other 'anys' whom I held aught against. There was a woman in South Carolina who had lied about me. She had done it deliberately and it had caused deep hurt to my wife and my children. And would you believe I even discovered resentment against a little boy, a neighbourhood bully, who had punched my son in the nose fourteen years before. I had quickly controlled my anger in that situation, but in reality I had not dealt with it for I had never forgiven the boy. All I had done was push the memory of the incident down beneath the surface of my conscious mind into the reservoir of my subconscious. When I began probing around, I quickly realised it was there. Still unforgiven. I handled him, along with the woman from South Carolina, the same way I took care of the mechanic from Georgia. In each case I was so immersed in love that I found myself weeping in conviction as I saw them through the eyes of Jesus. I was experiencing what Paul was talking about when he said:

> . . . *the love of God is shed abroad in our hearts by the Holy Ghost which is given unto us* (*Romans 5:5*).

But the biggest aught was yet to come. My father was an astute and honourable businessman. He had moved to Florida from Indiana at the close of Word War I and become a pioneer in the citrus industry. The east coast of the state was virtually uninhabited in the early 1900s and he helped carve the niche where the little town of Vero Beach now rests. One of the advantages of pioneering is you get to pick up some excellent real estate. Besides the various citrus groves he owned or had an interest in, Daddy purchased forty-eight acres of choice property as his own personal homestead. He cleared part of the land and had it planted in select citrus. There was every imaginable type of fruit: oranges, grapefruit, tangelos, tangerines, kumquats, limes, and many varieties in between. Part of the sector was left in virgin foliage, called a 'hammock' in Florida. Another part of it was fenced-in pasture to take care of the several cows and small herd of Shetland ponies which we raised and sold on the market. Although our pasture adjoined the municipal golf course, which one day would make it extremely valuable, our nearest neighbours were more than half a mile away. It was 'country living' at its best.

The crowning glory of this beautiful piece of property was the house Dad had built. Dad never believed in borrowing money – for anything. His business acumen helped him save, however, and when he learned an entire consignment of California redwood had been mistakenly sidetracked in Vero Beach and was for sale, he waited until the price was right and bought it to build his house.

What a house it was. Solid redwood. Two storeys with sixteen big rooms. The floors were of hard oak and the formal staircase, extending up from the living room, was of birdseye cypress – polished to a gloss. Walls and ceilings of all the rooms were lightly stained in green, red, brown, or pale yellow to preserve the grain of the double-notched, tongue-and-groove six and eight-inch planks. The outside was redwood siding, painted to preserve it against the salty air which blew in from the nearby ocean. Inside the only place we saw paint was on the bathroom and kitchen ceilings. Everything else was wood, beautiful wood.

One of Dad's greatest innovations was the raised bath in the big upstairs bathroom. There were five of us children, four boys and a baby girl, and Dad knew the rigours of having to bend over a bath to scrub backs and then get rid of the ring on the bath. So he instructed the carpenters to raise the big six-foot bath thirty inches off the floor. Underneath were drawers for towels and at the end was a set of steps, guarded by a handrail, for entering and departing.

The entire house was like that. An upstairs clothes chute emptied into a dirty-clothes cupboard downstairs near the kitchen, which was a fine place to romp and play (or to be locked in for disciplinary purposes). A huge attic added another floor to the house and provided a wonderful place to work on model aeroplanes, make toy soldiers from a hot lead smelter, or rummage through Dad's old World War I relics.

The wooden walls and ceilings acted as sounding boards so that even though my two older brothers, Walter Jr and Clay, were in a room down the hall from the room where my younger brother and I slept, we could still talk through the house after the noise of the day subsided.

In those night hours I loved to lie on my bed next to the open window and listen to the outside noises: the steady whirr of the crickets harmonised with the percussion sounds of the frogs. The melody was sung by the plaintive calls of the whippoorwills, and sometimes, when the nearby hammock was bathed in moonlight, the solo parts were carried by the great owls hooting as they answered each other back and forth through the woods.

It was on a night such as this, when I was thirteen years old, that I overheard a conversation between my mother and father. It was long past the time when everyone should have been asleep and the only sound in the house, other than the occasional creaking of the boards as they cooled off, was the echo, of the deep tick-tock of the grandfather clock which hung on the landing of the stairs. For some reason I was still awake, dreaming those wonderful dreams of early adolescence which spring from a happy and secure child-hood. I could tell by his steady breathing that my younger brother, John Ladd (we called him Laddie then, although now that he has picked up a string of impressive medical degrees he goes by his formal name of John), was asleep. Just as I was drifting in and out of slumber, I recognised my mother's voice coming through the slightly ajar door.

My older brother, Clay, was the apple of her eye. Five years my elder, he was in his last year of school and was by far the most popular boy in the school. An all-state football and basketball athlete, he had just received a Congressional appointment to the U.S. Military Academy at West Point. I almost idolised Clay, for he was all the things I wanted to be when I entered high school. Clean cut, disciplined in his studies as well as his athletics, deeply moral – it's no wonder my mother was so proud. He had given her his gold footballs and basketballs, awarded him for stellar athletic perform-ances, and she had them made into a necklace which she wore with unabashed pride. I think it embarrassed Clay a little, but he loved and honoured his parents. His mother could do no wrong – even when she was bragging about him.

That night I heard her talking softly to Dad, who was in the other bed. Still basking in the glory of Clay's appointment to West Point, she said: 'I'm so proud of Clay. He's the finest son we have.'

There was more, but that was all I heard. Already sensitive over the inordinate attention my older brother was receiving from my mother, I closed my mind. It was as though she had said, 'I love Clay more than I love Jamie.' And suddenly, as though it was built with concrete blocks, there appeared a wall between me and my mother – a wall which was to remain for almost twenty-five years.

The disease of unforgiveness spread until it infected my relationship with all women – especially those who bore authority. Women were to be used, manipulated. The thought sometimes occurred to me that had not God put his hand on my life in such a dramatic way, I had the makings of a Lothario. Fortunately this was buried so deeply in my lake, and covered so thoroughly with the grace of God and the love of my family, that it never did come to the surface. But deep inside I knew there lurked an exaggerated awareness and declaration of masculinity – a macho attitude – which was determined to assert itself over all female figures.

My relationship with my mother, seemed, on the surface, to be loving and healthy. When we did have clashes – as we usually did when we were together – we blamed it on 'temperament' differences. Now I realise that temperament is nothing more than the exhibition of the subconscious. If the inner lake is filled with unforgiveness, then your temperament will reflect it. If the subconscious has been made transparent through forgiveness, then things will be much, much different.

However, even though I was able to camouflage my feelings about my mother, others – especially those closest to me – noticed them. Jackie, in particular, recognised it. Often when I would flare up at her, she would quickly analyse the situation and say, 'I remind you of your mother, don't I?'

She was right. Especially was this true when she tried to assert herself against my will. In the deep places of my mind I had long ago disqualified my mother's right to assert herself in my life. In my thinking, if she didn't love me, then she had no right to tell me what to do. Across the years, as this lie got buried deeper and deeper in my lake, it finally took on the shape of 'no woman has the right to tell me what to do'. It was for this reason that Inez Thompson, and a host of other strong-willed women, caused me to react with hostility – even though I thought I loved them deeply.

Yet, strangely, on the other hand, I was putty in the hands of a woman who was tender, gentle, and submissive. I recognised this, and in the midst of some of the raging arguments which often erupted between Jackie and me, I would abruptly stop and say, 'Just love me, Honey. Don't shout at me, just come and hold me and I'll be all right.'

Recognising that my personality suffered from a kind of spiritual malnutrition caused by the shut doors of unforgiveness, Jackie learned that I could be brought into a semblance of emotional balance through a great deal of affectionate coddling. But we both knew this was sick. I was still a little boy demanding to be my mummy's favourite.

Thus, as I ran this deep inventory on my subconscious, checking out the aughts and anys, I eventually got to that massive closed door – my relationship with my mother.

However, recognising it existed only heightened the confusion. I knew I had to forgive her. But how? She was now in her mid-seventies, and over the years our relationship had improved to the extent that I loved her far more than I ever dreamed possible. In fact, not only did I love her, but I had grown to respect her judgement and appreciate her deep commitment to the Lord. She was by far my strongest supporter and biggest fan. If it were possible, I think she would have had the dust jackets of my books reduced to miniature form, gold-plated, and made into a necklace. How she delighted in bragging about me, loving my children, and showering her affection on Jackie. In fact, as I examined that door more closely, I saw it was only a shadow. Somewhere, across the years, it had distintegrated. Perhaps it happened when I received the baptism in the Holy Spirit, perhaps long before. Now all that remained was an image. Yet that image was just as real as if the solid door were still there, for it had kept her out of the inner place of my life, and kept me from reaching out to her in genuine love and trust. My mother wasn't the problem, I was.

'Let me show you something about those kind of doors,' God seemed to say to me one morning when I was praying. 'None of them are real. Once a door like that is bathed in the blood of my Son, Jesus, it disintegrates. True, it may look as if it is still there. But it's there only in your imagination. I have set you free.'

I was reminded of the experience of Simon Peter in Herod's prison. Arrested following the execution of the Apostle James, he was chained in a prison dungeon between two soldiers who kept constant watch over him. Between him and freedom were three massive gates and sixteen soldiers charged by the king to guard him specifically. Yet that night an angel of the Lord appeared in the cell, opening the doors, loosening the chains, and causing a deep sleep to fall on the guards. Even so, Peter was not free until he got up from the dungeon and walked through the open doors and out into the city (Acts 12:1-19).

I realised I would never be free from the spectre of that dark night when I imagined my mother no longer loved me, until I walked through the door of forgiveness – a door already opened by the work of Jesus in my life.

'But how do I do it, Lord?' I asked. 'Surely you don't expect me to go to my mother, after all these years, and say, "Mum, I forgive you for leaving the impression you loved Clay more than you loved me. It's caused me years of heartache and problems, but I forgive you for Jesus' sake." Surely, Lord, you don't want me to say anything like that. That would be cruel.'

'You're right,' the Lord said quietly. 'Besides, most of those problems were of your own doing. All I want you to do is look at your mother the way I look at her, and love her the way I love her.'

'I do love her,' I answered.

Then it was I discovered how to tell a person you forgive them. You do it by telling them you love them. Genuine forgiveness will always manifest itself in love. In fact, if it doesn't cause you to love the person forgiven, there is good reason to doubt the sincerity and genuineness of your forgiveness. You love because you forgive. Forgiveness is an act of the will. Love is the result. The fact that I really loved my mother was evidence that I had already, sometime in the distant past, forgiven her. There was nothing more that needed to be done – except express that love through action and word.

The way to say, 'I forgive you', is to say, 'I love you'.

Several years ago I attended a three-day retreat at the Methodist Youth Camp near Leesburg, Florida. Even though the retreat was scheduled during an extremely busy time of my life, I welcomed the opportunity to withdraw with members of our church family and spend a relaxing time in fellowship and prayer.

Shortly after we arrived at the beautiful camp which is situated on Lake Griffin, one of those sparkling lakes which dot central Florida, I began to feel uneasy. As the first day wore on I gradually became aware that my uneasiness was in some way connected to the fact that the camp was owned and operated by the Methodist church. In fact, just seeing the signs on the buildings, and walking into the chapel and seeing the Methodist hymnals in the pew racks, gave arousal to feelings of bitterness. Why, though, should this make me feel uncomfortable? After all, some of my earliest childhood memories were related to the Methodist church where Dad taught in the Sunday school.

That evening, as I sat in the back of the chapel listening to one of my friends lead the Bible study, it slowly dawned on me that I still held aught against the Methodist church back in Vero Beach. During my school years I attended, along with many of the members of the football team, Sunday

evening activities at the local Methodist church. We enjoyed
the fun and food served by the Methodist Youth Fellowship
(MYF) and especially was I drawn to the personable young
pastor who often joined the football team during afternoon
workouts. He was a 'swell guy', in the vernacular of the high
school athletes. He came to football practice dressed in track
suit, ran wind sprints with us, and acted as the unofficial
chaplain for the team. Coaches and players alike appreciated
his presence.

But his relationship with the boys never went any deeper
than that. When one of the boys on the team got one of the
cheerleaders pregnant, he went to the pastor – only to be
referred to a social worker in the community. The boy later
told me that he really wanted an experience with God, he
wanted to be forgiven for his sins, but the pastor seemingly
missed that point altogether.

One night after MYF the pastor asked me if I would speak
during a youth night service. I was thrilled and scared. But
later, when I went to him for help, the best he could do was
give me a book of devotions and suggest I memorise one of
them for my talk. At the last minute I called him and told
him I didn't think I could speak. He laughed and said I was a
terror on the football field, but a chicken in church. I agreed,
and we left it that way. Gradually I dropped out of the
Methodist church and drifted across town to the Baptist
church where my girl friend attended.

However, across the years I began to blame much of my
lack of spiritual understanding on that Methodist pastor. He
had an ideal opportunity to turn a whole football team towards God, but rather than run the risk of losing some by
getting too spiritual, he had opted to cling to his role as a
'swell guy'.

Somehow I transferred his failure to reach me to the
church he represented, the Methodist church. In my mind it
was really a denomination which had failed me, not just a
minister. Working on this premise I began to see many other
flaws in the Methodist church. When some of my friends

said their literature no longer honoured Christ, I agreed. When a renegade Methodist pastor accused the church of turning from the heritage of John and Charles Wesley to a social Gospel orientation, it gave additional fuel to my fire. For years this thing had smouldered deep in the back of my mind, sending up dense clouds of smoke which prevented me from ever seeing any good in the entire Methodist denomination. Now, closeted away for three days in a Methodist camp, all these memories came floating to the surface. I knew they had to be dealt with. But how?

The last morning at the retreat I rose early. Tiptoeing out of my cabin in the grey of the dawn, I wandered down a wooded path to a secluded spot beside the lake. There, under giant overhanging oaks, I found a seat of cypress stump in a spot designated 'the chapel in the woods'. Chin in hands, I sat brooding, wishing I could forgive and clean my mind, but not knowing how. After all, the literature *was* socially oriented, and there was a lack of emphasis on spiritual things. How could I forgive when the very things I held as aughts seemed to be true?

As the sky turned from grey to rose and the first rays of the sun reflected off the rippling waters of the lake, I became aware of a life-sized cross which had been erected near the water's edge. At least the Methodists still held to the 'form' of Christianity, I conceded.

For a long time I sat, looking. The only sounds were the noises of nature – the twittering birds, the lapping water, the swish-swish of the limbs in the trees. I couldn't get my eyes off that cross, silhouetted against the rising sun. What would it be like to touch it? To place my arms against the outstretched beams? No one in the camp was yet stirring. If I was ever going to do an odd thing like that, now was the time.

I don't know how long I stood there, arms outstretched, hands pressed against those rough, splintering beams. Gradually, though, I began to tire. My shoulders ached and my arms were weary. But I would not take them down. I wanted to stay on forever, where my Lord had hung.

I felt my arms falling and reached for the top of the cross-beams to hold on. Each second seemed meaningful. But as I gripped the tops of the crossbars, I noticed something strange. The texture of the wood was different. On the sides it was rough, rugged. On top it was smooth.

Painfully, I realised what it meant. I was not the first to put myself against that cross. Countless others – those Methodists whom I had criticised as 'un-godly' and 'un-spiritual' – had been there before me. By the hundreds. Perhaps thousands. It was their tired hands which had worn the wood smooth.

I returned to camp, chastened. That morning in the Bible study in the chapel, as we sang from the Methodist Hymn Book, the words took on a new meaning. I saw things from a different perspective. By the time we left that afternoon to drive back to the east coast, my whole manner of thinking had changed. In a final time of devotions, before we broke camp, I led the group in a prayer of thanksgiving for our Methodist brethren who had built that camp for the glory of God.

Everything, I discovered, looks different when you view it from the cross. It's there that inner healing begins – and finds its fulfilment.

6

MY WORLD UNDER WATER

It was a strange group, the sixteen of us who gathered that quiet August morning in 1971 in the big, sunny living room of the Bethany retreat house of The Community of Jesus on Cape Cod. Some of the people I knew, some I had only heard of through Len and Catherine LeSourd. We were all there for a common purpose, to surround Catherine's son, Peter John, and his wife Edith with our love – and to pray for tiny Amy Catherine who was in the Boston Children's Hospital, ninety miles away, slowly dying.

None of us knew how long we were supposed to stay, nor had any plans been made other than we were to eat our meals in the big community house where we were meeting. There was no leader, although we were looking to John Sherrill, who had made the arrangements for us to stay at the Community, and to Len who, although very soft spoken and easy going, was by nature a leader. The Community of Jesus is made up of several houses situated on the edge of Cape Cod Bay at Rock Harbor, a little fishing village near Orleans. In some vague way it resembled a Protestant monastry composed of both single girls who committed themselves to chastity and service, and families which maintained their own homes in the immediate vicinity and were deeply submitted to one another and the Community leadership. We were simply using their facilities.

After breakfast that Monday morning we gathered in the

big living room with its large windows facing the undulating waters of the bay. Seated in a rough circle around the room, we listened while Len suggested we take turns introducing ourselves and stating any personal needs. I welcomed this approach, for it would give me an opportunity to meet those I was seeing for the first time. On the other hand, it seemed a bit strange to begin this way, since we had gathered primarily to pray for the baby.

Each one of us took a few minutes to state where we were spiritually. Several in the group were exactingly honest and talked about their need for inner healing. All seemed to believe God had called us together so we could be cleansed in the deep areas of our lives.

About mid-morning we took a break and enjoyed tea and biscuits served by one of the 'sisters' of the Community – a beautiful young woman dressed in a simple blue and white uniform who padded in silently with a tray, smiled, and disappeared back into the kitchen. A few moments later we rejoined the circle and listened as Peter gave us the latest report on Amy Catherine. Several of the group expressed a desire to drive into Boston and lay hands on the baby, praying for her healing. Others were more cautious, feeling we should do nothing until we had direct 'guidance' from God. We agreed to wait, pray, and do only that which had the approval of the entire group. Already, in those few short moments, we had taken on the aspect of a church: a group of called-out ones, committed to the lordship of Jesus Christ and submitted to one another. We sat silently, waiting . . . praying.

Outside I could hear the Indian summer wind blowing in off the bay and moaning around the eaves of the big house. The brown and tan sea oats, which adorned the sand dunes between the house and the water, moved gracefully in the wind. A brilliant red cardinal pecked at the sill of the large picture window, sharpening his beak on the stone. I glanced around the room and felt that strong familiar surge of love for each one present, I closed my eyes and blended my mind with theirs, and with God, seeking his guidance for that hour.

Something was happening. A firm impression was forming in my mind concerning the woman sitting across the room in a wingback chair. I had met her for the first time only that morning. She was the wife of a well-known American businessman who could not come to the retreat, but had urged his wife to take his place. I knew, from her brief introductory statement as we shared earlier in the morning, that this kind of retreat was a new experience for her. Yet I had the strongest feeling she was to be a vital part of what God was doing this week. Since we had agreed to share any impression of guidance with the entire group, I spoke out.

'I feel a small group is to drive into Boston and lay hands on Amy Catherine. I also have the strongest impression that you – and I pointed my finger at the woman and called her name – are to go along and hold the baby while the others pray for her.'

I heard a gasp from across the room. The woman's face blanched. 'How can you say that? You don't even know me.' She was obviously frightened. This concept of sitting quietly and hearing from God was strange and unfamiliar to her. She looked across the room at Catherine, who was the only person in the room she knew well, and said, 'I can't do a thing like that. All the rest of you people are Christians. I don't even know what is going on here. I'm just here because my husband sent me. I'm not worthy to hold that baby. I don't even know how to pray . . .' She was weeping by this time and suddenly every mind in that room focused away from that tiny baby in the Boston hospital, and centred on this other child, sitting in our midst, who was also dying – not physically, but of far worse spiritual malady.

Catherine got up from the sofa where she had been sitting beside Len, crossed the room, and knelt down beside the woman's chair. In just a few moments, using passages of Scripture which had been familiar to her since childhood, Catherine led her to the place of committing her life to Jesus Christ. The rest of us in the room watched, in delight, as the gloom and fear on her face gave way to joy, much as the darkness of night is dispelled by the coming of dawn. She looked across the room as though she were seeing us for the first time – her eyes brimming with tears of happiness.

Charles Hotchkiss, a young Episcopal priest from Florida and a long-time friend of the LeSourds, left his chair and stood behind her. I sensed what was about to happen. Gently he laid his hands on her head and began to pray softly. The rest of us in the circle joined hands, forming a ring of prayer around Father Hotchkiss and the one for whom he was praying. She was slowly lifting her hands above her head and then out of her mouth, softly at first, but plainly audible, came unintelligible sounds, a heavenly language. Gentle and beautiful, the sounds flowed from her lips like the trickling of spring water over smooth rocks. Her eyes were closed and after her face was bathed in a soft glow, the light of peace. I bowed my head and held back the tears, tears that always seem to come when I am in the presence of one so gently touched by the Holy Spirit. For a moment I sensed what it must have been like, those many years ago, when Simon Peter came to the house of Cornelius and this identical thing happened. Yet this wasn't the Book of Acts, nor was it the City of Caesarea – it was the twentieth century and we were on Cape Cod.

Nothing had been said about 'praying in the Spirit.' No one had coached her. To my knowledge this was her first experience in any kind of group where something like this might occur, yet none of us had indicated we used a prayer language. It had come directly from God.

As the ecstasy subsided, the rest of us moved in to embrace her, then to embrace one another. The room seemed saturated with love and joy. Then John Sherrill, in a cheerful voice, asked a staggering question.

'Why don't we go all the way? We have witnessed conversion and the baptism in the Spirit. Why don't we have a water baptism service as well. After all, we have access to the biggest baptistry in New England, Cape Cod Bay. Surely it's deep enough for her to be immersed.

It was a fabulous idea – at least to a confirmed Baptist like myself – but I was astonished that it came from John, whom I knew as a rather traditional Episcopalian.

John gave me an 'oh-I-thought-you-knew' laugh and proceeded to tell me that he and his wife, Elizabeth, had recently been immersed in Charles Hotchkiss's Episcopal church in the little Florida town of Clewiston.

It was no wonder the group was excited over the prospect of another water baptism service. Peter John and Edith both injected that they, too, had been praying about water baptism and felt this was their time also. We agreed to hurry and change clothes, for the tide was beginning to ebb in the bay. If we didn't get to the water quickly, all we would find would be miles and miles of exposed mud flats until the tide returned.

I had a kind of inner excitement about the matter. I knew I was the only baptist in the group and even though Father Hotchkiss had immersed a few people recently, his experience at conducting water baptism services was nothing compared to mine. It seemed natural that I should 'officiate' at the service, a position which seemed very important to me because of my personal insecurity about being among these giants. These others might be experts in their fields – writing, editing, or the healing ministry – but I was an expert baptiser.

But God had other ideas and as the group left the house to make our way over the sand dunes and through the waist-high sea oats towards the water, I suddenly found myself in his presence. It was one of those rare times when I knew the Holy Spirit was teaching me. It developed into a dialogue as we headed towards the bay.

'You're not going to do the baptising,' he said. The voice, although not audible, was just as real as if I had been standing in a classroom talking to a teacher.

'But I'm the most qualified. Beside, I want to. I *need* to.' I had so little I could hold out as trophies to make others notice me. Surely God would recogise my experience and not take this one claim to fame away from me. After all, it would be quite a feather in my cap to say I had officiated at this historic baptismal service. How blind I was to the deeper things of the Spirit. How desperately my inner man needed healing.

'No, I am not going to let you do the baptising, because your own water baptism was out of order.'

I knew, of course, what he was talking about. It had bothered me, on and off across the years, but like a lot of other things which were not quite right, I had stuffed it down beneath the surface of my lake and tried to forget about it. It was only on occasions like this, when the Holy Spirit stirred the waters, that the question ever surfaced.

During my teenage years I had joined the First Baptist Church of Vero Beach, Florida. A lot of kids joined the church during adolescence, and the fact that the girl I later married was already a member was all the incentive I needed. In order to become a full member of the church, I needed to be immersed. I talked to the pastor and then on a Sunday morning, prodded by my mother who also felt it was proper that I join a church, I walked down the aisle and was received with what Baptists called 'the right hand of fellowship'. A week later, on a Sunday night, the pastor ushered me into the church baptistry and, suitably adorned in a white robe, I was immersed.

But there had ben no accompanying spiritual experience, no surrender of my will to Jesus Christ's. Even though the words were used, they were simply words. It wasn't for several years, when I found myself at that campfire service on an island in Shroon Lake, New York, that I made the necessary spiritual commitment to the lordship of Christ.

Across the years I knew my water baptism had been 'out of order.' I had known this, and at times it had bothered me. However, after a number of years in the ministry, my pride became strong enough to keep those troublesome thoughts from rippling the surface very often. After all, what would people think, if after all those years of baptising other people, I admitted I needed to be baptised? Wouldn't they lose confidence in me if I let my mask down and confessed this spiritual tangle in my life? No, it had seemed best to simply leave it alone. No one really cared when I was baptised and as long as there were no questions, why should I stir the waters and cause confusion.

But God is never finished with a man until he is conformed to the image of his Son. In this case I knew the matter of water baptism was second in importance to the fact I had been living a lie all those years – and was satisfied with it. Some matters can be handled by confession and absolution. In other matters confession is not enough, a person needs to set things right. My water baptism was one of those things that I could no longer push beneath the surface of my lake and pretend all was well. It was time to make the correction. Publicly.

'But who will perform those baptisms if I don't?' I asked the Holy Spirit.

'Why, Charles Hotchkiss, who else?' he responded.

I dreaded asking the next question for I already knew the answer. 'And who will baptise me?'

'Charles Hotchkiss,' the Spirit answered – and I could almost hear him chuckle. 'You'll be the first candidate when we get to the bay.'

'Oh, God!' I moaned inwardly. 'He's an Episcopal priest and I'm a Southern Baptist minister.'

This time it seemed the Holy Spirit laughed out loud.

However, in my obedience to the command of God, something else had happened. In fact, it happened even before we reached the water. When the Holy Spirit decides to teach a lesson, he can do it in split seconds. In my case, he did it as I was gingerly making my way through the sea oats, making sure my bare feet did not step on something sharp.

Immediately I began to think of the sins I had served – the elements in life which had controlled me. For years I had been a slave to strawberry shortcake. While others might have been addicted to alcohol or drugs, I was addicted to food. In short, I was a glutton. I was also fat. Not 'stocky,' but blubbery fat. I carried around my waist more than twenty-five pounds of excess flesh. I had been on every diet imaginable, but all they did was set the stage for a subsequent weight gain.

I had taken up jogging, but a huge brown dog with blood-shot eyes and claws that went 'clickety-click' on the concrete behind me sent me into wind sprints for home.

'Your brother, who is five years older than you, does one hundred push-ups each morning,' my mother bragged. Having competed with Clay all my life, I decided to get the Royal Canadian Air Force list of calisthenics and start to work. It was hopeless. There never was any time, and when I finally got around to it, my teenage daughters went into hysterics. 'Daddy, it shakes like jelly!'

I had resigned myself to remaining fat; yet deep inside I knew I wasn't supposed to be that way. One of my positive-thinking colleagues said the answer was to 'think slim'. But it's hard to think slim when you have difficulty bending over to tie your shoes. One clothing store clerk even had the audacity to say, 'Sir, if you'll stop holding your breath, I can get a correct measurement.' No amount of thinking slim would take care of my problem. It was far deeper than that, stemming from an inner condition of insecurity and bondage which caused me to crave food even when I wasn't hungry.

Now I began to realise that water baptism was another key to inner healing, for in submitting I was actually appropriating the death of Christ to my own subconscious appetites:

. . . that like as Christ was raised up from the dead by the glory of the Father, even so we also should walk in new-ness of life (*Romans 6:4*).

Suddenly I was filled with a new excitement that this could be one of the turning points of my life; that in water baptism I was actually going to leave my old wordly appetites under the water of Cape Cod Bay – which, symbolically, was ebbing out to sea and taking all the old pollution with it.

We arrived at the water's edge and I pulled Father Hotchkiss aside, asking if he would grant my unusual request and baptise me first, even before the now-excited woman who, only moments before, had accepted Christ as Lord. (By the way, she later accompanied a small group of us to the children's hospital in Boston and did hold Amy Catherine while we prayed for her. And even though the child died just two weeks later, I understood that this new change in the woman's life, coupled with her willingness to hold that tiny baby while we prayed, brought about a marvellous new relationship with her own daughter – a relationship which had been strained for many years.)

Father Hotchkiss asked me a few questions, for he was as mystified over my request as I. However, he agreed to take me into the water first. He quickly made it plain that if I was to submit to water baptism, I would also have to submit to his method.

I had no sooner agreed than he turned to the group which had assembled on the beach and said, 'Jamie wants to go first, but before I baptise him he wants to confess his sins before you.'

I hadn't counted on that. But I had come this far and there was no use in stopping. If my friends rejected me on the basis of my sins, that was their problem, not mine. I was determined to go all the way and leave my world under water.

So I named them: gluttony, lust, resentment, unforgiveness, pride, self-righteousness . . . on and on the list went. It was difficult, and terribly embarrassing. If there was any group in the world I wanted to impress with my spirituality, this was it. Yet I knew God was pleased.

We waded out into the bay which by that time was visibly receding. I crossed my hands in front of my chest, waiting for Father Hotchkiss to lower me backwards beneath the water.

'On your knees!' the priest said.

I started to protest, but I remembered I had agreed to do it his way, no matter how strange it was. I dropped to my knees on the sandy bottom. The warm water came up to my chest. I felt the priest's hand on the back of my head and realised I was getting ready to go under face first. As he offered a brief prayer, I looked down into the ebbing water of the bay and repeated that prayer of commitment which Jesus prayed on the cross, 'Father, into thy hands I commend my spirit.'

I came up, shaking the water out of my ears, just in time to hear the priest say, 'That's for the Father.' Then, before I could catch a good breath, I was under again. This time for the Son, and finally, a third time, for the Holy Spirit. I guess he figured he'd never get his hands on another Baptist minister.

Something did happen out there in the water, something in my inner spirit which had to do with discipline. I had begun a fast that day which I expected would last three days – which was the longest I had ever been without food. Instead, it lasted twenty-eight days. During that time I began to experience a new surge of spiritual authority. Not only were my old 'appetites' being broken, but by the time I returned home at the end of the week, I felt like Moses descending from Mt Sinai with the tablets of stone in his hand and the radiance of God on his face. Apart from my experience with the baptism in the Holy Spirit, nothing had so visibly shaken and shaped my life as did my submission to water baptism. It was, fact, another step to the healing of the inner man.

Almost at once, however, I realised that testing always accompanies fasting. It was the same with Moses. After forty days of fasting and communing with God, he returned from Mt Sinai only to find the children of Israel had gone wild – rebelling against God, practising licentiousness, and worshipping a golden idol which had been fashioned by Moses' brother Aaron. Something akin to this happened following Jesus' water baptism at the hands of John the Baptist. He was led by the Spirit into the wilderness where he fasted.

And when he had fasted forty days and forty nights, he was afterwards an hungred. And when the tempter came to him, he said, If thou be the Son of God, command that these stones be made bread (Matthew 4:2, 3).

It seems there is a biblical principle here. Every mountain top experience is followed by a valley. But it is in the valley that the true temper of the steel is tested. It is only when a life is under pressure that a person can determine if there are leaks.

Several years ago we installed an underground sprinkling system in our garden. With the help of my children, I finally managed to dig up the garden and lay what seemed to be end-less miles of plastic pipe. Then, using an abundance of tape, glue, and clamps, we got the thing hooked up. Like repairing a locomotive that is underway, the job was technically inter-esting, but not much fun.

A friend gave me a rebuilt three-quarter-horsepower pump which I hooked to a pipe that ran into the lake behind our house. Presto, we had water on the lawn.

But something was wrong. The water was not evenly dis-tributed, and unless we had a strong east wind, a portion of the garden never got wet. The little pump simply did not have enough power to give pressure to all those sprinkler heads. I had a choice of blocking off most of the sprinklers or getting a more powerful pump. I opted for the pump.

After three months of fiddling with the system, I finally went out and bought a brand new three-horsepower pump. The salesman assured me it was big enough to water the lawn of the White House. I spent most of Monday running a larger intake pipe out into the lake and installing the new self-priming pump. Then came the moment of truth as I stepped inside the back door and flipped the switch. The pump whirred into life and we had water. I mean we really had water!

Where my old system – held together with glue, rotting tape, and rusty clamps – had been sufficient for the three-quarter-horsepower pump, it was totally inadequate for this new big pump which exerted more than four times the amount of pressure. Water squirted everywhere. Underground connections burst loose and erupted in the yard like geysers, blowing dirt and grass up with them. Tape peeled off and exposed connections, sending out streams of water. Tiny pinholes in the pipes, unnoticed before, suddenly opened and sprayed water in all directions. Loose sprinkler heads exploded off their connections as the water roared upwards in gushers higher than the roof of the house. Flaws, blemishes, and defects which had remained unnoticed were suddenly exposed as the new power surged through.

So it was when I came off my twenty-eight-day fast. All my spirituality was gone – in the testing time after that fast it just gushed out of my inadequate piping system. I found myself with a ravenous appetite and was constantly losing my temper over the most inconsequential things.

'If that's what being baptised in water does to a person,' Jackie commented one evening after I had just lost my temper and slammed a door, 'then you better not recommend it to anyone else.'

I was chagrined. Yet even so I knew that something had happened to me. It was not just an emotional kick, I had literally moved into another dimension of life. Despite the fact there was still much evidence of the old life, I suspected it was something like a snake shedding its skin. The old skin was still there, and quite obviously a part of the snake, but it was dead. And in due time it would come off and be left behind. For the first time in my life I began to look at my defects and flaws not as insurmountable problems, but as challenges to be conquered – and left behind.

Someone said, 'I don't care how loud you shout, or how high you jump, as long as you walk straight when you hit the ground.' I was beginning to understand that. It's not the start, it's the finish that counts; and until I allow the Holy Spirit to take total control of *all* my life, I will have to go through the times of testing. If it was true for Jesus, how much more so for me.

Paul told the Ephesians to be strong and *stand* against the trickery of the devil. In fact, he used the word 'stand' four times in that strong passage of Ephesians 6:

> *Put on the whole armour of God, that ye may be able to stand against the wiles of the devil . . . wherefore take unto you the whole armour of God, that ye may be able to withstand in the evil day, and having done all, to stand. Stand therefore . . . (Ephesians 6:11, 13, 14).*

There comes a point, he was saying, in your Christian experience when God has done for you all he can do. He gave you his Son. He gave you his Spirit. He gave you his Word. He emptied Heaven and gave it to you. There is nothing more God can do. It is at this time that God asks you to stand.

There are some situations that can be changed directly by prayer. There are other situations that can best be changed by personal counsel. Conversely, there are some situations that can be changed by healing or deliverance, but there are other situations in which God requires a person to *stand*. That is why Paul said four times: 'Stand therefore . . . ' (The Greek word means to stand as a conqueror.)

There is a teaching going out through the Church that you can praise your way out of anything. I believe in praise. It is a great and wonderful and powerful tool. But it can be a very injurious thing to teach people all they have to do is praise, no matter what is going on, and they'll come out of every situation bouncing and springing. It is more complicated than that.

The same is true with any mechanical device of religion: water baptism, healing of the memories, deliverance, even prayer. There will come a time in your spiritual life, if you walk deep enough with the Lord, when you will eventually run into the principalities and powers. At this time, when you are involved in spiritual warfare that is so deep and complicated that you can't even describe your feelings with accuracy, there is but one thing you can do. Stand.

One of my favourite Bible stories centres on Moses at the Red Sea. The Egyptian armies were closing in on the Hebrew people who were fleeing from Pharaoh across the desert when ahead of them loomed the Red Sea. There was no place to go. The enemy was behind them and the sea before them. The people, frantic with fear and anger, turned on Moses, their leader.

> *Because there were no graves in Egypt, hast thou taken us away to die in the wilderness? ... It had been better for us to serve the Egyptians, than that we should die in the wilderness (Exodus 14:11, 12).*

Moses' answer to their bitter clamouring must certainly be ranked as one of the great passages of all history. Turning to the people he said calmly,

> *Fear ye not, stand still and see the salvation of the Lord, which he will show to you today ... The Lord shall fight for you, and ye shall hold your peace (Exodus 14:13, 14).*

In so many words he was saying what Paul later advised the church at Ephesus: *Don't just do something, stand there.*

My own personal test came shortly after I returned from Cape Cod and the fast was finally over. During the four years following my baptism in the Holy Spirit, our Baptist church in Melbourne, Florida, had made rapid strides towards taking on the shape of a New Testament body of believers. However, the closer we moved to New Testament forms and patterns, the further we were removed from our denominational traditions – and the more we seemed to agitate the other Baptist churches in our local association.

The week I ended my fast I was called before the Executive Committee of the Brevard Baptist Association to explain our actions in dissolving our membership rolls in favour of an open membership.

I tried to remind these other Baptist pastors that Baptists had always believed in a New Testament structure for the local church. We were just trying to put that into effect, and since I could find no authority in the Bible for having a church membership – or for that matter, dividing ourselves into separate denominations in order to exclude other Christians from our fellowship – we were simply transcending the man-made traditions to return to the patterns of the Book of Acts.

The pastors were kind, but firm. They wanted us out of the Association. I suspected the real reason lay in the fact that many of the people in our rapidly growing congregation spoke in tongues and we often had public healing services. However, this was never mentioned since Baptists also believe strongly in the autonomy of the local church and these men knew if they began a doctrinal investigation of our church, they would open themselves to a similar investigation themselves. None of them wanted that.

So, on the basis of a technicality – the fact that the Associational Constitution and By-laws said that only 'members' of a local Baptist church could attend the associational meetings – they voted unanimously (I abstained from voting) not to seat any messengers from our church if they showed up at the annual associational meeting the following week.

I was crushed. Their action was tantamount to casting us out of the Southern Baptist Convention, since membership in the SBC was contingent upon membership in the local association of churches. My roots ran deeply into the Baptist heritage. I had attended a Baptist college and held degrees from a Baptist seminary. For fifteen years I had pastored Baptist churches. I had served on various committees and boards on both state and nationwide levels. My parents had donated the old homestead, those forty-eight acres of choice land in Vero Beach, Florida, as well as the beautiful old redwood house, to the State Baptist convention to be used as the Florida Baptist retirement centre for aged Baptist ministers and laymen. Now we were being thrown out, and the only reason given was we had departed from the Baptist tradition.

My old nature said I should make a fight of it. I knew we were on scriptural ground and felt if our people attended the annual associational meeting the next week, en masse, that we could probably prove our point and rescind the action of the Executive Committee. Even if the vote went against us, our action would surely cause enough commotion to get us space in both national news coverage and in the various state Baptist papers.

I called a meeting of the deacons of our church and their wives and told them of the action of the associational Executive Committee. Still riding the spiritual 'high' of my water baptism and lengthy fast, I naïvely assumed they would side with me. Instead I discovered several of them felt the same as the Hebrews at the Red Sea, 'Why have you brought us this far? We never did want to leave Egypt in the first place. We've been Baptists all our lives and even if you say there is some kind of Promised Land out there, we don't want to have to walk through the wilderness to get there. Why did we ever have to get into all this free worship and association with Presbyterians, Methodists, Catholics, and Pentecostals? It's all your fault.'

I was angry. I had followed God and I expected them to follow me. Instead I found that even though they were camping in Goshen, their hearts were still in Egypt.

However, four of the families, the ones I most suspected would have wanted to remain in the Baptist fold, took another slant. Inez and Woody Thompson, their daughter and son-in-law, Allen and Saundra Reed, Allen and Carilyn Aden, and another dyed-in-the-wool Baptist family, Brooks and Laura Watson, pulled me aside after the meeting and gave me some surprisingly sage counsel.

'Any time you start off through virgin territory,' Brooks said, 'you're going to run into obstacles. God has brought us this far; we can't turn back now.'

The others agreed. They had as much to lose as I, but were

determined, now we had done all, to stand.

We agreed together that we had more important things to do than fight our brethren. By common consent we decided not to send any representatives to the annual associational meeting. We would lie down and die without a struggle. God would fight our battles for us.

Like my water baptism experience in which I died to self, this turned out to be one of the greatest things to happen in the life of our church. Within a year our attendance doubled – and the offerings tripled. People were driving from miles around to attend the services because they knew that regardless of their former or present church affiliation, they would be welcome in this body where the only thing that held the people together was the love of God – not a doctrinal statement, a denominational charter, or even a membership roll.

None of us have regretted that we let God fight that battle for us. Inner healing, we discovered, could be just as meaningful on the corporate level as it was on the individual level. In this case, an entire church decided to take up the cross and die with Jesus. The results were the same as take place when an individual is buried with him in baptism – you rise to walk in newness of life.

7

DELIVER ME FROM EVIL

No study of inner healing or spiritual maturity is complete without a chapter on deliverance from evil spirits. Unfortunately, most studies on inner healing look upon deliverance the same way a physician might view a peddler of snake oil elixir, while books on deliverance have a tendency to lump all personality problems under the heading of 'demon possession'.

I have no illusions that, in this short chapter, I do the subject justice. However, there are certain areas of our lives which cannot be handled through the regular channels of prayer, forgiveness and commitment. These are areas of demon control and harassment and they must be met head on, in the name and under the authority of Jesus Christ. In short, demons are not prayed away, they are cast out.

I doubt if I would have included this chapter in the book had it not been for a conversation I had in Germany soon after I finished the rest of the manuscript. Jackie and I were staying with a United States Army chaplain in Wurzburg during a four day teaching conference sponsored by the Wurzburg Chapel. One evening, after we had returned from the conference, we were sitting in the chaplain's comfortable living room, sipping coffee and giving him a chance to catch up on news from the States. He asked me about a mutual friend.

When I mentioned things had not gone too well with him

he put down his coffee and said, 'Oh, in what way?'

I dislike being the carrier of bad news. In this case, however, since we were talking about a common friend, and since our motives were prayerful concern and not idle gossip, I felt free to mention a few things. His deteriorating family situation, his bad health and, just recently, my concern for his emotional and spiritual state.

The chaplain sat back in his chair and closed his eyes.

'Do you know ... ?' and he mentioned the name of another minister.

I nodded, wondering why he brought up a second name when we hadn't closed the first subject.

'Is it true that he, too, got into the same problem as our other friend?'

I was concerned. I had known this chaplain for a number of years, and this kind of muckraking was out of character. However, I nodded my head. 'That's what I understood,' I replied.

He called another name, a teacher I knew of. 'I understood she has just written a book,' he said.

'That's right,' I answered, still puzzled over this line of questioning.

'Have you read it?' the chaplain asked.

Something strange was going on, but I couldn't quite fit it together. 'Yes,' I replied. 'But there were some things that bothered me – ideas which bordered on the metaphysical and psychic. I'm afraid she is actually being led into deception.'

The chaplain named two more well-known ministers. One of them had fallen into severe moral disorder and the other, sadly, was teaching an obvious false doctrine.

'You're leading up to something, aren't you?' I asked.

He nodded his head seriously. 'All five of these people have been close friends of mine. Several years ago, when I was a junior grade officer at a military post in the east, we were all involved in a search for deeper spiritual truth. During their search, however, they became involved in the occult, attended seances and even used Ouija boards. Later they all received the Holy Spirit. Now, however . . . ' and he dropped his head before continuing, 'one by one they are turning from the truth. Deceived.'

'I don't understand,' I said honestly.

He then reminded me of something which I, myself, had once written for Corrie ten Boom. It was Tante Corrie's story of closing the circle. I sat back, remembering how Corrie, in her Dutch accent, had first told me her story of 'Closing the Circle'.

It would seem, after having been a Christian for almost eighty years, that I would no longer do ugly things that need forgiving. Yet I am constantly doing things to others that cause me to have to go back and ask their forgiveness. Sometimes these are things I actually do – other times they are simply attitudes I let creep in which break the circle of God's perfect love.

I first learned the secret of closing the circle from my nephew, Peter van Woerden, who was spending the weekend with me in our apartment in Baarn, Holland.

'Do you remember that boy, Jan, that we prayed for?' Peter asked.

I well remembered Jan. We had prayed for him many times. He had a horrible demon of darkness in his life and although we had fasted and prayed and cast out the demon in the name of the Lord Jesus Christ, the darkness always returned.

Peter continued, 'I know God had brought this boy to me not only so he could be delivered, but to teach me some lessons, too.'

I looked at Peter. 'What could that boy, Jan, so filled with darkness, teach you?'

'I did not learn the lesson from Jan,' Peter smiled. 'But from God. Once in my intercession time for Jan the Lord told me to open my Bible to I John 1:7-9. I read that passage about confessing our sin and asked the Lord what that had to do with the darkness in Jan's life.'

Peter got up and walked across the room, holding his open Bible in his hand. 'God taught me that if a Christian walks in the light then the blood of Jesus Christ cleanses him from all sin, making his life a closed circle and protecting him from all outside dark powers. But – ' he turned and emphatically jabbed his finger into the pages of the Bible – 'if there is unconfessed sin in that life, the circle has an opening in it – a gap – and this allows the dark powers to come back in.'

Ah, I thought, *Peter has really learned a truth from the Lord.*

'Tante Corrie,' Peter continued, 'even though I was able to cast out the demon in Jan's life, it always crept back in through the opening in the circle – the opening of Jan's unconfessed sin. But when I led Jan to confess this sin, then the circle was closed and the dark powers could no longer return.'

That same week the wife of a good friend came to me for counselling. After I had made her a cup of tea she began to tell me about all the people who had prayed for her, yet she was still experiencing horrible dreams at night.

I interrupted her conversation and drew a circle on a piece of paper. 'Mary,' I said, 'do you have unconfessed sin in your life? Is this the reason the circle is still open?'

Mary said nothing, sitting with her head down, her hands tightly clasped in her lap, her feet together. I could see there was a strong battle going on in her life – a battle between spiritual forces.

'Do you really want to be free?' I urged.

'Oh yes,' she said.

Suddenly she began telling me about a strong hatred she had for her mother. Everyone thought she loved her mother, but inside there were things that caused her actually to want to kill her. Yet, even as she spoke, I saw freedom coming into her eyes.

She finished her confession and then quickly asked Jesus to forgive her and cleanse her with his blood. I looked into her eyes and commanded the demon of hatred to leave in the name of Jesus.

What joy! What freedom!

Mary raised her hands in victory and began to praise the Lord, thanking him for the liberation and forgiveness he had given her. Then she reached over and embraced me in a hug so tight I thought she would crack my ribs.

'Dear Lord,' she prayed, 'I thank you for closing the circle with your blood.'

(Logos Journal, Mar./Apr. 1974, pg. 11)

Tante Corrie's principle was easily applicable to the situation described by the chaplain. Because the five people had been involved in the occult, the door of deception apparently was still open, a door which could only be closed through confession and repentence.

There is much discussion these days as to whether or not a Christian can 'have a demon'. One of my friends says a Christian can have anything he wants. But that's too simple. Perhaps it's more accurate to say that Satan has no claim on that part of the soul which has been crucified with Christ. But if there is a part of the inner man – the soul – which we deliberately refuse to surrender to the Lord, then that part of us is still open to receive demon spirits.

In a fine explanation of this matter Frank Longino, Jr, a pastor/teacher in Louisville, Kentucky, writes:

> . . . Recoiling from a word like possession, many have concluded that Christians are not invaded in any serious way by demons, they are just harassed from the outside. Doing away with the word, possession, we can then say that anyone, including Christians, can come under demon control in some area of his life. If it is just beginning, he can probably handle his own deliverance by taking authority over it. If it is a severe measure of control, he may need to be 'delivered' by someone with this ministry.
>
> In the Scripture, demons are always cast *out* of persons,

not 'off' them. In all of this, it is extremely important to know where one has left the door open to these spirits so as to be able to close it. Open doors are usually places where we are knowingly disobedient to God, or they may be unworthy habits and attitudes that we refuse to let God deal with in our lives ...

Disobedience to God's law for our lives is always dangerous. For a Christian knowingly to live in disobedience to God is to open the door wide to demonic control in that area of disobedience. Some Christians have a quick temper and do nothing to curb it, or to allow God to deal with it. This opens the door to demonic control. Some allow resentments to develop into bitterness and outright hatred until these attitudes and spirits are beyond personal control. This is demonic control. Some persons are controlled by habits of various kinds. A habit that is not dealt with could become an open invitation for demonic control. Paul says, 'I will not be brought under the power (authority) of any' (I Corinthians 6:12b) ...

(Logos Journal, Jan./Feb. 1974, pg. 19)

Frank's insight helped me understand a situation which arose in our church several years ago.

Elaine Randall was a 49-year-old, slightly greying wife of a retired military man. Childless, she and her husband were active in the church and eager to make a contribution to the kingdom. One Sunday night, after church, she stopped me on the pavement and asked if I had any typing she could do. I was, at that time, behind on a book manuscript. She was elated over the chance to help and insisted on doing it without pay. She stopped by the house early the next morning to pick up the first five chapters which were ready for final typing.

A week later I dropped by the Randall's small home in a quiet housing estate. Elaine's husband, Harry, was working in the garden. He waved and pointed towards the back door.

'Go on in. She's working in the den.'

Elaine glanced over her shoulder as I came in. 'You're just in time,' she said with a cheery smile. 'I'm just finishing the last page now. I don't know when I've had so much fun.'

I stood in the doorway, watching her tap away at her little electric portable. I hadn't noticed it before, but Elaine's fingers were stiff and swollen with arthritis. I watched as she struck the keys and could tell they were sensitive. She was in obvious pain, yet she continued to type.

I have suspected, for a long time, that arthritis has its roots in unconfessed resentment and bitterness. I let the thought run through my mind. Should I broach the subject with Elaine? Yet, she was giving me so much, should I not give her the benefit of this spiritual knowledge. I was naïve enough to think that everyone was as excited about deliverance and healing as I was. I hesitated, but as Elaine pulled the final sheet of paper from the machine, I asked the question.

'How long have you had the arthritis?'

She carefully stacked the paper with the rest of the manuscript and for a moment, I thought she had not heard my question. But she sat motionless, staring down at her brittle fingers which were now resting in her lap. I walked over and laid my hand on her shoulder.

'Elaine, I don't believe God intends for you to suffer with arthritis. Have you ever wanted to be free?'

'A million times,' she said softly, still looking down at her crippled hands.

'Could there be areas in your life, in your childhood even, where you still nurse resentment – areas where you've been hurt or wounded and the root of bitterness is still there? Arthritis is often the result of this kind of experience.'

I felt her stiffen under my hand. She turned and glared. 'I don't believe that,' she spat out. 'And even if it is so, what business is it of yours?'

Almost as if I had thrown a switch, her personality changed. Her eyes narrowed. Her lips were white and quivering. 'If you don't like my typing just say so. After all, I'm not getting paid, you know.'

It was a ruse. She was trying to throw me off, trying to set up a roadblock so I would detour. I almost took her bait, tempted to try to defend myself. Then I realised what was happening and once more I moved back in, knowing the authority of Christ in me was far stronger than the demonic force at work in her.

'There *is* something, isn't there. Some deep hurt. Some . . .'

I didn't have a chance to finish. She dropped her face into her hands and began to weep, convulsively. She finally looked up. Her mascara had run down her face and one eyelash was askew. 'I can't talk about it now. Give me some time.'

I took her hand, wet with tears, and prayed with her. She tried to apologise but I picked up the finished pages and started out. 'The battle's ninety per cent won,' I grinned. 'I'll be back.'

She nodded and squeezed my hand. 'I do need help,' she said softly. 'Thanks.'

It was just one month later when the opportunity arose. Elaine had finished the manuscript, and though she refused to accept any payment, she and Harry did agree to let Jackie and me take them to dinner. We chose a quiet little seafood place overlooking the Indian River and spent an enjoyable evening in the nearly empty restaurant, savouring a delicious meal. After we had finished, as we sat drinking coffee, I started probing again.

'Let's talk about your arthritis,' I said, looking at Elaine across the table. 'And about your past.'

For just an instant I saw that same evil spirit start to exhibit himself. But she had promised, and by an act of her own will she kept it under control. She glanced over at Harry, who nodded, and then looked back at me.

Gradually the story unfolded. Her mother had died when Elaine was four years old. Her father had disappeared soon after, leaving her to be raised by her mother's mother. The grandmother was bitter, and filled with hate towards the deserted father. She lost no time in passing it along to Elaine.

'She used to come into my room at night,' Elaine said

softly, 'after I had gone to bed, and tell me bedtime stories about my father. She told me how worthless he was. He never could hold a job. She said he was responsible for mother's death and then he ran away. He didn't love me. He didn't love anybody. She said he was as mean as Hitler.'

This hate, planted by a grandmother, was so real and deep in Elaine's life that even as she talked her teeth clenched.

In most cases, hate is an attitude brought about by unforgiveness. But in this case I realised the hate ran far deeper than unforgiveness, and remembering the hostile reaction of a month later, I suspected demonic activity. Elaine's grandmother had caused her to hate someone she couldn't even remember, and hate him so badly it was now destroying her body.

Forgiveness was not enough. In fact, years later, Elaine had set out to discover the facts about her real father. She couldn't believe he was as wicked as her grandmother had said. She learned her father had died. But she also discovered that he was actually a kind, tenderhearted man who had not been able to find work during the depression. When his wife died he had an emotional breakdown. Broken in heart and body, he left his little daughter in the hands of the only person he thought could care for her – his wife's mother. The father had spent time in a sanatorium, had become an alcoholic, and before he died wrote a letter telling his daughter, whom he hadn't seen in twenty-two years, that he loved her more than anyone on earth.

Yet, knowing all these facts, Elaine was still unable to love him. The demon, planted in her soul by the vengeful grandmother, caused her to hate her father with a fury.

I paid the bill for the dinner and the four of us walked out on a small dock behind the restaurant which extended into the river. The spot was deserted and we sat on a weathered wooden bench, watching the black ripples on the surface of the water reflect the silver of the almost full moon.

'Do you think I have a demon?' Elaine asked softly.

'That's not the question,' I answered. 'The question is, are you sometimes controlled by a demon – and does your arthritis have its root in the bitterness towards your father?'

'Will you minister to me?' she asked sincerely, her voice shaking. 'I want to be set free.'

'I'm not the one to do it,' I said, gently touching her elbow. 'Tonight, after you get home, I want you to submit to Harry's ministry. Let your husband be the one to take authority over this spirit.'

It was about noon, the next day, when I heard from them again. Harry came by the house so excited he could hardly talk.

'I've never seen anything like it,' he said. 'The minute I began to tell the demon to leave she turned on me. She told me we were all crazy, that the two of us were conspiring against her, that I was just as evil as her father . . . '

Harry glanced at Jackie who was standing in the door, listening. 'I know this sounds ridiculous, but I grabbed her and shouted at the demon to come out in the name of Jesus. She screamed so loud I thought she would wake the neighbourhood, and then just collapsed in my arms, weeping. Then she began naming other spirits which she said had come into her life. She renounced jealousy, envy, a spirit of control, a dominating spirit . . . we were up until almost three o'clock. But when we went to sleep there was peace in the house.'

Once the root of bitterness was plucked out and she was set free from the bondage of hate, she could deal with the other attitudes which had so long warped and twisted her personality. This kind of recognition and repentance is absolutely necessary in order to receive inner healing.

Three weeks later I stopped by Elaine's house to take her some revisions on the book. She met me at the door, held out her hands and said simply, 'Look!'

The arthritis was gone. Her fingers were slender and straight. She laughed as she clasped and unclasped her hands.

'I don't know when it disappeared,' she said. 'But when I sat down at the typewriter yesterday to write a letter, I noticed the swelling was gone.' Then she began to cry, only this time her tears were mingled with sounds of laughter and praise.

I wish there was a happy ending to this story, but instead it almost parallels the story Jesus told of the man who swept his house clean but refused to fill it with the Holy Spirit.

> *When the unclean spirit is gone out of a man, he walketh through dry places, seeking rest, and findeth none. Then he saith I will return into my house from whence I came out; and when he is come, he findeth it empty, swept and garnished. Then goeth he, and taketh with himself seven other spirits more wicked than himself, and they enter in and dwell there; and the last state of that man is worse than the first'* (Matthew 12:43-45).

During the next year, as our church moved into a free worship, I noticed Elaine resisting. I could see it in her face on Sunday morning. Harry was open, and seemed to enjoy the new freedom, occasionally raising his hands and singing the new choruses. But Elaine disliked the change, and gradually I saw her old bitterness and arrogance beginning to return.

One Sunday morning I was standing on the platform as the congregation began to sing a new, lively Scripture chorus. Elaine stiffened as the piano picked up a bouncy beat and the people began to clap in time to the music. Directly behind her was a tall, heavily bearded young man. He was singing loudly, and clapping his hands. Elaine's face was like a frozen mask. She turned slowly and gave the young man an icy stare. Fortunately, his eyes were closed and his face upturned in worship. But when Elaine turned back, I saw the old demon of hatred had returned.

Across the months it became worse. I tried to talk with her, but she refused to listen. Harry just shook his head, sadly. 'All she talks about,' he said, 'are those strange people who are taking over *our* church.' Then he added, 'And it's beginning to bother me, too.'

131

I realised the Randalls's spirit was affecting me, and, as a result, affecting the entire congregation. If the congregation began to sing some of the new choruses I would glance at Elaine to see how she was faring. If her face was screwed into a tight mask (as it usually was) I was tempted to quench the Spirit in order to keep her happy. Gradually it dawned on me that the evil spirit, now operating in the Randalls, was holding back the entire spiritual progress of the church.

Jackie and I went to their house for a talk. Harry was not there, but we sat and talked seriously with Elaine. 'We love you deeply,' I said. 'But we know you are unhappy with the way things are going.'

'Who's unhappy,' she snapped. Then she added with vengeful sarcasm, 'Don't you remember. I was delivered of all that?'

'We want your love and friendship,' Jackie said gently. 'But we also want you to be free. Even free to leave the church if you wish.'

'Now you're trying to get rid of me,' she snorted, her face contorted in hate. 'Well, we know when we're not welcome . . . '

We stayed a while longer, trying to work things out. But there was no way. Harry came in just as we were leaving and I put my arms around him. He stiffened, and I knew that he, too, was now infected. Deliverance was available, we knew that from the past, but unless a person wants to be set free . . .

The following week the Randalls were not in the service. A month later we received word, through a friend, they would not be back. Ever.

It was almost three years before I saw them again. I had stopped by the hardware store one Saturday morning to buy some new sprinkler heads for my infamous underground sprinkling system. As I was coming out I almost bumped into Harry, who was picking up a small bag of fertiliser from the display on the pavement. He was his old, affectionate self and I was suddenly suffused with love for him.

'How's Elaine?'

'Oh, she's out in the car. Come and speak to her.'

I leaned through the window to kiss her cheek, but she pulled back. She was talking through a mask, but beyond the façade I saw the demon spirit, still glaring back through her eyes.

We chatted for a moment and I started to leave. But as I did I glanced down at her hands. Her knuckles were badly swollen, much worse than before, and her fingers were bent and twisted from the arthritis.

I waded in. 'How are your hands, Elaine?'

For just a moment I saw her true self trying to break free. Her face went tender and in her eyes I saw instant tears. She knew what I was offering, and she wanted to reach out.

Then, like a cloud slipping over the sun, the evil spirit drew the blinds and her eyes went dark.

'Let's go, Harry,' she said. 'You wanted to get that stuff on the grass before it rains. Nice to see you Jamie. Remember us to Jackie.' And they were gone.

I wanted to hold them back, but in this case there could be no deliverance unless there was a desire. I had to let them go, but my heart still, to this day, aches with sadness when I think of what they had, and refused to keep.

Elaine had not closed the circle. Satan and his demons had been evicted from land they formerly occupied, but then, in a deliberate act of defiance, Elaine had once again stamped Satan's passport with a valid visa and given him entrance into her life. Only through confession could she cancel the visa – but her pride was too formidable a barrier to allow that to happen. She was trapped in a prison of her own making, tormented by a demon to whom she had issued a personal invitation.

The Bible has a great deal to say about a worldwide kingdom of darkness in which Satan is king and the fallen angels rule under him as princes over countries, cities and people. By their control over men they control both the world systems and in some cases, even the organised church.

Demons are under the lordship of Satan and he uses them

to oppress, vex, afflict and torment men. They are named, often, by the results they produce in the lives of men.

Some demons that are named in the Scripture include:

a blind and dumb demon (Matthew 12:22)
a dumb and deaf spirit (Mark 9:25)
a spirit of infirmity (Luke 13:11)
unclean spirits (Acts 5:16)
seducing spirits (I Timothy 4:1)
a spirit of divination (Acts 16:16)

These demons can come in through a variety of entrances. One of the most common is occult practices. The rise of eastern and oriental religions – all of which are demon orientated – has opened the door for a new wave of demonic oppression in the United States. These include not only the Jeanne Dixon, Edgar Cayce concepts, which are merely underworld practices dressed as angels of light, but the practice of many things considered by the general public as harmless fads. A partial list of such practices, all of which open the mind for entrance of demons, would include:

Ouija boards	astrology
palmistry	levitation
handwriting analysis	fortune telling
automatic handwriting	water witching
hypnotism	tarot cards
incantations	witchcraft
charms	black magic
necromancy	white magic
transcendental meditation	seances
hari krishna	spirit guides
yoga	scientology
extrasensory perception	crystal ball gazing
gazing	clairvoyance

Hypnotism may not necessarily be evil within itself, but it

is certainly a door through which evil spirits may enter. It demands the submission of the will to another person in a manner that belongs to God alone.

One of the saddest stories in my experience surrounds the former pastor in my community. Soon after I received the baptism in the Holy Spirit he contacted me to let me know he was in great sympathy with my new direction. In fact, he said, he had found a similar source of power in 'ethical hypnotism'. He went on to describe how a young man in his church, through posthypnotic suggestion, had been 'delivered' of fingernail biting. I was ignorant of the dangers of this type of thing back then, but something deep in my spirit warned me to stay clear. In less than a year the pastor had resigned and moved to Colorado to teach in a large institution majoring in hypnotism. The last I heard of him he had left his wife and children and moved to California where he was roaming the beaches as a fifty-year-old hippie.

Much of what we call 'harmless' is poison in a jar with a medicinal label.

Strange as it may seem, another avenue through which demons may enter is music. In fact, music is often called the 'language of the soul'. The 'soul' being that basic nature of mankind.

King Saul, when he was troubled by an evil spirit, was soothed by David's harp-playing, since David sang and played songs that were inspired by the Spirit of God.

Mother Basilea Schlink of the Evangelical Sisterhood of Mary in Darmstadt, West Germany, points out that in the final analysis, it is not the words of the song that are decisive, but rather the spirit behind the music. Hence Scripture prefaces its words about singing and making music in the church with 'be filled with the Holy Spirit' (Ephesians 5:18). Music written under the inspiration of the Holy Spirit remains, generation after generation, to bless and inspire. However, melodies which have been inspired by bad spirits, no matter how religious the words may seem, will not be able to impart a spiritual blessing.

One evening, when our oldest son, Bruce, was in his last year at school, he developed an excruciating pain in his ear. We were up with him most of the night, doing all the things we knew to do. We checked to make sure it wasn't a draught of cold air. We put hot compresses on his ears. And we prayed. We prayed a lot. But nothing seemed to ease the pain. By morning the pain had diminished and he was able to go off to school, although he was in poor shape from loss of sleep. That night, however, the pain reappeared, even more intense. The next day we took him to the doctor.

The doctor made a thorough examination and could find no evidence of infection, although his ears were red and inflamed. He told him to take aspirin, use some ear drops, and stay out of the water. That night the pain was even worse.

I went in and sat on the side of his bed, feeling helpless as I watched him clench his teeth and writhe on the bed. The only way he could find partial relief was to sit up in bed. So, we sat and talked, long into the night.

Finally, near midnight, Bruce said, 'Dad, there's something I want to tell you. But I don't know how.'

'Try me, Bruce, I don't shock easily,' I smiled.

'About a week ago something came into my room,' he said seriously. 'It was early in the morning. I was just waking up. I was lying on my back with my hands under my head and my eyes half open. I knew it was time to get up, but I wanted to just doze for a minute before having to get out of bed. Suddenly there was a face dangling in front of me. It was like a mask on a string, hanging and bouncing over my bed. Only it was alive. The face was horrible looking, and it was laughing at me. I knew it was a demon, but I was so scared I didn't know what to do. I tried to say the name of Jesus, but nothing came out. My lips were sealed. I tried to open my eyes, but they were glued shut. The face got closer and closer, laughing and laughing.

'I turned over on the bed and buried my head in the pillow, but the face was still in front of me. Dancing back and forth with a hollow, demonic laugh. Then I heard you and Mum moving around in the other room and the face gradually disappeared, laughing all the way.'

'Why didn't you tell us?' I asked.

'I was too scared,' Bruce confessed. 'And then that night the earache started and I forgot about the face until just a few minutes ago.'

'Had you ever seen this face before?' I asked.

There was a long pause and then Bruce said softly, 'Yes, it is the same face on the back of that stereo album I bought last week.'

I knew the album. I've always detested acid rock music, believing it was straight from the pit. But Bruce insisted on buying this album, saying that even though it was hard rock music, the words were religious.

'Where's the album?' I asked.

'In the cupboard,' he said. 'But Dad, you don't think it could be that, do you? I've only played it a couple of times and I really dig the music.'

I got up and went to the cupboard. Finding the album I took it back to the bed. The jacket was covered with symbols, leering faces and twisting bodies. Every figure had a demonic connotation. It was as though the designer had taken a walk through hell and come back to paint what he saw.

'Get rid of it, Dad,' Bruce said. 'I never should have bought it.'

Unlike idols which have been used in demon worship, I did not feel the album, or its horrible cover, were inherently demonic. By that, I mean I did not feel it was infested with demons, or that by handling it one of them would 'leap on me'. However, I did see the album – and the jacket – as a tool through which Satan had pried open the door of the soul of a Spirit-baptised young man. Therefore I destroyed the record and the next morning the dustmen hauled it off to the dump – where it belonged.

But even this was not enough to set Bruce free from the splitting earaches. One of our church elders, Lew Draper, a former Southern Baptist pastor, was visiting at the house when Bruce came in from school the next afternoon. After a few moments conversation Bruce excused himself to go up to his room and study. After he left I told Lew of the strange events which had taken place.

Lew listened seriously and then said, 'Where did Bruce listen to the music?'

'Up in his room,' I said. 'He knew we didn't approve of having that stuff played on our big stereo, so he used his small record player.'

'Then we should exorcise the room,' Lew said, rising to his feet. 'It's not enough for Bruce to confess and repent. I believe the demons may still be present in the room and will probably attack him every time he lies down.'

That sounded a bit strange to me, yet there had to be some reason Bruce was only bothered by the earache at night, when he was alone in his room.

Lew and I went upstairs to Bruce's room, intent on cleansing it in the name of the Lord. When we got to the door I saw Bruce lying on his bed, his books spread open on the floor beside him. He was holding his head with his hands and twisting back and forth on the bed. The earache had returned.

Lew didn't hesitate. He stepped into the room like David marching to meet Goliath. 'In the name of the Son of God, the Lord Jesus Christ, I command you evil spirits to leave this room!' he roared.

Bruce came up off the bed like a spring had been released. Startled, he looked around and saw us standing there, hands in the air, vocally worshipping the Lord. Then we prayed for Bruce, asking God to bring inner healing to the wounds which had been caused by the the presence of the demon, asking God to heal the memories and thereby close the door on fear. Finally, we bound the spirits so they could not return bringing guilt and doubt.

We sat and talked for a long time, but by the time Lew left the earache had gone – and never returned.

By this deception of music young people are drawn under Satanic influence, without being aware of it. In Bruce's case, since he was a child of God, the attack was frontal. Satan actually tried to destroy him. In most cases the demons will not manifest themselves so vividly, preferring to work through the subtle attitudes of rebellion.

When I was working with Nick Cruz on *Run Baby Run* he often spoke of the wild parties or 'jigs' held by the gangs in Brooklyn. These were always accompanied by hard rock music. While the kids listened, they would be worked into a frenzy. Finally, driven by the demons into the streets, the boys would wildly strip parked cars, slash at their enemies with knives or tear up the shops along the pavement. Or, they would withdraw to the shadows of a basement to spend the afternoon in fornication. One member of Nicky's gang, the Mau Maus, told me, 'After listening to rock music there wasn't anything I wouldn't do.'

In his book, *What's Wrong with Rock and Roll*, Bob Larson says:

'The electronic insistence of guitars accompanied by the neurotic throbbing of drums compels the shedding of inhibitions ... worst of all this music has become a religion. The message of rock and roll songs and performers is basically anti-Christian and opposed to Biblical standards of behaviour.'

The noted district attorney, Vincent Bugliosi, who successfully tried and convicted Charles Manson and his 'family' in the much publicised Sharon Tate murder trials in Los Angeles in the late 1960's, testified that Manson himself said he received his ideas by listening to music produced by the Beatles. In his book, *Helter Skelter*, Bugliosi quotes one of the family who said:

'Manson would quote, verbatim, whole lyrics from the

Beatles' songs, finding in them a multitude of hidden meanings.'

Especially was Manson influenced by a Beatles' record on which the singers quoted frequently from passages in Revelation 9, accompanied by a weird drumbeat, throbbing electric guitar, and that musical mantra – the synthesiser. The fact that these tunes and records were composed and produced by men under the influence of drugs and transcendental meditation, was obviously the key to the Satanic power contained in the music.

While I was in the Philippines completing my research on *Into The Glory*, several missionaries told me I should interview Nard Pugyao. Nard was a young Isneg tribesman from the rugged mountains of northern Luzon. After his conversion to Christianity, members of the Wycliffe team had helped him get his education and then financed his trip to the United States where he received training as an aircraft mechanic at Le Tourneau College in Longview, Texas. He then went on to the Jungle Aviation and Radio Service Center at Waxhaw, North Carolina, where he learned to fly. From there he planned to go to the Moody Bible Institute in Chicago and finally, hopefully, to return to the Philippines as a JAARS pilot.

When I returned from the South Pacific, I looked up Nard in the hangar at Waxhaw Center. I had a new Hitachi tape recorder, one of the best machines on the market, and I wanted to ask Nard a few questions. He had been working on the engine of a small aeroplane, but put down his tools to chat for a few moments. During this time I discovered he had been raised in the tribal village by an aunt who was a *shaman*, a witch doctor. Intrigued, I switched on my tape recorder and began to ask him questions about demon activity in the Philippines. He was reluctant to talk about it. When he became a Christian, he said, he had publicly renounced his heathen gods and been delivered from all demon influence. However, when I asked if he ever sensed any of the same demonic activity in the United States that he saw in the Philippine jungles, he said something of extreme interest.

'Demons never die, you know,' he said matter-of-factly. 'They just flit about from one place to another looking for someone who will invite them in. There are two places in America where I sense strong demon activity. One is around the pornography shops and theatres. My aunt, the *shaman*, used to take off her clothes to attract the demons. There is something in the American concept of nudity that invites demon spirits.

'The other is in rock music. In the tribe the witch doctor always used the heavy beat of drums to summon the demons. Today, here in America, when I hear rock music, I am aware it is a summons, an invitation, to the demons. It is the same beat we used in the Philippines.'

We chatted a while longer and then I returned to the administration building to meet with Bernie May, the executive director for JAARS. When I told him of my conversation with Nard he wrinkled his brow and said, 'Well, I hope you got it on tape. No one else has been able to so far.'

'What do you mean?'

'Nard has given that same testimony on three occasions in area churches, usually talking to young people,' Bernie said. 'Each time someone has tried to tape him, but something always goes wrong with the machine.'

I grinned. 'Well, I got it this time. I was watching the meter and it picked up everything.'

Bernie looked at me seriously. 'Did you pray, specifically, before you started the interview?'

'Well, no,' I hesitated. 'What difference should that make?'

'I don't think you're dealing with a normal force,' Bernie said deliberately. 'I think you'd better check, just to make sure.'

I set my tape recorder on the table and pushed the rewind button. I ran the tape back to the middle of the interview, then clicked it into 'play'. The sound was perfect. Not only could I hear my questions and Nard's answers, but I could hear the sound of an aeroplane taking off on the nearby runway and the clink of tools as the mechanics worked in the hangar. I ran the tape forward to the place where we began talking about Nard's aunt, the *shaman*. Again the reception was perfect. I started to shut off the machine, but something happened. Suddenly, just as Nard began talking about the demons in the United States, the tape recorder went haywire. There were a series of 'burping' sounds on the tape and suddenly it went into 'Donald Duck talk' – wild gibberish. After that it faded out completely. Everything he had said about demons in America was gone.

I stood looking at Bernie. Neither of us said a word. He handed me his own tape recorder and we transferred the tape. Once again I ran it back to the beginning of this particular segment of the conversation and switched it into 'play'. The sounds were identical. It was as though some outside, magnetic force had deliberately interfered with the recording.

I put the tape back in my machine and switched it to 'record'. 'Testing, one, two, three, four.'

I flipped it to 'rewind', then back to 'play'. The sound was perfect. Only that portion about demons was unintelligible. My conclusion: the demons simply did not want that conversation recorded.

To this day most of those who are converted to Christ in heathen cultures know they must burn their fetishes and household gods, turn their back on all demon attractions and submit themselves to deliverance from all demonic possession. This entails severing all connections with the occult and music of their former religions, and avoiding all demonic cult festivals and sites. Christ will not associate with that which is inspired by the enemy.

Don't be teamed with those who do not love the Lord, for what do the people of God have in common with the people of sin? How can light live with darkness? And what harmony can there be between Christ and the devil? How can a Christian be a partner with one who doesn't believe?

And what union can there be between God's temple and idols? For you are God's temple, the home of the living God, and God has said of you, 'I will live in them and walk among them, and I will be their God and they shall be my people. That is why the Lord has said, 'Leave them, separate yourselves from them; don't touch their filthy things, and I will welcome you, and be a Father to you, and you will be my sons and daughters (II Corinthians 6:14-18 TLB).

The methods of deliverance are as many and as varied as the methods of possession and oppression. I personally believe that a dynamic conversion experience should include total deliverance from the powers of darkness. In my own case, though, my conversion was not dynamic or total. Thus my experience of the baptism in the Holy Spirit also brought about deliverance. Likewise, when I was baptised in water there was additional deliverance. Some need to go through deliverance sessions which will certainly contain confession, repentance and perhaps even rebuking certain demons. Occasionally in our Sunday morning worship services, as we move into high praise, a demon will manifest himself and we will have to take immediate authority over it to keep it from disrupting the service or tearing some poor person's body. There is no set pattern, but the authority always rests in the name of Jesus Christ.

One evening, after Corrie ten Boom had spoken at our church, she was approached by a young lady who had been involved in witchcraft. Corrie took immediate authority over the demons and commanded them to leave in the name of Jesus. The girl was instantly set free. Afterwards Jackie asked Tante Corrie what method she used in deliverance. Corrie looked at her sternly and said, 'I do it however the Lord tells me to do it.'

And that settled the matter.

It must be remembered that Satan is a defeated foe. He has no authority, no right, to possess the soul of a Christian – or to leave his demons behind to do his dirty work. The only authority he has is that which we give him. Once he is ordered from the premises in the name of the Lord Jesus Christ, he is compelled to leave – and take his vexing spirits with him. Healing of the inner man may be necessary to patch up the wounds he caused, but in all areas, Jesus is victor.

8

GETTING YOUR MOTIVES STRAIGHT

The Lamplighter Cafeteria in Ft Myers, Florida, was humming with activity when I arrived to go through the evening serving line. I was to speak at the monthly meeting of the Full Gospel Business Men's Fellowship and had been instructed that after I ate, I was to meet with the believers in a side room.

It was the heart of the winter tourist season and most of the people in the cafeteria were of retirement age. The same proved true when I joined the group in the side room for the time of fellowship. In fact, looking around, it seemed I was the youngest person in the meeting.

We sang a few songs, there were some testimonies, and then, just before I spoke, the president announced a special musical number by the chapter's 'senior duet'. Everybody present seemed to know the two old men who stood to sing, so I sat back and relaxed, trying to collect my thoughts before I stood to speak.

But it was impossible to collect my thoughts. The two men, both of them well into their retirement years, were accompanying themselves musically. One was playing a guitar, the other a banjo with only three strings. One string had been missing for a year, he apologised, and the other had broken while he was trying to tune the instrument just before the meeting. To make matters worse, the three remaining strings were out of tune. But so was the guitar, so it didn't make much difference.

145

After some preliminary plunking and strumming, trying to get the instruments in tune, the men gave up and began to sing. 'When They Ring Those Golden Bells for You and Me'.

It was bad. They started, one of them singing lead and the other tenor, and then stopped. They decided to change parts and started again, this time with both of them singing lead. Finally, after an embarrassing exchange of comments over who was to sing which part, they began a third time – both of them singing tenor. Undaunted, they painfully strummed and plucked their way through the first verse.

There's a land beyond the river,

That we call the sweet forever . . .

Half way through the chorus another string on the banjo popped with a loud twang. This disconcerted the old man who was plucking. He forgot the words and started singing something else.

I could hardly believe what I was hearing. I shuddered, embarrassed for them, embarrassed for the visitors, present, and mortified that I was being identified with it all.

I tried to close my ears. I tried to think how I could overcome this horrible presentation when I stood to speak. It was, without doubt, the worst musical presentation I had ever heard. Yet the old men went on and on, oblivious of my red face and twitching hands.

'God help us,' I moaned inwardly.

Then, just as clear as the sound of those golden bells the old men were singing about, He answered me in the deep place of my heart.

'You think that sounds pretty awful, don't you?'

'Oh, God, you know,' I groaned.

'Would you like to know what I think about it?' he said gently.

I felt the hair begin to rise on the back of my neck. I had the feeling I had ventured out into an area where I had absolutely no business being. I was afraid to answer, afraid he would tell me what he thought.

It didn't make any difference. He told me anyway. 'Those

are two of my choicest saints. They stand and sing, knowing their voices are cracked and their instruments out of tune, because they love me. They are singing to my glory, and I have commanded all the angels in Heaven to be quiet so I can hear them.'

I could hardly breathe. 'Oh, God, what a fool I am. I was listening with *my* ears, rather than yours.'

'That's right,' he chided me gently. 'Not only that, but you were judging them by worldly standards, while I was judging them by kingdom standards. You were listening to *how* they sang. I was listening to *why* they sang.'

One of the primary reasons we are unable to enter into inner healing is we have never learned the importance of getting our motives straight. As a result we develop ulcers, bad attitudes, and grouchy dispositions as we strive to complete a task which we outwardly proclaim is for God's glory, but for which, inwardly, we plan to take the credit.

God, I have discovered, is far more concerned over *why* we do a thing than *how* we do it. The person who demands perfection at any cost has paid too high a price. If two old men with cracked voices and out-of-tune instruments can cause God to hush the angels so he can listen, it seems the rest of us had better do some deep checking of our own reasons for singing, preaching, writing, publishing, raising children, earning money, or anything else we glibly proclaim we are doing for the glory of God.

My first introduction to the importance of motives came on the publication of my first book, *Run Baby Run*. I really thought my motives were pure when I signed my contract with Logos International. Oh, sure, I enjoyed being introduced as a 'professional writer'. But at least I wasn't in it for the money. In fact, it never occurred to me until much, much later that there might be some financial rewards connected with writing. I was satisfied just to 'get the word out' – and to be known all over the world as the man who wrote the book.

Having already determined that he was going to bring me into the image of his Son, God decided to go to work with his sandpaper on that particular motive. When the book was finally published, Logos sent me the first copy via air mail, special delivery. It arrived on a Saturday morning when the entire family was at home. Jackie and the children eagerly crowded around as I ripped off the wrapping paper and exposed the brilliant red dust jacket with the name across the middle: *Run Baby Run*.

We passed the book around. Everyone handled it – or perhaps 'fondled' is a better word – looking at the type, the art work on the cover, the thickness of the pages, and the personal inscription written in longhand and signed by the publisher, thanking me for my part in the book.

But I was disappointed. Nicky Cruz's name was emblazoned in big letters across the top of the book. At the bottom of the front cover was Billy Graham's name, also in big letters, since he had written the foreword. And in the middle, in very small type, it said, 'As told to Jamie Buckingham.'

Our number two girl, Bonnie, looked at the book and said, 'Daddy, your name isn't very big, is it?'

I blushed and tried to explain that I was an unknown writer, that the book was actually about Nicky's life, that they needed Billy's endorsement to catch the eye of the booksellers and besides, I had written the book to the glory of God. In fact, it really didn't make any difference whether my name appeared at all – as long as God knew about it.

But it did make a difference. It made a whopping difference. That afternoon I took the book into my studio, closed the door, and sat for a long time – looking at the cover. It didn't seem right. After all, I was the fellow who had done all the work. I was the one who had taken time away from my family, my ministry, and a lot of other things to struggle to get the words on paper. I was even the one who had convinced Billy Graham to write the foreword. Why then was my name so small and everyone else's so large?

It's the same syndrome that affects a lot of executives in business when they *demand* their own parking space – with their name on the curb – or their own coat locker. It's the thing that causes ministers to *demand* their name on the sign in front of the church, painted on the side of the church bus, or their picture on their stationery with a list of their varied degrees. It's that thing in us that demands recognition, even when we say we're giving God the glory. It's called a sick inner nature and is caused by emptiness. Only the inner security brought about by the filling of the Holy Spirit will bring healing.

How well I remembered a former church I had pastored which went through a building programme to renovate the church interior. The money ran out just before they got the new pews paid for. The finance committee, playing on this sick area of man's inner nature, raised the money for the new pews by promising the people that anyone who contributed $350 would get their name on one of the long pews (on a little bronze plaque) while $250 would purchase a plaque on a short pew. They raised the money for all sixty-six pews in less than a month.

I had highly criticised that syndrome back then – feeling the action of the committee, while it proved successful, was really feeding a sickness rather than helping to bring people into spiritual maturity. Now I was caught in the same web, only this time it wasn't my name on a church pew, but on the cover of a book.

It took me almost a month to get over the hurt and disappointment sufficiently to hear God again. But as the wound began to heal, I realised God had allowed it to happen to teach me about the inner nature of man. Success corrupts. Proclaim a man famous, and apart from the grace of God, it will destroy him. Give a man a title, and suddenly his personality begins to change.

We discovered this much later in our church when we decided it was time to establish elders and deacons. As long as we didn't have any titled leaders, the people in the body were flowing with the Spirit, ministering to each other and generally enjoying their fellowship with God and one another. Then we decided to formally recognise our leaders and vest them with titles. There was nothing wrong with that, we just moved too soon, before the men were healed enough so they wouldn't revert to their former traditions, or start acting on the basis of reaction rather than responding to the Holy Spirit. Soon our new deacons were acting like old deacons, and our elders began to act like they thought elders should act. Before long we had not only a 'clergy' but a 'hierarchy'. It was the old problem of being placed in a position without first holding authority. It took us almost two years to undo that mistake, drop all the titles, and start over again (with some of the same men, incidentally), placing the emphasis on leaders being servants rather than dictators.

I could have my name in big letters on my books if I wanted. All I had to do was storm the publisher's office, make a nuisance of myself, demand my rights, and I'd get them.

I was chagrined over my attitude and found myself praying what I now realise is one of the most dangerous prayers in the kingdom. I prayed, 'Lord, I want to be a seed that falls into the ground and dies.'

Seeds, of course, can never reproduce unless they die. The only way they die is to be buried in the ground, covered with dirt, and then sprinkled with manure. Had I known all that, I might not have prayed that prayer, but I was determined to get my motives straight. I was sick of being motivated by selfish, sick things that belched out of my subconscious like brimstone out of a volcano. I wanted to be pure, and the only way I knew how was to die to self.

As usual, God immediately put me to the test. My second book was written for Kathryn Kuhlman – and my name didn't even appear on the dust jacket.

There is another story that surrounded the writing of that book, by the way. Dan Malachuk introduced me to Miss Kuhlman in her offices at the Carlton House in Pittsburgh, Pennsylvania. I knew almost nothing about her except that she had one book published called *I Believe in Miracles*, that she was involved in a healing and miracle ministry. She turned out to be one of the most gracious, charming, and genuine women I had ever met.

We went out to eat that night in a quaint little steak house overlooking the Ohio River. After dinner Miss Kuhlman, whom I soon discovered was an astute businesswoman as well as a person of great spiritual power, got right to the point. Was I willing to write her next book? Yes. How long did I think it would take? I estimated two months if I worked full time. (I sadly underestimated – it took six months.) How would I like to be paid?

I paused here for I knew almost nothing about the financial arrangements in book publishing. Miss Kuhlman was patient and explained that I had a choice. I could either draw a royalty on each book as it was sold or she would be willing to pay me a flat fee – whatever I thought was fair.

As usual we were in a tight financial situation. The little church in Florida was still struggling and I saw this as an opportunity to go off salary for a couple of months, give the church a chance to catch up financially, and at the same time get paid for writing. I did some quick mental arithmetic and determined I would need $1,000 a month to support my family for the two-month period it should take me to write the book. This was $200 a month more than the church was able to pay me, but I thought it seemed fair to draw a little extra since this was a special project.

I took a deep breath and told Miss Kuhlman I would write the book for $2,000. It was more money than I had ever asked anyone for in a lump sum.

She gave me a funny look and said, 'Is that enough?'

'Yes, ma'am,' I said, sensing that she was willing to go along with my offer.

'You feel you would be more comfortable with the flat fee rather than a royalty?' she asked.

I nodded. I was determined to write that book for the glory of God and was satisfied to get paid just enough to support my family and buy typing paper.

Miss Kuhlman smiled and patted my arm. 'I'll have my

secretary write you a cheque next week.' I left, feeling like I was the richest man in the world.

Funny thing about the book. It sold almost 400,000 copies the first year in the hardback edition. At $5 a copy, that added up to a gross sales of $2 million. A co-author's royalties on such sales would have amounted to many times more than the $2,000 I asked for.

For those living in the kingdom of God and who desire inner healing, there are some mysterious economic absurdities which open the doors to vast intangible riches and a deep inner satisfaction.

They are:

> *The first shall be last and the last shall be first.*
> *You are allowed to keep only that which you give away.*
> *In order to live, you have to die. To get high, stay low.*

The blessing of that single experience with *God Can Do It Again* has extended far beyond me to my family and church. It was unexpected and unasked for. In fact, had I entered into the project for that purpose, I would have been automatically disqualified. We are never to undertake a project for the purpose of receiving God's blessing – whether it is tithing our income, teaching a class, or giving our lives to go to the mission field. The only adequate motive for any project is 'for the glory of God'. Choose any other motive and you run the risk of receiving your reward here.

9

RELEASE FROM TYRANNY

One of the most critical of all relationships is the one we have with our parents. As strange as it may seem, for many of us this relationship does not need strengthening; rather it needs loosening. Too often our ties to father and mother actually form a bondage which enslaves us to the tyranny of ancestry and prevents us from entering into the single relationship with our Heavenly Father which brings inner healing.

This principle is vividly illustrated in a story from the Old Testament. Following the death of King Solomon, the kingdom of Israel was divided into two sections: Judah in the south and Israel in the north. There followed a line of kings, most of them so wicked they actually forbade the people to worship God. One of these was Ahaz.

Ahaz inherited the throne at the age of twenty and immediately came under the influence of men from Assyria who offered to help him fight the Philistines. Soon he was worshipping the idols the Assyrians brought from Damascus. Not only did he sacrifice to them, but he set up altars under every tree in Israel, and required the people to worship the 'devas', the evil spirits. He also set up stone altars and sacrificed children to the evil spirits, some of his own children included. In the final years of his life he was so obsessed with evil that he even took the sacred vessels from the house of the Lord and gave them to the Assyrians. He nailed shut the

153

doors of the Temple and proclaimed it an offence, punishable by death, for anyone to worship Jehovah.

It takes a great deal to make the Lord – the God of loving-kindness and mercy – angry. But the Bible says Ahaz was so wicked he 'provoked to anger the Lord God of his fathers'. He died, at the age of thirty-six, in a mad rage against God. The priests would not allow him to be buried in the royal tombs.

Ahaz had a son, a young teenager, who was destined to succeed him as king of Israel. There is no record of who raised young Hezekiah from the time his wicked father died until he inherited the crown. Perhaps it was the same people who denied his father burial in the royal tombs. We don't know. But when he was twenty-five, Hezekiah was crowned king of Israel.

Something had happened, though, between the time his father died and the time he became king. Hezekiah had turned from the ways of his father and developed a deep love for God. In fact, when he was crowned, his first official act was to open the doors of the House of the Lord and to repair the Temple which his father had tried to destroy. Aside from Josiah, his great-grandson, and King David, the Bible records no more godly king in the history of Israel than Hezekiah.

The Hebrews placed a strong emphasis on family ties. Jews did not even have a surname, but were simply known as 'the son of'. Peter, that great disciple of Jesus, was first known as Simon bar Jonah, the Aramaic word *bar* meaning 'son of'. The fifth of the ten commandments is the only commandment that contains a promise:

> *Honour thy father and thy mother: that thy days may be long upon the land which the Lord thy God giveth thee (Exodus 20:12).*

From the very beginning of Hebrew history the people put great stock in their ancestral lineage, their heritage – especially as it related to their father. Yet something had happened to Hezekiah which gave him the courage and the wisdom to break loose from this tyranny and hear the voice of God. In his opening speech to the priests and Levites, he called them into the open space east of the Temple and addressed them, saying,

> . . . sanctify now yourselves, and sanctify the house of the Lord God of your fathers, and carry forth the filthiness out of the holy place. For our fathers have trespassed, and done that which was evil in the eyes of the Lord our God and have forsaken him, and have turned away their faces from the habitation of the Lord, and turned their backs. . . . Now it is in mine heart to make a covenant with the Lord God of Israel, that his fierce wrath may turn away from us (2 Chronicles 29:5, 6, 10).

In the ears of many of the people this must have sounded as blasphemous as the words of his father when he commanded them to close the Temple and worship idols. For any man, even the king, to stand and confess that his father had sinned and led them into a place of destruction and shame was tantamount to denying God himself. Yet not only did Hezekiah proclaim his own father had sinned, but he said the fathers of the others had sinned also, and it was time to make a break and start afresh with God. He was, literally, renouncing an entire generation of fathers. What an amazing and bold statement for a young man to make as he begins his political career.

However, once the spiritual bondage of his father was broken, Hezekiah was free to hear from God in a way that no king had heard since David. He instituted many new reforms. When the Levites could not get the Temple purified in time for the April Passover, Hezekiah changed the date of the Passover to May – something that no king, or priest, had ever dared do before. Not only that, but when it became obvious the people could not go through the lengthy but necessary purification rites in time to meet the Passover deadline, Hezekiah lined them up and said, 'May the good Lord pardon everyone who determines to follow the Lord God of his fathers, even though he is not properly sanctified for the ceremony.' The priests were horrified, and fully expected the young king to be struck dead. But to their amazement, the Lord listened to Hezekiah's prayer and honoured his enthusiasm.

Having broken the tyranny of his father, he was also able to break senseless traditions. He was able to hear from God in a new way and for a number of years led the people to fresh commitments to the living Lord. In the end, after a long and noble reign, he died and was buried with great honours in the royal tombs in Jerusalem.

The story of Hezekiah is one of the most fascinating in the Bible – not only because of the conflict and change in his life, but because it contains some of the vital principles of inner healing. In particular, Hezekiah shows us that honouring our parents should not put us in bondage.

For years I was disturbed by Jesus' reaction to the men who approached him while he was teaching in the synagogue and said his mother and his brothers were waiting for him outside. Jesus' answer seemed so blunt:

My mother and my brethren are these which hear the word of God and do it (Luke 8:21).

In another place he said:

If any man come to me, and hate not his father, and mother, and wife, and children, and brethren, and sisters, yea, and his own life also, he cannot be my disciple (Luke 14:26).

How can we honour our father and mother and hate them at the same time? Could it be that Jesus was drawing a comparison and saying that the highest honour we can pay father and mother is to give our first allegiance to the Lord? In fact, that allegiance should be so strong that in comparison, our love for our parents would seem like hate.

Many of us are under bondage to our ancestors: father and mother, grandparents, uncles, aunts, or even older brothers and sisters. We may call the relationship love, but, if it keeps us from inner healing, it is really sentimentalism – a tyranny which exerts a far greater bondage upon our minds than the chains of a prison.

In 1800, Thomas Jefferson wrote to Dr Benjamin Rush and set forth his political concepts for the Republic. He said:

> I have sworn upon the altar of God, eternal hostility against every form of tyranny over the mind of man.

Jefferson's hatred of this kind of bondage was repeated in another letter, written sixteen years later to his friend Dupont de Nemours, where he stated:

> Enlighten the people, generally, and tyranny and oppressions of body and mind will vanish like evil spirits at the dawn of day.

Jefferson's solution to political tyranny – enlightenment – has deep spiritual significance as well. The old saying that 'love is blind' often means that love causes us to go blind, preventing us from seeing objectively. Of course such 'love' is not really love at all, but sentimentality. But the blindness is just as real.

Many a father, even though he says he loves his children, has played the role of a tyrant by binding his children to him in an unnatural way.

A dear friend of ours, Thelma, recently went through a tragic divorce. Thelma was still a teenager when her mother died. Her father, who was then in his fifties, went into a period of mourning which lasted twenty years. As the only girl in the family (there were three sons, all married), Thelma felt obligated to stay home and take care of her father. Across the years she had brief flings at romance, but somehow her father always managed to break things up. He didn't do it by violence, but by playing on his daughter's sympathy. 'I need you with me, Thelma. I don't think I can face life without you now that Mother is gone.'

Then, when Thelma was thirty-four, she met a fine young man who seemed to understand her situation. A widower with four small children, he was patient as he courted her. When she called to say she had to break a date because her father was 'sick', he understood. When she told him she could marry him only if he could provide for her father, he agreed. They were married in a small church wedding and Thelma and her father moved from the old home place to live with her husband in a nearby town.

The first year was happy. Thelma seemed to be making the necessary adjustments and the children responded well to her natural love. But then Thelma's father began to miss the old house. He begged Thelma to let him return home, where he could 'die in peace'. It broke her heart, but she finally agreed, believing her place was with her husband, but her father could not turn loose. Once home, he began to call. There was no one there to take care of him, he complained. He was afraid he would have a stroke and be alone in the house, helpless, for days before anyone found him. He never asked her to come home, his tyranny was far more subtle. He just played on her heartstrings until she finally returned to take care of him. 'It will be for just a short while,' she told her husband.

But once home she fell into the old routine and, unable to escape the bondage, finally wrote her husband and told him she could not leave her father to die alone. Brokenhearted, she asked him to get a divorce. She was not coming back. 'I'm too bound to the past to change,' she said.

How does one break the bondage of ancestral ties and find release from tyranny? The answer to this, as to all questions concerning inner healing, is found in the Bible. In this case we need look no farther than the life of Hezekiah.

The tragedy of sentimental love is that it binds us from reality, preventing us from seeing the truth about our family relationships. Thus the first principle of release is to look at our situation objectively.

After the death of Ahaz, Hezekiah was able to step back and look at the situation from a distance. He was able to see that even though he had been taught to honour his father, nevertheless his father was a godless man.

True love does not hide its head in the sand, it enables us to look facts square in the face. Confessing that his father was godless did not cause Hezekiah to love him any less. In fact, it should have caused him to love him more. It is sentimentality which binds us to the facts and prevents us from acting objectively. True love will bring enlightenment which will, as Jefferson rightly ascertained, cause 'tyranny and oppressions of the body and mind' to 'vanish like evil spirits at the dawn of day'.

The call of Christ is for the people of God to take authority over the bondage of ancestry – of those both living and dead – and 'quit ye like men, be strong'. We should rebuke any spirit that tells us we should not look honestly at all our family relationships. We need to see the weaknesses of our parents, as well as their strengths. Much of our godlessness is inherited, either consciously or unconsciously, from our ancestors. In fact, there is a type of generic bondage which extends all the way back to Adam – a bondage which is inherited from those long dead yet is a strong reality in our lives. It is such a generic relationship which not only causes us occasionally to look like a great, great grandparent – but even to act like him.

Release from such tyranny is found by following Hezekiah's example – making a personal covenant with God and renouncing the false idols of our fathers.

Hezekiah said:

Now it is in mine heart to make a covenant with the

159

*Lord God of Israel . . . to stand before him, to serve him,
and that ye should minister unto him, and burn incense
(2 Chronicles 29:10, 11).*

This was an open declaration that he would not serve the
god of his father, whoever that god might be, but would only
serve the true and living God.

In all probability, your parents never built an altar under a
tree, sacrificed children, or bowed down before stone idols.
But every one of us is guilty of having built altars which were
not of God. A young man in our church stood one night and
confessed the bondage he had to his father. His father had
never been able to pay his bills. An itinerant construction
worker, he had moved from one community to another
amassing huge debts. When his creditors came to repossess
what he had bought, he would move on. As a result, this
young fellow grew up watching his father pay homage to the
god of money. Every decision was based on finances. If the
family moved, it was because the father could get a better job
somewhere else with more money, or because his creditors
were forcing him to leave. The idea of hearing from God
and following his direction was as foreign as flying to the
moon.

The young man finally left home and joined a motorcycle
gang. Eventually he wound up in our town and somehow
came in contact with several young Christians. Through their
influence he too became a Christian. When he did, his violent
ways changed and he became a gentle, affectionate young
man who soon found a sweet young lady and married
her.

However, despite the tremendous change in his personality
the bondage of the past was still with him. Some of the elders
in the church began receiving complaints from the local
merchants. The merchants knew he was a member of the
church because he openly testified of his faith in Christ. But
he could not handle his money. He was deeply in debt, following the same path his father had taken. He had run up

huge accounts with his credit cards, had purchased luxuries (such as a colour TV) which he could not afford, and had finally gone to a loan shark who was now threatening to take him to court.

Some of the more mature men in church perceived that his problem stemmed from a bondage to his father. They counselled him and it wasn't long before he stood on a Sunday night and renounced the tyranny that carried over from his childhood. He made a public covenant with God that he would no longer serve the gods of his father. Following the advice of his spiritual counsellors, he tore up all his credit cards, sold or sent back everything he didn't need, and entered a programme of disciplined spending. It took more than a year for him to get out of the hole, but now he is operating in the black, saving money in order to pay cash for furniture and the like.

Only God knows the bondage we put on our children. An old friend of mine tells of the first forty years of her life and says it was like living in hell – even though her entire life was spent in church and the last fifteen years of it as a foreign missionary nurse in Africa.

As far back as she could remember, her mother had told her she was to be a foreign missionary. The mother even went so far as to say God had told her she would serve in Africa. Ignorant of spiritual matters, she didn't know such a call should come only from God, directly.

The young lady dutifully went to college, nursing school, and seminary – preparing for her career as a missionary. Yet deep inside she knew it was not God, but mother, who was directing her life. It took fifteen years in Nigeria before she finally came to herself and realised she was out of God's will. She resigned from the foreign mission board of her denomination and returned home.

Her action broke her mother's heart. As long as her daughter was a missionary in Africa, the mother had enjoyed a special type of respect in her local church. Others knew her as the 'missionary's mother'. But now that her daughter had

161

resigned as a missionary, 'left the ministry' so to speak, the mother was crushed.

Eventually the mother confessed that when she herself was a young girl, God had spoken to her and nudged her towards the mission field. Instead, she had married early and gone with her husband to the Midwest rather than to Africa. When she discovered she was pregnant, she promised God if he would give her a daughter she would dedicate her to the task originally asked of the mother, that of being a foreign missionary. But in the 'dedication' she had bound the child to a false call – and effectively blocked her from hearing God's voice in her own life.

However, after all those years, the daughter was finally free. She took a job at a hospital and is now the director of nurses' training. Ironically, some of the girls in her classes are preparing for the mission field and she is a great help to them. But she herself will never go back. That was her mother's call, not hers.

Bondage to parents and their ideals can come in many ways. Even our 'confessions' bind a child. Countless numbers of children have been established in life patterns by parents who called them 'dimwit'. One man says he grew up with a worthless concept of himself because his father, time and time again, said, 'You'll never amount to anything. You'll always be a troublemaker.'

Actually that confession was a curse which followed him throughout all the years of his life. The boy eventually wound up in prison remembering – and hating – the curse put on him by his father.

Such curses are not easily broken. As in the case of Hezekiah, it often takes a public declaration that you will no longer recognise the godless ways of a parent, but will submit only to the direction of the heavenly Father. Since this crosses the grain of all that we esteem honourable and noble, since it breaks the chains of sentimentality, it is extremely difficult. But often it is the only way we can gain release from tyranny and move into inner healing.

There are other altars at which our parents have worshipped which need to be renounced. Altars of expediency, self, and pride. Or perhaps it was an altar to some kind of family heritage. As a boy I can remember my father grilling me, saying, 'Remember, you are a Buckingham. Never do anything which will bring disgrace to the family name.'

After my father became a Christian I never heard him talk about the 'family name'. However, I often heard him refer to the fact that I was a child of the King and an ambassador of Jesus Christ. 'Remember,' he said, 'you carry the banner of the Lord wherever you go. You are the only Bible some people will read. Represent your Lord well.'

All sons are not as fortunate as I, however. Many boys and girls grow up having been taught to worship at the altar under the family tree. In animal husbandry a pure blood line is referred to as a 'thoroughbred'. Tragically, that concept often extends from dogs and horses to the human race, until people take great pride in who their ancestors are, claiming some kind of present position based on the fact that their uncle was a bishop or their grandfather a governor. We use the term 'blue blood' to give us status which is supposedly inherited through the lineage.

There are, in America and the United Kingdom, investigative companies who do nothing but trace family trees, redesign coats of arms, or determine which totem or tartan represents our clan. The altars we build under these family trees are just as real as the altars Ahaz built under the trees in Israel. We dote on our heritage, and in many homes huge pictures of ancestors stare down at us as we eat, study, sleep, or procreate. It's no wonder that our offspring grow up in such bondage to the past. Such bondage is often a curse.

Others may not trace the family tree back to the Mayflower but take great pride in saying, 'My granddad built this church,' or 'Our family have always been Catholics.'

My first church after I left seminary was a large old downtown congregation in a textile community in South Carolina. Pride and tradition and family heritage ran deep. The church was ruled by a small handful of people who had inherited their power from their fathers. Men were elected to important positions in the church on the basis of their ancestral line rather than their relationship with the Father. Many of the families occupied the same pew on Sunday morning as their forefathers had occupied. To consider changing, or sharing, was as unthinkable as swapping wives.

One Sunday morning I took my usual place on the platform and looked over the congregation at a strange sight. The sanctuary was laid out with three sections of pews extending from front to back. The long pews in the middle row held twelve people each, while the short pews on both sides were five-seaters. A professor, his wife, and three old maid sisters who lived with them had occupied the same pew – one of the five-seaters – for many years. It was the same pew, or at least in the same vicinity (since we had recently renovated the sanctuary), that his father had occupied before him. In fact, there was a bronze plaque on the end of the pew that had his name, his wife's name, and the names of the three sisters, indicating he had 'donated' $250 which went to purchase a pew in the newly renovated church – no doubt that very one.

No one ever sat in the professor's pew but the professor. If he or his family were sick, or for some reason – which was rare indeed – missed the church service, the pew always remained vacant in his honour.

But on that particular Sunday morning when I took my place on the platform, seven people were crowded into the professor's five-person pew. The professor, his wife, and the three sisters were there – along with a couple I had never seen before. They looked absolutely absurd, squeezed into that tiny bench in obvious discomfort, maybe even pain. It was even stranger since there were plenty of empty seats close by.

It wasn't until after the service that one of the ushers told me what had happened. The professor had been late arriving that morning and somehow a visiting couple had inadvertently slipped into 'their' pew. When the professor arrived, rather than taking another seat or splitting up his clan so part of them could sit one place and the rest in their usual place, they all squeezed in on the visiting couple and remained there throughout the service.

The bondage of the past was too great to break. Tradition, established by the tyranny of ancestry, was more powerful than comfort or change.

Such ancestor worship is not only foolish, it is idolatrous. Paul says when a man becomes a new creature in Christ old things are passed away; behold all things are become new (2 Corinthians 5:17).

From that time on, family trees, national heritage, traditions, 'blood lines', and titles should mean nothing. For centuries people have justified their immature behaviour and volatile personalities by blaming them on their ancestral traditions.

'All us redheads blow our tops sometimes.'

'He's just like his father, always chasing after women.'

'Every woman in that family has been lazy.'

'I can't help it. My mother was the same way.'

Such excuses are not only contrary to the theology of the Bible, but actually become curses we place on each other – and on ourselves.

Equally devastating is our determination to convince ourselves, and others, that we are locked into a personality pattern by our nationality – a trait that millions of people accept with great pride.

'I know I lose my temper, but I'm Irish.'

'Sure I'm stubborn. So are all Dutchmen.'

'Those Germans are always so precise.'

'I can't help it if I'm emotional. I'm Italian.'

'I sure wouldn't let my daughter go out with a Frenchman.'

'Never trust an Arab.'

'If you were a Jew, and your ancestors had been persecuted like mine, you'd be bitter also.'

'All Scots are stingy.'

But I'm not a Scotsman, even though my ancestors were

born there. I am a child of God. What difference does it make whether one's ancestors were murdered by the Nazis, killed by the Japanese, raped by the Yankees or slaughtered by the Confederates. When a person becomes a new creature in Christ old things pass away. From that time on the only 'blood line' we have bypasses the Mayflower, it even bypasses father Abraham, and flows directly from the Father through his Son. It does not extend back to Ireland, or Italy or Russia. We have literally inherited a new character – the character of our heavenly Father.

In early 1974 I sat in on a press conference in Jerusalem prior to the First World Conference on the Holy Spirit. During the conference it was apparent the Jewish reporters were far more interested in finding the political opinions of the speakers than their spiritual concerns. When the answers were not forthcoming, a militant Jewish reporter turned to a Christian Arab pastor who was part of the local planning committee and asked, 'Tell me, pastor, who do you think owns this land – the Jews or the Arabs?'

It was a baited question, the same kind thrown at Jesus 2,000 years before. Yet the same Holy Spirit who imparted supernatural wisdom to the Son of God, inspired this Arab believer.

'I was born to hate Jews,' he said in halting English. 'I was taught from birth this land was ours and we should take it at any cost. Then Jesus Christ, the Jewish Messiah and Saviour of the world, entered my heart. Since that time I no longer quibble over the rocks and sand of this land. I am but a pilgrim passing through on my way to a new home prepared for me beyond Jordan. This is not my land – or yours – it is God's.'

There was a long moment of silence. Then the Jewish reporter – with just a trace of moisture in his eyes – slowly rose to his feet and began to slowly clap his hands in applause. There were no more questions.

In Jesus Christ we literally inherit a new ancestry. The old root which formerly extended deep into our traditions, our heritage, our family tree, is hacked off, and the indwelling Holy Spirit now sends our roots deep into the rich soil on the banks of the River of Life.

Sidney Lanier caught that spirit as he wandered through the Marshes of Glynn near Brunswick, Georgia. He wrote:

> As the marsh-hen secretly builds on the watery sod,
> Behold I will build me a nest on the greatness of God;
> I will fly in the greatness of God as the marsh-hen flies
> In the freedom that fills all the space 'twixt the marsh and the skies:
> By so many roots as the marsh-grass sends in the sod
> I will heartily lay me a-hold on the greatness of God.

It should make no more difference whether we had oriental parents, if our great-uncle was a Prussian baron, or if we come from a long line of Ku Klux Klanners. Once we are reborn into Christ, our ancestry is traced to the cross; our traditions are no longer bound in the old wineskins of the church, culture, or community, but take on the change of new wine; and it makes no difference, even if our ancestors were lords, earls, dukes, or kings, for now we are heirs to a far greater throne, joint heirs with the Son of God himself.

In the Bible the change was so often so dramatic, so literal, that the people underwent an actual change of name. In the case of Simon bar Jonah (Simon, son of Jonah), for instance, Jesus said that from that time on his name would be Simon Peter. No longer was ancestry linked to the sandy soil of an earthly heritage, but built upon the solid rock of the eternal Father in heaven.

Abram (exalted father) became who he actually was, *Abraham* (father of multitudes). The covenant relationship with God was literally built into his new name. *Jacob*, the trickster, became *Israel*, the soldier of God. And *Saul*, who longed to be great in the eyes of the world, became *Paul*, a name which means little and humble.

My own name is James William Buckingham II, indicating

that I was named after my grandfather on my father's side, who was also James William Buckingham. However, my mother, whose Thompson family hailed from Wales and Scotland, had a penchant for Scottish names. Therefore, from the very beginning I was both James William and 'Jamie'. I grew up disliking both names. James William reminded me of my grandfather who died before I was born. I can remember standing for long moments staring up at his musty picture in that great oval frame which hung in the attic, wondering if I would grow up to look like him – string tie, black bowler hat and all.

On the other hand, I winced every time I heard the name Jamie. Maybe it was the sound of my mother's voice calling out the back door, 'Jaa-mee!' Perhaps it was the fact that there were two girls in my class named Jamie (some of my friends said Jamie was a feminine name). I've often wondered just how much this reaction affected my life and drove me on to ruinous efforts to try to prove my masculinity when it didn't need proving at all. When my school-girl friend bought me a silver identity bracelet one year, I asked her to have the engraver use my initials, 'J. W. Buckingham' rather 'Jamie Buckingham'.

But even so, my motives were not pure. I was doing it to prove something to myself, and it wasn't until after I allowed Jesus Christ to take the reins of my life that I was free to accept my name. I didn't have to prove whatever it was I thought I had to prove. I belonged to his family and just as he had redeemed my nature and my body, so he had redeemed my name. Since then there has been real peace in simply being 'Jamie'. And when the mail sometimes comes addressed to Miss Jamie Buckingham (just as my wife's mail sometimes comes addressed to Mr Jackie Buckingham), I no longer feel resentment or even embarrassment. I'm free.

Last year I spent a few days in Japan with a small group of Christians from Kyoto. One of those in the group was the pastor of a Southern Baptist church. He gave me some additional insight into the problem of ancestor worship, which of course is deeply ingrained in many orientals.

It is not uncommon, he said, for a Japanese to become a Christian, join the church, learn the hymns, read his Bible, bring his children to Sunday school, and even serve as an officer in the church, while holding secretly to the religion of his father. This usually is not evident until there is a death in the family, at which time the Christian, not wishing to offend or dishonour his ancestors, often reverts to his old Buddhist forms.

The only way this kind of bondage could be broken, the pastor said, was for the Christian to make an open declaration in which he said: 'I renounce the gods of my father,' or 'I renounce the gods of my ancestors.' Of course this is tantamount to saying 'I hate father and mother,' but it is necessary in order to throw off the yoke and enter into wholeness.

Several years ago my wife made friends with a beautiful young woman whose father had been an American diplomat in India. Although he had been a member of an institutional church, he felt he should not offend his Indian friends by flaunting his religion. Instead, he embraced many of the outward accoutrements of the Hindu faith, filling his house with statues, idols, and various Hindu trappings.

When he left India, he brought these idols, many of them made of gold, jade, and carved teak, back to the States. After his death, his daughter inherited them and placed them in her beautiful home in the Pocono Mountains of Pennsylvania.

We became acquainted with her when she attended a luncheon where I spoke. Across the next few months we corresponded and the following summer we paid a brief visit to her lovely home. Shortly after she had become a Christian, her husband had left her, which only intensified her desire for inner healing. As Jackie helped her, it became evident that some obstacle held her to the past. She could not break clear of her father's powerful influence over her life.

As they prayed together, the woman realised her father's

influence was in some way connected to the various idols and statues which filled the house. Before the day was over, the two of them had an idol breaking/burning ceremony. Those which were made of flammable material were burned in the fireplace. The others were broken and smashed outside on the patio and dumped into the lake. Many of the statues and figures were worth hundreds, maybe thousands, of dollars. But the price was a small one to pay for the tremendous release that came from it.

Sometimes it is easier to deal with a living problem than a dead memory. A young widow moved to Melbourne from West Palm Beach where she had lived prior to her husband's death. Because he did not have adequate insurance, she was left virtually penniless. The only thing she salvaged from the estate was their large, expensive house in West Palm Beach which her husband, a contractor, had built shortly before he died. It was filled with a short lifetime of memories, but since she had been promised a job in Melbourne, she had moved her children up the coast to go to work.

When we learned of her, she had lost her job and was living on food stamps, trying to keep the three small children warm around a tiny wood stove in a cheap flat.

Some of our men visited with her, and after finding out her circumstances, counselled her to sell the big house in West Palm Beach which, because of its location, had remained empty even though she had tried repeatedly to rent it. They showed her how she could realise enough money from the sale, not only to purchase a nice house in Melbourne, but to put the balance in savings so she could live off the interest.

'You don't understand,' she wept, 'I can't sell that house. It's all I have left of my husband.'

Fortunately they were able to show her the need for healing in this area. She saw it and accepted their help. The house brought in more money than any of them had anticipated.

The renunciation of the idols of tradition and the tyranny of ancestors will always result in a time of trial. In the life of

Hezekiah, from the moment he was crowned king until he finally died, he was always being tempted to return to the way of his father. Even though he had been healed inwardly and set free from tyranny, many of those around him were unwilling to accept this new way of life. Thus the conflict and tension remained.

When King Sennacherib learned that Hezekiah was not going to follow the course of his father, the Assyrian king gathered his troops and marched on Jerusalem. They surrounded the walled city – 185,000 of them – and began to shout in Hebrew, 'Return to the gods of Ahab, return to the gods of your father.'

It was a tense moment. The people of Jerusalem, who wanted to be true to their new king, felt the pressure. All they had to do was renounce this new way of living and return to the worship of idols. If they did, the Assyrians would withdraw. If they continued loyal to Hezekiah and his God, the Assyrians would overrun the city and kill them.

Throughout the night the Assyrians milled around the walls of the city, crying out in Hebrew, 'Return to the gods of Ahab.'

Hezekiah sat in his chambers, listening, and perhaps at the same time hearing the murmuring of the people in the streets below.

'All you have to do is give allegiance to your father,' the tempter was saying.

That's a low blow, any way you look at it. But that is the way Satan always fights, playing on the sentiments, trying to bring us back into bondage by quoting Scripture. 'I know your father wasn't a godly man, but at least he kept the city from being overrun. The mothers were able to raise their children in peace and the men were free to support their families. Now, in the morning, the city is going to be sacked. The men will be carried off as slaves, the women raped, and you, the king, will be beheaded. The Bible says "Honour thy father and mother that your days may be long upon the land." Now, because you have broken that commandment, your days are about to be cut off. All you have to do is restore the honour due to your dear old father.'

But Hezekiah had already made his decision. 'I will not return to bondage,' he said. 'Nor will I lead the people back into idolatry.'

He called for his old friend, the prophet Isaiah, who had received his call the same year Hezekiah's grandfather, King Uzziah, had died. 'Come with me,' Hezekiah said. 'Let's stand on the walls and trust God to deliver us.'

Sometime during the night a host of angels appeared among the Assyrians. Frightened and confused the Assyrians began fighting with each other, and when the people arose the next morning to face what they felt was certain death, they found the entire Assyrian army had been slaughtered. King Sennacherib, seeing the slaughter, turned in fear and ran all the way back to Nineveh where his own sons killed him.

The final victory always belongs to God, but he seldom delivers his servants from their bondages in the flick of an eye. More often our initial commitments to him, like Hezekiah's decision to turn from Ahab's god to the Lord, are tested, and thereby deepened, unto our lives' ends. Every day we must choose anew to follow Jesus.

10

CONTENTMENT . . . NOW

We had just finished our evening meal and the family was sitting comfortably around the table, enjoying small talk and catching up on the day's activities. Summer was drawing to a close and in a few days the children would be back at school. Our oldest son, Bruce, had already left for college in Oklahoma, leaving behind a sadly vacant chair at the table. Tim, who had just come in from football practice, had eaten everything on his plate and was now systematically attacking and finishing every other bowl of food on the table. The two older teenage girls, Robin, who was in her first year at the local community college, and Bonnie, who was in her last year at school, were laughing at Tim as he devoured the last scraps of food. Trim and beautiful, they were very careful about what they ate and what they wore. If their younger brother wanted to act like a human dust bin, that was all right, but not for them. Our youngest daughter, Sandy, who at twelve thought she was twenty, but still acted as if she were at junior school, was eager for me to 'dismiss the troops' so she could go out and play with her friends. After all, there were only four days left of the summer holiday and then it was back to school. She needed to make use of every available second to play.

Suddenly there was a heavy knocking at the door. Sandy, looking for some excuse to leave the table anyway, shouted, 'I'll get it!' But before she could get her chair pushed back from the table the front door burst open, framing the lanky figure of one of the young men in the church fellowship. His face was flushed from the wind, having just got off his motorcycle. Removing his helmet, he stepped into the dining room and asked excitedly, 'Is it true? I mean about next Saturday?'

'You'll have to do better than that,' I shrugged, motioning him into the room. 'What about next Saturday?'

'You mean you haven't heard? Everybody I know is talking about it.'

The kids were all ears. Even Tim had stopped eating and was listening intently. Our caller looked around the room and finally realised we were ignorant of his great news. He shook his head.

'Well, I was on the phone to an old friend up in West Virginia last night. He told me that everybody up there was really upset. The world is supposed to come to an end on September 6. That's Saturday.'

Tim resumed his eating. 'So, what's the rush,' he said. Today's only Wednesday.'

It was the kind of answer I would have expected my children to give, the kind I would have hoped they would give. Sandy looked at me plaintively and said, 'Daddy, can I go outside now? I've got only an hour before I have to come back in and all the kids are out there waiting for me.'

I nodded my head and she was out the door. What was the end of the world when the neighbourhood gang wanted to ride skateboards in our driveway? I looked up at the young man and motioned him to sit down in Sandy's empty chair. 'Have a piece of pie, Tony, and tell me all about it.'

There wasn't much to tell. A lot of people were excited about a rumour that the world was coming to an end. It seemed some religious sect was going door-to-door across the nation – in fact, we later learned it was across the world – warning people to get ready. September 6, 1975, was The End.

Of course it wasn't. Since it was the last Saturday before

school, we crammed it full of all kinds of activities. I took Tim and Sandy water skiing, while Robin and Bonnie spent the day at the beach, trying to soak in the last drop of sunshine before they returned to the classrooms. Jackie went to the hairdressers and then spent the afternoon in the quiet house alone, catching up on everything that needed to be done before school started. In short, we did all the normal Saturday things. Of course, there was the possibility the prophecy might be right, but it would have been right only by accident. Our children knew this, and it really didn't make much difference to them. To be with the Lord was their final destination anyway, in the meantime they intended to enjoy life here on earth.

We hear a lot of reports these days about the end of the world. We shouldn't be surprised. The Bible says that as the end approaches there will be wild rumours of all sorts, reporting Christ has returned in one place or another. However, Jesus said that not even the Son of God knew when the end would come. The information belonged to the Father alone. Jesus did have a word to say to us about the last days:

These things I have spoken unto you that in me ye might have peace. In the world ye shall have tribulation: but be of good cheer; I have overcome the world (John 16:33).

History is fraught with tales of groups of people who sold all their belongings and fled to the mountaintops or hid themselves away in caves to await the end of the world. It seems that the unhealed man is always setting dates, hoping for the worst. Like the Broadway singer, he cries out: 'Stop the world, I want to get off.' Why? Because he has not experienced the contentment of life which is possible on this earth, and thus yearns for anything that will get him out of here.

Inner healing, however, produces a different type of person. As a person moves into transparency of soul, into maturity of the Spirit, as the inner lake is cleansed and the old wounds and hurts healed (and even our thoughts brought into captivity to the obedience of Jesus Christ), the discontentment fades away and life with God here on earth grows more meaningful. To the person who has experienced inner healing, the world itself grows more beautiful, friends are friendlier, loved ones more precious, life more abundant, and he sees the face of God in every dewdrop and hears his voice in every murmur of the breeze.

The great purpose of the Holy Spirit is to show us how to live every day to its fullest, to usher us into the kingdom of God right here on earth. There is no need to wait until we die to experience the joy, bliss, and security of heaven; no need to project our misery and insecurity on the world by setting false dates and making preposterous claims concerning the 'rapture'. There may be a rapture. There will certainly be tribulations. But that is all inconsequential when you are living in the joy of the Lord one day at a time.

Yet it is at this place that most of us have our greatest difficulty. An old friend of mine once told of taking a train trip down the eastern coast. At noon he made his way from his compartment back to the dining car where the steward seated him with a middle-aged couple who had already ordered their food. The husband seemed friendly enough, but his wife complained about everything. She complained about the silver on the table, she found a speck of dust in her water and demanded the waiter send it back, she grumbled about the bumpy ride, the food, and the service.

In an effort to try to lighten what was an extremely heavy situation, my friend asked the man what he did for a living.

'I'm a banker,' the man said, 'but my wife is in the manufacturing business.'

'Oh, what does she manufacture?'

My friend said the man had the most sorrowful look he had ever seen when he said softly, so his wife (who was complaining to the waiter about the lettuce) couldn't hear. 'Unhappiness,' the man said sadly. 'Every place she goes she manufactures unhappiness.'

We all know people like that. Maybe we are one ourselves.

It is the result of an unhealed spirit, the result of trying to cope with today's tribulation without the good cheer that comes by being filled with the Spirit of Christ.

At a dinner party recently I sat across the table from a distinguished attorney. When he discovered I was a minister he said, 'Oh, what a wonderful occupation. Some day you are going to grow old, and when you do you will look back with great satisfaction on the work you have done. I realise things are probably tough now, but when you get to be my age and look back, it will all seem worthwhile.'

I had to stop him. 'Friend, I hate to disillusion you, but I'm satisfied right now. I don't have to wait until I grow older and look back to find my joy. I'm living in so much contentment now I can hardly stand it.'

He said he understood, but I could tell from the expression on his face that he didn't. He was a typical mask-wearer, yet I knew behind his gracious smile and pleasing manner lay buried the anguish of a lifetime.

Jesus sent the Holy Spirit into the world to give us contentment now. That's difficult for some to understand. They cling to the Gospel as a life preserver to keep them afloat in a sea of despair. In one sense of the word, that's true. But the Gospel is far more than a life preserver. The Gospel is actually the good news that even though we have tribulation in this world, we have something to shout about: Jesus has overcome the world. He sent his Holy Spirit to bring us into the same fulfilment, the same inner health that he had when he was here on earth. Contentment, joy, wholeness – not later on, but now.

Tragically, many Christians miss out on all that because they reject the Holy Spirit. Seeing only the more sensational 'gift ministries' – the prophets, the healers, the miracle workers – they fail to understand that the real purpose of the coming of the Spirit is to lead us into abundant living through Jesus Christ.

It's strange, but the very things God has designed to bring us pleasure are often the things that cause us the most frustration. Why? Because in most cases we treat these things as a means to an end, rather than seeing them as a joyful end in themselves.

One of my favourite ministers is James Lee Beall, pastor of the Bethesda Missionary Temple in Detroit. In one of his little teaching booklets, Jim Beall pointed this out. He said, 'We read for profit, we party for contacts, we lunch for contracts, we bowl for unity, we drive for mileage, we gamble for charity, we go out in the evening for the greater joys of the municipality, we stay at home on the week-end to rebuild our home – always looking for some other reason for doing things.' What a rat race we have got ourselves into.

The Christian faith is extremely functional. The best example of how functional it is comes from the book of Philippians. Here Paul, chained in a prison cell, locked in a dungeon with shackles around his arms and legs, writes back to the church at Philippi and says, 'Wow, what a ball I'm having here, folks!' He had learned that real contentment is not based on our circumstances, but springs from inner healing.

Listen to Paul in Philippians 4 as he sings from his prison cell:

Rejoice in the Lord alway: and again I say rejoice.
Let your moderation be known unto all men.
The Lord is at hand.
[There's no need to wait for the second coming, he is at hand now.]
Be careful for nothing; but in every thing by prayer and supplication with thanksgiving let your requests be made known unto God. And the peace of God, which passeth all understanding, shall keep your hearts and minds through Christ Jesus.
[Inner healing, in a nutshell, is achieved when your heart and mind is 'kept' by the peace which God gives through Christ Jesus.]
Finally, brethren, whatsoever things are true,

whatsoever things are honest,
whatsoever things are just,
whatsoever things are pure,
whatsoever things are lovely,
whatsoever things are of good report;
if there be any virtue, and if there be any praise,
think on these things.

For several years I have been aware of the importance of going to sleep thinking on 'these things' – the things that are honest, just, pure, lovely, and of good report. And if it is important for my inner health, how much more important it is for my young children whose minds are still a fertile garden into which I have the opportunity of sowing weeds or productive fruit, tares or wheat. For the last several years, when I am home at night. I have made the rounds of the children in their beds, kneeling down beside them or sitting quietly on the edge of the bed, talking about things of virtue and praise. It may have been a bad day for them. Tim may have been told off by his coach at ball practice, but he needs to hear from me, his daddy, that I am proud of him. He needs to hear me recount some of the joys of the day and how good it is to have a son who is growing into manhood. I want him to go to sleep on that thought, for I know that during his sleeping hours the Holy Spirit will be much at work in his subconscious, bringing him to total inner healing.

In the case of Robin and Bonnie, their needs are different. Approaching the time when they will leave home, they are faced with the problems and frustrations of decisions. They may need to talk for a few minutes and allow me to respond, dropping into the garden of their heart seeds that will grow and produce lovely flowers which will bloom in sweet fragrance. I want them to know how much I love them, how proud I am of them despite any defects they may have experienced during the day.

It was because of this inner health that our seventeen-year-old Robin was able to go through a very trying experience last year. Driving our little car down a main street near the high school, she went through a red light and crashed into the side of another car. She was clearly to blame. The car was almost demolished and it was only by the grace of God that the boy in the other car was not killed. Most of the day was spent getting X-rays at the hospital, filling in police, insurance, and hospital forms. She was told she would have to appear in court, and of course our insurance company would have to pay all the bills.

That night I slipped into her darkened bedroom, expecting to find her unnerved, fearful, and crying. Instead she heard me coming and I heard her soft, cheerful, 'Hi, dad.' I sat down on the edge of the bed and took her hand.

'You okay, sweetheart?'

'I'm fine, dad,' she said. 'My knee hurts where I bumped it, but it's okay.'

'The angel of the Lord was with you,' I said softly.

'I know,' she answered and squeezed my hand. 'But he is always, isn't he?'

I nodded in the darkness, lay my hand on her head, and prayed for God's peace to keep her mind and heart during the night.

'Thanks, dad,' she whispered and leaned up and kissed me. Then with a simple 'Good night,' she turned over and went to sleep.

He giveth his beloved sleep (Psalm 127:2).

That's the evidence of a mind that has spent its waking hours thinking on 'these things'.

Every child's needs are different. My 'daddy responsibility', as the keeper of the garden of their hearts, is to make sure the right seeds are planted, the bushes trimmed, and the fruit harvested at the correct time. For instance, our twelve-year-old Sandy went through her growth period early. Last year she sprouted almost five inches and suddenly she was almost a foot taller than all her other friends, who would probably sprout up the next year. It was a grave cause of concern in her mind. Often when I would tuck her in and spend those few private moments which she knew were 'just hers', she would tell me about her fear that she was going to be a giant.

'What if I never stop growing?' she asked. 'What if I just keep on getting taller and taller? I don't want to be a freak.'

It was a critical issue with her, and the wrong thoughts could warp and twist her mind for years to come. So many young girls go through this same thing, but because they allow thoughts of fear rather than thoughts of cheer inside their minds, they try to cover their rapid growth by stooping. Stooping eventually becomes a lifestyle, evidencing itself not only in a bent back and drooping shoulders, but by stooping in areas of self-confidence. Many a girl has gone through life bent over, telling herself and others around her that she's just a 'freak', when actually she is a princess in the kingdom of God.

Thus it was often necessary for me to spend extra moments with Sandy, telling her how proud I was of her and sharing with her little stories of people who grew fast and grew slow, but all finally grew to be just the height God intended.

What a person thinks is extremely important. Especially is it important to control our last conscious thoughts before we go to sleep, thinking only on those things of 'good report'. It is often in the sleeping hours that the Holy Spirit is most active in his work of inner healing.

The great book on inner healing is the book of Proverbs. Its thirty-one chapters lend themselves ideally to daily reading, one chapter a day for the month, which means one could read the entire book twelve times a year, or over a ten-year period (which I recommend) it would be read one hundred and twenty times.

It was the writer of Proverbs who said:

For as he thinketh in his heart, so is he (Proverbs 23:7).

Positive thinking and positive living are necessary if we expect to enter into inner healing. This is also true if we expect others around us to have inner healing, for our negative thoughts can be just as damaging to them as if we had opened their minds and poured in poison.

Last month our daughter Bonnie, in her last year at school, came home bubbling with excitement. She had received an invitation from a friend to spend the spring holidays in the mountains. There was only one catch. They would have to drive one of our cars.

Ordinarily this would have presented no problem and I would have shared her joy and excitement. That morning, however, after Bonnie had left for school, I had discovered oil leaking out from under the estate car. I carefully drove it to the garage and was told we had serious engine problems. Thus when Bonnie came bouncing in and broke her good news, I reacted, and tossed her a negative thought in exchange. Before I realised it, I had destroyed all her happy plans, outlining reason after reason why such a trip was out of the question. Moments before she had been 'all joy', now she was filled with despair. She finally muttered, 'Oh, let's forget it,' and walked out of the room.

I stood there for a long time, thinking. Was it possible that I had wounded her with my negative spirit? That's not to say I should not say no. But I should have at least listened to her story, and then told her our circumstances. I should have allowed her the dignity of reaching the right conclusion without it being forced on her from the outside. Instead I tried to control her.

In Paul's letter to the Philippians he talks about his own positive example which he hoped would bring inner healing to his friend in Philippi.

Those things, which ye have both learned and received and heard and seen in me, do: and the God of peace shall be with you (Philippians 4:9).

Then he injects something else which we often miss. The Roman prison system felt no obligation to feed the prisoners. All they did was lock them up. If a prisoner starved, that was his bad fortune. Therefore, the only way a prisoner could stay alive was to hope someone on the outside would care enough to send food, or money to buy food. Paul was in this situation. In this case, he was looking to the church at Philippi for his support. He was at the financial mercy of his friends. He writes to them saying:

> But I rejoiced in the Lord greatly, that now at the last your care of me hath flourished again; wherein ye were also careful, but ye lacked opportunity (Philippians 4:10).

It's hard to believe, but it seems that for a time his friends had actually forgotten about him. A man can get very hungry in a situation like that. Now, though, they had begun to help him again and Paul was writing to thank them, and to let them know that he understood the reason they had neglected him in the past was they 'lacked opportunity'.

From his letter, and his attitude, we begin to understand something of the open, loving, transparent nature of this man Paul. Yet, if ever a man had reason to live a life of reaction, it was Paul. He had been stoned, rejected, cursed, and was now in prison for something he didn't do. He was having to depend on friends who often forgot about him – yet he responded only in love.

> Not that I speak in respect of want: for I have learned, in whatsoever state I am, therewith to be content. I know both how to be abased, and I know how to abound: every where and in all things I am instructed both to be full and to be hungry, both to abound and to suffer need. I can do all things through Christ which strengtheneth me (Philippians 4:11-13).

While he appreciated the material gifts and possessions he

had, Paul made it very clear that he was not dependent on these things for happiness. Contentment, he said, goes far beyond financial security, good health, a job, or respect in the community. There is no way to equate external prosperity with happiness and contentment. These things spring only from a mind that has been transformed by the renewing presence of the Holy Spirit.

Jim Beall once talked about a man who has everything. His clothes are given to him, he has three good meals a day furnished without charge, and a private room of his own. He is protected from those who would try to harm him by armed guards. He has no rent to pay and no major decisions to make. He has maximum security with a guaranteed future of minimum risk. But no man in his right mind would want to trade places with him because he is serving a life sentence in prison. He has all the external trappings of security, but he is the perfect illustration that contentment is not found in outer circumstances. It has to come from within, from the renewed mind that brings us into a state of happiness and contentment designed for every situation.

I found myself observing one of those situations in the summer of 1975. I took off a few days so I could accompany my parents on a trip they needed to make from their summer home near Asheville, North Carolina, to Rochester Minnesota, where they were both to undergo medical check ups at Mayo Clinic. At eighty-five, dad could not walk without two sticks and could not climb stairs at all. Mother was in her late seventies and could navigate a bit better. Both of them, however, indicated they would feel better if I flew with them to Rochester. Since I was supposed to be in Minneapolis the next day, I found it easy to arrange my schedule.

Travelling was difficult for dad in particular. The muscles in his legs had atrophied, making it necessary for him to use a wheelchair if he had to walk more than just a few steps. This was their first aeroplane trip in more than a year, and he was apprehensive about getting on and off the plane, the use of a wheelchair when they changed planes in Chicago, and a dozen other matters. I knew my presence would ease their anxiety.

Both mother and dad are very orderly persons. Dad's workshop behind the house is as well appointed and organised as a surgical clinic. Every tool has its special place. All the nails have been sorted according to size and shape and put in separate glass jars. The same is true with nuts, bolts, washers, and screws. Cans of paint are labelled and sealed. Bits of string and wire are carefully wrapped and kept separate. The floor is spotlessly clean.

Inside the house things are the same. Mother's pantry is better organised than the grocery store. Clothes in the wardrobe are on hangers all spaced two fingers apart. Things in the drawers are neatly folded. There is no dirt under the carpet and no dust on the top of the window sills. They live a very ordered, regulated life, rising at the same hour each morning and going to bed at the same hour each night. They have lived this way for years, and even today I know if I visit their house I will find the broom hung on the same nail where it was hung thirty years ago.

Even though this kind of regularity is commendable, it gave me an uneasy feeling when I thought of the trip to Rochester. They had planned it for weeks, packing and repacking their bags. Mother insisted they take along their breakfast bran and canned prune juice which had been their breakfast diet (often supplemented with fresh fruit) for the last twenty years. She also packed their pillows. 'Those pillows in the hotel and clinic just aren't comfortable,' she said. She would have taken their bedboards, but the manager at the hotel in Rochester had assured her they would be provided.

Friends drove us to the airport at Asheville. I checked their bags and arranged for the special chair so the attendants could carry my father up the steps of the plane. The only luggage they carried with them was a large shopping bag with some books, grapes, raisins, dry biscuits, and mother's knitting. We were scheduled to change planes in Chicago in order to arrive in Rochester by 5.00 p.m. This would give them plenty of time to check into the hotel and get ready for their appointment at the clinic two days later.

Then the very worst thing that could possibly happen, happened. Like Job, 'that which I feared came upon me.' We arrived at Chicago's O'Hare Airport, the busiest airport in the world, only to discover Northwest Orient Airlines had gone on strike. There was no possible way to get to Rochester that night.

With mother and dad in wheelchairs, we were caught in an angry mass of shoving, shouting people in front of the Northwest counter.

'No planes, no planes,' the agent was shouting. 'Come back tomorrow morning and we'll get you on a commuter flight.'

I looked at my folks, virtually helpless. I finally got to the agent and asked if there was any way we could claim their bags, since it looked as if we would have to spend the night in Chicago. He shook his head in a futile gesture. 'This place is a madhouse. The baggage handlers are threatening to go on strike themselves. There's no way to get their bags. Just pick them up in Rochester after you arrive.'

A taxi took us to a nearby motel. We had to take special pains helping dad in and out of the car and then helping him as he leaned heavily on his sticks down the long corridor to their room.

Having travelled extensively, I always carry the necessities with me. Thus I had my toilet kit in my brief case, along with a change of socks and underwear. But for my parents, it was an entirely different matter. They had nothing with them except a few grapes, raisins, and their Bibles. No night clothes. No toothbrushes. Nothing. Besides this, the beds in their motel room looked as if they had been used by elephants. They were lumpy and sway-backed with the flattest pillows I had ever seen.

'Oh, Lord,' I prayed, 'what are they going to do?'

I learned something that evening. All those years my parents had walked with the Lord had brought about an inner healing I never dreamed existed. When the chips were down, they revealed their real natures – and it so resembled Jesus it took my breath. Yes, mother and dad had grown comfortable in their daily routine. They liked everything in its place and fussed a little when things weren't proper. But when all those things were taken away, I discovered they were just as much at home with nothing as they were with everything. In fact, they were far more yielding than I was. When I expressed my deep concern over having to spend the night without any of their regular comforts – even pyjamas – it was my eighty-five-year-old father who para-phrased Paul's motto back to me:

For I have learned, in whatsoever state I am, even with-out a cup to put my false teeth in, therewith to be content.

The Gospel of Jesus Christ is the most functional philosophy in the world.

Back in the autumn of last year I saw how that same principle had been worked into another family. Jackie and I attended a wedding rehearsal party for a young couple in our church. At our table were a retired couple who had recently moved to Florida from Pennsylvania. We chatted amiably and I found them to be charming, sensitive people. During the conversation, they mentioned their son, who they said was retarded. Half of each year was spent in an institutional school, the rest of the time he lived with them.

'How old is he?' I asked.

'He's forty-three,' the father answered. Then he added, 'He's our only son and the doctors say he will never change. Sometimes he's dangerous to himself and others, but we have found that through love he can be controlled.'

'Forty-three,' I thought. 'That's my age. And he's been that way all his life.'

The woman, soft-spoken, grey-haired, with an air of great

tenderness about her, spoke. 'He's a very loving boy. Very gentle. It's only when he's frustrated that he acts violently.

'You've kept him at home for forty-three years?' I asked.

'Yes, only he is in the institution half of the year.'

'Then you have actually patterned and programmed your entire lives around his need, haven't you?' I asked.

I saw the man, dignified, yet very warm, reach over and take his wife's hand. 'Very few people understand,' he said. 'But he is our son, and nothing is more important than loving him into happiness and healing. We believe that somehow, through our love, God will bring him into wholeness.'

We sat for a long time, not speaking. I could feel the moisture gathering in my eyes and suddenly was afraid I would embarrass them by crying. I changed the subject and we chatted on about something else, but I felt like I had been treading on holy soil. Deep within me was a desire to take off my shoes.

'God must be something like that,' I said to Jackie as we left to drive home.

'No, they are something like God,' she corrected.

Whatever the case, I knew I had been in the presence of people who had learned the secret of contentment. They could say with Paul, 'In whatsoever state I am – even if it means I have a retarded son who is forty-three years old who will live with us until he is seventy – therewith to be content. Because I can do all things through Christ which strengtheneth me.'

God doesn't promise us a rose garden. He promises us tribulation. But in the midst of that – perhaps even because of it – we can be of good cheer because he has overcome the world.

This is what 'risky living' is all about. A person can seek the kingdoms of this world or the kingdom of God. If he chooses this world he will go after things: houses, real estate, position, reputation, popularity, sensual gratification – all the things the world calls security. Or he can seek the kingdom of God, risking everything on Jesus' promise to bring us into happiness and maturity.

To move into this realm of maturity calls for a total death to self. It means you are willing to be expendable, to give up all self-rights for the happiness of others. It means you submit yourself to the loving hand of God much as a pawn submits to a chessmaster: 'In whatsover square you choose to place me, there will I be content.' So even if you are surrounded by knights, rooks, and bishops who desire to destroy you, you will raise your hands in praise and say, 'Hallelujah! I'm expendable. I choose to give up my life for the glory of the King.'

Risky living. But in dying we find life.

When I was a boy, people used to talk about the 'poorhouse'. I never knew what the poorhouse was, I had never seen one, nor had I talked with anyone who had seen one. Everybody knew, though, that it was a terrible place on the back side of a lonely hill where a family went when they ran out of money.

As a result of the horrible fear of the poorhouse, I grew up hoarding my money. Every penny I earned was stashed away and we spent money only for bare necessities. I still have some of that tendency left, for we have continued, across the years, to live frugally. However, when we were exposed to some of these kingdom principles – especially the one that states that in order to receive you must give – it presented an acute crisis in my spirit. If I gave, even if I gave away only the tithe which is the basic minimum, I was running the risk of winding up in the poorhouse.

I was encouraged by the story of William Carey, a young English cobbler of the late eighteenth century. Carey believed God wanted him to carry the Gospel to the people of India. The leaders of his church in England ridiculed him. Finally, with stern, theological authority they told him if God wanted the people of India saved, he'd do it sovereignly – without the help of a shoe cobbler. Carey, however, was a man fashioned in the likeness of the Apostles. He left England and sailed to

India to become the first modern day Protestant missionary –
daring to do that which others called impossible. Even after
all these years, Carey's motto still excites men who dare to
step out in faith:

Attempt great things for God;
Expect great things from God.

The Christian takes his direction from a different King.
He is not motivated by money, fear, or public opinion. Nor
does he shrink just because his way is blocked by a mountain.
He is like Thoreau's marcher who, hearing the sound of a
different drummer, 'steps to the music which he hears, however measured or far away'.

The worst of all heresies is to despair of those childhood
ideals, those dreams that stimulated us when our minds were
still young. How many of us have reached the crisis of middle
life and, disillusioned, put aside our resolves of faith because
of the fantasies of fear?

'Too impossible,' we say sadly. 'Too foolish. Too risky.'

No wonder Whittier wrote:

Of all sad words of tongue or pen,
The saddest are these, 'It might have been.'

In our home we are challenging our children to invest
their futures in something that will cost them their lives – for
the glory of God. We are challenging them to go out and,
even at an early age, run the risk of dying for Jesus. Why
settle for the poorhouse when you can go all the way and die
on the cross.

The world does not understand this. The world says
parents should protect their children from pain, hardship,
and death – not point them towards it. But we know there is
no joy anywhere outside that which is done strictly for the
glory of God. Abundant life comes only when we give our

lives totally and completely to that which God has called us to do.

The most exciting and whole people I know are those who leave the comforts and security of home, who turn their backs on well-paying jobs and worldly fame to go to the remote areas of the earth as missionary doctors, pilots, translators, and teachers. Many of them die on foreign soil, unrecognised by men. But the price of death is very small when compared to what they purchase by their risky living. After all, what's the use of living if you don't attempt the impossible.

Risky living puts you in the position where God will eventually take off your mask, peel back all your layers, and lay you bare for the world to see. However, if the process of inner healing has been thorough and complete, those who look into your life from the outside will not see your nakedness, but instead – through your transparency – will see the glory of the One in whose image you have been created.

Where Eagles Soar

JAMIE BUCKINGHAM

KINGSWAY PUBLICATIONS
EASTBOURNE

To my dear friend and first publisher
Dan Malachuk
who not only pushed me
out of the nest but belongs
to that rare fraternity of
those with ice on their
wings who dare ride the
mighty *ruach* of God—
soaring above the storms

Contents

Preface

The engine on my ancient Cessna airplane was purring as I took off from the little grass airstrip near our home in Melbourne, Florida, to fly to Augusta, Georgia. It was a cold, blustery February morning. Other than the noise from the engine and the whistle of the wind past the rattling windows, the cockpit was quiet. My antique radio had stopped working moments after takeoff. That didn't bother me. I never did trust radio navigation anyway, having learned to fly by the seat of my pants in an old Piper cub on a dirt runway. All I needed was a compass and a map to get me to my destination.

But over south Georgia the ceiling began to drop. I was forced to climb out "on top"—over the clouds. It was beautiful up there, and the flying was smooth. But without landmarks—and without any kind of radio navigation to guide me—I was in critical danger of getting lost. Even though my compass was reliable—inerrant, to use an orthodox word—it gave little help and was basically ineffective without visual contact with the ground. I could be blown miles off course and never know it.

Within minutes I had a distinct sensation that the plane was drifting eastward, out over the Atlantic Ocean. In fact, on one occasion I lined up the nose of the plane on a distant cloud and could actually "see" the plane turning toward Spain. Every instinct said to apply the left rudder to keep from drifting out over the water. I yearned for some contact with the ground, even for some friendly voice through the speaker from a radar operator telling me where I was. It was not enough to know which direction I was *pointed*—the direction I was *moving* was the critical factor.

An hour later the clouds began to break. To my horror, I saw water below me. I began an immediate descent, hoping I would not meet someone else coming up through the same hole. Once again I found myself wishing for something more than my compass and basic instruments to give me guidance and direction. The need for "control" beyond my own was vital.

It was not until I broke through the bottom layer of clouds that I discovered the water I had seen was actually the Savannah River. I was off course about 15 miles, but to the left I could see the skyline of my destination and knew that Augusta's Bush Field was nearby.

After I landed and parked the plane on the apron, I was met by an agent from the Federal Aviation Authority who had been in the tower when I came in—sans radio.

"You caused quite a stir up there," he said kindly, "coming in without a radio. We've been watching you on radar for 20 minutes and tried to contact you for landing instructions."

"Sorry," I said. "Mine is broken. Besides, I never have trusted radios. As long as I got that blinking green light from the tower, I figured it was okay to land."

"Things are changing," the inspector said. "It used to be all a pilot needed was a compass and a map. Now aviation has speeded up. Planes are faster and there are a lot more of them in the air. If you're going to fly into a controlled air space—get a good radio."

He paused. "In fact," he said, "I'm not going to let you take off without special permission. Call the tower on the phone when you're ready to leave, and then come out and wait in your plane. They'll signal you with the light when it's clear to taxi."

Then he added, "And don't come back to Bush Field until you have a functioning radio. This is controlled air space."

For a number of years I committed myself to the Bible as my compass in life. The radio of the Holy Spirit was a nuisance. It could not be trusted. Especially inaccurate, I thought, were messages from those who claimed to have various "gifts" of the Spirit. I preferred to fly by the seat of my pants—good old carnal sense— and stick to the Bible as my sole guide in life.

Now comes additional revelation, oddly, from the Bible itself. The Bible is not enough. In fact, it is ineffective and may even lead you astray unless it is interpreted by the Holy Spirit. I am not talking about "extra-Biblical" revelation. I am simply saying that if the Holy Spirit does not bring life to the written Word, the Bible at best is nothing more than beautiful literature. At worst it is bondage—producing legalism. Jesus, as reflected in John's Gospel, and Paul in his letters to the new Christian churches have much to say about this.

The Bible is known as the *logos*—the written word. But there is another word, equally important, known as the *rhema*. This is the "now word" of God to each individual. It is what brings the Bible alive. It is what makes the Bible meaningful to each individual life. It is the word of the Holy Spirit.

To say all a Christian needs is the Bible is an orthodox-evangelical fallacy which has been fostered upon us by generations of people who feared we might be pulled off course if we listened to the voice of the Holy Spirit. The Christian needs to check every voice against the Bible's infallible direction. But to live by the Bible alone means your doctrinal nose could be pointing true north while your entire life is moving out over the ocean. You'll never realize how critical your situation is until you run out of gas and have to ditch at sea—or you're hit from behind by a jet liner full of singing charismatics.

My friend, Bernie May, has a twin-engine Beechcraft that is full of sophisticated radio gear. Several weeks ago he flew down from his home in Waxhaw, North Carolina, and picked up our family to fly us back north for a skiing weekend. We left Melbourne early in the morning in a driving rain and were in rain, fog and severe turbulence all the way to our destination. But flying in bad weather is no problem to Bernie—because of all those navigation aids. He took his direction from the tower, found his course on his compass, climbed to his assigned altitude and set the automatic pilot. From that point on, the radio—and the compass, working together—flew us safely to our destination.

That's what this book is all about. Balance. And the joy—and the risk—of the Spirit-controlled life. It is a book about the necessary venture—often tough, sometimes joyful, always fulfilling—that the believer must take to reach that life beyond his own control. The life in the Spirit.

JAMIE BUCKINGHAM
Melbourne, Florida

Where Eagles Soar

I

The Breath of God

"Watch the eagle," our Israeli guide said, pointing high above the Sinai desert at the silent figure, soaring close to the mountains. "He locks his wings, picks the thermals and rides the breath of God above the storm."

I was on a research trip in the Sinai Peninsula, collecting material for a book on the wilderness experience. For seven days our small group of men had been trekking the desert sand, making our way through the awesome wadis (dried riverbeds) and climbing the rugged stone mountains in the footsteps of Moses. Now we had reached Jebel Musa, the Mountain of Moses. Struggling in the darkness, we had climbed the backside of Mount Sinai to reach the summit by dawn. Now we were on our descent, following the steep path downward toward St. Catherine's Monastery, nestled far below against the base of the huge mountain.

It was then we spotted the eagle.

A huge storm, one of those rare phenomena of the desert, had built up over the Gulf of Suez and was now moving inland. The mighty thunderheads towered around 30,000 feet. It was awesome to behold as it moved to the south of us across the triangular-shaped peninsula toward Saudi Arabia where it would doubtless dissipate.

But it was the eagle which drew the attention of our guide. We were near the summit of the 7,600-foot mountain, and the eagle was already 10,000 feet above us. And climbing.

"That's what the prophet meant when he said God's people would mount up with wings as eagles," the tough, dark-skinned Israeli said as he squatted on the pathway, waiting for the rest of the men to catch up. I squatted down beside him, Bedouin fashion, and together we watched the eagle confront the massive storm clouds.

"How high will he go?" I asked.

"Over the storm. Twenty-five, thirty thousand feet. He is now beyond his own control. He locks his wings, here," he said—pointing at his shoulders—"and rides the wind of God."

Again he used that magnificent Hebrew word *ruach* to describe the thermals of the desert. It was the same word King David used in Psalm 51 to describe the Holy Spirit—the breath of God. "Take not thy *ruach* from me."

In the New Testament the word is softer, more gentle. There we find the Greek word *pneuma*, meaning breath or spirit. It is the same word from which we get "pneumatic." In the New Testament it is often used to describe a filling experience. So the Holy Spirit fills, much as one would blow air into a balloon. The thought is one of lifting—from within. But in the Old Testament, the Spirit of God, the *ruach*, is anything but gentle. Here it is a roaring wind, howling through the canyons and moaning over the mountains. It is the mighty winds of the storms blowing across the wilderness accompanied by flashing lightning and rumbling thunder. It is the hot air thermals rushing upward. And upon it rides the eagle, ascending to unbelievable heights, using the air currents which destroy things on the ground to carry him over the fury of the storm to safety on the other side.

I watched, fascinated, as the eagle circled and ascended until he was but a tiny dot against the onrushing storm. Then he disappeared altogether.

"He fears nothing," the guide said as we rose to greet the other men coming down the steep path. "Even though we no longer see him, he can see us. He can see for 50 miles. He will go so high he will be covered with ice—his head, his wings, everything Then he descends on the backside of the storm and the ice melts. Who knows, if it were not for the ice, he might just keep going up, touch God and never come down."

Our guide grinned, stretched and padded off barefooted down the rocky mountain trail.

It's interesting how I keep thinking of that eagle—and the breath of God upon which he rides. I think of him when storm clouds approach. I think of him when it seems I'm being swept, beyond control, to some dizzy encounter. I think of his determination, in the face of impossible odds, to lock his wings so that nothing can deter him from his upward climb. I think of him, even now, as I start work on this book.

It has been a dozen years since I had that exhilarating experience the Bible describes as the baptism in the Holy Spirit. I wrote about that experience, and the many lessons learned from it, in my earlier book *Risky Living.* For a while I was able to stay spiritually airborne on the enthusiasm alone. "Enthusiasm," by the way, comes from two Greek words, *en theos,* meaning "in God." But if the Christian walk is mere enthusiasm, we become nothing more than spiritual grasshoppers, going up and down but never learning how to soar. I need more than being "in God"; I must have God in me. Once airborne, I need some power to keep me aloft.

It was then I discovered there was more to the Christian life than living on experiences. Being born again is an experience. Being healed is an experience. Being baptized in the Holy Spirit is an experience. But if the experience does not open the door to an ongoing process, then we soon fall to earth again—battered, flattened, and often in worse shape than when we made our upward leap.

Conversion—turning your back on a self-centered way of life and allowing Jesus Christ to take total control—is an experience. But a man needs more than conversion, he needs salvation, which is an ongoing process. Salvation, in its truest sense, is becoming who we really are. And that process is never complete—at least not here on this earth.

Healing is an experience, and I am so grateful that thousands of people are experiencing divine healing in their bodies. I am grateful the healing ministry is once again being recognized by the church as a valid experience. I am grateful that in liturgical and evangelical churches alike, men and women are discovering that one of the purposes of the redemption was not only to save us from sin but to save us from sickness. The same Jesus who healed 2,000 years ago is alive and, through His Holy Spirit, still healing bodies. But while divine healing is an experience, it is not enough. The people of God must move upward to the ongoing process of divine health. And that, like the process of salvation, demands discipline, exercise, determination and the supernatural power of the Holy Spirit.

Thus, when we come to the ministry of the Holy Spirit—as we will in this book—we find the same concepts. The baptism in the Holy Spirit is an experience. For many of us it was an exhilarating, revolutionary experience. It opened our eyes to understand the Bible. It was the instrument which allowed us to call Jesus lord in all areas of our lives. It brought freedom from the bondage of legalism and set in motion the various charismatic gifts which had laid dormant ever since the Holy Spirit first entered at conversion. But while the baptism in the Holy Spirit is an experience, the Spirit-controlled life is an ongoing process. It consists not only of allowing the breath of God *(pneuma)* to fill and expand you to the proper size and shape, but it consists of allowing the wind of God *(ruach)* to bear you aloft—and keep you there. The *ruach* not only controls your path of flight in the face of oncoming storms, but He enables you to soar the exalted corridors of heaven and brush your wings against the face of God.

There are certain things you must do, however, before that is possible. For one, you must recognize who you are. You are an eagle, not a grasshopper. Then you must be willing to cooperate with God, to put yourself in takeoff position for God to fill—and send you soaring. To remain on your nest when the storm blows is disastrous. Your only hope is to launch out in faith against all insurmountable obstacles, lock your wings and let God do the rest

That's the reason I'm writing this book. To take you with me on some of my own flights (and some of my mountain-smashing experiences). I am writing to encourage you to soar like the eagle: be filled with the Holy Spirit and ride the wind of God.

II

Dealing
with the Awful Sins

For two months I had this particular week scheduled on my calendar to lay aside everything else and finish work on this book. Yet it seemed the world was not going to turn me loose. All week long I have been bombarded with intense, exhausting situations—situations which have forced me to relive much of my own dark past. And though I am no longer ashamed to uncover these black pits of my personal history when I see similar traits emerging in the lives of others I deeply love, their vicarious suffering is almost as bad as the actual pain of personal experience.

It has been a week during which the lid has been pulled back on the lives of three other ministers—all friends of mine—to reveal the murky shadows of adulterous relationships. As if by divine design they have come to us at this particular time, writhing and suffering in the same fires I've been through. And I've found myself virtually helpless to do anything but love and pray.

Our stories are not pleasant. I tell them to illustrate our mutual need to get beyond ourselves, beyond our own control and into the searing light of holy exposure where we can at last discover the comfort of knowing our lives are lived completely through the Spirit's guidance.

23

One of my closest friends is the former pastor of a large denominational church. Four months ago he called on the phone. He was being forced to leave his church. For some time he had been involved with another woman in an extra-marital relationship. It had been discovered and his kingdom had fallen around him.

Such disclosure should not shock or dismay Christians, for ministers—even Spirit-baptized ministers—are no less susceptible to the surging drives of sex and passion than anyone else. If anything, they are more susceptible. They are exposed to every kind of emotional and spiritual sickness. Only those who are spiritually empty seek their help. Like medical doctors who are daily exposed to deadly germs of disease, if they are not constantly on guard, constantly inoculated, under constant control of the Holy Spirit, they fall. Satan always seems to aim his biggest guns at the man on the point in spiritual warfare. Thus it should never come as a shock that shepherds are usually the first ones to bleed when the wolf comes after the sheep.

After a great deal of weeping and praying (mostly over the shame of being caught; for true repentance does not come easily, nor rapidly), my friend finally confessed to his wife, to his children and to a few select leaders in the church. There was a genuine attempt on the part of the men to work things out, to keep it quiet and bring healing to their shepherd. But the rumor spread rapidly. In a horrible moment of disclosure, he stood in the pulpit one Sunday morning and confessed to the entire congregation.

The desire to fight, the desire to minister ever again had been squeezed from him by the public recognition of his own imperfection. In shame and confusion, he fled the city. He and his family still smelled of the fires of hell when he arrived at our little city of refuge in Florida.

Healing—no more than repentance—does not come quickly in such situations. What at first may seem to be only a moral slip or an indiscretion is usually nothing less than the emerging tip of an iceberg of spiritual emptiness. The more you examine the thing, the bigger it is. Woe to the man who attempts to minister in such a situation unless he is thoroughly committed to the risk involved, and thoroughly controlled by the Holy Spirit in all his actions. The fool forgives and forgets. The wise man forgives and remembers and stands beside the wounded one with support and direction as the Holy Spirit administers His chastening whip and His purging fire.

Since Jackie and I had opened our lives—and our home—to the healing of wounded warriors, shepherds and sheep alike, there was no way we could back down from this challenge. Fortunately God had provided, in the elders of the Tabernacle Church, a community of love and trust, an atmosphere not based on judgments but on the anticipation of healing. All nine of the elders had emerged, to some degree or another, from similar fires. Jackie and I were with my friend—and his wife—almost daily. On Sundays they sat in the back of the auditorium, hidden in the crowd. Although he had preached for me on several occasions across the years, and many in the congregation knew of his famous work in the other city, we never recognized his presence. Nor did he want me to identify him, so intense was his shame, so deep his sense of failure, so depressed his mood. However, because we recognized him as a man of God, a spiritual leader, albeit a fallen leader, the elders confirmed he should join us in our all-day weekly meetings. Just to sit. And listen. And by being exposed to spiritual health, be encouraged and medicated toward healing.

Some of my friends, hearing he was in Melbourne, called and said, "Don't touch him. He'll drag you down with him." But that is one of the risks a man runs when he reaches out to help. It is the risk a lifeguard has to face when he goes after a drowning man, that he, too, may be pulled beneath the waters—used as a vain stepping stone for another's carnal salvation. Fortunately, I wasn't out there alone. The other ministers in our church were standing with me—counseling, loving, accepting, correcting. It was a perfect example of the Body of Christ reaching out to an injured member, surrounding him with love in an attempt to support and care while the Holy Spirit brought healing.

Any man who commits adultery also lies. Like alcoholism, the two sins always exist side by side. The very nature of any sin which grows in darkness calls for lies to support it. Yet there is no way for a man of God to lie to his Creator, any more than Adam

25

could keep his sin from the Father. Still there remains that eternal desire to hang on to the dregs of sin, to turn loose only as much as you are forced to release—always holding to the vain hope that sometime, somewhere, you can return to the garden where you violated God's command and once again taste of the forbidden fruit. The mere fact that the door is forever closed, that there now stands an angel with a flaming sword prepared to burn the life out of any who attempt to return, is a truth too large to comprehend, too heavy to bear. So healing—and forgiveness—must be administered bit by bit, with love and yet with sternness by men who, themselves, have conceded to the demands of God and have no desire to go in any direction except that directed by the Holy Spirit.

So I struggled with my friend, knowing at times he was lying to me, yet understanding. For to make full disclosure of all the darkness in his heart would expose him to the full light of healing—a light which he was not yet prepared to receive. Thus Jackie and I found ourselves, on the eve of my intention to pull aside and finish the writing of this book, deeply enmeshed in the twisted relationships of a man with his wife, with his mistress (and her husband) and with God. It was exhausting, yet we sensed always that if he could be plucked as a brand from the burning, he would emerge as a giant in the Kingdom—for black sheep always make the most understanding shepherds.

Gradually we began seeing evidence of his restoration. I knew my friend would not only be totally restored by the loving Body of Christ in Melbourne and through the grace of God, but I knew he would eventually take his place in pastoral leadership among our elders (something which has indeed taken place just recently). However, until that happened, I knew we were in for intense, fierce battles as he and his wife fought their way to the surface of their deception where they could breathe the fresh air of truth spoken in love. But even as this was developing, a second minister friend burst on the scene with a similar situation.

It was early one Wednesday morning when he called. I had met him a number of months before when I was speaking at a conference in one of the Gulf states. He had come to me after the service, following a message in which I had alluded to God's forgiveness as experienced in my own life. We sat in the back of the darkened church auditorium while he confided in me. He was in deep trouble. Rebelling against a strained relationship with his wife, he had turned to a woman half his age—a single girl who was the daughter of a prominent family in the city. Now she was pregnant. He had confessed to his wife and resigned his ministerial charge. He knew, if he was ever to serve the Lord again, he would have to do it through reconciliation with his wife—despite this horrible mistake. We sat and talked for a long time. I finally told him to go to another pastor in town, confess to him and seek his guidance. I had returned to Melbourne and forgotten about the whole matter.

Then, Wednesday morning. I had been out of town the day before and had not gotten to bed until long after midnight. I was still asleep when the phone rang at 8 A.M. He was in town. He needed to talk to me.

I agreed to meet him in a private place, and we sat and talked. Although he had been reconciled with his wife, he knew he could no longer remain in the same town with the pregnant girl. The entire community was aware of the situation. The girl had decided to keep her baby; her parents were going to help her raise it. Even though he and his wife had agreed he should pay all the medical expenses for his child, he realized neither of them could stand the stress of remaining in the same community. Their only leading was to move to Melbourne. Would we accept them?

We talked for hours. It was time to speak tough love. If he came, he would have to find a job. He would have to submit to spiritual authority. I suspected this was not just a single experience in his life. Like the others, when we got to know him better, we would find the brown spot on the peeling was the result of a rotten core. He nodded and wept.

But I was asking too much. I watched him, sadly, as he got in his van and left town. I knew he would not be back.

When I returned to the house Jackie was waiting, sitting at the breakfast room table. "Are you ready for another one?" she asked.

"Who now?" I said.

"Bill Patillo*," she replied. "He called from the airport. Someone has gone to pick him up."

I slumped into a chair and said, "You better get ready. There are some things about Bill I haven't told you."

A dynamic preacher with Italian ancestry, Bill had been an evangelist before taking a small church and building it to a large congregation. The first time he and his wife visited us in Florida he was near an emotional collapse. Like the others, he was emotionally involved with several women in the congregation. It was tearing him apart, for he recognized his life style was in diametric opposition to the teachings of the Bible concerning marital fidelity

I had listened, counseled briefly, and then kept my mouth shut. I had seen him on several occasions since, but his situation had been worsening. No one else knew, but he was fearful his secret would eventually leak out. Now it seemed I should at least share this with Jackie before Bill arrived.

The rest of the afternoon was spent in intense counsel with this great preacher whose life was a torturous sham. Like the others, he was determined to either break from the demonic bondage which clutched at his viscera or break from the ministry. Long into the evening we talked, wept and prayed. The next day he spent most of the time with a fellow minister in our church who has a ministry of deliverance. That night we were together again. He was rejoicing over what seemed to be a new freedom but still fearful of what he would face when he returned to his church. When I put Bill on the plane early the next morning, he said, "I may have to resign my church and leave the city." Then he asked, "If I come here and get a job, will you receive me?"

That night Jackie and I lay awake for long hours. I needed to talk. "Why me, Lord?" This intense time with my wounded friends had uncovered areas of spiritual scar tissue in my own life which, although healed, were still capable of being inflamed. "Why bring me these fallen shepherds?"

Jackie let me talk, long into the night, for she knew I was hurting. Not for myself but for my friends. Lying on my back beside her, hands clasped under my head, I stared up into the darkness of

---

* Bill's name has been changed. The facts are true.

28

our bedroom. "Surely there is some way a man can come to whole-ness without having to be exposed to the purging fire of hell."

"All fire is not from hell," Jackie said softly. "Remember our God is a consuming fire. Sometimes it is He who purges His children. Have you forgotten?"

I had not forgotten. I would never forget. I recalled my own fiery pits, when the flames were so hot I thought surely I would be consumed. I wished that on no man, especially such great and talented men of God as I had been with the previous few days. Yet how else could they be separated from that which was slowly strangling them—knowing if they did not release it they would surely die?

"Is there not some other way for the Holy Spirit to take control of a person's life without forcing him through such agony?" I moaned out loud, feeling the tears gathering in my eyes.

"All people are not the same," Jackie said, her voice still sooth-ingly soft. "Some grow up good. Think of Corrie ten Boom. She accepted the Lord at the age of five and never turned from Him—not a day of her life."

"But even she had to go through the horror of a Nazi concentra-tion camp," I countered.

"True," Jackie answered. "But her struggles were external—with forces from the outside. Not with internal forces like you—and your friends who are being drawn to you like magnets—have to face. You have to fight your battles on a different level. Yet the final conclusion is always the same—God brings you to that place in life where you have no choice but to turn loose."

I remembered the passage of scripture I had quoted to one of the men the day before:

See that ye refuse not him that speaketh: for if they escaped not who refused him that spake on earth, much more shall not we escape, if we turn away from him that speaketh from heaven . . . And this word, yet once more, signifieth the removing of those things that are shaken, as of things that are made, that those things which cannot be shaken may remain. Wherefore we receiving a kingdom which cannot be moved, let us have grace, whereby we may serve God acceptably with reverence and godly fear: For our God is a consuming fire (Hebrews 12:25, 27–29).

God, it seems, judges His ministers by a higher standard. That means He chastens those whom He loves and shakes those for whom He has special purpose, until all the loose things are shaken out and only the firm structure remains—a structure upon which the Holy Spirit can hang the flesh of Jesus Christ. It is a special purpose realized only beyond the control of individual design and desire.

"There was a time," Jackie said gently, reaching over and touching my shoulder in the darkness, "when you thought your world had come to an end. Remember?"

This time the tears overflowed. I remembered. Yet that day was the finest day in my life. For it was that day I turned loose. I relinquished control. I look back to that day of relinquishment, that day when in total and utter desperation I said to God, "Take me. I am worthless." It was the day when the Holy Spirit began to move in greatest power. Perhaps there is no other way. Even so, the knowledge that God is always in control, always standing and waiting for us to get beyond our own control so He can direct our footsteps, is all the hope one really needs. If He could set my feet upon a solid rock and give me a new song, then He could do it with my friends also.

The events, the sensations, the feelings of my own pain are forever etched on my mind. How foolish I had been those long years before. Fresh out of seminary. Flushed with the knowledge I was a success in the ministerial profession. Pastor of one of the largest churches in the state. Yet it had all fallen around me. As I thought back, I knew what had taken place was inevitable, for something always moves into a vacuum. There was no one else to blame. I could have blamed my seminary professors for not teaching me about the baptism in the Holy Spirit. But what guarantee is a charismatic experience to galvanize against sin? Was another baptism necessary—a baptism of fire? The gnawing for love which was deep inside of me had been almost cannibalistic—seeking to devour any around me who seemed willing to be consumed. All ministers (indeed, most ministers) do not turn to other women. Some fill the vacuum with their work. They build great cathedrals, they are nominated to important positions, they are recognized by the media or they lose themselves in legitimate ministry to the poor, the underprivileged, to those in foreign lands. They may join a community or submit themselves to some disciple-maker. Yet even these, eventually, have to examine themselves and face the fact they are created empty. No horizontal relationship will ever satisfy that vertical longing. And no experience—not a salvation experience, not even the baptism of the Holy Spirit—will satisfy that hunger. It can come only when one is *filled* with—and controlled by—the Holy Spirit.

And that is not an experience—it is a daily process.

The psychology of why I turned aside will have to be left to another book—and another time. The point I must make here is that because of a prior commitment to God through Jesus Christ, when I did fall I was not utterly cast down.

I trace that commitment and my subsequent spiritual journey back to a time when I was 21 years old. My father and mother, having come into a new and dynamic relationship with God, had insisted their number three son accompany them on a spiritual retreat sponsored by evangelist Jack Wyrtzen at his Word of Life Camp at Schroon Lake, New York. That week, during the summer between my junior and senior years of college, I had made a willful decision to commit my life to Jesus Christ. It was not a dramatic thing. I did not do anything. I did not answer an invitation, walk an aisle or even raise my hand. Rather, alone on a hillside on an island in the lake, I looked up at the stars and said quietly in my spirit, "Jesus Christ, I give you my life. You are my Lord."

At that time several spiritual principles went to work in my life. One of them is covered in some detail in *Risky Living*. When a man commits his life to Jesus Christ as Lord, he voluntarily surrenders the right to choose or the power to vary the consequences of that decision. He is called to move beyond his own control. In other words, from that time on, God can do whatever He wants

31

with that life to bring it to the place it conforms to the image of His Son, Jesus Christ. That is what the Lordship of Jesus Christ is all about. Whatever forces God chooses to bring to bear on that life, external forces like the Nazi concentration camp in Tante Corrie's life or internal forces like the raging sexual and emotional drives confessed by my friends—all are designed and directed by God to bring us to a place of total submission to His Holy Spirit. If that sounds like God allows a person to fall into adultery or allows him to kill someone and wind up in prison so he can hear the Gospel and be saved, then interpret it as you will. Perhaps that is what Augustine called the *felix culpa*—which loosely translated means the "happy sin." I do not have the final answers on whether God causes a thing to happen or allows it to happen. But I do know that once a decision is made to commit a life to Jesus Christ, whether it is in a foxhole, in a jail cell, in a Sunday school department or on the side of a hill on an island in a northern lake—God takes that commitment seriously. If a man drifts, or tries to run away, or even attempts to break the contract—it is indissoluble as far as God is concerned.

The other spiritual principle which I believe went to work in my life back in 1953 is found in that passage on the eternal nature of vows in Deuteronomy 23. Here Moses is giving the children of Israel a new look at the unchanging nature of God.

> When thou shalt vow a vow unto the Lord thy God, thou shalt not slack to pay it: for the Lord thy God will surely require it of thee; and it would be sin in thee . . . That which is gone out of thy lips thou shalt keep and perform . . (Deuteronomy 23:21, 23).

Therefore, even though there was a long period of time—12 years to be exact—between the time I made the vow and the time God required it of me, the spiritual principle was never invalidated. God was just waiting for the right time in my life, waiting until I had run my ego course, waiting as He did with my own parents, until I had to face the fact I could not make it on my own; waiting as He does with alcoholics who all have to come to that point of admitting that life has become "unmanageable" and must be turned over to a higher power, before He chose to step in and require that vow which had gone out of my lips.

As with Moses, who was discovered after having killed the Egyptian and driven into the desert, so I was discovered. I knew it would happen, eventually. There is no way that sin will not eventually come to the surface, especially when it involves a man of God. If Moses could not escape the exposure of his sin, if David could not escape his adulterous relationship with Bathsheba and had to stand exposed before history, why should I expect special favors? That which God seems to tolerate in some, He will not tolerate in those He has thrust into leadership. Thus exposure comes, not for the sake of punishment, but for the sake of salvation. Fortunate is the man who is exposed early in life. Pity the man who is smart enough to hide his sin until the judgment.

Etched forever in my memory are the events that took place the night of exposure. Like Jacob at Peniel, I wrestled—and lost. October 1965. I sat in the beautiful conference room of that large Baptist church in South Carolina, surrounded by a group of 20 deacons, all with stern faces. They had tried over the last few months to convince me to resign. They knew something was wrong but until this dreadful night had found no evidence. As the months of suspicion continued, I hung on. To leave would mean admission of guilt. Worse, it would mean leaving behind a relationship in which I reveled with the same degree of intensity an alcoholic does with his bottle.

Twice before I had stood before the church at the monthly business meeting and gone through a "vote of confidence." Twice I had bluffed my way through. But this time there was concrete evidence. One of the deacons had discovered a note. I had been laid bare. My insides were churning. Desperately I tried to hold the façade of false confidence.

They asked me to leave the meeting and wait outside as they discussed the matter. Instead of at least a pretense at a sedate exit, I bolted. Fled. I stumbled into the darkened sanctuary and knelt at the front, weeping in fear and confusion. Back in the conference room the men were deciding my fate. In the next room

33

was a small office. I called Jackie. "Come get me. I can't take it anymore." I hung up and in a state of near shock, shame and faced with the awfulness of it all, I wandered down a flight of stairs lit dimly by only the quiet redness of an exit light.

She found me, the shepherd of the flock, crouched in a fetal position in a basement hallway, huddled against the landing of the stairs. "It would be better for you, for the children, for this church if I were dead," I sobbed.

She comforted. She soothed. She never asked for details. There was no need. She led me by the hand through the dark hallways of the house of God to our car parked under the lighted window of the conference room. I did not realize it at the time, but those men were God's servants—sent by the Holy Spirit to perform the unpleasant task of shaking a man of God until only the unshakable remained.

That night I walked into the front yard of our beautiful parsonage. Standing under the autumn sky, I looked up into the heavens and screamed: "Take me! Take me now! Quickly!" In a desperate move, I grabbed my shirt and ripped it open at the chest, tearing the buttons and hem as I exposed my bare chest to the heavens, waiting for the inevitable flash of lightning which I knew would come and split me asunder, carrying me into the hell where I belonged.

But there was no flash of lightning, for the purging fire had already begun to burn. And besides, God does not punish sin the way we punish it. As ranchers often burn off a pasture to kill the weeds so the new grass can sprout, so the consuming fire of God burns away the dross without consuming the sinner.

There was more to follow, of course. For one thing, we had to leave. Then there was the fear of going to sleep at night because I could not stand the thought of waking to a new day. Better to sit up sleepless nights than sleep and start a new day without trumpets in the morning. There was the desperate reaching out for friends, only to find they had all deserted. I was like a leper. Unclean. I wrote letters—more than 90 of them—to pastoral and denominational friends. Only one man dared respond and that was with a curt, "I received your letter and shall be praying for you."

Perhaps God was working here too; comfort or encouragement

34

at that agonizing time could have moved me even deeper into a continuing self-deceiving sense of feeling justified.

And anyway, what else could anyone say?

We returned to my home state of Florida, to a small but rapidly growing church—the only opportunity that was open. But as Vance Havner once remarked, it doesn't do any good to change labels on an empty bottle. Nothing inside me had changed. I was still the magnificent manipulator, the master of control, the defender of my position. I was still pushing people around. I was far more politician than a man of God. The Holy Spirit was not controlling my life

Soon echoes from the past began drifting down to Florida—rumors of adultery, of manipulation, of lying. The old undertow of fear sucked at my guts. I was about to be swept back to sea for I had not been honest with the committee which had interviewed me for the Florida position. I could feel the insidious inevitability of confrontation creeping upon me again. I continued to fight, to brave the growing onslaught of fact that kept building the case against me. It took 15 months of a stormy relationship before the Florida church cast me into the waves to calm the sea—just like Jonah

The crisis exploded one Sunday morning when I stepped up to the pulpit to preach On the pulpit stand was a petition asking me to resign. It was signed by 350 people, many of whom were sitting, smiling in the congregation. A group of men had hired a private detective and checked into my past. The detective's report—all 47 pages of badly distorted facts—had been duplicated and handed out to the congregation. The deacons demanded I take a lie detector test. Even though I passed it—declaring I had no intention of perpetrating upon that new church the sins of my past—it was not enough. I had no choice but once again to slink home and huddle with my wife and children while the fire of God continued its purging work.

Often, I have discovered, we cannot hear God when we are busy. Hearing comes only when we have taken—or are forced to take—times of quietness. With Moses it took 40 years of wandering in the burning sands of the Sinai, tending the sheep and goats of

Jethro, his father-in-law and the priest of Midian, on the backside of the desert. It took that long for the fire of God to purge him of all the pride of his Egyptian prestige. Only then was he able to hear. Only then, when everything was quiet, did the angel of the Lord appear in the flame of fire out of the midst of the bush which burned but was not consumed. When a man has many things to do, he often does not have time to turn aside and see great sights. His time is consumed with busyness, his mind with activity. But Moses had time. So when the bush burned on the side of Mt. Horeb, he left his grazing flock and climbed the side of the rocky mountain to investigate. Then it was that God spoke to him and gave him direction.

So it was with me. All activity had ceased. No longer did I have to attend important committee meetings. No longer did I have to supervise budgets, direct visitation programs, promote an attendance campaign or even prepare sermons. All that I had felt was important was taken from me. There was nothing to do but tend the few sheep and goats who had pulled out of the church with me and were huddled together on the hillside grazing. I was beyond my own control. Then my bush burned.

Someone, perhaps my mother, had entered a subscription in my name for *Guideposts* magazine. I seldom read *Guideposts*, but in my idle time, which I now had in great abundance, I picked it up. Someplace in that particular issue I found a half-page announcement of a writers' workshop to be sponsored by the magazine. The stipulations were simple. Submit a first-person manuscript of 1,500 words following the basic *Guideposts'* style. This would be evaluated and judged by an editorial committee who would then pick the best 20 manuscripts. Those selected would receive an all-expense-paid trip to New York and would attend a one-week writers' workshop, conducted by the magazine editors, at the Wainwright House at Rye, New York, on Long Island Sound.

Several years before I had befriended a young man who was preparing to go to South America as a missionary pilot with a group known as the Jungle Aviation and Radio Service, the flying arm of the Wycliffe Bible Translators. I had been intrigued with

36

Tom Smoak's story. As an Air Force pilot, his jet bomber had exploded in midair over Little Rock, Arkansas. He alone had escaped the burning inferno, falling to the ground with a flaming parachute and barely escaping death as his parachute snagged on the tops of two trees in the backyard of a Christian woman. A friend of Tom's had jotted down the facts and sent them to me. Then along came the *Guideposts* offer. Since I had nothing else to do, I wrote the story and sent it in.

My bush burned on October 1, 1967. I was stretched out on the bed in the back room of our little rented house when the phone rang. It was the Western Union telegraph office. Jackie took the call and copied the message on a scrap of paper. It was from Leonard LeSourd, editor of *Guideposts*, stating I was one of the 20 winners—out of more than 2,000 submissions.

I didn't realize it at the time, but my life was about to take a tremendous turn. There were no outward indications. All I knew was for months I had been floating with the tide, buffeted by whatever circumstances God sent along. I had no sensation of direction, no indication this telegram was anything other than another event which had cropped up in the river. I could either dodge it or confront it. I chose confrontation and sent a return wire stating I accepted their offer and would attend the workshop the following month. Only as I look back on that event—now years in the past—do I realize I should have taken off my shoes. I was on holy ground.

The rest is recorded history and has, to some degree, been covered in my book, *Risky Living*. At the workshop John and Elizabeth Sherrill, both editors for *Guideposts* at the time, were approached by Dan Malachuk, a book publisher who was looking for a writer to compose the story of Nicky Cruz. Nicky was a former Puerto Rican gang leader from New York, now a Pentecostal preacher, whose conversion had played a major part in *The Cross and the Switchblade*, the book John and Elizabeth had written with David Wilkerson. The Sherrills were not interested in the project but recommended me. Before the week was out I had signed an agreement with the publisher and was on my way back to Egypt with a new sense of direction. I was going to become a writer.

Four months later I had an encounter with the Holy Spirit whom,

37

up until that time, I only recognized as a boring phrase in the Doxology. Almost everything about me was revolutionized—instantly. All that has happened since is material for other volumes. The important point I want to make is, I had nothing to do with it. Everything within me had been striving against God. Like Jacob at Peniel, I had been vainly wrestling with the angel of the Lord, trying to have my own way, yet at the same time unwilling to turn loose until he blessed me. Now the blessing had come. And with it, a limp. Yet even the limp—and the scars—are badges of His glory.

Perfection still eludes me. I am still vulnerable. But most important, I am no longer satisfied with my imperfection. Nor, thank God, am I intimidated by it. I have reached the point of recognizing that God uses imperfect, immoral, dishonest people. In fact, that's all there are these days. All the holy men seem to have gone off and died. There's no one left but us sinners to carry on the ministry.

If I had my way I would never again do anything wrong. Yet, like Paul:

> For I know that in me (that is, in my flesh,) dwelleth no good thing: for to will is present with me; but how to perform that which is good I find not (Romans 7:18).

Dissatisfied with imperfection, I am now determined to move toward that goal of "conforming to Christ"—knowing at the same time it will never come because of my obedience—but out of my submission to the Holy Spirit. It is that obedience that leads to the fine art of living beyond control—beyond self-will and into the comfort of the Spirit's control.

If I can convey this message to the three friends I mentioned earlier or to anyone else who feels there is no hope, then this book will not be in vain. Yet, at the same time, as I look back over my own life, I wonder if any truth becomes valid or personal until it is burned into our souls by the branding iron of God. I admit I do not know.

Malachi draws the picture of God sitting in front of the melting crucible under which burns the refiner's fire. The fire has been stoked to white heat. In the crucible is silver ore, representing, Malachi says, the "sons of Levi"—those chosen for special service in the Kingdom. The fire is burning, purging the dross until only the pure metal is left. Only when the refiner peers into the crucible and sees the reflection of his own face is the heat turned down and the pure metal poured into the forms which bless the world.

My old friend Seabury Oliver says the only way man—any man— ever comes to know God intimately is through trouble. Perhaps he's right. On the other hand, when I realize that most of my problems, perhaps all my problems, have been self-inflicted, I wonder if all this fire has been necessary. I suspect not. I look at others around me, those who have served God without the rebellious spirit which seems to be so much a part of my makeup, and see they seem to have passed through the fire at very low temperature and intensity. Without much pain or suffering they have come to a beautiful, simple, yet valid understanding of the deep truths of God. Others of us must pass through the very Valley of the Shadow of Death before we can say with a certainty, "My head is anointed. My cup runneth over."

Yet it is in these places, where the awful sins of life threaten to consume us, that we learn God can be trusted. Locking our wings in faith, we soar on the thermal of His Holy Spirit, out of control, yet in His will.

III

Finding Your Place

When I was five years old, my father built what I felt was the most wonderful house in all the world. It had 16 huge rooms and was located on 48 acres of rural Florida woodlands and pasture, with a big citrus grove behind it and a free-flowing, sulfur-water well nearby.

The house was all redwood—inside and out. The floors were knotty pine and the huge staircase was birdseye cypress. Everything else was stained redwood, walls and ceilings. To me it was the most beautiful house in the world—and the most liveable.

A huge attic covered the entire house. There were places to hide under the stairwell and behind the furnace. There were secret closets, dark clothes chutes and woodbins in the kitchen and next to the fireplace in the library.

Nearly all my childhood memories relate to that big house and the property surrounding it. It was my place.

Daddy and Mother had five children, and Daddy said if he had to give them baths he wasn't going to break his neck. So he built a raised, six-foot-long bathtub in one of the upstairs bathrooms. It was three feet off the floor with a set of steps on one end and storage drawers underneath.

It was a marvelous house. It was my fortress, my home, my

security. Behind the house were barns for the cows and ponies we raised, a huge haybarn where the tractors which worked in the grove were kept and lots of little sheds and other ideal places to play and hide. During World War II, when milk and butter were rationed, we had plenty for ourselves and our neighbors. Our chickens gave us eggs, our ponies provided pleasure and occasional money through a sale and the orange and grapefruit groves always produced a good crop.

Through my school years, into college and seminary, I knew I could retreat to the big house if I felt the need. It was warm and filled with life and memories. My mother and dad were always there to protect me. Even if they were not there, the house itself seemed to have a protective personality. I could go up the stairs to my old bedroom, sit on the floor with my arms on the windowsill, look out over the pasture and feel like I was home. The house was everything four boys and a baby sister could ever want.

But when the last of the five children moved away, my parents decided it was time to be practical. Daddy had surrendered his life to the Lord at the age of 60. That meant all he had belonged to God—including the big house and the 48 acres. When there was no more practical reason to maintain the redwood home, he gave it—including most of the 48 acres—to the Florida Baptist Convention to be the home for the Baptist Retirement Center. Mother and Daddy then built a much smaller house nearby and released the big house to be used as the headquarters and home for the administrator. A number of smaller cottages, motel type units and a nursing home were later built in the old pasture and among the citrus trees.

I was in graduate school in Texas when the letter came that the house was gone. Even though I approved of what he had done, there was still a great sense of loss, of sadness. I felt as if my roots had been clipped. For the first time in my life there was no place to go back to. It was a true grief experience as I mourned the passing of the old house.

A number of years later, after our own children were well on their way to adulthood, Jackie and I had a unique experience over a Christmas holiday. We were back in Vero Beach to spend Christmas with our parents.

"How would you like to sleep over in the big house?" Daddy asked, with a twinkle in his eye.

"Do you mean it?"

"They have changed administrators at the retirement center," he explained. "The new director hasn't arrived. The big house is empty if you'd like to stay there for a couple of nights."

It was quite an experience being back in the big house. It was bare except for a few mattresses on the floor. Though most of the furniture was gone, it was still the same house. The electricity had been shut off but there was no need for lights—at least not for me. I had, as a child, memorized every inch of the house. I knew which way the doors opened. I remembered that the third step above the landing on the stairway creaked when you stepped on it. (I had discovered, back in high school when I came in late at night, I should step over that step or run the risk of waking my parents who slept in the bedroom at the top of the stairs.) I knew a certain broom closet would smell of Old English furniture polish where I had spilt an entire bottle when I was a boy. That evening I took the children by the hand and led them from room to room, explaining all that had happened there in years gone by. We looked at the marks on the bathroom closet door where Daddy had measured each of us on New Year's Day to check our growth. We climbed the ladder to the attic and peered down the clothes chute.

Yet it wasn't the same. Nostalgic, certainly. But when I went to bed that night I realized something was different. I didn't belong there anymore. My roots no longer extended backwards into the redwood house. They went in some other direction. It was like looking on the body of a loved one. It looked like it used to. It felt like it used to. But it was dead. My mother and dad, my brothers and sister—they were what made that home alive.

That night I lay awake in the darkness, listening, waiting to hear the whispered voices of my mother and dad in the next room, wondering if I would hear my older brothers laughing down the hall, listening for the gentle breathing of my younger brother in the other bed. But they were gone. My parents lived in another house. My brothers and sister had married and lived in other states. I listened for the sound of the sulfur-water well in the yard, but

43

it had long been capped. I listened for the gentle tick-tocking of the old grandfather clock which had hung on the stairway landing, but it had long since been removed to my parents' new house. Maybe I would hear the shower running or smell the orange blossoms. But the water was shut off and the orange trees had long been bulldozed up to make way for the retirement cottages. The house was still there, but the life was gone.

I realized, though, as I realize even more now, that with the passing of that old house something good had happened in my life. For the first time I was able to have a clear look backward. The house had been a barrier in my life. It had been a place of security, a place where I could run when I was afraid. I always knew, even after I married, that if anything ever happened I could retreat to the big house in Vero Beach. There was always a place where I was welcome. A place where I could belong.

The removal of the house gave me a new perspective into the past. For the first time I was able to look backward beyond my parents, all the way to my true dwelling place—the dwelling place of God.

The same thing happened to me several years later when my father died. He was 87 years old and in declining health, yet his mind and spirit remained clear and lucid. When my mother called, that Sunday after church, and said, "Daddy B has just gone to be with the Lord," Jackie and I were there within the hour—driving down to Vero Beach from our home in Melbourne. We drove past the big house but didn't give it a second look, going directly to the smaller house where my folks had lived the last 20 years of their lives together. We went back into the bedroom where Daddy's body was still warm on the bed. But it wasn't his habitation anymore. The life was gone, missing from the body. I realized that afternoon that somehow another door had been opened to me, a door which would enable me to understand spiritual things even deeper. I would no longer depend on him for guidance. Now I would go beyond him to my heavenly Father.

"I do not wish him back," I said to Jackie, fighting back the tears. "But why do I miss him so?"

"You miss him because you have always gone to him for advice and direction," she said. "But like the big house, he is gone now. And you will be a better man because of it."

She was right. He had become my resting place. My security. If there was something I was getting ready to enter, some kind of business proposition, I'd turn to my dad. I would drive down to Vero Beach, sit beside his bed, make the presentation, and then wait. "Well, what do you think about this?" If I had some kind of spiritual revelation, I'd bounce it off of him. When I finished a new book, I always sent him the very first copy. I would wait a few days and then drive down to Vero Beach, sit beside his bed and wait for a response—like a little boy coming home from school with a picture drawn with crayons waiting for his dad's approval.

But because the big house was there in my past, because my dad was in my past, I never could get all the way back to where I belonged. Enjoying the pools along the way, I never would go all the way to the spring—the source.

Bit by bit these things need to be taken away until we become like Jesus with no place to lay our heads. Foxes have holes, birds have nests, but the true man of God has no place to lay his head but on the bosom of the Father. Places—geographical places—are necessary for service. But not for security.

It was good to go to my dad while he was here on earth, to seek his wisdom. Shortly before he died I drove down to his home in Vero Beach and went back into the bedroom where he was resting. His body, at that time, was almost gone. His old friend, P. J. McGriff, the black man who had long worked as one of his picking crew foremen in the groves, had returned in the latter years to give himself to my daddy during the final years of his life—picking him up off the bed and moving him to the wheelchair, then back to the bed, using arms and shoulders made strong by years of picking up heavy boxes of fruit in the orange groves. P. J. had put Daddy on the bed to rest a while, and I sat down beside him to talk.

I had a scheme which seemed foolproof. It involved making a lot of money—most of which I wanted to return to the Lord. Daddy lay on the bed, his eyes closed, listening as I rattled on, explaining my scheme in great detail. He could tell I was excited.

It seemed to be the answer to the prayer I had been praying for years. But when I had finished and asked him, "Well, what do you think?" he cleared his throat, asked for a tissue to wipe his lips, and spoke. He began by asking questions. Pointed questions.

"Has God specifically told you to do this?"

I stammered.

"Has God told you to stop doing other things which have been extremely productive, in order to spend your time with this?"

I could feel my eyes dilating as he struck at the heart of the matter.

Finally he closed his eyes again and said softly, "Son, never move away from the proven things of God for that which is mere speculation."

I left Vero Beach and drove back to Melbourne a shaken man. My dream castles had been shattered by his keen and incisive questions. But I knew he was right. I knew had I followed through on my scheme, I would have become a businessman, a financier, and would have never had time to write another book—much less carry on my ministry.

I was grateful for my dad's wise counsel, but I also knew—deep in my heart—that God was eager for me to reach the place where I did not have to turn to my earthly father but could turn directly to Him. He was bringing me to the place where I could walk directly into the courts of the Living God and say, "Father, what do You think of this?" and then receive His correction when He said, "Son, I have better things for you. This is the way. Walk ye in it."

As meaningful as my dad and mom are to me, more meaningful are the tabernacles of God. Now I have no old homestead. I have my own home instead. Now I have no father; I am a father instead. All the things which were so precious to me are being taken away so I can find my true place in life, my true security, which always lies in a house not made with hands.

Recently I was in Denver, Colorado, for a business convention. While I was there my old friend Harold Bruce, in town for the same convention, asked me to have breakfast with him. I had known Harold for a number of years, and I was impressed with his Christian commitment as a wealthy businessman from Tucson, Arizona.

Early Tuesday morning I met Harold outside the Brown Palace Hotel promptly at 7:30 A.M. We each had a 9 A.M. engagement in separate places, so I didn't want to be late.

Harold greeted me warmly and we went into the rather plush restaurant. The coffee shop was filled, but we found a table—although the dirty dishes had not yet been cleared. This didn't bother me, since I was happy to see Harold and eager to talk over some exciting business items. Harold, however, was agitated that the table was dirty. I noticed him gingerly pushing away the plate in front of him as though he were afraid the remnants of another person's breakfast still on the plate—the yellow residue of what had once been a fried egg and half a piece of toast—might somehow contaminate him. While I was chatting he kept looking around for the busboy, rapping his fingers on the table. Impatiently.

I didn't pay much attention to his agitation since I was engrossed in our conversation. Occasionally he would seem to forget the dirty dishes in front of him and relax. Shortly however he would glance at his watch, scowl at the table, then look anxiously around the room. Where was that waitress?

"Relax, Harold," I joshed. "They seem to be shorthanded this morning and with the convention in town . . ."

He smiled at me nervously, looked back at his watch, and said, "I guess it doesn't matter if we don't get breakfast, does it?"

"It won't bother me," I said. "The only reason I was going to eat anyway was to be with you. I'm satisfied just to sit here and talk."

But Harold was not satisfied. He kept drumming on the table with his fingertips and glancing around the room. Finally he interrupted me in the middle of a sentence. "There's no sense in waiting around like this. I'm going to find a waitress." And he was gone.

He had no sooner disappeared than a waitress appeared—with the busboy. While he cleared the table and replaced the tablecloth, she apologized. They had a capacity crowd and two of the waitresses were sick. She was handling the entire dining room by herself.

I ordered, looked around for Harold, and apologized back to her.

"I don't know where my friend is," I said.

"Oh, I know where he is," she said, nodding toward the cash register. "He's over there complaining." Moments later Harold returned. The waitress reappeared, took his order and left. After she had gone I told him what she had said.

"Do you know what the waitress said about you while you were gone?"

He blanched and just looked at me.

I continued. "I apologized because you were gone and said I didn't know where you were. She said she knew where you were. You were over there complaining."

Very slowly he pulled off his glasses and looked at me. Then tears came to his eyes. "I don't know why I can't hold still. I don't know why I'm so restless. I feel insecure—as if I can't settle down in *my* place and feel comfortable—secure." The rest of the morning was spent discussing real security—that which one can find only in Christ.

The Swiss psychiatrist, Paul Tournier, said: "Every man needs a place to be." A place where we're secure. A place where we belong. A place that is comfortable to us. Every person needs a place of some kind.

In Psalm 84, David captures the heart cry of all men when he writes:

How amiable are thy tabernacles, O Lord of hosts! My soul longeth, yea, even fainteth, for the courts of the Lord: my heart and my flesh crieth out for the Living God.

The New English Bible translates it like this:

How dear is thy dwelling place, thou Lord of Hosts! I pine, I faint with longing for the courts of the Lord's temple.

My favorite translation is in The Amplified Bible:

My soul yearns, yes, even pines and is homesick for the courts of the Lord; my heart and my flesh cry out and sing for joy to the living God.

48

After Adam's sin, man became a wanderer, a gypsy, a pilgrim. His place in perfect fellowship with God was shattered. His home in the garden denied. A great angel was put at the door to deny him entrance. Ever since then man has been a wanderer—striving to discover who he is and where he belongs.

No baby is born peaceful. Babies are born grasping, looking for a place. We grow up restless. We can't stay still. We have to jump up and find the waitress. It is the spirit of the wanderlust.

Not being able to find our place in God, we try to localize Him. We build buildings and call them "houses of God." Unable to have a personal relationship, we insist on formalized prayer, bowing our heads, closing our eyes, going into the chapel, dropping on our knees—trying to nail God down for a few minutes so we can have a temporary place.

The Episcopal priest, Malcolm Boyd, worked his way through the rigid requirements of the church to ordination. Then, unfulfilled, he became involved in social activism. Later he dropped out of any kind of Christ-centered ministry and finally wrote a lurid book describing his homosexual way of life. Always looking. Never finding. But anger is not the right emotion to express toward the Malcolm Boyds. It should be pity. For there is something of them in every one of us. It's what I was looking for in those early years of my ministry. It's what my three friends in the last chapter were looking for. It is the story of Everyman—always looking for his place.

Jesus, in a magnificent briefing with His disciples, told them He had a job for them. "I send you out as sheep in the midst of wolves," He said in Matthew 10:16. But as we read on, we find Jesus gave them absolutely no instructions on how to contact Him in case of an emergency. What discipler would send his disciples out without giving them the hot-line number back to the church? But Jesus had a purpose in this. He was training them for the time which was to come when He would be gone and they would have to depend entirely on an invisible Spirit to lead them. Now He was there in the flesh. But the time was soon to come when He would no longer be among them. No longer visible. He wanted each man to have an independent relationship with God Himself.

That was the whole purpose of Jesus' ministry among men—to bring men to a place of independent relationship with God. He did not want them related to an earthly disciple-maker the rest of their lives. He knew His followers would have to function everywhere. Alone in courtrooms. In jails. In the quiet of their homes. In the jungles, when nobody else was within a hundred miles. They needed to learn to stand alone, if necessary, simply having fellowship with the invisible Spirit.

When you go out with Jesus, you burn all the bridges, you relinquish the past, you willingly venture toward a new place. Only then can the Holy Spirit have complete control.

The Bible pictures life as a pilgrimage. We are here for a season, then we move on. All incidents on earth are but training sessions for that which comes later. If we stop at any given place—at a house, at a relationship, even at an experience (no matter how wonderful it is), then we miss what God has for us down the line.

Let our hearts be homesick for the courts of God—not for what lies in the past. If there is to be nostalgia, let it be for what is yet to come, not for what was.

The night before He died, Jesus called His disciples together in an upper room and said, "In my Father's house are many mansions: if it were not so, I would have told you. I go to prepare a place for you. And if I go and prepare a place for you, I will come again, and receive you unto myself; that where I am, there ye may be also" (John 14:2, 3).

Notice. Jesus is not the place. He is the One who prepares the place. Neither is Jesus our refuge. In Psalm 46 David says, "The eternal God is our refuge." Who then is Jesus? Jesus is the Son of the eternal God. Jesus is not the place. Jesus is the way. No man comes to the place but by Him. What then is the place? The place is the courts of the Lord. "My soul yearns, yes, even pines and is homesick for the courts of the Lord; my heart and my flesh cry out and sing for joy to the living God."

We seldom talk about the Father anymore. We do a lot of talking about Jesus—and in some circles even more talking about the Holy Spirit. That is wonderful. But the purpose of Jesus' mission on earth was to reconcile men to the Father—to make the rough places plain, the crooked places straight—so we could enter into the courts of the Father with Him. When the child of God understands that he is as welcome in the presence of the Father as the incarnate Son of God is welcome, then he has an entirely new concept of who he is. It is magnificent. Much more magnificent than most of us can grasp. The eternal God is my refuge, my dwelling place, my place of security—where soaring is a venture in safety.

God allows His children certain crutches to lean upon—spiritual training wheels, so to speak. We find them all the way through history, for God knows we are a weak people. The Ark of the Covenant was a crutch. The Temple in Jerusalem was a crutch. But God was constantly weaning His people away from the crutches to teach them to stand alone in their place. God is not contained in buildings. He is spirit. He is your place.

I was with a Roman Catholic priest in Bangkok last year. He was working in the most miserable situation I had ever seen, in the slums of Bangkok. He lived in a slaughterhouse, sleeping in a tiny corner and spending his time with the people. The smell was abominable. The conditions too ghastly to describe. He took me around, showing me where he worked, introducing me to his Thai friends.

I finally stopped him. "Father, where are you from?"

He looked at me in amazement. "I'm from Bangkok."

"No," I said, "I mean, where is your home?"

"Oh," he said, "Bangkok is my home."

I finally had to pin him down with good plain American lingo. "I mean, where were you born?"

"Oh, now I understand," he said with a grin. "I was born in Portland, Oregon. I went to college in Oregon and seminary in Chicago. But I'm from Bangkok. This is my place."

No wonder he could sleep in that stinking slaughterhouse. He had found his place—not in Bangkok, but in God.

It's difficult to understand that—for God is invisible and we are looking for something tangible. A roof over our heads, someone to hold our hand, a lap to sit on. That's the reason we want to return to the old homestead, or visit the cemetery and place flowers every Saturday morning on our mother's grave, or carry the torch for some old flame vowing we'll never marry. That's the reason many widows refuse to consider a second marriage; their dead husbands remain their "place"—rather than the living God. But the call of God is to move upward: beyond mother and daddy, beyond that aunt or uncle who was so meaningful to us, beyond that gray-haired grandmother who let us sit on her lap or snuggle into bed beside her, beyond that old house where we were raised as a child, beyond the childhood romance and all the misspent dreams of how it could have been, beyond all that to the tabernacles of God. In the abiding place of God there is satisfaction for every need. "My soul is homesick for the courts of the Lord."

Heaven is not precious to me because my dad is there. That is a precious hope, but that is not the thing that draws me to Heaven. The great drawing toward Heaven is because it is the final court of God, the ultimate in entering into His tabernacle. It is the abiding place of Him who has loved me, sustained me, carried me through, given me dreams and hopes, filled my life with happy memories, led me through the rough places and given me light in the darkness. That's who I long for.

The writer of Hebrews says we are strangers in exile. We are wanderers, travelers. We are like Abraham who was called of God to leave his "place" in Ur and go out, not knowing where he was going. He became a wanderer. Why? Because God wanted a man whose place was in a relationship—not in a location. We are all cast in the design of Abraham, modern day Hebrews, nomads living in temporary lodgings. Earth is not our home; we are just passing through.

In Hebrews, Paul had already warned that little community of Christians that they faced two dangers. He said the first danger was drifting away from the faith. The second danger was failing to mature in the faith. Then he warned them of the greatest peril of all—losing your sense of direction in the faith. He constantly had to remind his readers they were citizens of two worlds. They were not bound by traditions nor obligated to those who had gone on before: they were moving on toward a tabernacle whose builder and maker is God. Again we are being asked to move beyond our own control—to venture into a Spirit-controlled relationship with God.

The quest of man for his place—and his penchant for localizing it with something concrete—is perhaps the biggest spiritual problem mankind faces.

In *Fiddler on the Roof*, Tevye says that the thing which is most important in life is "Tradition!" That's the reason, he says, the Jews have been able to live through all their persecutions and keep their identity. Yet, as necessary as tradition is, it is also the thing which keeps us from moving on. For man is constantly in danger of stopping to dig a well, build an altar, and settle into some kind of overnight tradition—much like those groups who brashly announce "first annual meetings."

Men in business and industry vie for place. Security for many comes by having a "V.P." after their name, their name on a parking sign in the executive lot, or their own washroom connecting to their office. All these are more than status symbols—they are symbols of having "arrived"—of having a place.

So we put crosses on our lapels, or dove tags on our cars, to signify our arrival at "place."

(I have a friend who had a dove tatooed on his chest. He says, "When they take me into the funeral home, they will know I'm charismatic.")

There is nothing wrong with dove tags, lapel crosses or having our name on the sign—as long as it does not become traditionalized and become our "place" of security. The first thing King Hezekiah did when he took office in the nation of Israel was to destroy the bronze serpent which had been passed down from generation to generation. It was the same bronze serpent Moses had lifted up in the wilderness to protect the people from the snakes. It had been preserved as part of the tradition, passed down through the generations as a good luck charm. But by the time Hezekiah took office the people were actually worshiping it. It had become their place. So he had it destroyed, for he wanted the people to find their place in God.

It is all part of mankind's problem in trying to localize God.

For almost nine years I was the pastor of a very traditional Baptist church in South Carolina. When I took over as senior minister, however, following a building program, the finance committee was deeply worried about paying for the new pews. They were beautiful pews—28 rows of them—mahogany colored with white ends. We had long pews in the middle—20-seaters—and short pews on the sides—five-seaters. But they weren't paid for and the bill was past due.

At an emergency meeting of the finance committee, someone had a good idea. "Let's put bronze plaques on the ends of the pews," one of the men suggested. "We can put the people's names on them. We'll sell the pews—$250 for the long ones and $150 for the short ones."

The church had tried for a year to raise the money unsuccessfully. But when they agreed to put the names of people on them, they raised the money in four days. And there were another 30 families who offered to give money, but it was too late.

God allows us crutches. Putting bronze plaques on pews is a crutch. It takes time to recognize we serve a God who is capable of healing cripples.

Once the pews in our church were paid for, we noticed a strange thing beginning to take place. The people who had their names on the pews began to sit in them—as though they actually belonged to them. No one said anything about it, but several of us noticed it. However, since all the rest of us in the church—including my-self—were busy establishing our own place, we did nothing more than notice.

As for me, I found my place in more subtle ways. On Sunday mornings the church staff entered the sanctuary in ascending order of importance. First came the organist and pianist who took their seats at the instruments. Then the choir filed in from two special doors in the back of the choir loft and stood before the congregation. Then from the right, front corner arrived the ministerial procession. First came the educational director, next the minister of music, followed by the associate pastor and then me. All of us had our place.

One Sunday morning we went through our little ritual (it was something like firing the cannon at dawn), and I arrived on the platform and stood, as usual, looking out over the congregation. The auditorium was comfortably filled (which, according to Charles Allen, means everyone had room to lie down). But when I glanced to my left, I noticed something strange.

The regular seating place for the professor, his wife, and the three old maid sisters was four rows back in one of the five-seater pews—the one with the professor's name on it, of course. The professor was actually a retired sixth grade school teacher, but like many in the congregation, he was still vying for place. It was natural for him to cling to the title of professor.

That morning, however, not only were the professor and his wife and the three old maid sisters in the pew, but there were two other people squeezed in beside them. And I mean *squeezed*. The five-seater pews were meant for five people—and that's all. Adding two more was next to impossible. But there they were, all crammed in there like vienna sausages in a can. And the odd thing was, there were a number of other seats close by.

When they stood to sing, they all had to stand up at the same time. To sit down meant they had to go down in unison—as if they were welded together.

It wasn't until after the service that one of the ushers told me what had happened. "You won't believe this," he said laughing. "But those two strangers came in early. They didn't know that pew 'belonged' to the professor, and they sat down there. When the professor and his group arrived, instead of splitting up or moving to another pew, they crammed in there with them."

At the time I thought it was ridiculous. Now I understand. The human drive for man to find his place is one of the strongest of all forces.

"I've got my friend. That makes me secure."

"General Motors is my place. That is where I belong."

"I've joined the labor union. The Teamsters will take care of me from now on. They are my place."

It's built into all of us. Little girls want to play house. Little boys have their secret clubs. College students have their sororities and fraternities to which they pledge themselves for ever and ever.

The secret handclasp, the password, the fraternal ring: they all signify that we belong.

When I was checking out of the hotel in Denver, the fighting men of the 94th Infantry were checking in. These were the men who had fought under General Patton in World War II. There they were. Fat men crammed into their old Eisenhower jackets complete with shoulder patches, wearing their 30-year-old army hats. That was their place—the memory of the past. Once a year they would get together, calling each other "Sarge" and "Captain" and get so drunk they couldn't remember anything. The 94th Infantry was their place.

With others it's the Volunteer Fire Department, the Masons, the Rotary, the Lions, the Kiwanis or even the church.

"What do you mean, I can't play the piano anymore? That's my place."

"But we've got a much better pianist now, and you hit all the wrong notes. Besides, you get mad and slam the lid down during the sermon if the preacher says something you don't like."

"I don't care. My daddy gave that piano to the church, and I have always played it. That's where I belong, and I'll stay there until hell freezes over."

Maturity is the ability to move from the downstairs concepts of things we can touch, smell and taste—to the upstairs concepts of things spiritual.

I recently read an article on "executive mobility." That's a system top corporation executives use to produce people as singlemindedly devoted to their corporation as they are. The idea is to move the junior executives around so often that the only things left in their lives are money, work and power. If you keep separating a man from his friends, his community, even his family, after a while he will begin to believe the only stable thing in life is his job— and he'll throw himself into his work with total abandon for the sake of rising to the top where he won't have to move anymore. The trouble with that is, he'll either die at an early age—burned out for Amalgamated Fertilizer Corporation—or in his effort to get ahead quickly, he'll make a horrible mistake and be fired.

It happens all the time.

Rare is the business executive who is able to determine his place apart from his next job offer. For that reason, people in America are constantly on the go—moving from city to city, transferred by their job or seeking a new job. A few of these carry their "place" with them. Most of them are still searching.

Recently I visited in the home of an old man who had been in the nursery and greenhouse business all his life. "I'm an author, too," he said seriously.

"Oh, I didn't know."

"Oh, yes," he said, pointing to a yellowed clipping which was framed behind glass and hanging near the fireplace next to an award for growing the finest nasturtiums for the county fair. I walked over to the frame. It was a letter to the editor giving an opinion on why people should not vote for Franklin D. Roosevelt for a third term for president. His name was printed at the bottom.

It was his place.

We see it in church—this desire to belong. "If I can only be elected president of my Sunday school class." "At last, I've been elected as a deacon." Or, "Hey, everybody! I'm the person who washes the communion glasses."

It's not wrong to feel this way. The problems come when that place is not provided, or worse, when it is taken away from us.

How do we find our place?

First, we find it by confessing we are lost and looking. Salvation is a process which starts at an experience and continues for the rest of our earthly lives. There is a sense in which things are settled, finished, at salvation. This is true of our eternal security, for instance. But when it comes to finding our place on earth—to moving into maturity—then salvation is a process which continues until death. It is a never-ending process—this process of being saved.

Second, we find our place by recognizing the basic difference between a citizen and a tourist. A citizen has a sense of permanency, a sense of belonging. If you are a citizen, you buy a home. You settle down. You register and vote. You may even run for public office. You buy a cemetery lot. You put your name on the end of a pew. That is your home.

But citizens of the Kingdom are a different lot. This earth is not their home. They are just passing through. They are pilgrims. They keep their eternal passport in their pockets at all times.

That is the reason God warns His people about being unequally yoked with unbelievers, about being in debt to no man, about staying clear of the world systems which would put us in bondage. God doesn't want us with roots so deep in the earth that when the trumpet sounds, we can't go.

When we moved into the country, my 18-year-old son Tim insisted we buy a pickup truck. "Dad, we can't live out here in the country unless we have a pickup." We started shopping for trucks. Of course the kind Tim wanted had great big oversized tires, roll bars, lights on the top and four-wheel drive.

The kind I wanted was a used truck of any nature which would get at least 30 miles to the gallon.

As a result, we did a lot of shopping. Finally Tim said, "Dad, there's a place over in Orlando where they sell trucks that have been used by rental car agencies. I understand you can get a real good buy on one of those. Let's go look."

I vetoed the suggestion. I didn't want to buy something which had been rented by someone else.

"Why?" Tim asked.

"Have you ever watched a person drive a rental car?" I asked. "You ought to see them pull out of the airport parking lots, tires squealing, gears clashing. You never treat your own car that way. But for some reason, folks seem to think when they rent a machine they can treat it any way they please."

We finally compromised for a used truck which had belonged to a local fireman. It has oversized tires, roll bar, lights on the top, CB radio, four-wheel drive and gets eight miles to the gallon. Even so, that's better than buying an ex-rental.

When you are a pilgrim—when you are just passing through— you put a much lower value on material possessions. Things are to be used for God's glory, but not hoarded. We are to possess them, not let them possess us. Material possessions are not wrong— but they must not occupy the premium place in our lives. Possessions are to be used for God's glory, not misused for selfish reasons.

Third, one never finds his place until he enters the Kingdom with utter abandonment, slamming the door forever on materialistic and selfish goals as a way of life.

Several years ago, driving through Norfolk, Virginia (in a rented car, of course), I pulled up at a stop light beside a big yellow school bus filled with nuns. Glancing out my window, I saw written on the side of the bus, "Sisters of Divine Providence."

I thought, *That's great. A whole bus load of people living on faith—divine providence.*

Then the bus pulled out in front of me, and on the back door I saw, in much smaller letters, "Emergency Exit."

People of divine providence have no emergency exits. Trusting God means sealing up all the other ways out. It's like those teenager friends of Daniel who said to Nebuchadnezzar, "O King, we will not serve thy gods, for our God is able to deliver us from the fiery furnace. But even if He doesn't intervene, we'll still not disobey Him."

To them, trusting God meant sealing off all emergency exits. And so it does with today's pilgrims. It means welding all the doors shut. It means burning all the bridges so we cannot go back. It means turning your back on everything but the tabernacles of God.

Recently I had a bedtime conference with my 18-year-old son, Tim. He's a very special fellow, as is each of our five children. I was sitting on the side of his bed in the darkened bedroom, talking, as we often do just before he goes to sleep. He said, "Dad, do you remember several weeks ago in church when you were talking about heroes?"

I nodded in the darkness and said, "I remember."

"Well," he continued, "you asked us to make a list of the heroes in our lives. You asked the men to write down the male heroes and the women to write down their female heroines. Then, when we had finished, you asked the women how many of them had written down their moms as their number one female heroine— and how many of the men had listed their dads as their number one hero."

"I remember," I said.

"Well, there were about a thousand people present, and you

said only five of the men raised their hands when you asked who had listed their dad as their number one hero." Tim paused. I waited. Then out of the darkness his voice continued. "I was one of those five."

I was too choked up to reply and was grateful for the darkness.

I reached out, put my hand on his muscular shoulder, and prayed for him. But even as I prayed, I knew there was something greater than naming his dad as his number one hero—and that was finding his place in God.

I am eager for Tim, and all the Tims of this world, to look beyond their dads to the eternal God who is their refuge. Our hearts are homesick for the courts of the Lord.

IV

The Joy and Danger
of Discovery

The desire to belong—to find a place—is basic in our nature. However, the Spirit-filled man will never be content to remain caged, despite the safety that bars seem to provide. Once aloft on the winds of God, the spirit of man is activated to adventure. It will never be satisfied unless it is moving upward—exploring, discovering, venturing.

I am sure this drive for adventure is one of the reasons I have been drawn back to the Sinai on an almost annual basis during the last several years. My stated purpose for these trips was to collect data and photos for a book on the wilderness experience—following the footsteps of Moses. However, when a 47-year-old man, who spends the majority of his time behind a typewriter or sitting in comfortable living rooms talking with overfed Americans, starts making out bivouac equipment lists and then heads off into one of the world's most desolate and remote areas, you can assume that book research is only an excuse. The real reason is to fulfill that God-given sense of adventure which is common to all men—especially those controlled by the Holy Spirit.

Last year, dressed in shorts and Arab headdress, the *kaffiyeh*, sitting crosslegged in the sand of Wadi Feiran and sifting small pebbles through my fingers, I realized I was "home." Yet it was not the rocks and sand which called me back but the relationship When God descended upon Mount Sinai, He was accompanied by thousands of angels—some of whom are still resident in that place. Moses, the lone figure, clung to the craggy sides of the mountain overcome by what was taking place in front of him. Even the mountains around him were illuminated by the divine glory. Despite the passage of 3,200 years and the constant shift of political power, that glory remains. And whether sitting in the sand or climbing the mountains, I somehow seem to be a part of that remaining presence.

There is within me this drive to explore. It is more than the spirit of the voyeur: it demands participation—accompanied by an element of risk. Yet like the eagle, unless one spreads his wings and soars, he will never see more than the bars of his cage—much less be able to experience what lies beyond the ranges.

The last trip was made with 12 men in an open, four-wheel-drive truck which bounced across the rocky desert and through the sometimes narrow, sometimes wide wadis which wind their way among the towering mountains. We would often dismount to climb mountains or, taking our canteens, trek through the narrow gorges and meet the truck on the other side many hours later. We cooked our own food and slept under the stars.

Rain in the Sinai is rare. But when it comes, it is an awesome experience. The water roars off the barren mountains, fills the huge wadis, and rages toward the sea in a mighty tidal wave of fury and force. Entire Bedouin tent villages and herds have been swept away when this happens. The wise guide always checks the sky before leading his group into one of those dried riverbeds, for a sudden flash flood could be disastrous.

The third day out we cut inland from the Gulf of Suez and made our way through a wide wadi, bouncing along in the ruts of other vehicles which had gone before, perhaps months in advance. Late that afternoon one of the men beside me in the back of the dusty truck pointed at the steep side of a mountain on the opposite side of the riverbed. He had spotted an abandoned turquoise mine, thousands of years old.

"There may be turquoise bits still in the mine," I said.

"Let's explore," the others suggested

I asked the Israeli driver to stop and explained our group wanted to climb the mountain and explore the mines. I asked if he would leave the sandy ruts and drive us closer to the base of the mountain.

He scowled, wrinkled his brow, and shook his head. "No way!" he grunted. "Too dangerous."

During an earlier Sinai campaign, he told us, the Israelis had placed explosive land mines in that particular wadi, knowing it was the only way the Egyptians could escape through the rugged territory. They had kept a chart of the mine placements, intending to return and retrieve them after the war. However, at the height of the campaign, one of those rare cloudbursts flooded the Sinai. Torrents of rain fell on the desert mountains, pouring off the sides of the treeless cliffs and roaring through the ancient riverbed in destructive mayhem on its way to the Gulf of Suez. The land mines had been swept out of the ground and scattered all over the broad wadi. Some had exploded in the force of the water, but others were still buried in the trackless sand. Experienced drivers knew the only safe place was in the ruts made by a previous truck or military tank. In fact, just a few months before, an Israeli colonel had been killed when his jeep ran over one of those old land mines and it exploded.

Our driver said the only way we could explore the turquoise mines would be to dismount from the truck and walk across the sand. But he—and his truck—would remain behind.

"Just walk lightly," he added, slouching down in the seat and pulling his cap over his eyes for a nap. "I'll be waiting here—if you get back."

I glanced at the other men. It was too much of a challenge to pass up. But we walked gingerly.

When we got back to the truck with our pockets full of beautiful turquoise nuggets, our driver said most pilgrims choose to stay in the safety of the ruts. He then reminded me it was "tradition!" which had kept the Jews alive all these centuries. "But," he smiled, "we don't have any turquoise either."

Ruts are safe and comfortable. But Christians must grow. Or die. And nothing is worse than death from sameness.

Growth demands change. Change demands movement, sometimes across the trackless sands of the untried. But to venture from the road and run the risk of being blown up—just to make a new spiritual discovery—well, no thank you; I'll just remain with the truck.

There is nothing more distracting to a denominational program rumbling along in the ruts of yesteryear, or to a pastor asleep behind the wheel of his stalled church, than to hear a group of people on the other side of the wadi shouting, "Hey, look what we've found!"

Just one man in a congregation who decides to raise his hands in praise; just one woman who prophesies; just a small Tuesday night prayer group where the people study the Bible and lay hands on the sick for healing—can cause an entire congregation to stampede across the mine field. Therefore, rather than lead the way, many leaders prefer to chain the offender to the truck—or if he persists, run over him. If we can just still that voice which keeps talking about spiritual discoveries, we can get on with the busyness of our lives.

Most leaders know how to handle a fanatic. But what do you do with someone who is genuinely bent on spiritual discovery, who has as his goal in life to be under the control of the Holy Spirit?

The question, you see, every person must face is: Who (or what) controls my life? For none of us is the captain of our soul or the master of our fate. We are controlled by our senses, our traditions, our habits, our reactions, our feelings. Some are controlled by demons. Others are controlled by the Holy Spirit.

But daring to live the venturesome life of the eagle is risky business. When Jesus closed the book in the synagogue in Nazareth and sat down—after having defined His purpose—the religious people rose up in furor and tried to kill Him. He had threatened them by saying He was leaving the ruts and heading out across forbidden territory.

It's dangerous out there. And sometimes lonely. Yet, as Kipling said in "The Explorer," there is a voice beyond the mountains calling, which somehow keeps us going, pioneering, searching:

Something hidden. Go and find it. Go
and look behind the Ranges—
Something lost behind the Ranges.
Lost and waiting for you. Go!

Thus, despite our timidity, our hesitancy, our proneness to make mistakes, we know there is more, much more than we have experienced in our dusty ruts of traditional religion. The call of spiritual adventure grows louder the closer we move to God. So we venture out.

"Because it is there," said George Leigh Mallory earlier in this century when asked why he wanted to climb Mount Everest. "Because it is there."

As long as I can remember, I have been challenged by people with purpose. Those who dream impossible dreams—and then bring them into being.

A while back, a friend of mine, Bob Burdick, a senior pilot with United Airlines, took his vacation to fly a small, single-engine airplane across the Atlantic Ocean. The Wycliffe Bible Translators in Nepal needed the plane for their ministry. With his teen-age daughter as his only passenger, Bob flew across the stormy North Atlantic to France following the same route Lindbergh used years before. Then he went beyond Lindbergh. He picked up his wife in France, and they flew over the Alps, across the deserts of the Middle East, across northern India and up into the Himalayas to Nepal—flying to the glory of God.

Dangerous? Sure! But there is something inside me that wants to do the same thing. To do something nobody else has ever done— to the glory of God. After all, what's the use of living if you don't attempt something impossible—even if it kills you.

Several years ago I read of a man who had listed 100 things he wanted to do before he died. They were exciting things. Daring things. Impossible things. He wanted to scale the Matterhorn, write a book, go on a lion safari, sing in Carnegie Hall, paddle the length of the Amazon in a canoe, sign up as an Indian in a cowboy and Indian movie. He was 68 years old at the time he wrote the article, and he had already accomplished 92 of his 100 things. They were the things all of us dream of doing but never attempt because they are "impossible."

The late Dawson Trotman, founder of the Navigators, used to set up difficult but attainable goals for each new year. One year he learned to speak a foreign language. Another he learned to play the organ. He was able to do this same thing when he memorized the Scripture—and taught thousands of others to do it—through discipline.

It seems that those of us in the Kingdom, more than any other people on earth, should be willing to discipline ourselves to achieve the impossible, to do the daring, to fulfill our expanded sense of adventure.

There is a place in the Christian community for the dreamer. Most of us dream dreams, however, then put them aside as impossible. Yet God never puts a desire in our hearts, or beckons us to walk on water, unless He intends for us to step out in faith and at least make the attempt. Whether we achieve or not is almost immaterial; the passing of the test lies in whether we try, in whether we're willing to be obedient to the inner call to greatness—the onward call to spiritual adventure.

I think of the people Jesus challenged while He was here on earth. To a man who never walked Jesus said, "Rise and walk." To a blind man who had never seen before He said, "Go, wash in the pool of Siloam and see." To men who had never done anything but pull fish nets out of the water Jesus said, "Go ye into all the world." To all He said, "Put that dream into action."

Caleb, Joshua's old friend and fellow warrior, was such a man.

Forty-five years had passed since Caleb, at the age of 40, had been appointed by Moses, along with Joshua and 10 other men, to scout the land of Canaan. The land of the Sinai was familiar to Moses. He had lived there 40 years tending the flocks of his father-in-law, Jethro. But he had never been up into Canaan. So when the children of Israel reached Kadesh-Barnea, Moses sent out 12 men to scout the land, discover the best paths and bring back a report.

Their purpose for spying out the land was not to see if they could possess it. God had already told them the land was theirs. Their purpose was to scout out the roads, discover where the cities were and draw a crude map so Moses could lead the people into the land promised by God.

The 12 returned with conflicting opinions. Ten of the spies brought a majority opinion.

"It's a magnificent land that flows with milk and honey. But you ought to see who lives up there. They have people 14 feet tall. Giants. The sons of Anak. And their cities have walls around them. We'll never be able to make it. We're like grasshoppers in their sight."

Only Joshua and Caleb had the vision. "There are giants all right," Caleb said. "But we can take the land, for God has already given us the promise."

But the people raised their voices against Joshua and Caleb, and they barely escaped with their lives.

In disgust, Moses withdrew. God told Moses He was disgusted also. He was going to wipe out the entire nation of Israel and start over again with just Moses and a few men of faith—like Joshua and Caleb. Moses quickly interceded for his grumbling, faithless people, and God agreed to withhold His wrath. But, He said, of all the people, only Joshua and Caleb would enter the promised land. The rest would remain in the wilderness until everyone over the age of 20 had died. Then, using a fresh new generation, He would send them in to claim that which was theirs.

It was a sad day for the people of God. Within weeks a great plague struck the 10 spies, and they all died. The rest of the people were doomed to wander for an entire generation. Joshua would be charged with leading the people upon Moses' death, and Caleb was to inherit all the land he had covered on his initial scouting trip into Canaan—all the land from Hebron to Eschol, where the giant grapes grew, to the springs of Ein Gedi near the Dead Sea.

Forty-five years passed: Moses had died and Joshua had led the people into Canaan where they had conquered the land—city by city. Then came the important but difficult task of dividing the land among the tribes. In the midst of all this parceling, Caleb stepped forward. He was now 85 years old, but he reminded Joshua of the promise of Moses.

"Remember what God told Moses at Kadesh-Barnea about you and me," he said solemnly. "I was only 40 years old when we returned from exploring the land and brought back our report. But on that day Moses promised me: 'The land on which your feet have trodden shall be an inheritance to you and your children forever—because you have wholly followed the Lord my God.'"

"I remember," Joshua answered, smiling at his old friend. "I remember well."

Caleb continued. "The Lord has not only kept me alive these 85 years, but I am just as strong today as I was when Moses sent me out. And I am just as eager to take on the giants of Anak as I was then."

Then, turning and pointing at the mountain to the south, toward the walled city of Hebron, Caleb's eyes glistened when he said, "Now, old friend, give me this mountain."

Joshua looked at old Caleb. His face was leathery from the long years in the desert sun. But his huge arms still bulged with muscle, and his body was that of a young man. Caleb was not cocky. Just confident. He was resting on God and had now stepped forward to claim that which had been promised.

"I know the giants live there," Caleb said. "I know you chose to bypass the city when you took the land rather than run the risk of heavy losses fighting the sons of Anak. But with the Lord helping me, I shall drive them out of the land, and they will never bother you again."

Joshua hesitated no longer. Reaching out, he laid his hands on the shoulders of the old warrior, and blessed him in the name of Jehovah. Then Caleb called his sons and nephews around him— the young men who had come out of Sinai and helped capture the land of Canaan—and told them what to do. With a mighty shout they marched on Hebron, drove out the giants and killed the three sons of Anak: Sheshai, Ahiman, and Talmai.

Caleb was a man who answered to a higher authority than military science and tactics. It did not make good sense to take Hebron.

Joshua had figured the odds, said it wasn't worth it, and bypassed the walled cities. There was no sense fighting the giants of Anak.

But Caleb was not content with that. He was marching to the sound of a different drummer. He had been confident 45 years before. He was confident now. The promises of God never change. All that was needed was a man of adventure.

Every child of God has a promised mountain in his life. It may be a childhood dream or vision. It may be a teen-age desire which has now been tossed aside as too impossible. It may be something God gave in prayer which seemed so impractical it was never tried. It may be some seemingly insurmountable obstacle. But every child of God has a promised mountain.

It's easy to be content with the valleys. Ruts have a great appeal. If it's not giants on the mountain, it's mines under the sand. So men snuggle into ecclesiastical gowns, bury themselves in their libraries of musty books, talk about the way things were, recite the creeds, build the cathedrals, draw charts of end times, but never venture out into the arena of the impossible, never taste of new wine, much less experiment with a new wineskin.

My friend Roger Wilson says he is building his life and his family so that if the Holy Spirit were ever removed, everything would fall apart.

That's real mountain climbing.

That's the way churches need to be built: so if the Spirit of God is ever removed, the walls will fall down, the roof will cave in, the money will disappear and all the people will leave.

I have a printed sign, in a big frame, which hangs above my desk. It says: "Attempt something so big that unless God intervenes it is bound to fail."

That, too, is mountain climbing.

The saddest of all people are those who taste the power of God, discover it will change them if they swallow—and then spit. They fear the result of digesting the power of God and are content to live in the proximity of commitment.

My friend Peter Lord, a Baptist pastor in the nearby community of Titusville, Florida, tells his church: "We practice daily what we believe. All the rest is religious froth."

There was nothing religious about Caleb.

As a college student at Mercer University, I was challenged by a soft-spoken southern preacher who visited our campus one day. Clarence Jordan had taught New Testament Greek at Southern Baptist Seminary for a number of years. Then one day he began to realize he could teach Greek the rest of his life—and never put the Kingdom into practice here on earth. Life was too short, he said, to spend it in a classroom—as important as that is. He would leave that for others, but he had a call on his life. God had given him a mountain.

So he went down into Southwest Georgia, found a piece of property near Americus and founded a little community farm. But this was the early 1950s and communal farms weren't very popular among Georgians—especially those where blacks and whites lived and ate together.

Folks in that section of Georgia couldn't handle it. So they burned his buildings. They dynamited his peanut barn. They boycotted his people so they couldn't buy cottonseed, hay or feed for their cattle. Clarence and his people had to drive all the way to Columbus to buy food, and often when they returned at night and drove down the long dirt road to Koinonia Farms, they were shot at by neighbors with rifles and shotguns. They were called communists—for that was the worst thing you could call a person back then.

I sat at the feet of Clarence Jordan all that afternoon, listening as he quoted the words of Jesus about the Son of Man having no place to lay His head, about leaving father and mother and brother and sister to follow, about taking up the cross daily. He was the only man I had ever heard who was willing to die for what he believed. I had met lots of folks who were willing to kill for what they believed—but never a man willing to die. I was 22 years old and looking for a cause.

I know now that if Clarence Jordan had pointed at me and said, "Jamie, lay down your nets, and come follow me," I never would have hesitated. I would have walked away from my college classes, from my planned career, from my friends—to become his disciple. Why? Because he was unlike any other preacher I had ever met. He was not just talking about brotherhood from the leafy boughs of his safe pulpit, he was living it. Even if it killed him. I would have followed him because he was the only man I had ever heard who blew a certain sound on his trumpet. He knew where he was going. And men like that were rare in those days.

Now there are a number of men coming forth who know where they are going. These are men who are unafraid of the land mines, unafraid of the giants of Anak and willing to lay claim to the mountain God has given them.

They are men who have discovered the five-word secret of Caleb: he *wholly followed the Lord God.*

Nevertheless my brethren that went up with me made the heart of the people melt: but I *wholly followed the Lord my God* (Joshua 14:8).

. . . Surely the land whereon thy feet have trodden shall be thine inheritance . . because *thou hast wholly followed the Lord my God* (Joshua 14:9).

Hebron therefore became the inheritance of Caleb . . . because *he wholly followed the Lord God of Israel* (Joshua 14:14).

But my servant Caleb, because he had another spirit with him, and *hath followed me fully,* him will I bring into the land . . . (Numbers 14:24).

No divided loyalties. No murmuring or complaining. Only a steady obedience to light received—and a willingness to wait 45 years to see the promise fulfilled.

The worst of all heresies is to despair of those childhood ideals, those dreams that stimulated us when our minds were still young and innocent. Too many of us have reached the crisis of middle life and, disillusioned, put aside our dreams of youth.

"Too impossible," we say sadly. "Too foolish. Too ambitious. Too dangerous."

On the island of Mindanao, in the southern archipelago of the Philippines, is a small coastal barrio called San Jose. A number of years ago an evangelist by the name of Gonzalez founded a church there. The church grew and a number of people accepted Jesus Christ as Lord. Soon nearly all in the community were Christian, and a school was started. When the elder Gonzalez died, his son Aley carried on the ministry. Aley believed in a God of miracles and told the people in the barrio and church that the age of miracles had not passed. Many believed him and were baptized in the Holy Spirit. Both the church and the school continued to grow.

One afternoon the second grade teacher announced a test. He told all the children to be sure and bring a pencil and paper the next day for the exam. Since most of the children were very poor, they did not ordinarily carry pencils and paper to school.

The following morning all the children showed up with pencil and paper except one. This little eight-year-old, brown-skinned Filipino boy came from an extremely poor family. He lived in a palm thatched hut and had no shoes or shirt—only a ragged pair of shorts to wear to school. He had found a single sheet of notebook paper but he had no pencil. The teacher told him he was sorry, but he could not sit in on the examination since he had no pencil. He would have to wait outside until the test was over.

Heartbroken, the little boy walked out the door and sat on the front steps of the little school building which also was used for a church on Sunday. He remembered Pastor Aley Gonzalez's sermons on miracles, on the great God who did impossible things.

"Dear God," he prayed, closing his eyes and raising his face toward the sun, "please send me a pencil. I want to take the test."

He opened his eyes and looked all around, expecting that God would drop the pencil out of the sky. But there was nothing. Only the shiny white pebbles on the sand, the sound of the wind rustling the branches of the coconut palms and the gentle lapping of the surf on the nearby beach.

His eyes filled with tears as he sat, his arms folded around his knees, his single sheet of notebook paper in his hand.

As children will do, he rolled the notebook paper into a small cylinder, rolling it back and forth between his open palms, tears dripping down his cheeks. Then, as he twirled the paper in his hands, he felt something hard—round and hard—inside the paper.

He quickly unrolled the notebook paper, and there in the middle was a bright shiny yellow pencil. It had a brand new eraser on one end, and the other end was machine sharpened—even though there was not a pencil sharpener within 30 miles. He quickly ran into the schoolhouse, waving his pencil. The teacher asked him where he had gotten such a magnificent pencil, and the little boy paused, thought, and finally said, "The impossible God gave it to me."

I was in San Jose the following year, a guest of Aley Gonzalez. I talked to the little boy. He showed me his pencil. He had used it over and over and had broken the lead a number of times and sharpened it with his father's machete. But it was still a good pencil. And there were no other pencils like it in all the barrio.

The reason pencils appear to little Filipino boys, the reason Davids kill Goliaths, the reason unlearned fishermen preach with power while learned theologians often elicit nothing more than yawns from their listeners, the reason old men capture walled cities and slay giants—is childlikeness. They believe in a God who fulfills dreams and does the impossible.

Do not despair of those childhood dreams, those visions which came in adolescence. They are the fiber of life, the stuff which holds us together. Dangerous? To be sure. Foolish? Never.

In the Buckingham home we are challenging our children to invest their futures in things that will cost them their lives—for the glory of God. We are challenging them to go out, even at an early age, and be willing to die for Jesus.

The world does not understand this philosophy. The world says, "Be in control." But God says, "Be out of control." The world says parents should protect their children from death, not point them toward it. But we know there is no glory anywhere outside that which is done strictly for the glory of God. Abundant life comes only when we give our lives totally and completely to that to which God has called us.

As a young man, Dwight L. Moody was challenged by someone who said, "The world has yet to see what God can do with one man who is totally committed to Him." Moody was an unlikely candidate. His English was atrocious. He had no formal education.

He made his living as a shoe clerk. But he had a dream—a vision. And he said, "I'll be that man." Twenty years later he stood with one foot in Chicago, the other in London and shook two continents with the Gospel of Jesus Christ. He had learned to put aside all those urgent matters which pulled at his coattail and do only the important things God had called him to do. He was an overcomer.

The climax of my Sinai excursions has always been the climbing of Jebel Musa, the Mountain of Moses. Rising 7,500 feet out of the desert sand, the magnificent, three-peaked mountain stands not only as mute testimony to our triune God but as a challenge to all who dare ascend its rugged flanks as Moses did to receive the law.

On my last trip, with 12 other men along, we reached Sinai on the seventh day. In order to get to the summit by dawn, we had to begin the climb no later than 2 A.M. Climbing in the dark can be a stumbling, groping experience. Or it can be the adventure of a lifetime. I had hired a 12-year-old Bedouin boy to guide us up the backside of the mountain. I knew, from past experience, that the moment we left the desert floor and our eyes adjusted to the darkness—away from our campfire—there would be ample light to see by starlight. The Sinai is one of those rare places of the world entirely free from air pollution. Only during certain times of the year are there any clouds. At night, once your eyes adjust to night sight, the light from a billion stars provides ample light to climb the mountain. But the first several hundred feet of climbing are the hardest as you stumble over sharp stones and cling to the larger rocks to keep from falling.

After about 10 minutes I stopped our group, allowing the slower ones to catch up as we bunched in the chilly darkness of the steep mountain trail.

"We are going to walk alone," I told them, "rather than as a group. I'll go ahead with the guide. Leave at least a hundred yards between each of you as you climb. Climb in silence, listening for the voice of God as it still resounds from this mountain. Put your flashlights in your pockets. Let your eyes adjust to the night, and you will enjoy one of the most fantastic physical and spiritual adventures of your life."

Having caught our breath, we proceeded up the steep mountain trail, ascending the mountain in the quiet darkness of the desert. The higher we got, the more the panorama of the dark desert spread out before us. The air was clear and cold. And silent. For there are few living things in the desert. None of the usual night noises; just total silence and the beating of your own heart.

I was overjoyed, not only for what I was again experiencing on that sacred place but because of the deeply personal, spiritual stirrings I knew were taking place in each of the men stretched out behind me. Halfway up I paused for breath. I stood in silence, letting my eyes take in the mighty shadows of the mountains, now faintly outlined by the coming dawn. I turned and looked back over a ledge. Far below me, coming up the same path, I could hear the men, their footsteps echoing in the stillness of the canyons. Then I noticed something else: two of the 12 had pulled their flashlights from their pockets and were using them to see the way. Perhaps they had already bruised a shin or stubbed a toe. Rather than run the risk of additional damage, they had sacrificed the beauty of climbing by starlight for the safety of climbing in the small, artificial, yellow circle of light directly in front of them.

I was saddened. These men would reach the summit like all the rest and would join in the magnificent and indescribable spiritual experience which awaits all who attain the pinnacle, but they were missing something of even greater value—the joy and adventure of the ascent.

Despite the glory that awaits all of us when we are transformed from this earth into heavenly places, the adventure of the climb is the thing that makes it all worthwhile. I am grateful for crutches—and flashlights—but I yearn for the time when I can climb without them, experiencing the sheer joy of the Spirit-controlled life.

In 1948 God spoke to a young student at Wheaton College, a small liberal arts college near Chicago, and promised him a mountain—a mountain which would turn out to be a lonely beach on an uncharted jungle river in Ecuador.

One day, sitting alone in his study, he read the first chapter of Hebrews. There, in verse seven, he ran across the phrase: "[God] maketh . . . his ministers a flame of fire." Jim Elliot picked up his journal and wrote, paraphrasing something Amy Carmichael had written many years before.

"Am I ignitable? God deliver me from the dread asbestos of other things. Saturate me with the oil of the Spirit, that I may be a flame. But a flame is transient, often short-lived. Canst thou bear this, O my soul—short life? In me there dwells the Spirit of the Great Short-Lived, whose zeal for God's house consumed Him. Make me thy fuel, Flame of God."

Jim took his mountain and it cost him his life. On January 9, 1956, a rescue party found his body, along with the bodies of four fellow missionaries, floating face down with Auca spears protruding from their backs.

But because those five men gave their lives climbing their mountain, not only have many in the Auca tribe been converted, but literally thousands of young men and women have stepped forward to answer the call of missions and fill their vacant places. And that section of the Ecuadorian jungle, once alive with tiny sons of Anak, is now full of praises coming from the brown lips of the sons of God.

If a man is going to die—let him die climbing.

V

Living on the Growing Edge

When I got married and left home to enter seminary in Texas, I never dreamed I would ever again live in a house like the one my daddy built. In Fort Worth, Texas, Jackie and I lived in a tiny duplex and shared the bath with the landlady and her spinster daughter. Later we moved into a little frame house near the school. Our first child was brought home to that small house with an even smaller front yard with the one spindly poplar tree we had purchased at the garden department of Montgomery Ward.

Later we moved to Greenwood, South Carolina, where we lived in a small two-bedroom house which the church provided for associate pastors. After I assumed the duties as senior minister, we moved into the elegant parsonage—complete with formal living room, formal dining room, paneled den, plush carpets and drapes. It had been decorated by the ladies of the church and was always viewed as their pet project. As a result, even though we lived in an elegance far beyond our means, we never could change anything about the house—for it was not ours. It belonged to the entire church and in particular to a committee chaired by a woman who was the best friend of the former pastor's wife—and who always resented the fact we had moved in with our children. It was a very artificial situation, one in which we could never feel comfortable or "at home."

When we returned to Florida after those difficult and heartbreaking circumstances demanded our move, we were forced to live in a series of rented houses in the little community of Melbourne. Our furniture, which we had purchased to fit the huge parsonage in South Carolina, would not fit into the postage-stamp-sized rooms of the little Florida houses. So much of it languished (and mildewed) in a nearby warehouse. We lived in three rented houses, moving and bashing our furniture in the process until even that which did fit in the small houses was damaged beyond any utilitarian value. Finally we bought a subdivision house and after several years added an upstairs with a big bedroom and writing studio. At last we got our old furniture out of storage. But by then it seemed out of place in our life style, and we wound up giving most of it away—after having paid storage on it for almost four years.

Then, after living in the subdivision house for seven years, I began to feel we should move. It was a strange thing, for we were comfortable where we were and had saved up enough money to pay off the mortgage on the house. The children were growing up and leaving home, and there was no need to expand to anything larger. If we had any needs at all, it was for a smaller, less cumbersome house. Yet, for an unexplained reason, I had a strong feeling we should move into an even larger house—with surrounding property.

It was as if God was requiring of me another venture—albeit one without so much pain this time.

We had arrived at a financial station in life where we could live almost any place we wanted. I was 45 years old and no longer dependent upon the church for a salary. I had become well enough established as a writer and speaker to live on my royalties and honorariums.

The pastoral role I had formerly occupied in the church had been assumed by several other qualified men. My role had become apostolic, that of the spiritual overseer. The council of elders recognized me as the spiritual head of the Body. In turn, I submitted to them. It was a very satisfying situation. Jackie and I had found

78

great contentment in Melbourne, something I had never believed possible in my days of struggle in the crush of institutionalism.

For years I had wrestled with being a "hireling" to a group of people. As a minister I had always been paid by the church. I was controlled by an official board. There was no spiritual privilege which did not have a string attached—a string securely fastened around my wallet. I was told how to live, what days I could take off, how many Sundays I was required to be "in the pulpit," what to wear and what not to wear. Even my wife's wardrobe had to meet the approval of official and unofficial groups within the church. My life style was under constant scrutiny by any number of people—all in some kind of official capacity—who asserted some degree of control over my life.

Now our situation had changed. The new church had grown up around me. In some respects I could be looked upon as the founder. But we had majored on relationships rather than buildings, and I had been able to direct attention away from me and was really no longer looked upon as the "main attraction." At the same time, I had been able to impart many of my own attitudes of tolerance, mercy, love, and forgiveness to the Body. I realized the need to submit to other men and did so because I wanted to—not because I was forced to. Other leaders appeared around me, men who ministered without condemnation, who were filled with love and understanding. Jackie and I had "friends" in the church—people who would die for us, even if we were wrong. There had been occasional friends like that in the past, but like myself they were hamstrung by the unreasonable rules and regulations of the institution. Now we were free.

Yet there was this growing feeling we were to move. Not out of the community, just into a different house. The idea that we were being directed by God to buy a big house in the country was frightening. To me it meant moving beyond personal control of my finances, for despite my comfortable childhood, my father had always been an extremely frugal man; somehow I had grown up thinking that to become very spiritual, one had to become very poor. Therefore we made every effort to hide the fact that we had made money. When one of my books brought in a healthy royalty check, it so embarrassed us that neither Jackie nor I would tell anyone. It was one blessing from God I just didn't want others to know about, for fear it would cause us to look worldly—or separate us from our dear friends who had not made as much.

We found great satisfaction in giving away large amounts of money. We bought several cars for friends. We helped a number of young people go to college by paying their tuition. We made a down payment on a lot for another friend who was struggling to find a place to raise his family. We helped another purchase a house. We gave away large amounts of money to missionaries working in difficult places and at the same time continued to give at least a tithe of all we made through the local church. All in all, we were giving away far more than half our income—yet still living as rich people.

Thus, when it became obvious God wanted us to find another house (I say obvious, for the desire of our hearts was growing every day), we wanted to be very careful we did not buy something pretentious—something which would leave the impression we were wealthy and would thus separate us from our dear friends all of whom were far more meaningful to us than any place to live. For we had long come to realize that nothing on this earth is as valuable as relationships.

We had always been careful to drive inexpensive automobiles, wear department store clothing, and eat far more chicken than steak. We had not employed a housekeeper nor did we hire someone to cut the grass. We did not do it because of external pressures; we did it because we felt comfortable in that life style. Besides, this released additional money to give away—something we thoroughly enjoyed.

It was New Year's Eve morning when my friend, Jim Underwood, came by the house. "I've found your next home," he beamed. Jim had been looking for a house himself and knew we had been thinking about moving. I drove with him out into the country. We pulled into a long, winding drive through the pines. There, sitting on 20 acres of land, was the house I knew God intended for us to have. It was surrounded by towering southern pines and a few cabbage palms. The two-story house was red brick, fronted by white Georgian columns. Behind the house was a fenced pasture and a beautiful two-bedroom guest cottage.

It was a beautiful day. The Florida air was crisp. The sky bright blue. We stood in the front yard, looking and listening. Birds flitted in the branches of the trees. Squirrels chattered and scampered back and forth. I closed my eyes and could almost imagine myself back home—35 miles and 35 years away. And I heard, deep in my heart, the voice of God.

"Take it. It's yours."

Jackie and I had looked at dozens of houses—all much smaller and far less pretentious. Each time we had commented to one another: "It's too big. Too grandiose." I looked at Jim. "What will Jackie say when she sees this mansion and hears me say, 'This is to be our new house'?"

It was unoccupied at the time, having been built only months before and lived in only a short while before the owner—a bank president—was transferred out of town. The determining factor was the adjoining guest house, for we had long dreamed of having a prophet's chamber, a place where we could host those in need and minister to them without having our own lives disrupted.

Jackie reacted as I suspected. "What will people think? We'll be isolated way out there in the country. Besides, it costs twice as much as we want to pay."

Yet, despite Jackie's misgivings, I was certain. We prayed and debated for two weeks. The debates between us grew stronger and more heated. The more she argued against living in a big house which would drain all our savings and would probably consume everything else we would make just for maintenance, the more I was sure God was saying: "Take it. It's yours."

Finally, one evening, after we sat for the twentieth time examining the facts, Jackie used a phrase which sent shivers up my spine. "You are not using reason or common sense in this matter," she said. "It's as though you have no control of this—as if it's beyond your control."

It scared me, for during all those years of walking in the Spirit I had always thought of myself as being a "controlled" person—level-headed, reasonable, well-balanced in spiritual matters. Now

I was being classified by my own wife as devoid of all those attributes I so admired in others and, admittedly, in myself.

"Think of all those missionaries overseas you love and support," she said. "How can you stand the thought of living in a house which is better than theirs? How do you think it will look here in this church if the spiritual leader lives in a mansion while all the rest live in much smaller places? We will be accused of being false shepherds who shear the sheep and live off the proceeds from the wool."

Rationally, I knew her arguments were invalid. We already lived in a house finer than any missionary I knew. The people of our community would not misunderstand; they loved me and would be happy for us if we chose to buy the big house—for they knew it would be open for ministry just as our smaller houses had been. Besides, I was not buying it with money which had come from the church but with money which I had earned as a professional writer. In fact, we had not taken any money from the church for several years. Yet I was stung. I knew that Jackie would submit to my final decisions, but I was afraid to step out unless I knew for sure God was leading.

"We'll move ahead," I told Jackie. "But we'll not sign a contract until all the lights are green."

Our personal friend, Gail Whitley, who was acting as our broker, called early one morning in late January. "Everything is approved," she said. "I'll be at your house at 11 A.M. for you to sign the final papers."

I walked back into the breakfast room where Jackie was finishing her cup of tea. "That was Gail," I said. "She'll be here at 11 A.M. for the final signing."

Jackie reached out and took my hand. "If you're certain, then I'm with you."

I began to pace the floor, voicing my own misgivings. We were getting ready to invest all our savings—plus money not yet earned—in a house and 20 acres of land.

"I thought you said God directed you to buy it," Jackie said. "Why are you now so uncertain?"

"It is one thing to be certain when it doesn't cost you anything," I said. "Now, in less than two hours, we will be penniless again."

"But we'll be in the will of God, won't we?" Jackie encouraged me.

I was astounded how the debate had reversed itself.

I sat down at the table and we did what we had done many times in the past few weeks. We prayed. But this time there was no reassuring feeling when the prayer was over. Just continuing doubts. What if I have written my last book? What if the publishing company goes bankrupt and cannot pay my royalties on the previous books? What if all Jackie's fears about the people rejecting us if we act affluent were correct? What if . . .

Confused and bewildered, I left the house and drove to the post office to check the mail. I told Jackie I would be back at 11 A.M. to meet Gail. "But if I don't have any more assurance than I have now, the deal is off."

There was only one letter in the box at the post office. It was hand addressed in a plain white envelope. The return address, in the top corner, was from a woman I did not know in Jacksonville, Florida. *Odd*, I thought, *usually the box is stuffed with mail.*

I stood at the high table in the post office and opened the letter. Inside were two sheets of paper typed with a manual typewriter. The first was a short note of explanation.

"You don't know me," the writer stated. "But three weeks ago I received this prophecy from the Lord and He told me it was for you. I wrote it down and submitted it to my husband and to my pastor. Both of them confirmed it was of the Lord and encouraged me to send it to you. I hesitated, since it was so strange to send a prophecy through the mail to a man I had never met. But this morning God said I should send it. I feel I have now satisfied my obligation and leave the results in the hands of the Holy Spirit." The letter was signed by a woman I had never met— and to this day have not met.

The other sheet was typed, double-spaced. Across the years I had received a number of prophecies through the mail. Seldom, if ever, did they have meaning. This one was radically different:

Questioning me does no good of late, my son. Have I not taught thee to follow by thy spirit and lean toward that which is unquestionable and right to thee? Why have you worried? Am I not God? Do I not own the cattle on a thousand hills? How fruitless is doubt. Henceforth, lift up high thy head, thy hands, sing again thy songs to me, for I am God. I send to thee a word to say only that I love thee with a love beyond what ye comprehend. Surely as I love thee with such might, shall I send to thee all thy direction. Thy concern and worry can ye now give up, for I am God and my answer and direction is even now on the way.

Therefore shall ye further expand the temple, my temple, and be ye prepared to raise a roof of love. Full of understanding and compassion shall be its walls. Call out to my wounded sheep to prepare themselves deeply in my word, for they shall direct lives that have never heard my word until now. From henceforth ye shall expand and send people throughout the country and to lands afar, and fruitful shall be their labors for they have received refuge in your place.

December 28, 1976

I stood immobilized, clutching the sides of the table in the post office. I tried to stifle the sobs but could not quench my tears. They poured down my face. My nose began to run. I looked for a handkerchief but did not have one. I was back where Jackie said I had been earlier: beyond control.

It really didn't seem to make much difference that people were walking by, checking their mail, and giving me strange looks. I wiped my face with my shirt sleeve and read the prophecy again. The tears began again. It was as though God Himself had written the note and stuck it in the post office box. I sensed the prophecy had far more meaning than my relationship with the house, but that would come later. It was the immediate message which overwhelmed me. It did everything but say, "How many times do I have to tell you, stupid, buy the house!"

I made my way home, crying and singing at the same time. Gail was in the living room with Jackie when I entered. She took one look at my tear-stained face and said, "Listen, I love you all too much to get you into something you're not sure of. If God has not spoken to you and told you to buy the house, let's call off the deal right now."

She stood to leave and I said, "Sit down. I want to read you something that was in the mailbox this morning." I read the prophecy, or at least tried to read it, to the two of them. It took me a long time for I kept crying. "On the way home all I could think about were the cities of refuge."

"Like those in Canaan?" Jackie asked.

"I'm not sure," I answered. "But over and over the word 'refuge' kept coming to my mind. And so did the word 'Hebron.'"

"What's a 'Hebron'?" Gail asked.

"It was one of the cities of refuge," I explained. "I've been there. It is located on a high mountain at the edge of the Negev Desert a number of miles south of Jerusalem. It's noted for its grapes."

I opened my Bible to Joshua 20 and read to Jackie and Gail the story of the cities of refuge. Earlier, in the books of Numbers and Deuteronomy, God had told Moses about such cities which Joshua would establish after he had conquered Canaan. In these six cities, scattered all over the land of Canaan, any man who had been unjustly accused of a crime could flee and find refuge. Even if he had actually committed the crime, he could find protection. He would plead his cause to the elders. After they judged him, they would protect him until a certain time had passed after which he could return to his own city or his own house from which he had fled.

Again, as had happened when I read the prophecy, I cried my way through Joshua 20. "We are to sign the contract," I said. "Price is no longer an object of consideration. And we are to call the place 'Hebron,' for it will become a place where the accused can flee and find refuge and healing."

All that we were given that morning has not yet come to pass. I am not worried about it. I am certain—beyond doubt—that God directed and controlled the events to insure I would be obedient. Now, sitting at my typewriter in the upper room of the house, overlooking the backyard, I can envision not one but a number

85

of guest houses. How they will be built I do not know. I can envision a vineyard. And an orange grove. I can envision wounded shepherds fleeing from the wolves which would not only devour their flocks but devour them also, coming for refuge and healing. And I dare not say no to that which God has set in motion.

All that had happened had been a Spirit-controlled venture into the will of God for us; I can only feel confident it will continue to be so.

VI

The Other Side of God

The Spirit-controlled man will eventually take on the nature of God. He will know and trust God because of who He is—not because of what He does for him.

A lot of people have not had the advantage and benefit of loving earthly parents—the kind who discipline as well as encourage. My father was that kind of man—the kind mentioned in Psalm 37 whose "steps are ordered by the Lord." He was the only man in my life about whom I cannot remember having ever spoken a single unkind thing. I loved him deeply and recognized him as a noble, generous, honorable man. By looking at him, I found it easier to understand and appreciate and know my heavenly Father.

Although my dad was the kindest, most tenderhearted, generous man I have ever known, he was also an exacting disciplinarian. Born and raised in Indiana of what my mother called "stern stock," he moved to Florida after World War I and went into the citrus business. He divided his time between his office and his groves—feeling that sweat was just as anointed as a balanced journal. It was hard work in those early years in Florida. Citrus trees were planted and pruned by hand. Few of the roads were paved. The machinery was often limited to a grubbing hoe, a machete and a brush hook. If there was a fire in the woods, you didn't put it out—you beat it out. And you spent a lot of time hoping you would not get bitten by a rattlesnake—or an alligator. It was hot, dirty work, and only the tough survived.

But through it all my dad remained a gentleman. Even though he supervised hard-drinking, iron-mouthed men, he never took a drink himself, never smoked, and I never heard him utter an oath stronger than, "Well, I declare!" Even when he was at work in the groves, his leather snake boots laced to his knees, his dusty khaki pants and shirt soaked with sweat, he always wore his black bow tie. It was his trademark as a former English professor, an army officer and a gentleman member of a society which he believed should consist of more than men with red necks.

He never lost his temper. I never heard him speak a harsh word to my mother or to any of the children. But he knew how, with a well-modulated voice, to let us know that next to the wrath of God, the wrath of a father is greatly to be feared.

Smoking was a cardinal sin. If you can't eat it or pick your teeth with it, don't put it in your mouth, he said. Bad language, of any kind, evoked instant punishment. One night at the supper table, I decided to pull an it's-time-to-let-you-know-I've-grown-up trick. I described a football injury which I had suffered at practice that afternoon as hurting "like the devil." My dad reminded me that any reference to the devil was profane, and I should leave the table. It was great vocabulary training, for it forced me—if I was going to get to eat with the family—to learn to be expressive without being vulgar. Even to this day I refer to my dictionary second only to my Bible.

Only once did he use a strap on me—and even then it was with much forethought and planning. I had been caught stealing money from my mother's purse. It was bad enough that she had caught me with an unexplainably large amount of cash in my pockets, but far worse was the fact I had lied about it and tried to cover up by blaming the whole event on my younger brother. That night my father came to my bedroom, pulled the study table out in the middle of the room and instructed me—with well-modulated voice—to climb up on the table and lie on my stomach. Moments later he pulled up a chair near my face and sat there with the

88

razor strap across his lap. I had seen the razor strap many times hanging on a hook in the closet of the big bathroom with the raised tub—the same closet where my father marked our height and weight once a year on the back of the door. He never used the razor strap, preferring to shave with a safety razor. The strap just hung there like a hangman's noose, a solemn warning that crime was not tolerated in the Buckingham household.

This evening, however, the strap was off the hook, and my heart was in my throat. I had heard my older brothers tell horrible stories of its prior application. Now it was my turn. Daddy didn't touch or refer to the strap to begin with. He just talked. But I heard nothing. All I could do was stare at that horrible instrument of torture—a wide piece of slick leather with another piece of heavy, woven fabric behind it.

After he finished his long monologue, he got up and closed the door of the room—the strap hanging loosely in his hand as he walked back to the table where I was lying on my stomach. He told me to grip the sides of the table with both hands, because, he said, what was about to happen was going to be extremely painful. Of course all that did was tighten up the muscles of my buttocks so he would not have to strike me nearly as hard to produce the needed amount of pain. I do not remember him striking me because, under conviction of my evil-doing and having already seen the instrument of punishment close at hand, nothing could compare with the pain I had already experienced in my mind.

I never stole money again, although the problem of blaming others for my wrongdoing was not so easily purged. That would take years of discipline by my heavenly Father.

My dad, you see, knew how to administer justice in ways to accomplish his purpose. That was the only time he whipped me. The rest of the times he used a similar psychological approach to administer justice. His favorite method was to come home from work early on the days I had been bad. I knew that only a very important issue would cause him to leave his office, and the mere fact I had pulled him away from his desk spelled doom and disaster. Pulling up in the driveway, he would send for me and tell me to climb up in the cab of his pickup truck. Then we would drive slowly around the grass road which took us behind the orange grove to a lonely spot on the back side of the 48 acres. Not a word was spoken. He would stop and turn off the engine. We would sit silently for a long time, both of us staring through the windshield. Finally, when the tension and suspense were so thick I could hardly breathe, he would turn and tell me what was on his heart—his disappointment over my actions, his despair at being an inadequate father, his grief over the way I had treated my mother, or my younger brother, or the fact I had been caught smoking behind the toolshed. It was all a very deliberate—and extremely effective—approach to justice.

Yet even in the administration of punishment, he was kind, gentle, and loving. I never knew him to be otherwise with anyone else either—until my senior year in high school.

I was deeply involved in high school athletics. Especially football. My senior year we had the meanest football coach in the nation. What he lacked in meanness, he made up for in vulgarity. The players hated him and dubbed him "The Monster" behind his back. I called the offensive plays that year, and the nights I got hit in the head a lot, we ran some weird formations. As a result, we didn't win many games.

One Friday night I called a particularly bad play which allowed the opposing team to intercept a pass and score the winning touchdown. As I came off the field, the coach met me at the sideline, shouting vulgarities and hitting his fists on my shoulder pads. Even though he was a large man—well over six feet and a hefty 230 pounds—I was too well-padded to be hurt. I shrugged it off as a temper tantrum and went to the dressing room.

The next Monday after school we were back on the practice field. During a break in the scrimmage, I left the field to get a drink of water. As I walked to the sidelines, I saw my dad's pickup truck near the end of the bleachers. *That's strange*, I thought. Although my father never missed a game, I had never known him to come to practice.

Curious, I walked over and peeked behind the bleachers. There was my father—59 years old, five feet nine inches tall and weighing less than 165 pounds—giving the coach an awesome tongue-lashing.

He had backed The Monster up against the bleachers. Looking up into his face, his finger tapping his chest and the veins standing out in his neck, he unleashed a storm of fury which had the coach pale and shaking.

My little old daddy! I had never seen anything like it. His anger was fierce to behold.

I was scared. I knew, in an instant, what was going on. My father did not tolerate even one word of vulgar language. Nor did he approve of injustice—especially in front of a Friday night crowd which included his business associates. His reaction was to wait patiently until Monday afternoon and then vocally skin this huge coach—much as a top sergeant would dress down a recruit.

I was not afraid for my father. I was just frightened because I had not seen that side of him before.

I ran back on the field and never mentioned it to anyone. That evening at the supper table everything was normal. Daddy never mentioned it to me, and I certainly did not bring it up to him. But always, in the back of my mind, I knew there was far more to my father than I had experienced as his son. To me he was one thing, but to my enemies he was something else.

As I evaluate the character of God, I remember that incident. Most of us have a very low concept of God. We believe He can fail us. We believe we can slip from His grasp and fall into hell—even after He has committed Himself to us. We believe we can offend Him, and He will cast us out. We judge His love for us on the basis of earthman's love for his children. We do not understand His patience, His love, His mercy, His grace, His provision, His protection, His healing power, His glory. We cannot comprehend how He welcomes, even invites us into His presence, despite our sins. There is so much about Him we do not know.

It is good to know one's ancestry. One's roots. But earthly ancestry can become bondage. Spiritually, my roots do not go back to my dad's Indiana. They go back no farther into history than my twenty-first year, when I made a commitment to Jesus Christ and was admitted into the family of God by adoption. At that time my entire ancestry makes a 90-degree turn to the right. My heritage no longer extends back to the native soil of my ancestors in England and Wales. Rather it goes to Galilee, to the Sinai, to a garden eastward in Eden, and eventually to the courts of the Most High God. As much as I admire and respect my earthly father and mother, I desire the characteristics and traits of my heavenly Father even more. As I grow older, people who knew my dad often tell me I look like him. That is a high compliment. But far more complimentary would be to say I was taking on the image of my heavenly Father.

Sometimes I think I would like to go to the doctor's office for a physical exam and when the nurse pulls out the medical history form and asks: "Did your father have diabetes?" answer with a straight face, "No, ma'am, my Father is very healthy."

"Did your father have any fainting spells?"

"No, ma'am, my Father fainteth not."

Of course, I would have to be careful, for not all nurses understand such a lineage. But it's comforting to know—even if they won't record it on the medical history form—that my ancestral roots go back to the Father of all health and that in my blood flows the very nature of God.

As a man grows into the knowledge of God, as he is filled with the Holy Spirit, even his physical characteristics change. The life cells of his body take on the characteristics of the Creator. Even the genes and chromosomes—those unchangeable and unalterable factors in the human body—can be controlled by the Holy Spirit. Facial expressions change. Eyes twinkle. Mouths smile. Sexual drives are redirected. Vocabulary changes. The respiratory system, the cardiovascular system, the digestive process—all these things can take on godly characteristics. As the Holy Spirit takes complete control, we become like our Father.

So it is very important that every Christian establish his identity.

The man who has no earthly roots, the man who doesn't know who his earthly father is, is often a floundering person. I think of that pathetic bard, whose sad poetry and songs touched the American generation of the early 1970s, wandering the earth in his twisted homosexuality, searching for his father. The sad part is, it doesn't really make any difference. If he would allow the Holy Spirit to take control, if he would recognize Jesus Christ as God's Son, he could then join that magnificent family and find his heritage under the Fatherhood of God.

Even though I came from a happy family relationship, there was always a nagging feeling that I was incomplete, rootless, without real heritage until I came into a relationship with my spiritual family—and in particular with the Father of that family. I can share with you the happy experiences of my childhood and tell you about my meaningful relationship with my earthly parents, but it does very little for you. You say, "That sounds like a very happy family. I am glad you had a good father and mother. But that does not help me, except make me wish I had been raised in a home like that."

And that is true. For when it comes to entering my earthly family, no matter how badly you may want to join or how much I would like to invite you in, the door is closed. My earthly father had only four sons and one legally adopted daughter. Now he is dead, and it is impossible for him to have any more children or adopt any others. So I cannot have additional brothers and sisters in my blood family. The ranks are closed forever.

But when I talk to you about my spiritual family—which, in many respects is even closer than my blood family—well, that is a different matter. For my spiritual Father is not dead. He does not even sleep. Not only that, even though He had only one Son—an only begotten Son—He is constantly adopting new children into His family. In the adoption process you receive all the privileges and benefits of the bloodline. In fact, you become heirs of God—joint heirs with His Son Jesus Christ. All that is His, is yours. Through Jesus Christ we can know our Father even as Jesus knows Him, and we can become as close to others in the family as I am with my earthly brothers and sister.

The words of the scripture are so strong in this passage that even most Christians have backed off, afraid of becoming blasphemous. But John tells us that "as many as received Him [Jesus Christ] to them gave he power to become the sons of God . . ." (John 1:12). When we become as He is, then we are not only fashioned into His image, but we become—to a real degree—little

Christs. (Which is the literal meaning of the word "Christian.")

Most of us have stopped, in our Christian walk, with that beautiful confession that Jesus is Lord. We pray to Jesus as our intercessor. We thank Jesus as our Savior. We praise Jesus as the worthy Lamb of God. All this is good and proper. But the highest New Testament truth is not that Jesus is Lord—but that God is our Father.

We don't talk a great deal about that, for it smacks, in many fundamental circles, of heresy. I am not promoting the "Fatherhood of God and the brotherhood of man" theology. We cannot legitimately say God is our Father unless we accept His Son, Jesus, as our Lord. But even Jesus told us not to glorify the Son but to glorify the Father in Heaven. Jesus is not the Father. He is, by His own admission, "the way" to the Father. In fact, He is the only way. Through Jesus we now have the privilege of entering the throne room of the Father, communing with Him, loving Him, worshiping Him and abiding with Him.

That's a bit scary, for to know Him means we run the risk of becoming as He is. I knew, when I entered the presence of my earthly father and asked for his advice or opinion on some matter, that I would have to do one of two things—accept it or reject it. And if I rejected his word, it was the same as rejecting him as the authority. There was no in-between.

And so it is with God. If we come into His presence, hear His word, then we must accept or reject Him. God does not make suggestions. Nor does He give options.

The Bible describes God as holy. If we abide in His presence, we, too, must eventually become holy. But very few of us are eager to take on that attribute of God, for, as Wordsworth once said, "The world is too much with us."

This is the reason any kind of "holiness" revival threatens churches and church leaders. It will require, in the long run, that people become holy, too. Separated from the world. Godlike.

Most Christians do not believe God really controls things. They look at their churches and see they are controlled by men. They see the infighting, the divisions, the jockeying for position, the political machinery, the worldly shepherds—and they conclude God cannot be trusted with important matters.

There seem to be two major areas in which Christians have problems with the Father. One is in the area of *concept and control*. The other arises from the fact we see God as a *characteristic* rather than a person.

Most church leaders have a very low concept of God. To relinquish control of their lives, their finances or their churches to God's Spirit would be the equivalent of mayhem and devastation. Most church leaders, unfortunately, operate off a broad basis of insecurity. Just as surveys prove that many doctors who specialize in psychiatry have severe emotional and psychological problems, so many of those who enter the ministry are spiritually insecure. Their entrance into the ministry, submitting themselves to the rigors of seminary study, the forced procedure of living Godly lives, the disciplines of the church—all are ways of seeking something which will fill the inner void where the Holy Spirit seeks to reign.

I was a prime example of this insecurity syndrome. During the years I was the pastor of a denominational church, I prided myself not only on my self-control but on the fact I was in control of the functions and activities of the church organization. Staff meetings, council meetings, deacons meetings and long range planning sessions were all designed to keep matters under control. As a friend of mine once quipped, we were so organized that if the Holy Spirit dropped out of the church we would not miss Him for a year and a half—for we already had the calendar planned that far in advance. At weekly staff meetings we discussed in great detail the order of service, the location of hymns, prayers and announcements—and, most important, how to begin on time and close the service at one minute before noon. Everything was designed to promote order. The services ran like clockwork. And even though we cast disdainful looks at our Episcopal and Catholic acquaintances who ran their services by the age-old tradition of prayer books and liturgy, we were no better. Everything was always in its proper place.

I now understand such over-emphasis on control was evidence of my own emptiness and insecurity. Much as an insecure father will often physically mistreat his children, so I "ran a tight ship." I was always fearful, although I never voiced it to anyone, including myself, that some outside force could take control and wrest my position—which was my place of security—from me. It was this emptiness, of course, which caused my eventual downfall and allowed all sorts of things to rush into the spiritual vacuum of my life. For despite my attempts to control the outer organization, I was helpless to control my own emotions. Thus, as I began my downward slide, all I did was tighten the outer controls on the church. (This, by the way, has the same effect as tightening one's buttocks just before a father administers the razor strap.) But that, too, I now understand, was part of God's purpose and design for my life. For only through pain and suffering does one learn he cannot control God—he can only submit to Him.

Let me recall an incident which happened during the better days of that early ministry which will illustrate the tightness of control. One Sunday morning I entered the sanctuary for our morning worship service, coming through the side door in our weekly "Parade of the Pious." There, just inside the door of the sanctuary, sat a bedraggled looking man, slumped forward in one of the front side pews. I recognized him as a man I had seen a number of times at the local Alcoholics Anonymous meetings. My friend Ed Seymour, the old alcoholic who taught me "applied theology" the first two years after seminary when I had come to that church, had finally persuaded him to come to a morning service. I was glad to see him, but his presence at the front presented a threat to my idea of what an orderly church service should be. The organ was just chiming the hour. (We always began the Parade of the Pious on the second chime which allowed all the platform personages to reach their proper place by the last chime.) I was last in line, of course, since we always entered in ascending order of importance. Now suddenly I was waylaid as this wretch of a man reached out and tugged at my coat sleeve.

My mind was a torrent of emotions. I wanted to stop and talk, but what would happen if I was not standing at the pulpit by the time the organ finished chiming the hour? I had not trained anyone to take over in such an emergency, so I knew that the entire service would come to an embarrassing, silent halt. I could picture the confused look on the face of the minister of music. He was supposed to lead the choir in the call to worship—"The Lord is in His Holy Temple, let all the earth keep silent . . ." But he could not do this until I had stood at the pulpit and motioned for the people to stand and had read the morning scripture. Everything depended on my being up there to make things work.

Yet here was this man, tugging at my coat sleeve. I wondered, in that instant, if the priest and levite who passed by on the other side, in Jesus' story of the good Samaritan, went through this same turmoil.

"Please, pastor," the man said haltingly, "I need help."

I glanced at my old friend Ed Seymour, who had brought this foul-smelling man into the church sanctuary. Ed was sitting beside him, dressed as usual in his rumpled suit with coffee-stained tie. I loved and respected Ed Seymour as much as any man I knew. He had been sober three years and during that time had not only taught me how to fly an airplane but how to walk into a jail and speak to men behind bars without preaching or condemning. But there was no way Ed could understand the mechanics and psychology of an order of service. He was just an old drunk. He knew how to handle an alcoholics' meeting; in fact, he was a master at that. But he had no concept of the necessity for dignity and order in a worship service. So looking at Ed was of no help. He was grinning and nodding. I am sure he expected me to take his drunk buddy right up on the platform with me and ask the people to pray for him.

But I could not. Instead, I put my hand on his shoulder and said, "Glad you're here, Stan. Sit here beside Mr. Ed. At the close of the service, when I give the invitation, step forward, and we'll receive you into the church."

I turned and moved rapidly toward the platform, arriving at the pulpit just in time to ask the people to stand for the invocation as the organ finished chiming the last note at 11 A.M. Inwardly I was relieved. I had handled that rather nicely, I thought.

But when I opened my eyes after the prayer and glanced in the direction of the front side pew, Stan was gone. He never returned. In fact, he resisted all efforts on the part of Mr. Ed to get him back. Shortly afterwards he was jailed and sent out of town on a work gang. We never heard of him again.

It was unthinkable, at that stage of my ministerial career, to believe God could be so brash as to interrupt anything as sacred as a worship service—or that He might want me, instead of asking the people to stand for the invocation, to kneel and surround this poor man in prayer, allowing brothers and sisters to hear his confession and welcome him into the Kingdom. Even though I was nagged by guilt, I was able to justify my decision to ask Stan to wait until the "appropriate time" to accept Christ. It all came because I was in control.

It was a year or so later, during another Sunday morning service, that I got a second taste of the danger of being in control. The hymns had been sung and the offering and special music were over. I had just stood to preach when I saw, in the far back of the auditorium, a man on the back row with his hand raised. For years I had been running scared in the ministry. Any threat to the routine was a personal threat to me. Just as we did not have a place in the order of worship for people to repent at the beginning of the service, neither did we have a place for people with their hand raised. I did not recognize the man and had no idea what he wanted. Fortunately, since he was seated on the back row, only those in the choir and the people on the platform saw him. He was not causing a disturbance; he was just sitting there, dressed in his coat and tie, with his hand raised.

Several months before we had discussed, in the deacons meeting, what we would do in case there was some kind of "disturbance" in the worship service. In particular we were afraid of what might happen if a black person tried to enter our all-white church. This had happened in several locations across the south in the early '60s, and our local white Christians were afraid it just might happen in our community. Black people were still viewed as mentally and spiritually inferior by many southern whites at the time.

"I don't mind 'em as long as they keeps their place," was the typical answer to my urging to reach out to the black community. Fortunately, things have changed radically over the years and blacks and whites now sit together in many of those former bastions of segregation.

But this man, with his hand up, was not black. He was white—like the rest of us. Yet his presence was just as disturbing as had he been of a different race, for nobody ever raised their hand in our church—even to go to the bathroom. When the initial racial scare hit us, the deacons suggested we install a warning system in the church. This consisted of a button on the pulpit which, if pushed, would flash a red light in the vestibule so the ushers could be alerted to a pending problem.

I pushed the button. Within moments two ushers walked through the swinging back doors of the church and spotted the man seated on the back pew with his hand raised. In absolute control, I waited in the pulpit in something which resembled a dramatic pause, while the ushers converged on the man and whispered in his ear. He immediately lowered his hand, and I began my sermon. That morning I chose not to go to the front door to shake hands with the people as they departed, as was my custom. I had no desire to meet or speak to a man who had raised his hand. It was better if I just let him go out with the crowd.

He did. He never returned. To this day I have no idea who he was. Perhaps he had a cramp in his arm and needed to stretch. Perhaps he was praising God—although, frankly, as I think back about those dead services, I cannot imagine anyone getting excited enough to raise his hand in worship, even a visiting Pentecostal. On the other hand, I sometimes wonder if he was a prophet sent from God. Or an angel. Even so, it made little difference, for we had no place in the order of worship for messages from God which emanated from the congregation. Even from prophets. Or angels. For in those days the Spirit was hardly recognized in the service—much less given control.

Last week I spent the day with my editor, Len LeSourd, in his home in Boynton Beach. After lunch we sat for a long time and chatted. For years Len has been an active Presbyterian layman. Recently he has had a vital part in helping establish a new Presbyterian church in South Florida, one of the fastest-growing Presbyterian churches in the nation. But along with such rapid growth have come problems. Hundreds of them. So Len and I sat, comparing notes between his church and mine. We talked about a lot of other situations across the nation, about what was happening in the big denominational circles.

"It seems the entire church is in a stage of ferment," Len concluded.

I thought about that on my way back to Melbourne. New wine, it seems, is always in the stage of ferment. Bubbling. Expanding. If there is not some outlet, some elasticity in the structure around it, it will either cause the structure to split—or it will pop the cork from the container and go foaming across the floor. Either way is messy. A divided church, even though it may bring multiplication of numbers in the long run, is always a sad situation. And to have a pastor ejected because he does not allow the Spirit to take control, is tragic. No wonder pastors and denominational leaders accuse the "Holy Spirit movement" of being divisive. It is. But it is divisive only if the people—individually or corporately— do not allow Him the room to expand their lives, to push out their old walls of tradition and bring them to freshness of discovery, to lift their sights to new vision of understanding, to deepen their roots into the word of God and to move them closer to God's infinite purpose on this finite earth. New wine cannot be contained by old wineskins. It must grow.

A church will never grow spiritually beyond its leadership—and beyond its pastor in particular. But what should a people do when they have been visited by the Holy Spirit and received a new revelation of the nature of God, only to find their pastor reluctant to move, fearful of any kind of movement which might rock the boat? What if he is theologically opposed to the various manifestations which always accompany such a visitation by God? Or worse, what if he is scared because he's emotionally insecure—and afraid to admit it? Speaking from personal experience, I know he must be confronted. Not once, but hundreds of times if necessary, by the sheep of the flock who are determined to move to higher pastures. However, the confrontations must always be in love, never with the threat of rejection. At the same time, since sheep are priests also and therefore as responsible to God as the shepherd, it is often necessary to gang up against him and push him forward, gently prodding him in the right direction. The shepherd, you see, may be dull and uninterested. He sips from his theological tomes, attends his stuffy meetings, prepares his boring sermons and in general is fed by tidbits. On the other hand, the sheep are starving. But their senses are now quickened by the Holy Spirit. They sense there is new grass on the higher slopes, and they know they will die if they remain in the dry valley. So they shove on, hopefully persuading their pastor to go with them, praying he will one day break out of his stiff structure and take active spiritual leadership, going before them into the presence of God as Moses did with the children of Israel, and returning with a shining face to say, "Follow me!" But even if he refuses to move, the sheep must go on. For they, like him, are commanded to "quench not the Holy Spirit." Sad is the pastor who lies in the dust, trampled by sheep who wanted nothing more than for him to lead them.

The second major problem area in our relationship with the Father lies in the area of trust. We do not trust Him because we do not know Him. We see him as a *characteristic* rather than a person. God is holy, we say. But holiness is a characteristic—one open to much interpretation. Yet we force people into our concepts of outward holiness, totally ignoring the fact that holiness is an inner matter—not outer. We force them to dress like our concept of God, speak like our concept of God, and wear their hair the way we think God wears His. Since God would never be caught dead in a movie theater (unless it is to view a Walt Disney film), then we deny ourselves and our children that right. Since we visualize sex for procreation only, we try to make it as unenjoyable as possible and do everything possible to keep references to that dirty act out of the holy places of our lives. And since God is always fully clothed, we abstain from all remarks about nakedness. In short, we draw up our concepts of God according to western culture (flavored with Victorian morality) and, seeing God as a "holy" God, we try to fashion ourselves and those around us in the image of that characteristic. We remain disdainful (yea, sometimes even a bit proud) that it was the "holy" people who burned the reformers and stoned the prophets.

Others see God as the characteristic of love. Imitating this philosophy, flavored with mores garnered from the cesspools of Hollywood and the New York TV studios, we set out to convince the world we no longer have to abide by the law of God—now we live in a dispensation of grace which gives freedom to love and be loved. This understanding of God begets people who demonstrate on the streets in behalf of social justice, who join marches for "gay rights" and "women's lib," who feed the hungry, clothe the naked, and open their arms to every despicable thing which comes down the pike in the name of Jesus. But their character is so raunchy and their behavior so undisciplined, that even the heathen suspect they are poor representatives of God.

Still others have never seen God other than the characteristic of the stern judge. God is a god who punishes sin—and calls on his children to punish it also. Unfortunately, punishing sin invariably involves punishing the sinner also. Thus while those who see God as justice spend much time fighting liquor-by-the-drink, picketing the porno theaters, lobbying in Congress to have prayer returned to public schools, demanding their civil rights and proclaiming that God's chosen people live mainly in the United States, there is often a great lack of love and almost a void when it comes to an understanding of the true meaning of holiness. In short, they are as difficult to be around as the God they seek to portray.

Several months ago I caught an early morning flight from Tampa to Atlanta. The plane was packed. I had a seat on the aisle in the tourist section. Directly across the aisle from me was a distinguished-looking, miserable-looking man. He was dressed in black suit, white shirt, black tie and shiny black shoes. He had a large briefcase in his lap and was busy sorting out papers as soon as we were airborne. I took one look at him and said to myself, *Preacher.*

Moments later he reached into another briefcase under his seat and pulled out a large Bible—the kind with numerous study aids, maps, and an encyclopedia in the back. He pulled down the little tray on the back of the seat and laid his Bible on that—his briefcase still in his lap.

It was too much for my curiosity. Leaning across the aisle, I said, "Glad to see you reading the Bible this morning." I expected him to take the lead and respond.

"Hrumphppp!" he said, looking at me over the top of his horn-rimmed glasses. He quickly returned to his busyness.

I tried once again. "You don't see many people reading the Bible on airplanes."

This time he didn't even respond. Perhaps, I thought, it was because he didn't speak to people wearing dungarees and tennis shoes. However, I suspected it ran far deeper than that.

Shortly the stewardesses were in the aisle serving breakfast trays. Since every seat on the plane was full, and it was a relatively short flight, they were in a hurry. When she got to our row, the stewardess asked the Reverend Miserable if he wanted breakfast. All he did was glance up over the top of his glasses and then continue with his work, flipping through his Bible and shuffling his briefcase full of papers. I assumed he was on his way to some kind of conference and needed to make notes ahead of time. However, it seemed he should have at least had the courtesy to respond with a, "No thank you, I'm a holy man and I don't eat breakfast."

The stewardess just shrugged and asked the two people sitting next to him if they wanted breakfast. They were an older couple; the elderly man sat next to the window and his heavyset wife was in the middle seat next to the preacher. They both beamed at the stewardess and said, "Yes, indeed. We're famished."

The young stewardess smiled and tried to hand them their trays. But she could not get them around or over Reverend Miserable. Twice she tried to hand the trays over him. The elderly couple had trouble reaching up to grasp a tray. Reverend Miserable, obviously irritated by all the activity surrounding his throne, looked first at the stewardess and then at the older couple. He scowled.

"Sir, I cannot reach the people beyond you. Would you mind helping me for a minute so they can have breakfast?" There was a note of exasperation in her voice. I watched as Reverend Miserable leaned back enough so the stewardess could pass the trays over to the elderly couple next to him. Not once, however, did he offer to help. When the couple finally had their trays, he gave them another scowl over his glasses and returned to his holy work.

After breakfast was served, I got up and walked down the aisle of the airplane. When I returned to my seat, I stood for a moment directly behind Reverend Miserable and peered over his shoulder into his briefcase which was still open on his lap. By that time he had put away his Bible and was doing something with his computer—probably figuring out how many years left before the Judgment.

It's amazing how much you can learn about a man from glancing into his briefcase. It was filled, among other things, with brochures about himself. Interestingly enough, his name was not Reverend Miserable. On top of the papers was a schedule of the conference he was to attend in Indiana. His name was listed as one of the speakers. There was also a little biographical sketch which told which school he graduated from, which church he had been associated with, how many buses he had in his bus ministry and all the places he had served—that is, if you can call such a life style one of service.

I took my seat and remained in deep thought. Here was a man who had been trained from early childhood, through his fundamentalist college and Bible school, and by his present associations, that God was a god of justice. It exuded from him and made him unapproachable, stiff, unbending and stern. When the plane landed, I let him push on ahead. I didn't want to be close to him. Nor, did I suspect, would other sinners be attracted to him.

I wondered, as I walked through the airport, what kind of god I exuded.

How easy it is to fall into the trap of seeing God as a characteristic, then imitating that characteristic to the exclusion of all others. Ministries take on the favorite characteristic of God as taught by the minister. As a result, we have developed, even inside the church, a number of cults. We have the Prosperity Cult, the Deliverance Cult, the Submission Cult, the Praise Cult, the Fall-Down-Under-the-Power Cult, the Water-Baptism-in-Jesus'-Name-Only Cult, the Discipleship Cult, the What-You-Say-Is-What-You-Get Cult, the Suffering-for-Jesus Cult. On and on.

None of these are wrong. None are complete either. God is all of them and more. If we stop at any stage, pause at any doorway of life and do not enter in and take the whole gospel, then we have limited God and created Him in our own image. God is more than a characteristic. He is a person. Like my dad, He has sides I'll never see but which others see vividly.

How desperately we need to know Him as Father, remembering there are more sides to Him than we will ever recognize. To us He may be love and grace. But to our enemies He may be over behind the bleachers, roaring vengeance and causing them to quake.

The prophet Nahum gives us brilliant insight into this other side of God, helping us enlarge our vision and understand there is so much about Him which is incomprehensible.

Once before God had sent a prophet to the city of Nineveh. The first to go was the reluctant prophet Jonah. God said He loved the Assyrians, however, and was eager to bless them. But He could not bless them unless they repented of their evil as individuals and as a nation. So the Lord sent the Hebrew prophet Jonah to the capital city of Assyria to call the people to repentance. They did repent, from the king to the lowest peasant. God honored their repentance and blessed the nation for 150 years. But after five generations, the nation once again slipped into idolatry and wickedness. They became the destroyer of the people of God, the archenemy of the people of Judah. Once again God sent a prophet. Nahum went to speak the word of God to the wicked nation. Only this time it was not a call to repentance, it was a cry of vengeance. God was angry at the Assyrians for humiliating and destroying His chosen people, Israel, and promised to destroy them.

God is jealous, and the Lord revengeth; the Lord revengeth, and is furious; the Lord will take vengeance on his adversaries, and he reserveth wrath for his enemies. The Lord is slow to anger, and great in power, and will not at all acquit the wicked: the Lord hath his way in the whirlwind and in the storm, and the clouds are the dust of his feet. He rebuketh the sea, and maketh it dry, and drieth up all the rivers . . . The mountains quake at him, and the hills melt, and the earth is burned at his presence, yea, the world, and all that dwell therein. Who can stand before his indignation? and who can abide in the fierceness of his anger? his fury is poured out like fire, and the rocks are thrown down by him. The Lord is good, a stronghold in the day of

105

trouble; and he knoweth them that trust in him. But with an overrunning flood he will make an utter end of the place [of the wicked] . .

Behold upon the mountains the feet of him that bringeth good tidings, that publisheth peace! O Judah, keep thy solemn feasts, perform thy vows: for the wicked shall no more pass through thee; he is utterly cut off (Nahum 1:2–8, 15).

Here is our Father standing behind the bleachers with His finger against the chest of the enemy. No more shall they curse and humiliate and destroy the children of God. This time the Assyrians were not just dealing with children, they were face to face with the Almighty God, the Creator of the universe, and His wrath was mighty to behold. Yet that night, back in the Father's house, God had only words of peace and comfort for His children, Judah.

God has two faces—one which is presented to those who would harm and destroy His children, and one He presents to His children. So Nahum is a horrible book, but it is accurate. For in it we see the other side of God, a God of terror to His enemies, who destroys them with His mighty arm and the flame of His wrath. But at the same time, who reaches out in tender mercy to those who would trust Him—to those who would turn to Him for help.

In our desire to discover the person of God, we need to make an occasional trip behind the bleachers and see Him standing against our enemies. Who are the enemies of God's children? Disease. Deception. Sin. Demonic forces. Satan. When these come against the people of God, our loving heavenly Father builds up a storm, and He rides that storm with the host of Heaven against the entrenched forces, and He grinds the seed of Satan to the earth, and He utterly destroys those things which would oppose Him. He is God, and there is no force in the world capable of destroying Him or destroying His church.

There are occasions when I want to step into all the pulpits of the world, to cry from every steeple, to stand on the balconies and stages of the nations and shout: "Lift your vision. Know Him! Do not be afraid He will destroy you. He wants to take over your life and bring you meaning and purpose."

We have a great God. We do not need to fear what is happening in His Kingdom. We need to be willing to move out beyond our own control so He can be in total control. God does not have to be convinced to be separated from His blessings. He wants to bless all His people. He wants to bless every church. And in the midst of the blessings, He will protect His children from evil.

Moses came outside the tabernacle, lifted his hands in the air, and cried with a great voice, "Let God arise! and His enemies be scattered!"

That cry still echoes through the corridors of time as the enemies of God are scattered before the mighty power of His Holy Spirit. That is the reason I am not afraid. To be sure, there is tension and stress in every situation. The church is indeed in ferment. But it is a healthy fermentation as the yeast of the Holy Spirit permeates every facet of humanity and calls us to change and growth.

There is no fear when we approach God through His Son, Jesus. God is our daddy. He loves us. He is protecting us. And even though His hand may be against our backside on occasion, it is not there to punish but to direct. His voice is constantly saying, "This is the way, walk ye in it."

And "the way" is always a venture controlled by the Holy Spirit.

VII

Abiding in the Shadow

I was on the middle leg of a four-week nationwide tour, going from city to city to promote one of my books on TV and radio. It had been a lonely tour. In some of the cities I had made contact with old friends who had met me at the airport and chauffeured me around. Now I was coming up on a blank weekend. I finished my last television interview in Seattle on Friday afternoon and was free until Sunday night when I had another TV interview in Las Vegas. Las Vegas is one of those cities where powerful spiritual forces are at work. I had been there twice before and each time felt under severe attack from the moment I arrived until the moment I left. I did not look forward to going back. At the same time, my loneliness was catching up with me. Everyone on the plane seemed excited. Very few people go to Las Vegas on the weekend for any purpose other than gambling, entertainment or recreation. This planeload of people was no different, and I seemed to be the only man without a beautiful woman on his arm. It only increased my loneliness. I had been away from home too long.

The feeling continued after I reached Las Vegas. I called my only Christian contact, but he was cool. Preoccupied. I shrugged it off, rented a car, and decided to drive out of town. I did not relish the thought of submitting myself to the garish temptations which parade the strip of America's best known center for gambling and prostitution. Even though both professions are repulsive to me, nevertheless I did not feel strong enough to expose my life to the spiritual forces at work, especially in my lonely situation. So in my rented car I drove north toward Utah—and Zion National Park.

Ever since I was a small boy and my father brought back little 3-D slides of Zion Park, the kind you could look at through a viewscope, I had wanted to visit. But not as a tourist. I wanted to do it at some season of the year when the park was deserted. The red and purple rocks, the towering cliffs, the high mountain trails all had a special attraction to me. Besides, Saturday was my birthday—March 28—and the park would be deserted. What better way to spend it than walking.

Spending the night alone in a small border town, I rose early the next morning and drove into the empty canyon, parked the car, crossed the little swinging bridge over a rushing river and started my climb up the steep path along the side of the mountain. As far as I could tell, I was the only human being in the park. Even the ranger house at the entrance was closed. Usually there was snow in the high mountains, but this was a brilliant, cool day. The sky was cloudless and azure blue, giving stark relief to the towering red, gray and lavender natural stone monuments. It is the only place I have ever been in America which equals the grandeur and awesomeness of the Sinai—but on a much smaller scale.

I walked alone, breathing the clear Utah air, lifting my face to catch the bright sunshine. For two weeks I had been traveling, going from one city to another, spending the nights in lonely motel rooms and the days rushing breathlessly from one television studio to another, from one radio talk show to another. Then hurrying to catch my plane to the next city. The loneliness which had almost consumed me on the crowded plane and which had followed me as I drove out of Las Vegas to Utah, soon disappeared as I began to talk to God in conversational tones.

I walked for two hours along the narrow mountain path high above the rushing river. There was not another soul in the valley below. I stopped and sat on an outcropping of rock, 500 feet above the floor of the canyon. The only sound was the soft rustle of the wind as it blew among the gnarled and weathered spruce trees rooted deeply in the rocky soil. Starting back, I began talking to God about the deep things in my heart. It made me feel good to confess my flaws out loud, to tell Him of the deep burdens of my heart, to intercede for those dearer to me than life itself—family and friends. Finally, having cleared all the problem areas from my heart, I said aloud: "What I really want more than anything else is to know You. I want to know You. I want to know You."

Then I was quiet. Walking. Listening. Deep in my heart I heard Him respond. "You are not ready for that. You cannot know Me until you first abide with Me."

I felt sad and fought back the tears, so real was His presence. Yet I understood the spiritual principle involved. You cannot know someone unless you live with them. Like Martha, I was too busy working in the kitchen to sit in the living room.

I have many friends in Melbourne and others I call my friends across the world. But I *know* only a few of them. I cannot know a person unless I have eaten at his table, played with his children, entered into his life and his problems. I know a lot *about* a lot of people, but I *know* only a few. That's the reason I am constantly probing, asking questions, trying to get beneath the surface of those I associate with—for I want to know them and am eager for them to know me. Jackie knows if I spend the night at someone's house I will invariably go through their closet before the night is over, rummaging through all the stuff on the shelf, opening boxes and drawers. If I use their bathroom I will peek in the medicine cabinet, open the linen closet and look under the sink. Why? Because I want to know people, and the only way to do that is to get beneath the guest towels and fancy pillowcases and see how they live when I'm not around. You can discover a great deal about people by opening their refrigerator and checking their bookshelf; for what people eat and read is a good barometer to their personality and character.

But you cannot know God by just opening His closet or reading His Book. For God is immortal, and we are made of different stuff. Simply going to church and hearing about Him, taking the sacraments, singing His hymns, reading the Bible—even if you memorize it in its entirety—will not open the door of knowledge to God. That comes only when you abide in His presence. But such a relationship is not formed overnight. It takes a lifetime. And beyond.

The prodigal son—and his elder brother—lived with their father all their lives, yet neither of them knew him. When Moses was on Mount Sinai with God, the Lord told him to hide himself in the cleft of the rock and He would pass by. But all God revealed was His backside. Moses had not done enough abiding.

Nor have I.

So as I walked that lonely mountain trail in Zion National Park, my hands raised in praise, my voice crying out in the wilderness seeking to know Him, His answer continued in my heart, "You are asking for that which you are not prepared to receive. You don't even know the people around you. You barely know your wife and children. How can you know Me? All you can do is obey Me."

Behind me, as I walked and prayed, I heard footsteps. I was momentarily startled, for I hadn't seen anyone else on the mountain path that entire morning. Embarrassed, I quickly lowered my hands and turned around. There was no one there. I could see far back up the trail, and it was empty. Only the clouds, the sky and the magnificent red and purple mountains. I started to walk again, this time reluctant to pray out loud or raise my hands. Again I heard the soft *crunch, crunch, crunch* of feet on the gravel behind me.

Once again I paused and looked. The path was empty. I smiled. Perhaps it was my imagination. Perhaps it was not. I turned and started on down the path, my hands once again raised in praise, my face up, catching the full rays of the early afternoon sun. Deep in my heart a passage of scripture, once committed to memory but long forgotten, came to life.

And though the Lord give you the bread of adversity, and the water of affliction, yet shall not thy teachers be removed into a corner any

112

more, but thine eyes shall see thy teachers: and thine ears shall hear a word behind thee, saying, This is the way, walk ye in it, when ye turn to the right hand, and when ye turn to the left" (Isaiah 30:20–21).

I would never see Him—at least this side of Glory—for His face is too much for me to behold. To His enemies He bares His arm, but His children hear only the soft sound of His voice behind saying, "This is the way, walk ye in it."

The higher way of guidance is not to follow the Lord but to go before Him as He directs. He longs to bring His children into such maturity that they can walk alone. He does not desire to hold us with a tight rein as a horse or mule but with freedom, guided only by His eye upon us. If at any moment we misstep, if our ear is tuned to His voice, He will speak softly and say, "No, not that way, this is the way—walk ye in it."

We need to tune our spiritual ears to the voice behind us.

The loveable Dutch woman, Corrie ten Boom, once taught me something about abiding with God. She was in our home while I was working on *Tramp for the Lord*. One afternoon we took a few hours off and went down the coast to see our old friends, Will and Eloise Orr, with whom she had stayed on a previous visit. After chatting a while, we walked out into Dr. Orr's beautiful yard overlooking the Indian River. We had reached a difficult place in the book, and our personalities had crossed. I thought she should go in one direction, but she was determined the book should head in another. I was terribly frustrated, and in the midst of this bread of adversity and water of affliction, I finally confronted her.

"Tante Corrie, you do a great deal of talking about walking in the light, but I don't see any light now. All you have done is walk over me in this matter. I want to go one way, and you are a stubborn old Dutch woman who insists we go another. I don't think you're walking in the light at all."

It was a difficult thing for me to say to a woman whom much of Christendom revered as not only a living legend but as a literal saint. She looked at me, gave me her old Dutch smile, and shared with me the secret of Psalm 91:1, "He that dwelleth in the secret

113

place of the most High shall abide under the shadow of the Almighty."

"There comes a time," she said, "when you don't walk in the light anymore."

"I do not understand."

"Well, you don't walk in the light when you are walking through the valley of the shadow, right? There is no light in the valley. All there is in the valley is the promise of His presence."

I understood that principle. I knew the artificiality of lighthearted smiles and happy hallelujahs when a person is going through a period of deep darkness, grief or repentance. There are few genuine hallelujahs when all the lights go out.

"Neither can you walk in the light when you are *abiding* under the shadow," Corrie said, looking deep into my face. Then she shared a little gem which has changed my life. "The closer you get to God, the less you understand Him. But the more you believe Him."

Months after Corrie had gone, that nugget stayed with me. We are called to walk, not by sight, but by faith. The man who knows God nominally, who has a hat-tipping experience with Him, who meets Him twice a year at Easter and Christmas—that man can tell you volumes about the nature and character of God. The same is true with many learned theology professors and puffed-up preachers who spend long hours with books but seldom come into His presence. They, too, have much to say about the God they've never met. But come into the presence of a person who abides under the shadow, and all that person can say is, "Shhhh. Be still and abide." He knows very little. He just believes.

You can write a systematic theology, but you cannot diagram God. Neither can you draw out a schematic pattern of His Kingdom. But he that dwells in the secret place of the most High, who abides under the shadow of His wings, does not walk by sight, he walks by faith. And that cannot be diagrammed—it can only be demonstrated.

Sometimes I wonder whether the abundance of books and articles and sermons about faith is not an unhealthy sign. True, the Bible has much to say about faith. But the faith spoken of has no intrinsic

114

value; it merely links us with the Lord. Sometimes the teachers of faith leave the impression that faith is more important than the object of our faith. As a result, many people worship the promise rather than the Promiser. But it is not the promise of God which heals; it is His presence. Neither the quantity nor the quality of our faith matters. What is of primary importance is the object of our faith. To take our faith apart, much as a doctor does to a corpse during a post mortem, either indicates our faith is already dead—or soon will be. The sooner we leave it alone and start demonstrating it, rather than diagraming it, the sooner it will come into being. The young man who is constantly trying to figure out whether he is in love or not, is sure to destroy whatever love he may have—and will surely discourage any young lady to whom he may be drawn or attracted. After all, who wants her emotions analyzed? Emotions, like faith, are to be experienced—not blue-printed.

It is easy to be deceived in this matter. It would seem the greatest believers are the ones who speak much about their faith, who are always preaching and writing about faith, analyzing it, praying about it, exhorting others to have it and bragging about how much their faith produced for them. The fact is, such conduct actually reveals a sick faith, an academic rather than an active faith. That is why God chooses the foolish over the wise, the babe instead of the prudent. Those who trust God most seldom say much about it. At times they seem unenthusiastic, even unresponsive. When approached by those anxiously wanting more faith, they often seem blunt. They live it rather than talk it.

Some years ago our oldest son came into our bedroom one evening and sat on the edge of the bed, distressed. "I don't know whether I love you as much as I should," he said. "I want to love you. I think I love you. I know I'm supposed to love you. But I don't think I love you enough. How much should I love you?"

We had a long discussion, far into the night, and he finally left feeling he didn't need to do any more than he was doing—unless it was try to obey a bit more. The very fact he was worried about his love for us was sufficient reason to prove his love was adequate.

Across the years his love has matured—and grown far more spontaneous. It is now unstudied and natural. And that is what makes it precious.

One does not get love by taking stock of himself or attending lectures. And the same is true with faith. The people who were blessed most by Jesus when He was on earth were the simple people. They had no time for Bible conferences. They did not send Him offerings on a regular basis to increase their faith, they did not spend hours listening to tapes and making notes on Scripture references, they did not repeat various "promise verses" over and over each morning to increase their faith: they simply believed Jesus, walked with Him, and that was all. The ones who missed His deepest blessings were the smart folks who had to analyze everything He said.

Vance Havner, spicy old Baptist preacher, used to tell the story of the mother bear who told her cub, "Shut up and walk!" when he wanted to know which foot to put forward first. It's a perfect illustration of faith. If we waited until we understood, it wouldn't be faith. Faith doesn't wait until things are just right or until things feel right; it just does.

Much of what we call "faith" is merely irreverent brashness. Healing, like joy, does not come from the promise but from the Presence. It does not depend upon our faith but upon His faithfulness. His command to us is not "have more faith." Rather it is to come before Him with clean hands and a pure heart. In this position of obedience and repentance, beyond our own control, He takes control of us—and of our circumstances.

In the tabernacle of Moses, when the smoke from the sin offering went up from the altar, there was joy throughout the camp. However, after the people settled in Canaan, they compromised their obedience, and God said the smoke of sacrifice had become a stench in His nostrils. Obedience, Samuel told Saul, was better than sacrifice.

But that is always the danger when men grow strong, their ministries grow popular and miracles become commonplace. There is an advantage in being a minority, numbered among the persecuted: for in that stance you must depend upon God as your source. It is, as Havner once quipped, only when Christianity moves from the realm of the persecuted to that of the popular that the power goes off.

It doesn't take much to get started if you want to believe in a God of miracles. Just look to Him. Walk with Him. Commune with Him. Read His Word. Occupy your thoughts with Him. And suddenly you're a faith person. It's His presence which makes it all possible.

When I first started writing this book, a year ago, we had only two of our five children left at home. The other three were students at Oral Roberts University. That left our 17-year-old son, Tim, and our 14-year-old daughter, Sandy, at home. Any time you mix this kind of brother-sister combination you have potential dynamite. Our case was no exception.

Shortly after we moved into our big house in the country, Jackie and I were invited out for a dinner party. Sandy was still not too happy over our move out of the city. The sound of whippoorwills, crickets, and frogs did not give her the security she had in the subdivision with street lights, honking horns and a nearby police station. However, we assured her we would not be far away and left the phone number of the home where we were visiting. Besides, her big brother Tim was there to protect her.

At 10 P.M. the phone rang at our friends' house where we were having dinner. It was Sandy calling for me. "Come home!" she almost screamed into the receiver. "Come home, quick!"

I was able to calm her enough to find out nothing serious had happened, but she was, for some reason, terrified. We quickly excused ourselves and rushed back to the house. Every light in the house was on as we pulled up in the driveway. And every door was locked. Peering through the den window, we could see Sandy sitting on the sofa, staring straight ahead, a huge butcher knife in her hand.

She finally let us in and fell into our arms, shaking with fear. "Honey, what in the world is wrong?"

Then she told us what had happened. Shortly after it got dark

117

and all the night sounds were tuned in symphony, she went to the den to watch television. Our son, Tim, who is the fuse on the dynamite, had sneaked upstairs and gone out on the balcony above the den windows. He had taken a bed sheet, let it down over the balcony and then moved it slowly back and forth across the outside den windows. Sandy, sitting on the sofa watching TV, saw the white, ghostly apparition and panicked. Rushing through the house, she turned on all the lights and locked the doors— including the door to the balcony. When Tim realized he had been locked outside, he came down the back stairs and with his finger wrote in the dust on the windowpane, "I'm going to get you."

Returning to the den, Sandy saw the message on the dust and went into shock—calling us on the phone and screaming for us to get home as fast as we could.

It was a precarious situation. While Jackie comforted our daughter I went outside to find Tim. He was sitting on the balcony, doubled over in laughter. I had to admit it was a pretty good trick and chuckled with him. Then I reminded him that if 17-year-old boys were big enough to pull a stunt like that, they were certainly of the right age to be spanked. He didn't think that was too funny, but after a long conversation he understood my point of view and submitted himself to the belt—in Sandy's presence.

It was almost midnight before the house was settled and quiet. Tim was in bed, still chuckling, although his bottom was burning from the strap. Jackie had just tucked Sandy in bed and headed down the hall to our bedroom. I told her to leave Sandy's light on for a moment while I talked to her.

She was lying on her back, only her head poking out from under the covers, her eyes, still moist, looking at the ceiling. "Honey, let me pray with you."

"Okay, Dad, but please don't turn out the light."

"Sweetheart, it's midnight. It's time to go to sleep."

"Daddy, just don't turn out the light. Please."

"Sandy, you know it was only Tim moving a sheet back and

forth. And he was the one who wrote that stupid message on the windowpane. And he's already been punished. Now it's time to go to sleep."

"I know, Daddy. But please leave the light on tonight."

I sat on the side of the bed and prayed with her, then got up and started out the door. "Please, Daddy," she said. I looked back at her pleading eyes. "Honey, I'm going to turn out the light." I flicked the switch and then came back into the darkened room, pulled back the covers on her bed and quietly crawled in beside her. She reached over, put her arm around my chest and whispered, "Thanks, Dad," and drifted off to sleep. She didn't need the light. All she needed was her daddy.

The only thing necessary to stand the bread of adversity and the water of affliction is the presence of the Father. I can walk through the valley of the shadow of death and not fear—for "Thou art with me." I can handle anything incomprehensible, any calamity, any disappointment—just as long as His rod and staff are there to give me strength and comfort.

When Jesus appeared the second time in the room where the disciples were gathered following His resurrection, Thomas, who had not been there for the first encounter, was present. Earlier Thomas had doubted, telling the other men he found it impossible for Jesus to have come back from the dead. This time he could see with his own eyes. Seeing, he cried out, "My Lord and my God!"

Jesus' response to this man who needed proof was classic—and still speaks to those of us who must walk by faith alone:

Thomas, because thou hast seen me, thou hast believed: blessed are they that have not seen, and yet have believed (John 20:29).

That is what "abiding" is all about.

The Holy Spirit is in the business of weaning us from bottles that we might eat meat, strengthening us so that we no longer have to lean on the crutch of knowledge but may walk alone in the power of faith. He wants to bring us upward to that place of spiritual maturity where we no longer have to explain God in terms

119

of systems or formulas, but rather we are satisfied to know Him as our heavenly Father. For there will come a time, said the prophet Jeremiah, when there will be no more need for knowledge, nor shall we need teachers to say to every man his brother, know the Lord: "For they shall all know me . . . I will put my law in their inward parts, and write it in their hearts . . ." (Jeremiah 31:34, 33).

That day is now, as the Holy Spirit not only etches the law of God upon our hearts but ushers us into the presence of the heavenly Father where we may, once again, walk with Him in the cool of the Garden.

My friend, Peter Lord, pastor of the Park Avenue Baptist Church in Titusville, Florida, is one of the few men I know who has designed his life so his first priority is to abide with God. As a result, he is constantly probing those of us around him to realign our priorities. Last year Peter and I joined our old friend Mickey Evans on a three-day hunting and camping trip together in the Everglades. Each of us brought a son to share in the time of fellowship. One afternoon Peter and I sat under an oak tree while our sons wandered off into a deep hammock looking for wild turkey. Peter, who came to the United States from Jamaica, began his usual spiritual probing.

"Don't give me your answers," Peter said. "Just think about them as I ask you five questions."

Peter's first question was this:

Why did God make you? I knew what he was driving at. He wanted me to define why I was here. What was the reason for my creation? What was my primary reason for being on earth? If the primary purpose of a pen is to write, if the primary purpose of a chair is to provide seating, if the primary purpose of a trombone is to make music—then what was my primary purpose for being on earth? I made a mental note—true to the Westminster Confession: "I am here to glorify God and enjoy him forever."

Second: *What is the thing you love more than anything else?* I was tempted to give a religious answer, but I knew better. One of the best ways to test your greatest love is to determine what you can't do without. I have a friend whose greatest love is his head of hair. He won't even let his elders put their hands on his

120

head for fear they'll mess up his hair. I did not think I was that vain. Inwardly I answered: "My greatest love is my family."

Peter's third question: *What is your greatest fear?* Again, I was tempted to give a religious answer about being delivered from fear—but that's just not so. In fact, everyone is afraid of something. My greatest fear, I thought, was losing my family and being left without their love.

Fourth: *What is your greatest ambition?* Deeply spiritual people are always ambitious people. Not worldly or egotistical ambition but an ambition sanctified and restored to its proper dimension. Peter was asking about my goal in life. That was easy. For years, ever since I started writing professionally, I yearned to write a book that would touch the world for Jesus Christ.

Finally, Peter asked: *Why do you want God?* That took more thinking than the rest. He was asking, in essence, what I expected to gain by being a Christian. That was easy: I wanted God so He could help me accomplish my goal for Him—for without Him I was nothing.

All my answers seemed sound. At least I seemed to have my spiritual pyramid down pat: God first, family next, career last.

"If your answer to question number one is not the same as your answer to question number four, you are a mixed-up person," Peter said matter-of-factly.

He continued. "If God made you to harvest apples, and you are busy planting oranges, you are going to be confused when it comes time to pick the fruit."

"But I said my reason for being on earth was to glorify God and enjoy Him forever," I said.

"That's fine," Peter answered. "Then your greatest ambition better be to glorify God and enjoy Him forever."

But I had not said that. I had said my ambition was to do something for Him, rather than to abide in Him—to have fellowship with Him. Slowly it dawned on me. I am here on this earth for no other reason but to have communion with Him and to renew that wonderful relationship that took place in the Garden of Eden when Adam walked alone with God in the cool of the evening.

If I have any ambition other than that, I am missing God's purpose for my life. If I have been placed on this earth to abide in God, then my greatest ambition should be to have fellowship with Him.

Peter continued: "Your answer to question number two ought to be the same as your answer to question number three."

Again I was trapped. I had the right sequence, but the wrong answers. If my purpose for being on earth is to abide in God, then my greatest love should be the person of the Father—not my wife, children or my ministry. Likewise, my greatest fear should be the fear of losing that precious fellowship with God. Paul said that was the thing he feared most, that after preaching the Gospel, he himself might become shipwrecked and lose fellowship with God. He had seen it happen in a number of his associates. "For Demas," he said, "hath forsaken me, having loved this present world . . ." (2 Timothy 4:10). King David prayed so eloquently in Psalm 51, "Cast me not away from thy presence; and take not thy holy spirit from me." If God has placed us on earth to have fellowship with Him and to abide in Him, then our greatest love must be for Him, and our greatest fear should be losing that fellowship.

"I will not ask you how you answered question five," Peter said. "But if you said you wanted God for any other reason than the fact He *is* God, then you are a materialist and an idolator."

He needed to say no more. I was cut to the bone. I had said I wanted God to help me accomplish something I wanted to do for Him—notably, to write a book for which He would get the glory, and I would get the money. That put me in the position of the bomber pilot in World War II who coined the slogan: "God is my co-pilot." Yet I don't want to fly with a man who has God in the co-pilot's seat. I want to fly with a fellow who is co-pilot to God. Too long I had been in the position of giving orders to God, telling Him to go and fetch, so to speak. As I look back over my life and all its problems, I see they all began when I saw myself flying in the captain's seat—with God relegated to crew status or perhaps strapped in a passenger's seat (first-class section, of course). In fact, there had been times when I had taken off without Him, telling Him I would be back in a few hours (or however long it would take to fulfill my selfishness) and would renew acquaintances then.

Many people want God in order to be healed, to be happy, to get out of debt. Others, like myself, may want Him to help out in their ministry. All are unworthy and secondary motives. I must want Him because He is God.

Why do I want my wife? Because she is a good cook? A good mother? A good sex partner? Because she scratches my back when it itches, washes my dirty underwear, answers the phone, gets me out of trouble? But what if she were physically incapacitated? Would I want her then? Not if my reasons were any of the above. I must want her because she is my wife. And so with God.

I have grown cautious about giving God directions—even directions to heal, mend broken families, help folks with finances or give them power for ministry. For years I looked upon God as my servant, my helper, rather than my Lord. I asked His help with various projects rather than submitting myself to His will. I gave Him directions, and I had even been guilty of shouting His promises back at Him in an attempt to blackmail Him into action—when I should have been prostrating myself before Him in grateful submission.

There is nothing wrong with recounting the promises of God when we pray. But we need to remember it is not God who forgets—it is we who have forgotten the promises. Thus mentioning the promises of God when we pray is for *our* benefit—not His. God is not a servant for us to order around. He is Lord of the universe and we bow before Him. He controls our lives and we must want Him because He is—and for no other reason.

My old friend and first publisher, Dan Malachuk, introduced me to Kathryn Kuhlman back in 1969. She was searching for someone to write her second book. I had just finished *Run Baby Run* and had become intrigued by the uniqueness of this woman evangelist whose methods were so radically different from my own. After several days together, she invited me to stay over in Pittsburgh and attend her regular Friday morning "miracle service" at the Carnegie Library on Pittsburgh's north side. It was one of the most mind-boggling experiences of my life. I arrived a full three hours before the service was to start, and there were already thousands of people thronging the doors, packing the steps of the building and blocking the street. After the doors opened and the people pushed inside, there were still a thousand people left outside trying to get in.

It must have been this way when Jesus walked through Galilee, I thought, as I noticed the sick, the lame and the crippled who had come hoping to be healed. I was able to squeeze inside the building and lean against the back wall of the auditorium. The room was packed, including the balconies. The sick were mingled with the well. It was my first time, ever, to be in such a meeting, and I was almost overwhelmed by the press of humanity—and by the awesome sense of faith and expectancy which permeated the room. Coming from a Baptist heritage where not only were miracles and healings relegated to the first century but where women preachers were strictly forbidden, this first service was a deep, soul-shattering experience.

I wanted to believe it was true. I wanted to believe that God still healed as He did when Jesus was here. I wanted to believe all those words I had been reading in the Bible, words which only recently had come alive to me following my own personal encounter with the Holy Spirit. But there was so much doubt. Yet how could I deny these people? I had already spoken to several who gave dramatic testimony of healings at previous services. Nothing could keep them away ever again. And how could I defend my old position where the pews were half empty and the people half dead, compared to the life and vitality that flooded that room?

There was a man standing next to me in a police captain's uniform. About halfway through the three-hour service, Miss Kuhlman pointed toward the back of the auditorium and said, "The Holy Spirit is moving in great power back there." This burly policeman, who had been standing at attention through the entire service, gave a little gasp and fell to the floor. I thought he had died, but the people around us simply raised their hands and started saying things like, "Praise the Lord! Hallelujah!" Later I discovered the reality of the experience of being "slain by the Holy Spirit" myself. But that morning it was awesome, breathtaking. The policeman slowly climbed back to his feet, his lips moving in quiet praise, and took his stance beside me.

Even as I was watching all this take place around me, I noticed nearby a beautiful young black-haired woman standing against the side wall. She was holding a small child in her arms, perhaps eight or nine months old. The child had a horribly deformed head. I could not tell whether the baby was a boy or girl, for the head was almost twice normal size. I tried to pull my eyes away from the pathetic sight of the beautiful mother and her small child, but I could not. I began to pray, *Oh, God, please heal that child. God, if you don't do anything else in this meeting, I pray you heal that child.*

Then I did something I have long since regretted. I began to bargain with God. Murmuring half out loud, I prayed, "Lord, if you will heal that child, I will stand on every street corner in America and speak of your greatness. I will tell strangers. I will go into the churches. I will write books. I will proclaim for all the world to hear that you are a God who still does miracles. Please, Lord, let me see it with my eyes so I may believe."

For the rest of the service my eyes were fixed on that tiny baby, its head lolling on the mother's shoulder. Occasionally I would catch my breath as I thought I saw the head shrinking in size. I was prepared to shout, even prepared to fall prostrate to the floor as the policeman had done. But it did not happen. The service closed, and the mother took her child and made her way through the crowd until she was lost from sight.

It took me months to recover from that. I had laid my life on the line, as seriously as I had ever done before. I had made God a promise. It took me a long time to realize that man is not allowed to make conditional promises to God. Instead, God makes conditional promises to man. It is God who tells us, "If you will, then I will . . ." Not we who tell Him. It slowly became apparent to me that God could have let me see that miracle—and I have seen many since that time—and then I would have gone out and become His spokesman. But how much better to go out and tell the world about God's power, about His ability to control lives, when I have not seen but only believed. How much better to walk by faith rather than by sight. How much better to abide in Him and let the signs and wonders follow—as He deems fit.

I am not a healer, although I have seen people healed. I am not a miracle worker. But I have seen miracles. Many of them. But it no longer bothers me when I pray for someone to be healed, and they are not. The older I grow, the less I know. But I love Him. And I am available. The results—and the glory—belong to Him.

All God requires is that I become a seed that falls into the ground and dies.

> But you will not mind the roughness nor the steepness of the way,
> Nor the chill, unrested morning, nor the searness of the day;
> And you will not take a turning to the left nor to the right,
> But go straight ahead, nor tremble at the coming of the night,
> For the road leads home.

Author Unknown

VIII

How to Let Your Dreams Come True

Be delighted with the Lord. Then He will give you all your heart's desires (Psalm 37:4, TLB).

Edwin Markham once said, that everything in which we glory was once a dream. Everyone has at least one basic dream—something you believe God has laid on your heart, something that has not yet come to pass, but which you fervently believe will happen one day.

All great things are born in dreams. Art. Music. Architecture. Family. Relationships. Even books. All started with a hope, a glint in the eye, a desire in the heart. To the believer whose life has moved into the Spirit's control, the fulfillment of dreams is a profound venture.

Some have already experienced the realization, the fulfillment of their dream. They are the happy ones. The Bible is filled with stories of happy people. These are people who, despite their hardships and sufferings, realized happiness by the fulfillment of their dreams. Hannah was a mother without children who dreamed and prayed for a child. She was ridiculed not only by her husband, Elkanah, but by the priest Eli. But her dream came true, and she gave the world Samuel. Ruth lost the husband of her youth and found herself in a strange land, forced to glean from the fields in order to live. But her desire for a man to love was fulfilled in Boaz, and that union produced men like Jesse and David and finally the Messiah Himself. The Apostle Paul, beaten, imprisoned, condemned to death, wrote back to his friend Timothy that not only had he fought a good fight, but all his dreams had been fulfilled. He was a happy man. And I love to picture old Simeon. For years he had come to the Temple in Jerusalem believing he would see the Savior of Israel. Then on a day like all other days, he suddenly looks up and sees a young teen-age mother holding an eight-day-old baby in her arms, awaiting her turn to have the baby circumcised. And Simeon approaches in awe, reaches out gently, and whispers for only Mary to hear: "Mine eyes have seen thy salvation . . . a light to lighten the Gentiles, and the glory of thy people Israel" (Luke 2:30, 32). His dream had come true.

But to most of us the fulfillment of our dream is still far off. My friend and fellow elder, Herman Riffel, says happy people are those who know they are at least moving toward the fulfillment of their dream. The unhappy, frustrated ones are those who feel their dream has passed them by or that what they long for is impossible. They are the ones who believe life is only a cruel trick, designed to make a mockery of the desires of our heart.

All great men have had their dreams, for dreams are the stuff of which life is made. Take the dreamers out of our civilization, and the entire structure of history tumbles to the ground.

Joseph was a dreamer. Despite his foolishness, his dreams finally came to pass. Moses dreamed of freedom for his people. Joshua dreamed of a nation under government. Isaiah dreamed of a suffering Messiah—750 years before the event came to pass. Peter dreamed on a housetop and the Gospel was given to the Gentiles Paul dreamed at Troas, and the message of Christ was carried to the mainland of Europe. Columbus dreamed. Galileo dreamed. Edison dreamed. Pasteur dreamed. Firestone, Henry Ford, Wilbur and Orville Wright, and Martin Luther King—all dreamed. Markham was right: all that we glory in was once a dream.

The dreams God places in our hearts are all attainable. Grace is the supernatural power which God gives the believer to accomplish His will, to bring those dreams to pass. This is difficult for us to grasp, for we have been conditioned to believe that if we do not bring a thing to pass in our own strength, it will not come to pass. But if we are the living, breathing, acting, loving extension of the man Jesus Christ in the world today, then the things He did, we can do also. His mission is now our mission; His dream, ours.

There are two kinds of dreams: those we dream up ourselves which are nearly always self-centered, and those God places in our hearts. God gives each one of us the desire to accomplish His will, to fulfill the dreams He places in our hearts—and the power to do it. But the only legitimate dreams are the ones God places in our hearts.

The Holy Spirit accomplishes His work in this world by the measure of faith each man is given to express his personal spiritual gift. It is the process He uses to make the dreams He has placed in our hearts come true. This is best understood when we realize that *our loving God has created each one of us to do best that which we enjoy doing.* A number of years ago, I determined the best way to make this principle effective in my own life was to find the one thing I enjoy doing more than any other, then figure out a way to get people to pay me for doing it. In my case, that is what I am doing right now—writing a book. In your case it may be something else. Whatever it is, the Potter has designed something into each one of us which needs to be sanctified, some special gift which when discovered and put into use, will bring you happiness and satisfaction by fulfilling the desire of your heart.

The tragedy that surrounds most people is they are never able to do the thing they are gifted to do. A woman with great artistic talent winds up doing secretarial work in a law office—and painting only on the weekends. A man with a gift as a mechanic satisfies his guilt by going into the ministry. Forced by circumstances, misguided by prior educational direction, guilt or some kind of financial pressure, most of God's children never exercise their faith enough to do the thing they are called to do—the thing they are gifted to do. As a result, they live frustrated lives because their dream can never come true.

129

However, when a Christian is doing that which he is called to do, that which he is gifted to do, there is tremendous motivation and joy in his life.

If we are privileged to do the very things Christ did, to dream His dreams and see them fulfilled, then we must find out how He did what He did, for herein lies the secret of our own personal happiness.

The best place to start with this revelation is at the beginning of Jesus' personal ministry. He called 12 disciples, commissioned them and gave them "power against unclean spirits, to cast them out, and to heal all manner of sickness and all manner of disease." He told them "as ye go, preach, saying, The kingdom of heaven is at hand. Heal the sick, cleanse the lepers, raise the dead, cast out devils: freely ye have received, freely give" (Matthew 10:1, 7–8).

Later in Matthew 28, Jesus gave His disciples a final commission:

> All power is given unto me in heaven and in earth. Go ye therefore, and teach all nations, baptizing them in the name of the Father, and of the Son, and of the Holy Ghost; teaching them to observe all things . . . I have commanded you; and lo, I am with you alway, even unto the end of the world (Matthew 28:18–20).

The commission of Matthew 28 is simply an enlargement of the commission in Matthew 10. The first commission was to go to the "house of Israel." The second commission took in the entire world. However, the purpose was identical. John quotes Jesus' enlarged plan: "He who believes in me will also do the works that I do; and greater works . . . will he do, because I go to my Father" (John 14:12, RSV).

For years this bothered me, not because I did not believe it, but because I did not see it in practice. How could I do "greater works" than Jesus? Now, however, I understand Jesus was not referring to greater in kind but greater in degree. He was speaking of the fulfillment of the dream He had placed within my heart.

As a child I used to dream how wonderful it would be to speak to a sick person, saying: "In Jesus' name, be healed." But I was afraid to try—afraid I would fail in my task and the word would get around that I had made a fool of myself. Now, however, I have not only had my eyes opened to the possibility of this, but there have been times when I have been infused with such power from the Holy Spirit that these things have literally happened.

Several years ago I was invited back to my alma mater, Mercer University, to speak in chapel. Mercer is a Southern Baptist University, under the auspices of the Georgia Baptist Convention. Since I had become involved in the charismatic movement, and my church had been voted out of official Baptist membership, I had felt totally ostracized by most of my Baptist brethren. The invitation, then, to return and speak in chapel was a distinct honor. At the same time I was frightened. The evening before I was to fly to Macon, Georgia, I attended a small prayer group in Melbourne and asked the people to pray for me. During that prayer time a young housewife prophesied: "Do not prepare what you are to say. I will give you the words when you arrive."

That really terrified me. Even though I had been preaching without a manuscript for several years, this was one time I wanted to go fully prepared. After all, I would be standing in front of many of my old college professors. If ever I needed to make an impression for the Lord, this was the time. Yet, deep inside, I felt the prophecy came from God. I determined to walk it out.

Being told specifically not to do something is like telling a man not to think of a green-eyed monkey. It stirs every kettle of imagination. On the plane from my home in Melbourne all the way to Macon, I had to do fierce battle with my desire to let my mind run ahead and plan. At least my first sentence. At least the general topic. But I was determined to obey what I knew was the voice of God, no matter how hard or impractical it seemed.

That morning, when I stepped on the stage of the chapel and looked out over the student body and the solemn faces of the professors, I felt a strange peace. Following the introduction, I walked to the podium, opened my mouth and to my horror heard myself say, "I am a former Southern Baptist preacher who now speaks in tongues."

It was the best opening sentence I've ever given. From that

moment on, every ear was tuned—some to criticize, some to drink in what I said like water pouring from a cracked rock in the middle of a desert. The great and profound things I imagined I might say did not come forth. Instead, I simply shared my testimony.

At the end of the chapel period, a pale young man approached me as I stood in the aisle near the front of the auditorium. He seemed especially frail, his eyes sunk deep in his head, his hair silky and thin. He talked in a coarse whisper.

"I have leukemia," he said. "My older brother died of the same disease at the age of 19. The doctors have told me I would not live any longer than he. I am now that same age. Everyone I know tells me I am going to die. You are the first man I have ever heard who said God still heals. If you believe what you said this morning, will you pray that I may be healed?"

"I will do it now," I said, forgetting that the large crowd standing in the chapel had grown totally silent. Every eye, students and professors alike, was on us. I reached out, laid my hand on the clammy forehead of the emaciated young man and began to pray. I felt him staggering. Suddenly his knees gave way and he began to slump. I grabbed him under the arms and lowered him to the floor. There was not a sound from those standing around, although I am certain they had never seen anything like that.

For that matter, neither had I. For an instant I wondered if the boy had died. But I knelt beside him, and his eyelids were fluttering. He finally opened them, gave me a crooked smile and said softly, "I'm okay. I don't know what happened, but I'm okay."

I breathed an inner sigh of relief, helped him to his feet and stood there as he embraced me, tears running down his face. "Am I healed?" he asked me.

I answered him honestly, not with some formula but out of my heart. "I don't know. That's God's business. But I do know we have done what He has asked us to do. The rest is up to Him."

The boy picked up his books and slowly made his way, walking with a decided staggering gait, out the side door. I made my way through the group of students, who backed off to let me through, to a friend who was waiting outside to take me to lunch. The entire affair was never mentioned—not then, not ever again.

Two years later I was speaking at a Full Gospel Business Men's Fellowship meeting in Cocoa Beach, Florida, a small community a few miles up the east coast from my home. During the course of my message, I found myself telling the story—for the first time—of the incident at Mercer. Afterwards a handsome couple came quickly to the front of the room and embraced me fervently. Gradually they choked out their story. They were the parents of that young man. He had been completely healed of his leukemia and was, according to them, the picture of health. They were vacationing in the area, heard I was to speak, and made a special trip to the meeting. They had no idea I would tell that story, nor do I know why I told it, except to prove once again the greatness of God and to point out that those deep dreams of childhood do, indeed, come true.

We are the expansion of Jesus' mission in the 20th century, and, equally important, we are the fulfillment of the dream He has put within our hearts.

What does this mean—the expansion of His mission? To fully understand what is meant by the continuing and enlarging work of Jesus here on this earth, we need to look at the opening words of the Acts of the Apostles: "In the first book . . ." Luke wrote—and here he was referring to his Gospel—"I have dealt with all that Jesus began to do and teach . . ." (Acts 1:1, RSV). Give special attention to the words, "all that Jesus began to do and teach." The implication is that Luke's second book, The Acts, is a record of what Jesus *continued* to do and teach. Thus, even though the book is labeled "The Acts of the Apostles," a far more accurate title would be "The Acts of the Holy Spirit" or "The Continuing Acts of Jesus Christ on This Earth."

Luke points out it was "the Lord" who added to the church day by day (Acts 2:47). And when the lame man at the Beautiful Gate of the Temple was healed, Peter specifically points out that the disciples had nothing to do with the healing. ". . . why do you stare at us, as though by our own power or piety we had made him walk?" (Acts 3:12, RSV). Then there was that healing at Lydda. Aeneas had been bedridden, paralyzed, for eight years. Peter said to him, "Aeneas, Jesus Christ heals you" (Acts 9:34, RSV). Peter meant that literally. Jesus Christ was alive and at work in Lydda.

This of course presents a real problem to the rationalist or the humanist. It is difficult enough to believe that Jesus performed miracles when He was on earth. But how can He be alive and at work in all ages and in all places? Yet the very heart of the Gospel is the continuing ministry of Jesus Christ through His Body—the church—here on earth in exactly the same way, only greater than the ministry He had when He was incarnate in the flesh.

John the Baptizer appeared at the beginning of our Lord's public ministry, preparing the way. "After me comes he who is mightier than I," John said in one of his public addresses. "I have baptized you with water; but he will baptize you with the Holy Spirit" (Mark 1:7–8, RSV). Shortly after that, John spotted Jesus on the banks of the river and cried out, "Behold the lamb of God who takes away the sin of the world" (John 1:29, RSV). Then Jesus submitted to John's baptism.

> And when he came up out of the water, immediately he saw the heavens opened and the Spirit descending upon him like a dove . . . (Mark 1:10, RSV).

Jesus' baptism was composed of two parts: baptism in water and the descent of the Spirit. The term "baptized in the Spirit" also describes the second part, since those words are often connected with baptism when it is mentioned elsewhere in the New Testament. In fact, baptism in the New Testament is always related to both aspects—water and Spirit.

Now why Jesus needed to be baptized in the Holy Spirit remains a great mystery. For centuries the church has argued the point. But it seems even the Son of God was incomplete. His dreams could not come true without the fulfilling power of the third person of the Trinity—the Holy Spirit.

Jesus' baptism was the beginning of three years of intense conflict. Listen to the way Luke introduces the beginning of Jesus'. ministry:

"And Jesus returned [from the wilderness] in the power of the Spirit into Galilee . . ." (Luke 4:14, RSV). From there He went to Nazareth, His home town, and on the sabbath day went to the synagogue. During the allotted time, He stood with the scroll and read from Isaiah: "The Spirit of the Lord is upon me . . ." (Isaiah 61:1; Luke 4:18). Then He said the prophecy had just come true and sat down.

The people, who were frustrated because their dreams never came true, were angry at the man who seemed fulfilled. They would have killed Him on the spot but He escaped, withdrew to the seashore, called His disciples and began the ministry which we are called to continue—a call which still bubbles in the hearts of all Christians in the form of their dreams.

It is this dream which Paul talks about in 1 Corinthians 12. He says, "Now concerning spiritual gifts, brethren, I do not want you to be uninformed" (12:1, RSV). The verse could just as well be translated, "I do not want you uninformed about those who bear the marks of the Spirit."

Jesus exhibited the marks of the Spirit. In fact, all that He did can be summed up in the first seven of the nine manifestations listed in 1 Corinthians 12:8-10. These manifestations are also called graces—coming from the Greek word *charis*. We have added "ma," meaning a charisma is actually a "gracing"—the visible evidence of God's grace in our lives. It is all from the Spirit and by the Spirit. Such was our Lord's ministry before His ascension; such is His continuing ministry after His ascension in and through those of us who are now walking in the Spirit. In short, we are the continuing ministry of Jesus on earth.

Jesus was limited to one body and further limited to one era of history. How, His disciples wondered, could He overcome these limitations and acquire universal extension of His presence and power? The answer is through generation after generation of men and women who are filled with the same Spirit who filled Jesus at His baptism. It is God's divine plan for us to receive His Spirit and thereby overcome the physical and geographical and chronological limitations placed on Jesus—and thus extend Him into the entire world of all generations.

135

In John 15, Jesus Himself speaks the word of transferred authority to His disciples. "Ye are the branches . . ." He told them (John 15:5). It is a strange use of words. At least eight times in the Old Testament there are messianic prophecies in which Jesus is called "the branch." Zechariah said: "Thus speaketh the Lord of hosts, saying, Behold the man whose name is The BRANCH; and he shall grow up out of his place, and he shall build the temple of the Lord" (Zechariah 6:12).

Most Bible scholars agree this refers to the coming Messiah—Jesus Christ. Jesus was the fulfillment of Zechariah's prophecy. Why then does He confer this title upon His disciples? Is it not that He is preparing, within the next few days, to return to His Father in Heaven? Thus His continuing work shall be carried out by those who not only represent Him but actually go forth with the same power and Spirit that He had when He walked the earth.

Already in John 14, Jesus had told His disciples, "I am in the Father, and the Father in me." Even though He never pretended to be the Vine, He now says that since the Father—who is the Vine—is in Him, then He, too, is the Vine. And because of that He is able to confer upon His followers the identical title earlier conferred upon Him by the prophets. Now He is the Vine, but we are the branches—just as He was the branch while He was on earth.

Are miracles for today? Only if Jesus is for today. For He has not changed—and His Spirit in us is still the same, miracle-working Spirit as when He descended upon Jesus at the Jordan River. By giving us the same Spirit He received at His baptism, He indwells us and empowers us and in and through and by us presents Himself to every generation and every place.

So there you have it. Being filled with His Spirit, we may expect to function in our world as He functioned in the world of the first century. We are the thinking, breathing, feeling, acting Body of Christ in the world. It is His dream which still forms in us, awaiting final fulfillment in our own lives.

The world assumes that each of us is something to be taught or trained—that we are raw material ready to fit someone else's mold. The Bible teaches, however, that each of us has a unique design that can be fulfilled only when we find our place in God's purpose.

The reason there was such power in the early church was they were all in one accord. They were the literal presence of Jesus Christ on earth because they were an integrated, harmonious body—fitly joined together. As long as they remained that way, the same power operated in the church which operated in Jesus Himself. Only when they became divided did the power disintegrate—and only as we come again into unity will His power return in all its fullness.

It is up to each one of us to find God's gift in our lives—and then let the Holy Spirit fulfill His dream in us. As a boy, I dreamed of being a doctor. I yearned to be able to pull my car off the side of the road, rush back to an accident and save someone's life. Then I got to college and discovered there is more to medicine than putting broken arms in splints and administering magical potions which save lives. There is the matter of chemistry, and of mathematics, and of biology. These were my worst subjects, and when I barely squeaked through freshman chemistry and never did learn to use a slide rule, I had to admit I had misinterpreted my gift. Did this mean my dream was shattered? Not at all. Even though I knew I would never make it as a doctor, the desire to help remained. All I needed to do was align my dream with my gift—which, in my case, was that of showing mercy. As each man finds his place in the Body, develops his dream by aligning it with his gift, determined not to be anyone else but to be the person God created him to be—then the Body shall come together and signs and wonders shall once again appear—just as they did in Jesus' day. For it is then that believers, as individuals and in true oneness, will be within the Spirit's control.

Corporations believe it is possible to train a man to fit the needs of the corporation—salesman, management executive, technician, engineer. But if a man does not have the basic spiritual gift which underlies these departments, no amount of training will ever make him happy or effective in that position.

Seminaries often teach young ministers that the pastor of a church needs to be a "well-rounded" person. The minister, we were taught, should not only preach; he should be an administrator, an evangelist, a teacher, a shepherd and give spiritual oversight to the entire Body. In short, the seminary concept is that one man called "the pastor" should do the work that the Apostle Paul said should be handled by at least five men. Not once in my four years of training in a theological seminary was I told to find my place and fulfill my dream as either an apostle, prophet, evangelist, pastor or teacher. It was just assumed I would be all five—despite Paul's admonition to the Ephesians (Ephesians 4:11–16). But just because one has a pastor's heart does not make him a public teacher or an evangelist. Just because one has a burden for lost souls does not mean he is also gifted as a shepherd—or has the insight of a prophet.

Over the years, as I have watched men fail in the ministry, it is often because they have been forced into roles where they were not gifted. The prophet, who had a great gift of preaching and deep spiritual insight, was forced to be a pastor—or an administrator. When he failed in that, and since his preaching was often irritating and pointed, he was forced out of the church. Or perhaps it was a man with a tender, shepherd's heart, who loved his sheep as deeply as he loved his own children. Yet because he was not a prophetic preacher or was a poor evangelist, those in the congregation who wanted to build a bigger, more efficient organization would finally see to it that he was replaced—usually by some kind of human dynamo who shot golf in the high 70s, remembered jokes like Bob Hope and was the darling of the social circle—but knew God only as a distant cousin.

When the church recognizes that God never intended for the spiritual leader to be all things to all people and when the spiritual leaders become secure enough in their gift that they are not threatened by others who can supplement their ministry and succeed in areas where they are weak, then the church will once again grow strong and healthy.

A man is happy and productive only if his work life corresponds with his dream—with the desire of his heart. Self-inventory is absolutely necessary for every Christian, especially those in leadership.

Last year the 10 elders in the Tabernacle Church in Melbourne—

most of whom were in full-time ministry—submitted themselves to a series of vocational tests—the kind given to corporate executives in industry. The purpose was to help us discover our basic, motivational gifts. In short, how to let our dreams come true. After a week of thought and prayer, we withdrew to a small cabin on the beach to spend two days in intense personal evaluation. Each man had jotted down who he really thought he was. Brushing aside "Who do others want me to be?" and "What am I doing now?" each of us focused on such questions as: "What do I really want to do? What is the best contribution I can make to the Body of Christ? What are the real desires of my heart? What is God telling me to do with my life?"

It was an interesting and revealing session. Each man got extremely honest. "You men see me in *this* role," our church administrator said. "But if I were free from all restraints, I would get out of this office and spend all my time as a pastor—ministering to people's needs at the personal level."

Another man confessed he was tired of being thrust into the role of a pastor and counselor. He did it because it was demanded of him. But his real gift was in seeking the Lord in prayer, meditation and through the anguish of the soul, then coming back to the Body as a prophet to speak with strong authority, "This is what God is saying."

I myself confessed I had been playing the role of a pastor for a number of years—first by necessity because there was no one else to do it and later by tradition and habit and because it was expected of me by the people. But deep in my heart I knew my gift was not that of a pastor, even though I shared deep compassion for people. But my basic gift to the local Body was that of a spiritual overseer, fulfilling the apostolic office.

In describing the functions of the "five-fold" ministries Paul outlines in Ephesians 4:11–16, Bob Beckett, one of our pastors, likened it to a human hand. The apostle is the thumb, touching all the other fingers. The prophet is the index finger, jabbing and pointing. The evangelist is the long middle finger, reaching out to the lost. The pastor is the ring finger, calling people into covenant. And the teacher is the little finger, constantly digging for knowledge.

A lot of interesting things came to the surface during those few days in the beach cabin. We found we had asked each other to do certain things in order to fill needs rather than because that was God's highest will for the individual. We had not been sensitive to each other's dreams. All of us had assumed responsibilities greater than our capabilities. One of the men finally put his finger on the problem. "The question," he said, "is what are we willing to quit in order to do the things God is asking us to do? The problem is how to differentiate between what I *can* do and what I am *supposed* to do."

In *Up the Organization*, the president of Avis Rent-A-Car tells the story of the fantastic growth of the company. It started with the president saying, "We're going to define our objective." It took six months, but when the dust had settled they had a 23-word objective: "We want to become the fastest growing company, with the highest profit margin, in the business of renting and leasing vehicles without drivers."

To achieve their objective, they had to get rid of everything that didn't fulfill it. Some heads rolled, and a lot of folks got angry, but in the end—after they decided what they were not going to do—they became successful.

Deciding what you are not going to do is equally important with deciding what you are going to do. In fact, you cannot do what you are supposed to do until you stop doing what you are not supposed to.

Producers get life sorted out. They eliminate in order to concentrate. They set up priorities and put on blinders. They learn how to focus. And how to say no.

This is the difference between the achiever and the underachiever. I look around at the people who have achieved and notice all of them have learned the secret of focus. They have learned to say no to the trivial and yes to the important. They have learned to tell the "urgent" to wait until they finish the "important." They have learned to shut out all but the priority issues of life. Like the Apostle Paul, they forget those things which are behind and press on toward the mark of their high calling.

The major difference between a river and a swamp is that the river is going one place while the swamp tries to go everywhere. The river has a goal—an objective. It is determined to reach the sea. The swamp, however, rebels against the discipline of riverbanks and remains a constant underachiever, producing only undesirable things like snakes and mosquitoes—with maybe a few alligators. Although swamps are notorious for bragging about all the territory they cover, they never will experience that glorious satisfaction of achieving one thing—reaching the sea.

Swamps are like a friend of mine who is an expert in nine different areas—from engineering to theology—but can't hold down a single job.

The achiever learns to say no, especially to the good, in order to produce the best. He runs the risk of making people angry, of being called narrow ("What's wrong with breeding a few frogs and snakes?"), but he achieves his goal.

It's not a sin to be a one-talent person. The sin lies in wanting to do 10 things with your one talent and getting so frustrated you wind up achieving nothing at all.

Every so often we catch a glimpse of a man who knows where he is going—a man with a dream who dares invoke the authority of Jesus. In him we see Eden afar off. Through the mist of sin and corruption we say, "That's the way God intends for all of us to be. To live above the fog of perversion and procrastination and achieve, create, conquer."

The world is filled with terribly frustrated people who operate in these areas of illusion, fantasy and deception—never quite able to see the other side of God's purpose for their lives. Often they blame God, charging Him with teasing and taunting them with impossible desires. Yet the wise man soon learns that all dreams do not come from God. Many of them, like my dream of becoming a doctor, are but shadows of our carnal nature, haunting us, taunting us as they never come to pass. It is only when we dare to dig beneath the canopy of desire and tradition to the wellspring of our basic gift that we will discover who we actually are—and find our stream flowing to where we are to be. Until that happens, we continue with our struggles, crying out when our dreams are constantly broken and shattered on the rocks of circumstance which line the inlet to the safe harbor of contentment.

When I started to work on this chapter, I first entitled it, "How to Make Your Dreams Come True." But making dreams come true is the way the world system operates. In the Kingdom, if a dream is of God, and if we allow His principles to govern our lives, the dream will come true. Here, then, is a five-point outline of Kingdom principles designed to let your dreams come true.

Be willing to wait. The kind of dream I am talking about— your deepest hope, the desire of your heart—will not grow up overnight. Such a dream has to materialize, evolve, go through process after process until it is matured. Remember, you may have only one dream for a lifetime. That dream may hit several plateaus along the way, but for most of us there is only one basic dream per person. It is the wise man who is able to focus in and know what that is, to define it exactly.

If you have but one dream to a lifetime, then it's worth waiting a lifetime for it to come to pass. Simeon waited all his life to see the fulfillment of his highest dream—that his eyes would see the Messiah. Doubtless he had been tricked many times before. Surely people had pointed out great leaders and whispered, "That's the Messiah." But there had been no inner witness of the Spirit. So Simeon waited. Like Abraham and Sarah, who waited into old age for the fulfillment of God's promise of a child, hope had nearly faded away. But Simeon held onto his dream. And then one day in the Temple, going about his daily worship as he had for decades, his dream came true.

How much pain we cause ourselves, and others, by trying to fulfill God's best purpose for our lives ahead of time. Young men, young women, starting out into ministry, often feel they need to write a book to give them and their ministry credibility. A great number of these books are written—long before a person has anything to say. A book should grow out of credibility rather than expecting credibility to be established because your name is on a book. Sadly many are unwilling to wait. They hurry their book into production only to wish, years later, they had not said many of the things they earlier put into print. Corrie ten Boom's great books were written after she was 70 years old. Kathryn Kuhlman felt the true story of her life could not be told until after she died. In my own case, even though our church has been on the cutting edge of the Holy Spirit's thrust into this generation, I have resisted all temptations to write that story in detail. That book, like many others snuggling in the womb of creativity, must wait until gestation is complete before it is birthed on paper.

Immature sharing of dreams often brings unneeded heartache. Young Mary, the mother of Jesus, evidenced the wisdom of God when she "kept all these things, and pondered them in her heart" (Luke 2:19). So many of us believe that just because God has whispered something in our ear, it is supposed to be broadcast with our mouth. There is a time to speak—but also a time to keep silent.

There is evidence that Jesus knew as early as age 12 that He was the Messiah—the incarnate Son of God. Yet He willingly submitted Himself to the rule of Joseph and the care of Mary for another 18 years before He made a public announcement of His mission. There were things, necessary things, which needed to come to pass. A great part of His growing in "wisdom and stature, and in favour with God and man" (Luke 2:52) took place in the carpenter's shop. To have stepped out at the age of 12—or at the age of 20—and announced His role as Messiah to the world would have been folly. So He waited. And worked. Until another fullness of time had come and He heard the gentle whisper of the Holy Spirit saying, "Meet me at the Jordan."

Be willing to be misunderstood. Every dreamer is misunderstood by those who do not share his dream. If you have a dream, a vision, if your heart is set on something spiritual and you believe with every fiber of your being that God is one day going to bring it to pass, then you are going to be misunderstood. The Josephs with a far-off look in their eyes are always a threat to men and women living for today alone. Even if you say nothing, the very fact you have a dream will bring persecution.

Martin Luther King's great sermon on the steps of the Lincoln Memorial, "I Have a Dream," stirred more hatred than any sermon ever preached in the United States. He was cutting across the deepest values and traditions of white America. He dreamed of a time when black men would be addressed as "mister" rather than "boy," when black women would be treated with courtesy and respect on city buses, when black children would no longer be called "pickaninnies," when black people were not forced to drink from separate water fountains or use separate restrooms and could sleep in the same motel beds as white people. He dreamed of a day when a black man would be paid the same wages as a white man doing the same work, when children could go to the same public schools as white children, when "for whites only" would be a thing of the dark past. King, like a lot of other visionaries, died for his dream. He died because he was misunderstood.

Visionaries, those with a dream, often have problems with the present. Living out there in the future when the dream, to them, has already come true, often brings them head-on into the bloody facts of the present. Sometimes more practical people have to take them by the hand and lead them as they stagger and bumble through life. Fortunate is the man who has friends around him who at least love him, even though they may never catch his vision or hear the sound of his drummer.

Sometimes, like Joseph, the dreamer is misunderstood because he shares too much too soon. Some pearls should never be scattered across the barnyard—nor shared in the weekly prayer group. If a dream is of God, it will come true even if we keep our mouths shut. In fact, the more close-lipped we are, the better the Holy Spirit is able to work. Only when all the facts have come into place does a man like Jesus rise in the synagogue and say, "The Spirit of the Lord is upon me." Only then does a group of church leaders, fasting and praying and waiting before the Lord, finally lay hands on two men—Barnabas and Paul—and send them forth on the earth's first missionary journey of the early church.

To a real degree the ability to wait is directly involved with the amount of misunderstanding you generate. The classic example is the Apostle Paul. Converted on the road to Damascus—and blinded at the same time—he went immediately into the city where he waited three days in the house of Judas before he received his sight and was filled with the Holy Spirit. However, impatient, over-zealous, and filled with enthusiasm, he straightway went into the synagogues of the city and began preaching that Jesus was the Son of God. It almost cost him his life. In just a few days, when the other believers in the city discovered a plot on his life, they lowered him over the city wall in a basket so he could escape into the desert of Arabia. This segment of his life ends with Acts 9:25.

According to Paul's letter to the Galatians, he remained in the desert for three years—in the seminary of the Holy Spirit. When the story resumes in Acts 9:26, it is three years later. But Paul's nature is the same. Roaring into Jerusalem, he joins the local church and immediately begins to preach—as he did in Damascus. Argumentative in nature, he sought out Jews and Greeks to debate. After only two weeks the entire city was in a turmoil and despite Barnabas' intercession the church could take no more of Paul's immature visionary nature. Again, hearing of a plot to kill him, the Christians rushed him out of the city to the coastal town of Caesarea and put him on a ship for his hometown of Tarsus in Asia Minor. The very day he was kicked out of the church, a revival broke forth. "Then had the churches rest throughout all Judaea and Galilee and Samaria, and were edified; and walking in the fear of the Lord, and in the comfort of the Holy Ghost, were multiplied" (Acts 9:31).

Five years passed and finally the church at Jerusalem sent Barnabas as an apostle to minister to a number of new Greek believers at Antioch. Shortly after he arrived, he departed for Tarsus to find Saul and to ask him to minister with him in Antioch. For two years—from 42 A.D. until 44 A.D.—Saul worked quietly in Antioch, perhaps making tents as he ministered with the other men in leadership position. Finally one day, as five of the leaders were fasting and praying, the Holy Spirit spoke and said, "It's time to send Saul into public ministry" (Acts 13:1-3). Thus began the early church's first missionary journey—10 years after Saul's conversion on the road to Damascus. Interestingly, the change that had taken place in Saul's life was immediately recognized in a change in his name. From that time on, he was no longer called Saul, but Paul.

Paul's dream had not diminished over that 10-year period. If anything, it had enlarged. Neither had his enthusiasm waned. But his maturity was reflected in his ability to wait, patiently, for God to speak—rather than rushing out and trying to convert the world in one giant crusade.

Dreamers are misunderstood because very few people, even those close to them, understand what God is saying. The best you can expect is they will love you, even though they will not understand.

Be willing to work. While dreams come true for cripples as well as those whole in body, all are commanded to work until that dream is fulfilled.

Paul is blunt in his word to the lazy Christians at Thessalonica who seemed to think all they had to do was sit around and wait for manna to fall from heaven—or perhaps let the church feed them.

> For even when we were with you, this we commanded you, that if any would not work, neither should he eat. For we hear that there are some which walk among you disorderly, working not at all, but are busybodies. Now them that are such we command and exhort by our Lord Jesus Christ, that with quietness they work, and eat their own bread (2 Thessalonians 3:10–12).

The man who works with his hands, who labors with the sweat of his brow, opens up avenues for God to speak to him at the same time—avenues never opened to the lazy Christian. God never speaks to lazy people. A survey through the Bible indicates that God always called busy men when He had a dream to fulfill.

"You, Abram. You've been busy for 75 years tending the flocks of old Terah; I have a dream for you to fulfill . . ."

"You, Moses, busy for these last 40 years herding sheep and goats for Jethro, I have a dream for you to fulfill . . ."

"You, Gideon, over there behind the winepress working with the grapes, I have a dream for you to fulfill . . ."

"You, beautiful Ruth, busy gleaning the fields of Boaz, I have a dream for you to fulfill . . ."

"You, young Samuel, busy cleaning out the Temple at Shiloh and making sure the lamps are always burning at the altar, I have a dream for you to fulfill . . ."

"You, Amos, busy harvesting figs down in Judah, I have a dream for you to fulfill up in Israel . . ."

"You, Jesus, there in the carpenter's shop, it is time to lay aside your apron and hammer. I have a dream for you to fulfill . . ."

God seldom speaks to people to go off on long retreats and sit under trees with their mouths open, waiting for some especially tasty word to fall in. What He does is let you sit there until you get exceedingly hungry and for sheer preservation are forced to go to work with your hands. Then, in the process of hammering nails, digging fence-post holes in the swamp, driving a taxi or working behind a cash register, He calls you by name. At that time He may tell you to quit work but only because He has a far greater task for you to do. He never calls men to idleness.

If you want your dreams to come true, get to work. Do things with your hands. Sweat with your brow. Get to work 10 minutes early and work 15 minutes past quitting time—without asking for overtime. Walk the second mile for your boss. Give him your cloak when he demands your coat. Turn the other cheek when he slaps you with his insensitivity to your personal needs. Dream up new methods. Innovate. Improve the business. Go to school in your spare time. Come in and work when no one else knows you are working. Whatever your hand finds to do, do it with all your might.

And your dreams will come true. Not because you've worked and brought them into being, but because God honors the worker and will bless you accordingly.

Dreams come true when a man does an honest day's work for a full day's pay. Just because a man has a doctor's degree in theology does not mean he is disqualified from laying bricks or pumping septic tanks. Sometimes that's the best therapy in the world.

Recently a well educated man arrived in our community saying he needed work. We discovered he had taught history on a graduate level in a large university but had been fired when a student accused

147

him of immorality. Out of that he had come to know the Lord, even though he had lost his wife and family in the process. Now he was in Melbourne, asking us to help him.

"What is your biggest need?" I asked him.

"Money," he said a bit embarrassed. "I may go to jail if I cannot pay off some of my debts."

"Fine," I said, "I know how you can get money. Lots of it. I have a friend who owns a septic tank service. He needs someone to drive the 'honey truck' and handle the pumping. At the end of the week he pays you money."

The professor was insulted and soon moved on to another town. Somehow he had never related the fact that work and money go together. Perhaps he thought it just flowed automatically from the administration building, or he had been taught in his early days as a Christian that to trust in God meant to open your Bible each morning and there would be a 20 dollar bill tucked neatly into Romans. Fortunately that is not so. We live in a very practical world. God expects us to do practical things. If Paul, the Pharisee of the Pharisees and a member of the Sanhedrin with a doctorate of theology, could sit on the curb with his bare feet smelling of camel dung and sew tents for a living—in order to carry on his ministry—then it should not be below any of us, especially those of us with dreams yet to be fulfilled, to perform the menial if that's what it takes.

Be willing for God to twist you until you are the right shape to contain your dream. God cannot put round dreams into square containers. So He twists. Molds. Reshapes until we are prepared to hold all He has for us.

If Jesus Christ is Lord, then He can do with you what He chooses. To bring you to that place where the dream He has placed within your heart can come to pass, He often has to do a great deal of reshaping. That sometimes causes pain, humiliation, even death. Sometimes it means we are bruised or scratched. We can choose to blame Satan when we undergo tough times if we want, but if our dream is legitimate—if it comes from God—then it is not the devil who is twisting our life but the Holy Spirit. God allows these things to come into your life for the purpose of making

148

you a fit container for His dream. Plastic surgery is often painful, especially when it is done in public, but at the same time it is necessary if we are to reflect God's grace.

Last Wednesday morning, before I sat down at the typewriter to finish this chapter, the telephone rang. It was the wife of a former evangelist. We had known the family for several years, but things had not gone well in his family. He and his wife had divorced, and shortly afterwards he married again. He had dropped out of all church activity and gone into a lucrative business selling insurance to churches. Occasionally I would question him about his dream, but he would always shrug and say, "Later, after things calm down and I get out of debt." But I was unable to figure out how he could get out of debt as long as he was buying a new Mercedes every year and eating at the most expensive restaurants in town. I tried to be kind, but I knew I was speaking truth when I told him, "If you don't begin to cooperate with the purposes and principles of God, then God, who has a claim on your life, is going to twist you and bend you against your will until you do cooperate. You have no choice but to do His will or be broken as you beat yourself against that will."

That, you see, is the nature of God, the nature of His love. He loves us so much He will do anything to shape us into the image of His Son, Jesus Christ.

Then this morning his wife called.

"We're in trouble," she said simply, her voice quivering.

"I'm listening," I replied.

"Tom's son was involved in an accident last night. Two people were killed. One of them was a baby."

She went ahead to blurt out the details. Tom's 17-year-old son by his previous marriage, who was visiting with them for the weekend, had stopped by a bar after a teen-age dance. The bartender had refused to serve him since he was underage. Angry and embarrassed in front of his friend, he stormed out of the bar, got in his father's new Mercedes and roared out of the parking lot straight into the path of a small car carrying a young couple just returning from the hospital with their newborn baby. The mother and child had been killed instantly. The father was critically injured. Both cars were demolished. The son, frightened and alone, had fled the accident on foot and was later picked up by the police and was in jail.

"I know God is working in his life," the stepmother said. Then she paused, choking on tears, "and in ours, too."

The love of God does not let us go. When Samuel told Israel, "For the Lord will not forsake his people . . ." he also added, "But if ye shall still do wickedly, ye shall be consumed " (1 Samuel 12:22, 25). Sometimes God's people might wish God would forsake them, leave them alone. But once the commitment has been made, God never breaks His contract. He is always there, the mighty Hound of Heaven, tracking us down and arranging or allowing circumstances to take place which are designed to conform us to the image of His Son Jesus.

The Bible is filled with stories of men running from God. Samson. Balaam. King Saul. David. Jonah. Elijah. My friend, the former evangelist, was in good company. The Hound of Heaven was still nipping at his heels. But the man of God on the run from God is the most miserable of all people. And so, in the midst of crisis, my friend came the next day to say, with the Apostle Paul, "I can no longer fight God." He has a long way to go, but now with his spirit softened, he, his wife and his son are prepared soil for the seeds of the Kingdom to take root and grow. Just this morning he called, saying even though his son was out of jail, he was still committed to turn his back on the systems of the world and return to the true God.

Was God in all that? Did God design a tragic automobile accident where innocent people were killed, and a lonely boy was battered for life? Such questions cannot be answered, except with other questions. Are the sins of the fathers visited upon the children? Is God still in control of the world? Can it be possible that life on this earth is relatively inconsequential when compared with all that is before us in eternity? Can God take even a tragedy like this and use it for His glory? Is it possible that dreams have not been dashed into irreparable damage but rather are indeed being worked out despite those involved?

The answer to these questions, of course, depends on the size

150

and power of God rather than our ability to understand Him. Thus it is not fair to ask if God was responsible for the tragedy until you have the answers to the other questions. For our dreams are too small. It is only God's dream, in the long run, which counts.

Finally: *Be willing for that dream to come to pass through somebody else.* Let's return to old Simeon, wandering around the Temple, holding onto his dream. There is no way Simeon could have known the Messiah was going to come in the form of a tiny baby. No doubt like all others he pictured the Messiah as another Maccabean deliverer, riding into Jerusalem on a white horse with flashing sword to deliver the Jews from the hated Roman tyrants. So he had practiced his little speech for years and imagined how he would fall on his knees before that magnificent specimen of manhood who like Jupiter would spring in full maturity from the heart of God. But Simeon's thoughts were not God's thoughts, and one day in the Temple the Holy Spirit whispered to Simeon, "There! See over there! See that father talking to the priest? See that young mother holding the little baby right behind them? That little child is the Messiah of the House of Israel, the light to lighten the Gentiles, the Holy One of Israel. There He is. Take Him in your arms and bless Him. Your dream has come true."

So it is with us. So often we have our hearts set on one thing, and God shows us something else. But what He shows us is so much better than what we thought we wanted; it brings nothing but joy.

David thought his dream of the magnificent Temple would come true through him. But God had another plan. And the dream came to pass through David's son, Solomon.

Moses dreamed of a promised land and led his people to the mountain where they could look across and see the green valley of Jericho in the distance. But it was up to Joshua, who was like a son to old Moses, to lead the people into Canaan.

Paul dreamed of Spain—and wound up in a Roman prison.

John Hus dreamed of a time when the common people could drink of the cup of Jesus' blood. But he wound up at the executioner's block. Latimer and Ridley dreamed of a time when the Bible would be available to all people—and were tied to stakes and set afire. Martin King dreamed of a society without prejudice and was killed by an assassin's bullet. But dreams live beyond men, for the dreams coming from the heart of God are always bigger than the dreamers—and bigger than those who try to stop them.

In Hebrews 11, Paul lists the heroes of the faith. Then he closes out the chapter with a list of other men who never did see their dreams come true. They were tortured, mocked, imprisoned, stoned, sawn asunder, slain with the sword, wandered about in skins, were destitute, afflicted, and tormented. It is not the same picture often presented to us by mail-order evangelists who tell us if we send them money in an envelope, our dreams will come true. At the end of the chapter, Paul reminds us that they "received not the promise." Faith teachers often say that all the promises of God are for us. But we must remember the promises are always bigger than our comprehension. In this case, Paul says, "God having provided some better thing for us, that they without us should not be made perfect" (Hebrews 11:40).

We are the continuing fulfillment of their dream—just as we are the continuing fulfillment of Jesus' dream. So the question remains for all of us: Can we release even our dreams to God, to let them come to pass in His time and His way—not ours?

It's a venture we shouldn't miss.

IX

Our Times in God's Hands

I was sitting in the back of the large auditorium with some of the other conference speakers, enjoying the opening session. More than a thousand youth leaders had gathered at the beautiful 4-H retreat center at Rock Eagle, Georgia, for a three-day conference sponsored by the Tennessee-Georgia Christian Camps I was to teach a daily seminar and then speak to the large assembly on Saturday. However, like the other speakers on the program, I wanted to attend all the sessions to catch the "mood" of the conference as it progressed.

Rock Eagle is about an hour's drive from Atlanta and about the same distance from Macon. The camp is nestled in the heavily wooded red hills of Georgia, very quiet, very secluded. People had come from all over the Southeast for the conference and were staying in the various cabins scattered over the large retreat grounds.

We had arrived only a few hours earlier on that Thursday. In fact, some of the people were still in their cabins unpacking as the first session began in the auditorium. Larry Tomczak, a Roman Catholic lay-evangelist who is pastor of a large interdenominational youth-oriented group in Washington, D.C., was the opening night speaker. Larry is a special friend and, seated in the far back of the auditorium with the other speakers, I looked forward to his message for the evening.

But Larry was too excited to get right into his message. He had some personal stories he wanted to tell first. His wife was expecting their first child—due in a couple of weeks—and he was pretty wound up about the miracle of childbirth. I chuckled inwardly as he talked excitedly about the wonderful thing that was about to happen. After all, when you've gone through five such events, although the thrill remains, the excitement is not quite so intense.

But Larry's excitement was at the pinnacle, and he seemed determined to give the audience a blow-by-blow description of everything that had happened to them since the moment of conception, eight and a half months before. I was impressed with his enthusiasm over becoming a father but a little bored with his long discourse. After all, after you've had five of your own . . .

But there was no way to tone down his passion and eloquence of description. He shared what happened when his wife first discovered she was pregnant—his feelings and hers.

"I held her for a long time," he said. "Not only had she created new life, but I was responsible. My wife and I had created a new life which was already alive in her body—waiting to be born."

Larry was convinced the baby was a boy. So convinced he immediately picked out a name and began ministering to the baby. "Every night before bedtime, my wife would lie on the bed, and I would lay my hands on her stomach and minister to the child, speak to him, comfort him, remind him that he was a child of God, impart my love to him as his father."

Now that's interesting, I thought, sitting up a bit as I took notice. Larry said he had been doing this from the very first night they discovered his wife was pregnant. He would speak directly to the child, preparing him for the great event of birth, telling him not to be afraid, that there were some folks waiting for him who loved him and were eager to greet him when he arrived. Not only that, but he was going to be born into a much larger family of brothers and sisters in the Washington area, all of whom were eagerly awaiting his arrival.

"If John the Baptist could be filled with the Holy Spirit in his mother's womb," Larry said, "then why not my son?" So he had been praying that his son would be baptized in the Holy Spirit even before he was born. Now it was almost time for the baby to arrive. I began to understand why Larry was so excited.

Just as he was finishing his story and getting into his message for the evening, I felt a gentle tap on my shoulder. Looking back, I saw a man leaning over the back row and motioning for me to slip out and join him in the vestibule of the auditorium. The back rows were not crowded so I was able to leave without causing a disturbance. Once in the vestibule, the man said, "Could you come with me? A friend of yours, Bo Reed, sent me over from our cabin. We have an emergency going on and need your help."

Bo, a CPA from Boca Raton, Florida, has been helping me with my accounting problems for several years. I knew he and his wife, Carol, were staying in a cabin with a young couple from Macon, Georgia. I also knew he would not call me out of a meeting unless it was important, so I went with the man out into the darkness and down a long path to a lighted cabin.

Bo and Carol met me at the door of the cabin and explained the situation. The young wife from Macon was about three months pregnant and had begun to hemorrhage. They didn't know anyone else at the conference to call but me. Could I help?

"It sounds like she needs a doctor, not a writer," I said.

"I know," Bo said, putting his hand on my shoulder. "But somehow the Lord kept telling me I should call you first."

"Where is she?" I asked.

"She's in the bedroom with her husband. It's their first child, and he's frantic. She's been bleeding for more than an hour and is in a lot of pain. It's a pretty tense situation right now."

I slipped into the cabin, down the hall to the bedroom and stood in the door. The young wife was stretched out on a cot, writhing in pain. Her face contorted, her body twisting with intense cramps. Her husband was pacing the floor, dropping to his knees beside her, then up to the wash basin to get a cold cloth for her head. He looked at me, and there was deep anguish on his face.

"We're more than an hour away from her doctor in Macon,"

he said. "I don't know whether to move her or what. We need help."

I glanced at Bo. "Ask everyone to leave the bedroom. Including her husband. I want to be alone with her for a few moments."

I closed the door behind them and knelt beside the young woman on the bed. I had no idea what I was going to do, but I knew the intensity of all those people in and out of the room was not helping things. As I knelt, I remembered what Larry had been talking about just moments before in the auditorium. At the time I wondered why he was going into such great detail. Now I realized it was far more than coincidence. God was at work.

Kneeling beside the girl, aware she was in danger of a miscarriage, I put my hand on her stomach. It was hard and taut. I could feel the muscles rippling beneath her dress as they undulated back and forth in cramps. She was moaning, her body twisting and convulsing.

"Just relax," I said softly, as she looked down at me with eyes wide with fear. "God is in control here."

Fortunately she knew who I was and gave a little sideways smile. "I'm not going to talk to you," I said gently. "But you can listen if you want. I'm going to talk to this little life in your tummy. I'm going to minister to this baby who is trying to kick his way free."

She nodded and smiled again, then let out a scream of pain as her stomach once again convulsed in an excruciating cramp.

It seemed so natural. Having heard Larry helped; but what I was doing seemed the most natural thing in the world. As an adult I was taking authority over an unruly child. And even though I knew the baby could not hear me—or even if it could it could not understand—nevertheless I realized I was setting some spiritual principles in motion which would cause the child to obey. The fear and anxiety which had filled the room earlier had only caused the child to be more frightened. Now I was trusting that the spirit of love and power and a sound mind would cast out that fear, and it would be replaced with a spirit of authority and submission.

"Little baby . . ." It sounded so strange. Maybe I should talk a little louder. I raised my voice. "Little baby, you don't know

156

me. In fact, you don't know anyone. That's your problem. You're lost and lonely and afraid. But I've been sent here by your Creator to tell you that you are a child of God. You have been created by God. But you've not met Him because you're all closed up in there. But I want to tell you about Him. He's a loving Father. He's taking care of you. He put you there, and He wants you to stop all that fussing and kicking and rebelling. You don't need to be afraid. You don't need to try to kick your way out of that pocket you're in. Your life is in the hands of the heavenly Father. If He wants to come get you and take you home, that's His business. If He wants you to stay inside your mother and grow, that's His business, too. You don't have to worry about it. Now, in the name of God's Son, Jesus, I tell you to lie down and be quiet. You've got everything you need in there. Just relax and be quiet; God is in control."

As I was going through this little procedure, I kept my hands on the young woman's stomach, resting gently, not moving. Beneath my fingers I could actually feel her stomach begin to relax; the swelling went down, the tight muscles loosened. She had her knees pulled up, but as I ministered to her baby, she straightened out on the bed. The moaning and screaming had stopped. When I finished speaking, I looked up at her. Her head was back on the pillow. She was asleep.

I breathed a quick *thank You* to my Father and tiptoed out into the hall where her husband and his little group of friends were standing in an anxious huddle. I spoke to the young man.

"She's asleep. Relaxed. The cramping has stopped. I suggest you find a telephone and call your obstetrician in Macon and tell him what has happened. I am sure he is going to ask you to bring her to the hospital so she can be examined. But everything is all right. She and the child are in God's hands."

I returned to the auditorium in time to catch the last of Larry's message. The next morning I learned the rest of the story. The doctor had asked the husband to bring her to the hospital in Macon. They had put her in the back seat of the car so she could stretch out. She had gone back to sleep and sometime during that ride, before they reached the hospital, she miscarried. But she slept all

157

the way through the ordeal. The Lord, who had put the child in her body, had taken the child for reasons unknown this side of Glory. But He did it with decency, order and peace.

As I reflected on the entire event, I became aware once again of the sovereignty of God. Our times are indeed, as David said, "in His hands." It is God who gives life and God who takes it away. There is no reason for us to walk through life with a chip on our shoulder or our fists balled up, anticipating a fight. People who go through life like that always meet someone ready to take on their challenge. The Romans used to say, *Si vis pacem, para bellum.* (If you wish peace, prepare for war.) This is still the theme of our Department of Defense. But in the Kingdom of God the very opposite is true. He who is servant is leader, he who is last is first, he who ministers peace is the strongest warrior. As God's children we can walk through this world unafraid, for our times are in His hands. He is in sovereign control of our lives and of this universe.

We often forget that. We forget it when we are tense, anxious, when the money runs out, when our job is terminated, when the doctor says we have cancer, when the little baby inside begins to try to get out. We forget that God is in control of His world—and especially of His children.

There is an interesting story in Mark 4 which illustrates this. All day Jesus had been teaching along the shore of the Sea of Galilee. When evening came, He asked His disciples, most of whom were fishermen and had their own boats, to take Him to the other side of the big lake. But His request was more than a suggestion; it was a positive affirmation. "Let us pass over unto the other side" (Mark 4:35).

Since all the disciples could not get in the one boat, they took several other smaller boats also. Jesus, who was physically tired, settled down in the stern of the boat, put His head on a pillow and went to sleep. As still happens on the Galilee, a great storm arose without any warning and suddenly the tiny ships were in danger of being capsized. Water was pouring in over the gunwales. The disciples were bailing, but it looked like the ships were going down. Seeing Jesus still asleep in the midst of this horrible storm, one of the men cried out: "Master, carest thou not that we perish?" It was a simple, human cry. "Master, do something!"

Jesus woke up. Seeing the fear on the faces of the disciples, He spoke to the sea: "Peace, be still." Immediately the wind ceased to blow, the huge waves subsided, and the storm was over.

Then turning to His followers, Jesus rebuked them. "Why all this fear? Have you no faith?"

That remark used to bother me, for it seemed to be an unjust rebuke. Who wouldn't be afraid in a situation like that? But you cannot understand Mark unless you remember Mark. Before they embarked, Jesus had affirmed: "We're going to the other side."

Faith is believing God will do what He says, regardless of the height of the waves. Fear causes us to look at the circumstances. Faith causes us to look at God. It is the gift which enables us to go to sleep in the middle of a storm, knowing God has promised we will cross over—or go to sleep in the middle of a miscarriage, knowing God is in total control.

As the ongoing ministry of Jesus, not only do we have faith to believe God's word will bring us through, but we have the authority to speak to the elements—just as Jesus did—if they get in the way of God's intent and purpose.

Spiritual authority is one of the attributes which accompanies salvation and the Spirit-controlled life, yet it is so seldom used. How vividly I remember the reply Corrie ten Boom gave when asked about a certain missionary family who were under great attack on the mission field, harassed by circumstances, defeated by sickness, plagued by evil spirits. The fabled old Dutch woman shook her head sadly. "They have given all, but they have not taken all."

How desperately we need to take the authority God has given us and defeat the enemies which surround us. The authority to lay hands on the tummy of a young woman and speak to that life inside, kicking its heels and rebelling, and say, "In the name of Jesus, little baby, lie down and relax."

Shortly after I had been baptized in the Holy Spirit, I received a call from the principal of the high school in the community where we lived, asking me to preach the sermon to the graduating class at baccalaureate. The high school had never had a baccalaureate service before, but since several of the graduating seniors attended our little church, they put pressure on the school administration who agreed. It was to be a big affair in the football stadium the first Sunday night in June.

I gave little thought to it for we were having our own problems in the church about that time. We lived in a transient community and a number of our people were either associated with the nearby space center or stationed at Patrick Air Force Base. As a result, people were constantly moving in and out of the community—more out than in. Our church had grown even smaller than the original 40 families we began with a year before and now my open declaration that I had been "baptized in the Holy Spirit" had everyone on edge, wondering what was going to happen next. They did take some comfort, however, that I had been asked to deliver the first baccalaureate sermon at the big high school and, realizing that 80 percent of the young people in the high school were "unchurched," had been praying for me.

Three days before the scheduled Sunday evening service in the football stadium, the east coast of Florida was buffeted by a preseason hurricane which came roaring through the Caribbean and up the Atlantic seacoast until it reached the city of Melbourne. Mysteriously it remained stationary, about 10 miles off the coast, dumping tons of water on our city. It rained torrents for 48 hours straight. Sunday morning the high school principal called my house.

"We have almost three inches of water on the grass turf at the stadium," he said. "If it doesn't stop raining by four o'clock this afternoon, we're calling off the baccalaureate service."

I went to church that morning in an anxious mood. Ordinarily I'm not too eager to speak at community functions, but this was different. For the first time in my life, I felt I had something to share with the people. I had met a God of miracles, and I was eager to introduce Him to the students and their parents. But I couldn't do a thing unless the rain stopped. With the eye of the hurricane directly off the coast, however, there was no way. Even if the hurricane began to move, it would not be far enough away by evening for the rain to cease.

That afternoon I called five or six of the men in the church and asked them to meet me at the Tabernacle at 3 P.M. to pray. They sensed my urgency and agreed to be there. We arrived in the pouring rain and dashed to the shelter of the building. We stood in a circle in the side of our little meeting room and held hands. The rain was falling so hard we could scarcely make ourselves heard. One by one the men prayed.

"Lord, you control the weather. Please make it stop raining."

"Lord, you opened the Red Sea; now part the clouds so we can have the service tonight."

"Lord, we believe you ordained Jamie to speak tonight, but he can't do it in the rain. Isn't there something you can do about it?"

"Lord, you created the sun and the rain, and we sure need the sun right now rather than the rain."

They were all good, honest, sincere prayers. But nothing happened. In fact, I don't think we really expected anything to happen. We were just praying because we didn't know what else to do.

Then it was my time to pray. But when I opened my mouth, instead of the usual Baptist "sentence prayer," I heard myself saying something that was so ridiculous I was shocked. But the words just poured forth. I was shouting.

"IN THE MIGHTY NAME OF JESUS, I COMMAND YOU CLOUDS TO GO AWAY! I COMMAND YOU RAIN TO STOP FALLING! I REBUKE YOU, EVIL HURRICANE, AND COMMAND YOU TO DEPART! OPEN, CLOUDS, AND LET THE SUN SHINE THROUGH!"

My word! Had that come out of me? I had never spoken like that before. I looked around at the other men, still standing in our circle holding hands. They were all staring at me—and I could understand why. None of us, including me, seemed to want to hang around any longer. I choked out, "Let's go home." We all picked up our rain coats and umbrellas and headed for the door.

But instead of walking out into the rain, we walked out into brilliant sunshine. Water was everywhere. The streets were flooded up over the curbs and sidewalks. Water was dripping from the trees and plants. But overhead the sky was blue and the summer sun was shining through, reflecting off the water below

161

"Hallelujah!" one of the men shouted. Then, catching himself, he blushed. We dashed to our cars, but I knew something had happened in that room that would not only change my life forever, but change the lives of those men who were with me.

That night I preached the baccalaureate sermon to a group of kids who marched out on the field in caps and gowns, barefooted. All around us we could see the rain falling in sheets. But the football stadium was under clear skies. The Methodist pastor who gave the invocation asked me before I marched out on the field if I wasn't going to take my umbrella in case it rained. I'm sure he didn't understand my grin when I said, "Not after what I've just been through."

I had never preached with such power. And authority. And when I shared about the reality of a miracle-working God, I knew I was speaking from personal experience—not from someone else's testimony. By the time we were back at the car after the service, it had started to rain again—and continued to rain for another 24 hours before the hurricane moved out to sea and dissipated.

The idea that God is speaking today—and that we are able to hear Him—is foreign to most of us. People who "hear voices" are considered strange. If you "act on that voice," you are considered psychotic. Yet, when we stop and consider that God has not just set certain laws in motion by which the universe is run and then stepped back out of the way but still intervenes in the affairs of men through His Son Jesus Christ, and that we are the Body of Christ here on earth—well, how else will God speak unless it is through one of us?

Recently I was one of the invited speakers at a convention of Christian businessmen in a northern city. Several thousand people were in attendance, filling the ballroom for three days at the beautiful Hilton Hotel. The singing was beautiful, many of the messages were inspired and there seemed to be some genuine spiritual activity taking place as people committed themselves to the Lord, and some were even healed.

However, as is sometimes the case, some of the leaders got caught up in the spiritual excitement and began to think they were in control. I first noticed it at the Saturday morning meeting. I had spoken Friday night and the meeting had been good. Solid. But the next morning, as I was sitting on the platform with the other speakers and a number of Christian leaders, I sensed things were becoming commercial. It started with a series of marketing announcements in the worship service—selling books (including some of mine), tapes and records. I have always been uncomfortable when this happens. It is one thing to make the books and tapes available for those who want to purchase them but another thing to hawk them from the platform as one might sell snake oil from the tailgate of a covered wagon. Later in the meeting the same commercial spirit was exhibited when the platform leader launched into a long, emotional appeal on the sad state of finances in the organization. This was followed by an offering in which he asked people to pledge money on a monthly basis. "Who will give $1,000 per month? Who will give $500? Who will give $100 per month to keep this great organization alive?" People stood, to the applause of others, and waved their checkbooks to indicate the amount of their pledge. I was appalled. And saddened.

Then the song leader, a short man with a big voice, began playing the role of religious cheerleader. Employing a number of hackneyed gimmicks, including some "Jesus cheers," he tried to whip the people into an emotional frenzy. There is a place for joyful applause, dancing in the Spirit, even shouting. But such activity must be inspired, fueled and directed by the Holy Spirit—not by some grasshopper leading a cheering section.

I was sickened, but I held my peace. It did not seem appropriate for an invited guest, one sitting on the platform at that, to interrupt the meeting and bring correction. Besides, several of those in charge of the meeting served on the board of one of the publishing companies which was paying part of my salary. So, to a degree, not only was I a guest but an employee as well.

During one of the moments while the song leader was catching his breath between choruses, there was a sudden interruption in the meeting. From the back of the room came an utterance in tongues. The room grew silent as the man spoke, strong, forcefully, in an unknown tongue. I have never given a public utterance in tongues, and only on rare occasions have I felt I had an interpretation for such an utterance. But this time, as the man continued speaking, I began receiving the interpretation. It was as clear as any word I have ever received. I could almost hear what God was telling me to say when the utterance was completed. I was terrified, and knew I could not speak what I was hearing:

"I am appalled by what is going on in this place in my name. You have quenched my Holy Spirit who wants to lead you into holy places of worship. You are making a mockery out of praise . . . you have turned my house of prayer into a den of thieves . . . your sounds come before me as a stench in my nostrils. Be still, and I will move sovereignly among you . . ."

There was more. It was coming so fast I could scarcely remember it. I knew it was God's word for that group at that time. The man speaking in tongues stopped. Again there was a moment of silence. I knew I should speak out. But I was afraid. I was an invited guest. I was sitting on the platform surrounded by great men of God. Who was I, a newcomer, to inject such a harsh message of condemnation? I stood silently, my head bowed, hoping someone else would give the interpretation but knowing no one else would; for God had given it to me. Alone.

The silence lasted only a moment. The song leader, having caught his breath, seemed offended that anyone—including God—would interrupt his method of leadership. "How about another chorus?" he beamed. And he was off and running, thumping the pulpit and clapping his hands in time to the music.

Inwardly I was burning with relief—and shame. When we finally sat down, I reached under my chair to adjust some papers when the man next to me, an older minister from another state whom I had met only that morning, leaned over and whispered in my ear.

"You had the interpretation for that utterance in tongues. Why didn't you speak it out?"

I could hardly straighten up. It felt like someone had kicked me in the pit of my stomach and driven all the air out of me. I knew my face had turned crimson. I looked up and tried to speak, but nothing came out. "I-I-I . . ."

He shook his head and said with finality, "You should always be obedient when God tells you to do something. We all needed to hear His word at that moment."

I remember very little about the rest of that meeting. Later in my hotel room I sat with several friends and explained what had happened. They, too, had felt God was trying to interrupt the soulish activity to bring His order—but none of them had received the direct word. Only I. And I had been too scared to speak. However, as I prayed in my room with my friends, I made a fresh commitment to God. From that time on, if God told me to say something, I would do it. Better to be criticized by man than to disappoint God.

God is seeking men and women willing to be His voice, His hands, containers for His power, dispensers of His love. He is waiting for men and women to step forward saying, "Our times are in your hands—we trust you with our lives."

X

The Jonah Complex

I don't even remember what we were arguing about. It all seems so nonsensical now—but then it must have been a pretty big thing. It probably centered around the fact I pay more attention to other people than I do to her.

That particular day the children were at school and the house had been quiet most of the morning. I had been in my studio working and had emerged for lunch. While Jackie was putting the last items on the table, I made a quick phone call to my secretary to see if anything had come up during the morning which needed attention. When I hung up, Jackie commented something to the effect that it would have been nice had she been the first person I spoke to when I appeared from my study. I should have admitted I was preoccupied, apologized and given her a big hug—which was all she really wanted. Instead, I made some snide remark about the difficulties of moving into spiritual maturity. And suddenly we were in the middle of a fight.

I don't react very well when I am hungry—or preoccupied. And that day I was both. Before I knew it, I was angry. The argument moved, as most marital arguments do, from the original point of contention to numerous other subjects—including some of my past mistakes. Lunch was forgotten as we stalked each other around the kitchen, each trying to prove our point. Frustrated, I finally picked up a heavy salt shaker and, before I could think, smashed it against the wall above the breakfast table.

The salt shaker disintegrated into a thousand slivers of pottery, which, mixed with the salt, went everywhere—especially over the sandwiches and into soup already on the table. Fortunately, the beautiful yellow and white wallpaper was not cut, but there was a large, squishy indentation in the gypsum wallboard behind it— a scar which remains to this day.

As usual, Jackie decided that was a good time to leave the room. I got the whisk broom and a thin piece of cardboard and went to work, on my knees, cleaning up the mess. That is an ideal position in which to repent. Which I did. When it was all over and the kitchen was back to normal—minus one rosebud salt shaker from Jackie's favorite "Desert Rose" pattern and plus one squishy indentation in the wall over the breakfast table—I went to find my wife and apologize. She was upstairs, stretched out on the bed, reading her Bible.

"We both needed to skip lunch anyway," she said, after I apologized for my behavior and for showering our food with tiny slivers of pottery.

We sat and talked for a long time. I talked about my explosive nature, which was not nearly as bad as it used to be, but still an insult to me and others around me. She talked about her insecurities and petty jealousies and why she was always demanding from me more than was reasonable for me to give. We traced our actions back to various times in our past when we had been wounded. Then we prayed together and spent a little time making up. Forty-five minutes later, when all the emotions had passed, Jackie rather nonchalantly said, "Have you ever read the last chapter of Jonah?"

I lay back on the bed, thinking that arguments weren't so bad if they all wound up this way. I gradually realized she was talking to me, and I asked her to repeat it.

"While you were down there cleaning up your mess, I came up here, opened the Bible and was reading the Book of Jonah. Have you ever read the last chapter?"

I thought. Jonah? Well, it had been a long time since I had read the first chapters. Even then, I had to admit I had stopped at the whale.

"I think you ought to read the entire book," Jackie said. "I think it will reveal some things about your anger—and your inability to control it."

I felt myself growing tense again. Why did she have to spoil such a peaceful moment with preaching? Then I recalled our conversation, how we had been so honest with each other regarding our frailties and flaws. Why shouldn't I listen to her? After all, I expected her to listen to me. So I promised her that before the day was over I would sit down and read the entire Book of Jonah— all two and one-half pages of it.

After dinner that night and after the children had gone to town for a football game, Jackie and I were alone again. She was sitting at the dining room table with her checkbook and a big green accounting book which our CPA insists we keep in case we are ever audited again by the Internal Revenue Service. I pulled up a chair at the breakfast table, ran my fingers gingerly over the depression in the wall thinking I needed to get some kind of decorative plaque to cover it and opened my Bible to the Book of Jonah.

As I said, it is a short book. Four chapters long. Most of the story is familiar. Jonah receiving a call from God to preach in Nineveh. His running from God. The incident aboard the ship when he is finally thrown overboard. That infamous whale. Then Jonah picking himself up off the beach and, reeking of seaweed and caviar, heading out to Nineveh to preach the Word of the Lord.

But it was the rest of the story Jackie wanted me to read— and I did so with some care. It seems that when a prophet with seaweed in his hair shows up and preaches repentance, people take him seriously. Not only did the people repent, but so did the king. They all put on sackcloth, smeared themselves in ashes, and God honored their repentance and withheld His judgment.

Then Jonah went outside the city, and that's where the difficult part of the story commences. Jonah was angry. He was angry because his theology had been shaken. It seems Jonah, the Jew, felt all

Assyrians deserved to be destroyed. In fact, he was hoping they would not repent and he could sit outside the city and watch as God wiped them out with fire and brimstone. When the destruction was withheld, however, Jonah grew angry and cried out to God to take his life.

One of the best ways to discover what a man is really like is to discover what makes him angry. I guess that was the reason Jackie wanted me to read about Jonah—because it seems his anger was simply evidence of some other things inside him which were all messed up.

I paused as I read, thinking about the incident at lunch. It was just one of many, for I get angry at a lot of things. Big things seldom make me angry. It is the little things which cause me to blow my top. Just let someone scratch the surface of my life, upset my pet plan, disrupt my routine, interfere with my . . . everything seemed to be centered around the word "my." Just as it was with Jonah. He had come to Nineveh with a chip on his shoulder. He was prejudiced. He had hated the Assyrians all his life. After all, the Jews were God's chosen people—not the Arabs. Had it not been for that storm at sea and God's indisputable direction for his life, he would have been safe in Tarshish. Even so, he arrived in Nineveh convinced he was right—and they were wrong. He could not handle it when they became right too.

I thought ahead. What made Jesus angry? Or better, what didn't make Him angry? They tried to stone Him at Nazareth, right after He made His purpose known in public. That didn't make Him angry.

He did not become angry when He was feeding the 5,000, and His disciples didn't have any faith.

He did not become angry when He beckoned the men to walk on water with Him and only Peter had enough gumption to try it. Nor did He become angry when Peter lost his faith and began to sink.

He was not angry at the religious leaders when they rejected His healing miracles.

He was not angry when a group of men disrupted the preaching services and took the roof off and spilled dirt and debris all over the pulpit. It didn't seem to bother Him that they were tearing up someone's property.

He wasn't even angry when His disciples—after three years of teaching—asked Him stupid questions. Just the night before He died, Phillip interrupted one of His most profound teachings by saying, "We don't know what you're talking about. You keep talking about the way to the Father. We don't even know who the Father is, much less the way."

Jesus answered back so gently. Patiently. "You mean you've been with me for three years and do not know that I am the way— the truth and the life? And if you've seen me, you've seen the Father. For we are of the same spirit." No anger. Just eternal patience.

Even when the men who were closest to Him went to sleep in the garden after He asked them to watch for those who would come to arrest Him, He was not angry. Nor was He angry when they all fled—leaving Him alone. He was not even angry when He was falsely accused, mocked, beaten, and finally hung up on a cross to die. He was often sad. Sometimes, it seems, disappointed. But seldom angry.

What did make Him angry?

He was angry when the Pharisees, the religious leaders of the day, took cruel advantage of the poor, of widows and orphans. The entire 23rd chapter of Matthew is a fierce diatribe against people who act religious but are not spiritual at heart.

In the 25th chapter of Matthew, He was angry. Here it was a different kind of anger. He was angry at a man who did not use what he had been given for the glory of God. He called him wicked and slothful.

Another time He was passing down the road and spotted a fig tree covered with leaves but producing no figs. He cursed the tree and it died. His anger then was toward those who held out promises but made no pretense at delivering.

And of course there was that famous scene in the Temple the week before He was crucified when He drove out the moneychangers who had taken the house of prayer and turned it into a den of thieves and robbers. He was really angry that time. Yet He turned right around and healed both a blind man and a crippled man in the Temple.

I came back to Jonah, sitting under a big leafy gourd vine which God had caused to grow up almost instantaneously to give him shade. Now Jonah was angry again. This time because a big green worm came along, ate the vine and caused it to die—taking away his shade.

No wonder Jackie wanted me to read the last chapter of Jonah. That could have been me, sitting out there in the hot Assyrian sun. I'm angry at the Assyrians because they repented. I'm angry at God for not wiping them out. I'm angry at the worm. I'm angry at myself because I can't control my anger.

How like Jonah I was. How unlike Jesus.

I sat there in the kitchen at the breakfast table, looking up at the dent in the wall. At least Jonah had finally obeyed God and gone to preach to the Assyrians. And I hadn't done anything but lose my temper and bust my wife's best salt shaker all over the kitchen.

I could see her in the dining room, poring over those books. Her check stubs were scattered all over the table. Bills and receipts were in little piles on the floor nearby. It was 9:30 P.M. on a Friday, and she had been going since 6 A.M. when she got up to get breakfast for the children before they left for school. I felt a hot wave of shame sweep through me. How stupid can a man be? Here God had given me something far more valuable than Jonah's gourd vine—the most wonderful wife in the world—and I showed my appreciation by smashing her salt shaker against the wall. *Some man of God you are. You're more like those whited sepulchers Jesus condemned than God's man of faith and power.*

So getting out pencil and paper, I decided to use the rest of the evening, while Jackie was balancing the books, listing the things that made me angry and why. It was quite an experience.

First of all, I discovered that I seldom got angry at the things which made Jesus angry. Next I discovered that the things which made me angry were legion. I got angry at a whole lot of things. As a matter of fact, I spent a great portion of my life being angry at something—or someone.

Shortly afterwards I heard Jackie sigh as she closed her ledger,

172

pushed back her chair and came into the kitchen. She stood at the sink for a few moments, letting the water run over her hands, then dried them with a paper towel and came over to where I was at the table.

"Reading Jonah?"

"How'd you guess?"

"Well, I figured you were when I saw you making a list."

"Oh?" I felt the back of my neck growing red.

"I'll bet you're making a list of all the things that make you angry, aren't you?"

I was really blushing by this time. I tried to cover my list. "You think you know me pretty well, don't you?"

"I'm not as stupid as you think," she chuckled. "Let me see your list. I'll bet I can add some things you've left off."

I flushed with anger as she reached for my list. I yanked it away.

"See? There's one I'll bet you didn't add. 'I get angry when my wife looks over my shoulder.'"

I sighed, shook my head in resignation and pushed the list at her. "Go ahead. I might as well be hung up naked before the world."

She reached out, rubbed the back of my neck and the tops of my shoulders in a gesture that always brings peace. "Why don't we work on this together? Instead of your making a list, let me make one for you. And you make one for me."

Now that was something I could really get my teeth into.

It turned out to be a remarkably revealing procedure. I recommend it only if you can stand the white light of honesty and then only if the one making the list knows you well enough—and loves you well enough—to list everything. I guess, if I lived with my mother, I could have asked her to do it. (Although I'm not so sure she would have been as devastatingly honest as my wife—and I am certain she would not have enjoyed it as much.) As it was, Jackie seemed to enjoy listing—with my approval—all the things that, in her opinion, made me angry.

And I, in turn, thought it was a great opportunity for me to point out some of her anger points.

My list of things which made Jackie angry included:

—when I lie to her—and she finds it out;
—when I interrupt her while she's talking;
—my refusal to discipline the children;
—my refusal to back her up when she disciplines the children;
—when I leave the car windows open at night and it rains in and gets the seat wet and she has to take the children to school;
—when I invite people home to lunch—or home to spend a month as our guests—without asking her first;
—when some other woman makes a play for me;
—when I respond to some other woman who makes a play for me;
—when I promise to take her someplace special and then cancel out to help someone else;
—especially if that "someone else" is another woman.

Her list of the things which make me angry was much longer. It included things like:

—interruptions;
—incompetence (in the men around you or the wife beside you);
—intolerance;
—messiness (such as someone leaving the cap off the toothpaste or not wringing out a wet wash cloth);
—sickness;
—name droppers;
—injustice;
—laziness (such as when one of your fellow workers puts off an assigned task or when one of the children doesn't return the tools after they have used them);
—criticism by your wife;
—when your wife disagrees with you in public;
—betrayal;
—cruelty;
—compromise;
—liars;
—when you are caught in a lie;
—stinginess;
—ingratitude;
—egotistical persons;
—when your wife refuses to get you out of the mess you've gotten yourself into;

—blasphemy;

—lack of courtesy to a woman (unless it is your wife);

—your own ineptness.

I sat for a long time looking at her list—the one she had made about me. She was right in most instances. But some of them puzzled me.

"What's this bit about 'sickness'?" I asked. "What do you mean I get angry at sickness?"

"Oh, I don't mean sickness per se," she answered. "I mean you get angry when I get sick."

I've given a lot of thought to that. The Lord is forever revealing new areas of hard-heartedness in my spirit, and that is one of them. I recall, when I first entered the ministry, there were mornings when my young pregnant wife would be too sick to get out of bed. That meant I had to be late to work, staying home in order to fix breakfast for the children, get them dressed and clean up the house. That smoldering anger built up in me, and since I was not able to express it against the busybodies who were constantly checking but never helping, I vented it against my wife. "If you wouldn't get sick in the morning, you could do the housework, and I could get on to my office and be busy with the important things of God."

At first she reacted in anger. "If you hadn't gotten me pregnant, I wouldn't be sick!"

Later she gave in under my relentless attacks and would say softly, "Have you ever considered that your wife and children might be just as much the 'work of God' as sticking pins in maps in the church office, making sure the financial statements are mailed out and preparing the church bulletin?"

However, like all priests and Levites, it is hard to see the importance of binding up wounds when there are duties awaiting at the Temple. So I passed her by on the other side, fuming all the while at her occasional spells of morning sickness.

Across the years I learned to modulate my anger, to keep it under control. But it was there all the time, smoldering. Every time Jackie was sick, even though I no longer fussed about it, she could sense that deep attitude of anger which was always present in my spirit. What right did she have to get sick? Did she not realize that her sickness prevented me from doing important things and interfered with my way of life?

As I examined this one point, I realized that my anger, like so many other emotions, centered around and grew out of my self-centeredness. Jonah was angry because the worm destroyed his shade. He was angry because it was his prejudices which were called into question. I got angry at Jackie because her sickness, or her needs, disturbed the things I wanted to do. Incompetence on the part of those around me caused me to be angry because that meant I had to do not only my job but theirs as well. It all grew out of my self-centeredness.

Recently I got up early on Sunday morning, as I usually do, and disappeared into my studio in a far wing of the house to prepare myself spiritually and mentally for the Sunday morning service. Jackie and the children like to sleep later on Sundays, but I usually rise early, do some physical exercises, perhaps take a walk through the pine trees and then go into my study to make final notes for my teaching session at the morning service. I deliberately separate myself from the family and the normal confusion that goes along with getting ready for church so as to be in just the right frame of mind to teach the Word.

On that particular Sunday morning, I had followed the normal routine and emerged from my studio at precisely the moment we should get in the car and drive to church. As usual, I expected all the children to be perfectly dressed and sitting in the car, waiting for me to get in behind the wheel and drive us to church, singing and praising the Lord all the way.

Of course it never happened that way, but I found it better to have an unattainable goal than no standard at all. This particular Sunday morning things were worse than usual. Tim was still in the shower. Sandy was upstairs curling her hair. Jackie had opened the refrigerator door to get some milk for the cat, and a big bowl of jello had crashed to the floor. Our oldest son, Bruce, had just pulled up in the driveway announcing he was leaving his little two-seater car for us to drive to church so he could borrow the station wagon for a youth picnic, and the phone was ringing. One of our daughters, away at college, was calling to ask for money. It took about 20 seconds for me to evaluate the situation and lose all the spirituality I had been working on since six that morning. I stormed around a little, did some shouting, popped a button off my shirt and finally announced that everyone could get to church on their own; I was taking the car and leaving.

Halfway down the drive I had second thoughts and returned to wait for the family. It turned out we were still on time, but the tornado of anger which roared through my life and out again had left me washed out—empty. When I stood that morning and confessed my anger and asked how many others in the congregation had gone through similar situations, the show of hands indicated I was in the majority. Fortunately, God took my weakness and converted it to His strength—and gave us all a new revelation that morning about self-centeredness.

Anger is an effect. And for every effect there is a cause. The cause of anger is not hate. The basic cause of anger is fear. Our anger is a façade we raise to hide our insecurities. So when Paul tells Timothy that God has not given us a spirit of fear but of power and of love and of a sound mind—he wipes out all the reasons for self-anger.

All anger is not wrong, of course. The Bible talks a great deal about the anger of God. But God never got angry in relative situations. He was angry only in the area of absolutes. He never struck out at that which was relatively wrong, only against that which was absolutely wrong. What we often call losing our temper really means we have given way to the things which control us: insecurity, fear, jealousy, self-centeredness. Our "temper" is nothing more than the control valve which keeps us in check. But the man under full control of the Holy Spirit is no longer in subjection to the whims, feelings, appetites, passions and lusts which formerly controlled his life. Now all these are in subjection to the higher power of God working within. Instead of being a slave to your anger, anger becomes your servant—a tool in your hands to accomplish good things.

Last year we had a little situation develop which centered around our 15-year-old daughter, Sandy. One afternoon she came home from junior high school, where she was finishing the ninth grade, and announced that Thursday, May 25, was "Freshman Skip Day" at Johnson Junior High School.

I asked her the normal questions. Is this an allowable skip day? Is the school approving? Will she be excused? She answered no to all the questions. If it was allowable it wouldn't be any fun. Half the fun came in doing something which was against the rules. However, she reminded me, Freshman Skip Day was an old and honorable tradition. For years the graduating class at the junior high had participated in skip day. The school officials always knew it was coming and always made a big commotion about it, threatening to suspend any student who skipped, but in the end they always laughed, winked and took it in stride. "Besides," she asked me, "didn't you have a skip day when you were in school back in the 'roaring '20s'?"

I reminded her I wasn't even born during the "roaring '20s," but yes, we did have skip day, and yes, I guessed it would be all right for her to participate since it was an old and honorable tradition.

There were several things I did not know. One of them was the new principal at the junior high school was formerly an assistant superintendent of public education and was not in sympathy at all with skip day, or with any other old and honorable tradition which pulled kids out of school. The other thing I did not know was Sandy had invited all the kids in her class to come out to our house for a swimming party on skip day.

Two weeks before the infamous skip day was to take place, Sandy came home from school very excited. Someone had squealed. The officials had discovered that Thursday, May 25—a day which was supposed to be ultra-secret—was scheduled by the junior high underground as skip day. The rumor was spreading through the school that a number of police officers had been assigned to stations all over the city to arrest the kids as they skipped and put them in jail. So they had a little caucus meeting after school that day and changed skip day from Thursday to Friday. That made it even more fun.

By that time it was too late to back out, and Sandy then told

178

us she had invited a number of her friends out to our house on skip day to swim in the pool. We had no choice but to go along. We insisted, however, that any child who came to our house had to bring a note from the parents granting permission.

Friday, May 26, about 40 ninth-grade children appeared in our back yard—nearly all of them chauffeured by their parents. They were a well-behaved group and all had permission notes. They had brought sack lunches and, after receiving instructions from Jackie on what to do and what not to do in the pool, began their party. They seemed to be having a great time and Jackie left to run some errands, leaving me at home with the 40 kids. Our college-age daughter, Bonnie, was home at the time and agreed to act as the lifeguard.

I returned to my studio and was at work at my desk when I looked out the window and saw children running everywhere. Still dressed in their bathing suits, they were fleeing across the pasture and dashing out into the woods. I leaped up and ran outside only to be met by Bonnie, running toward the house with a breathless expression on her face.

"The principal and the dean of the school are here. They just pulled up in the front driveway."

I glanced around the corner of the house and sure enough, there came the principal of the school. And he had the dean with him—marching across the yard toward the swimming pool. They looked angry. The kids were still fleeing in all directions.

Before I knew it I, too, was fleeing. Back into the house. Up the stairs. It wasn't until I got in the upstairs clothes closet that I realized, *Hey, this is stupid! Why am I running and hiding? This is my house. I live here. I own this house. Why should I flee from the principal and the dean?*

Sheepishly I came back down the stairs, gave Bonnie, who was peeking around the corner of the den, a crooked grin and opened the front door. There were the two school officials. Sullen and angry. I invited them in and we had a little conversation. The principal was very pointed. "I want you to know that what's happened here is strictly against the school board rules. This is not allowed. You are aiding and abetting criminals in your house."

I really didn't know what to do, since legally he was right. I told him I was sorry he felt that way and even more sorry he didn't have a skip day when he was 15 years old. Looking at him, I suspected that he never had been 15 years old, but nevertheless I respected his authority and promised to send the children away.

After he left, I went back outside and called all the children together. I explained the principal was under the authority of the law, and I was under the authority of the principal, and they were under my authority, and they had to leave. They thought it was kind of fun that they had been caught and all came in and called their parents who came after them.

When it was all over, I went back in the house and sat down at my typewriter. My fingers were still shaking from the whole episode. I asked myself, *Why am I afraid of the principal?* After all these years of being out of school, all someone had to say was, "The principal and the dean are here," and I ran and hid.

It relates to fear. Fear of principals, deans and truant officers was built into me as a child. It is still with me. That fear of authority often eventuates itself in anger against authority figures. Once I grasped the fact that it was my house, that I lived there, that whoever was knocking at my door—even if it was the principal—could come in only on my invitation, then I was fine. But until that time, I had been running and hiding like all the rest of the children. Afraid.

People who are offended easily, who are edgy when someone or something rubs them the wrong way, who put up angry defense mechanisms, are usually very insecure, self-centered individuals. We don't want people getting close to us for fear they will discover what we are really like. Discovering that, we are afraid they won't like us any more. It is easier just to get angry.

As Christians come together in community, true koinonia, there will be even more rubbing and touching. We often reject this, afraid that if we are rubbed hard enough, others will discover we are only a thin veneer or that we're hollow inside. But it is only when the masks come off, when the outer layers are discarded, that we can be filled—and eventually, controlled—by the Holy Spirit. The purpose of our being rubbed and sandpapered and chiseled is not to expose us but to open us. A man cannot expand in the spirit if he has 19 coats of paint on him. Wineskins with that kind of covering never can hold the effervescing new wine.

Crusty people, those who get angry easily, are usually stiff and unbending. They have no elasticity. When confronted with situations they cannot handle, they blow up. Blood vessels in their head pop. Or their heart explodes. Or a stomach or colon ruptures or develops an ulcer. The Holy Spirit, however, is the spirit of health. His desire, in controlling us, is to bring us to that place where everything works in harmony with the Lord of the universe—our heavenly Father.

The week after my experience with Jonah, I hung a plaque over that big dent on the breakfast room wall. In the process, the Lord spoke, in the deep area of my heart, and said, "It's all right to hang the plaque, but I want you to remember what it's covering— and how it got there. I want you to remember you are still an angry person who can't control himself. You need the daily control of my Holy Spirit."

Recently I dropped a little note to the wife of a well-known minister who lived out of state. Her husband's newsletter, which I receive, had mentioned an incident in which his wife and her parents had been involved. It was an interesting experience, and I was eager for a little more detail. So I wrote her a note and asked if she would send me full details on the incident her husband had alluded to in his newsletter. At the bottom of the letter, I penned a P.S. which said, "By the way, if you are ever in need of a place of retreat or if you need a shoulder to cry on, Jackie and I would like to invite you to spend a few days in our guest house in Florida."

I didn't think anything about it, for it's an invitation I have given to several others. Ministers' wives, I have discovered, sometimes need to get away from home—and their husbands—for a few days. Two weeks later I got a blistering letter back from my friend, the woman's husband. Not only was he angry, but he was deeply offended. What right did I have to insinuate that he could not take care of all his wife's needs? Didn't I recognize him as her spiritual covering? Didn't I recognize he provided everything she needed? It was a very angry letter.

I spent four days answering that letter. I threw the first five or six answers in the trash, and finally I wrote one that Jackie could approve—one which did not psychoanalyze my brother and point out his reasons for being angry. But the question needs to be faced sometime. Why are we so easily offended? Why do we react with so much anger when things don't go exactly our way? Why will a housewife invariably snap at one child but treat another child gently? Why, when someone comes along and suggests a change in our life style, do we grow angry? Why would a minister assume I had accused him of being less than Mr. Everything to his wife—unless he was indeed deficient? Why have some of you reading this book gotten angry?

Last year I was invited by the pastor of a Presbyterian church in Atlanta to share with his session some of the new concepts being revealed by the Holy Spirit. I tried to be gentle and kind. I told them the story about the ruts in the Sinai. But even as I talked, I sensed one man in the back of the room was building up a full head of steam. His face was blanched and there was a little white ring around his mouth—a sure sign of a coming explosion. When I finished speaking, I opened the floor for questions or discussion. He was the first one on his feet, his eyes narrow, his voice shaking as he talked.

"I am highly offended," he said. "You have come into my church—the church my father belonged to, the church my grandfather helped build—and said we need to change our ways. Well, I want to tell you right now, I'm damn well pleased with the way we're doing things, and I don't intend to change."

Then he sat down.

Fortunately, he was the only one in the room who seemed to feel that way. Immediately others came rushing to my defense and by the time we finished the evening his ruffled feathers were smoothed. But underneath his anger, I knew, was a huge vacuum of insecurity, and I had almost taken away the shroud and exposed him to himself—and his peers. No wonder he had exploded. It was his only defense.

There is a fine line between self-centeredness and self-confidence, between egotism and security. The insecure man is always afraid.

182

The secure man, the man who knows who he is and is unashamed of his flaws—for he has faced them and confessed them long before the accuser gets to him—may be frightened on occasion but never afraid.

In the flyleaf of my Bible I have written a number of messages to myself—personal messages from God to me. One of them says: "Jamie, don't let the world—or the church—mold you into its image." Some of my friends do not understand my sometimes strange ways, but I am determined to hear and do the will of God for me—despite what others think I should do. This does not mean I do not fail and need the correction and adjustment of others. But it does mean that I shall not be ashamed—or afraid—of my imperfections. And I shall push on, despite my flaws, and present my body a living sacrifice, blemishes and all, and believe I am acceptable to His service. For it is far better to risk and fail than to count myself unworthy and not risk at all.

That means I must be willing to be myself—and live with others' anger and not grow angry in return.

One of the areas of my life which is constantly under examination is my relationship with tomatoes. I do not eat them. I never have eaten a tomato. This is not necessarily a religious practice, it is just that I cannot stand the thought of biting into one of those quivering, jellied, nauseating things. It is not that I have anything against tomatoes per se, for I love catsup. I eat catsup on everything from cheese to scrambled eggs. But a long time ago I made a quality decision—and for the life of me I do not know why— that I would not eat tomatoes. The thought of biting into one of them is as repulsive as biting into an earthworm. That's just the way I am.

I almost ate one several years ago. I had ordered a hamburger at a hamburger stand ("Skip the tomatoes, please") and took it back to my table. I had already taken a bite when I discovered I had that awful thing in my mouth. It wasn't the thought of swallowing the tomato which bothered me, it was the thought of chewing it up. Fortunately I was able to spit it out. Then I had to go through the process of getting it off my hamburger before it soaked into the bun—all those little seeds with mucus around them. Then

I discovered I had gotten some of it on my fork and had to wipe it off—much to the pleasure of my children who were watching and giggling. However, I maintained my virginity and can proudly state to this day I have never eaten a tomato (which some theologians, I understand, believe was the fruit Eve gave Adam in the Garden, thus contaminating all mankind).

It doesn't bother me that I don't eat tomatoes. I am not the least bit embarrassed to take the tomatoes out of my salad and put them in my wife's bowl when we go out to eat. I pick them out of the soup as well, for the only thing worse than a raw tomato is a cooked one—especially if it is boiled with okra. Just as I do not drink hard liquor, snort cocaine, dip snuff, sprinkle voodoo dust in my bellybutton or chant incantations to the devil—so I do not eat tomatoes. It is simply part of my way of living and comes as natural as saying "no thank you" when asked if I want a martini or a whiskey sour.

But while some of my Christian friends may applaud my abstinence from hard liquor, very few of them understand my decision to skip tomatoes.

"What? You don't like tomatoes? What's wrong with you anyway?"

"What are you doing, taking all the tomatoes out of your salad?"

"You eat catsup, don't you? What's the difference?"

I've heard these and every other remark during the 47 years I have not eaten tomatoes. The difference is I have chosen not to eat tomatoes. That's my way of life. I do not grow angry when questioned. I am secure. I am satisfied to remain that way.

The other day I visited the cafeteria in Vero Beach with my mother, my wife and a lady missionary friend the same age as my mother. We went through the line and I ordered a piece of ground steak. The woman behind the counter asked if I wanted mushroom sauce on it. I said yes. I didn't know the mushrooms were cooked in tomatoes and before I knew it she had smeared that awful stuff all over my meat—big hunks of quivering, pink tomato in lots of juice. I took it calmly and when we got to our table I began, as unobtrusively as possible, to take the tomatoes off my meat and put them on the bread plate. Well, the ladies at the table thought that was awful. All of them had loud things to say about my not liking tomatoes. My mother said it was a shame I was still like that. My wife said I embarrassed her every time I went to a restaurant. The elderly missionary lady said if I lived overseas long enough I'd learn to eat things like that—and be grateful. I managed to smile through it all and finally wound up pouring the tomato juice into the ashtray on the table to keep it from soaking into my cornbread. I enjoyed my dinner immensely, but the ladies never did seem to get back in the mood for eating.

In the areas where I am secure, where I know who I am and where I am going (such as in the area of my relationship with the despicable tomato), I never grow angry. In such areas I refuse to let the world—even the world of my wife and mother—mold me into its image. It is only when I am on shaky ground, unsure of my stance or afraid to take off my mask and let folks see me the way I really am, that I explode in the defense mechanism of anger.

Salvation, in its purest sense, is becoming the person you really are—the person God created you to be. It is possible, I can report, to live above the humanism of this world and to achieve the individuality and personal identity with God that each man yearns for. But it can be done only when a man comes to grips with the fact he is different, that God has a unique place and purpose for him in life, and he does not need to defend his status—just live it out.

A few years ago I was invited to be one of the principal speakers for a major Episcopal convention in Kansas City. It was quite an honor since I was appearing on the program with two bishops and the dean of a cathedral. Pretty high company for a defrocked Baptist who doesn't even like to wear a necktie. Several days before I was to fly to Kansas City, I bumped into an old friend, the esteemed rector of one of the Episcopal Churches in our city. I was to be the baccalaureate speaker at our local high school again, and the priest was also on the program. We had a few moments before the processional began in the high school gymnasium and he said, "I see where you are to be in high company this coming week."

"How did you know?" I asked.

"Oh, I saw it in one of the brochures."

"I have no idea why they asked me," I said honestly, and a little apologetically. "I'm the only non-Anglican in the line-up."

The priest grinned and said, "Oh, I know why they invited you. Because you painted out your sign."

It was time for us to move to the platform. I was still trying to figure out what he was talking about. Then I remembered. Several years before, when our church was just breaking out of some of the traditional ruts and heading across the desert, we put a sign beside the main road with an arrow which pointed toward our modest building. Feeling that every church needed some kind of slogan, we painted one on the sign. It said: "For those who want more than a Sunday religion."

Several months later one of our elders approached me. "I was in an interdenominational meeting this week," he said. "Some of the people from the Episcopal church were present. One of them told me, in a kind but firm way, that our slogan offended him—and a number of others in the parish as well. He said he didn't see anything wrong with a Sunday religion, and he was disappointed we seemed to be capitalizing on a cheap dig at their beliefs."

My first impulse was to shrug and say, "Tough luck." But that afternoon as I stood in my study, I glanced at another slogan, this one hanging in a frame on my wall. It was a needlepoint gift from some admirer who had heard me use the phrase at some conference, had stitched it beautifully on a piece of cloth, then shipped it to me in a frame. It had been hanging above my typewriter for several months. It said simply:

"It is better to be kind than to be right."

I evaluated that in the light of what I had just heard. My first reaction had been anger. The slogan on our sign was right. Our faith needs to be more than a Sunday religion. Actually, as I thought about it, I knew the priest believed that also. But he is a staunch sacramentalist and to him the most important event of the week is that which takes place when the sacraments are administered to the people. In fact, to him nothing has meaning during the week except that which is related in a dynamic way to the serving

186

of the sacraments. Even though I do not totally agree with that, I deeply respect his position and was eager to move even closer to it. But how could I do that if I was deliberately offending all the sacramentalists in our community with our sign? After all, while my concepts of rightness are a matter of relativity, there is nothing relative about kindness. It is an absolute command from the Holy Spirit.

And be ye kind one to another, tenderhearted, forgiving one another, even as God for Christ's sake hath forgiven you (Ephesians 4:32).

So I had asked someone to paint out the slogan. That's what the priest was referring to. Now the bread I had cast on the waters had come back, and I was to speak to the very group I had earlier offended.

There comes a time in the life of every Spirit-baptized Christian when he has to face the fact that character is more important than charisma. Charisma is a gift to us from God while character is a trait required of us by God. Character means turning the other cheek when slapped. It means walking the second mile after we are forced by another to walk the first. It means giving up our shirt after someone has forced us to give our coat. It means not eating meat or drinking wine in the presence of one who feels these things are wrong. It means reaching out to heal when everything within us says we should slash out with a sword in self-righteous anger.

This kind of character is dangerous, for it makes us vulnerable to the attack of others. There is an interesting story which appears in all four gospels concerning the night Jesus was arrested in the Garden of Gethsemane. Jesus had been praying while His disciples slept. Suddenly the garden was lighted with torches as soldiers and Temple guards came rushing in, led by Judas, to arrest the Son of God. There was very little warning before the soldiers were upon Him. Hearing the disturbance, Simon Peter leaped to his feet and drew his sword. Seeing Malthus, the bodyguard for Annas, the high priest, approaching Jesus, Peter stepped forward and with a single blow of his sword cut off the ear of the armed henchman.

Doubtless Peter intended to cut off his head, but in his sleepy condition he missed.

Jesus then stepped forward, laid His hand on Peter's muscular arm, and said softly, "That's not necessary, Peter. Put away your sword. If I needed to be defended, I could call 10,000 angels."

Then, reaching out to Malthus, He touched the side of his head where blood was gushing out and healed him. It was an extremely delicate moment. The angry Temple guard had already drawn his sword. Peter's wound had made him even angrier. And into this situation stepped the Son of God, exposing His chest as He reached out toward the wounded one. Perhaps Malthus sensed he was in the presence of God. Perhaps he was too shocked to move. The normal reaction would have been to thrust his short sword into the chest of the man who was reaching for him, for it is at that moment of healing that God's people are most vulnerable. But the soft word turned away the wrath of anger.

Here we are, busy defending the Gospel with our sword of the Spirit, slashing in all directions as we declare our rightness. Then comes Jesus, touching ears and healing. Running the risk of being killed—because it is better to be kind than to be right.

Anger is a barrier that blocks relationships. But until I can identify it as such, I will not be able to relate correctly to those I wish to heal. Thus I must constantly ask myself if I am willing to undergo periods of discomfort, even make myself vulnerable to pain and death, in order to bring about change. The self-expressionist says, "Don't inhibit yourself. If you feel it, do it." But it is far better to act your way into a feeling, than to feel your way into a course of action. In this case you can, by a deliberate act, expose yourself to the power of the Holy Spirit who will take that which you cannot control, bring it under His control and use it as a tool for the glory of God.

XI

Kissing Frogs

Perhaps my friend the prophet, Bruce Morgan, is right when he says, "The trouble with Christians is no one wants to kill them anymore."

Every place the Apostle Paul went, there was a revival or a riot. Today's seminaries teach a lot of good things, but few of them teach Christians how to react when rioted against—especially if the Christian is the instigator.

Maybe such things can't be taught and must be caught instead. But very few Christians seem interested these days in getting spit on.

Mike Evans, founder of the B'nai Yeshua Center on Long Island, sponsors a national conference for Messianic Jews called *Shechinah*. Last year's conference was to feature Ruth Stapleton, the sister of President Jimmy Carter, as the keynote speaker. The significance of her appearance and the recognition it would have provided for the evangelistic effort among Jews was too much to go unchallenged. Powerful Jewish and Christian political organizations combined to exert great pressure—and forced her to cancel out at the last minute.

Discouraged, Mike Evans called me at my home in Florida, wondering if he should call off the conference. I suggested he should first examine his motives. Maybe God wanted to send a prophet instead of a princess.

Mike agreed, and invited me.

I accepted and got spit on.

There were about 1,500 present that opening night—most of them Messianic Jews, some of them former rabbis. About 10 minutes into my message, 20 militant young demonstrators jumped to their feet and stormed the platform, shouting slogans like, "Death to Jews for Jesus!" All were members of the Jewish Defense League, led by the National Student Coordinator.

It was a nasty scene. They took over the platform and threatened to cut the microphone wires if not allowed to speak. The police were there, but Mike wisely refused to let them arrest the demonstrators. The more the JDL youth shouted hate and death slogans, the more the people in the audience responded by shouting, "We love you!" When the demonstrators began singing a lively Jewish song, the audience joined in, clapping and dancing the hora. They then went on to sing another six stanzas of the same song which the demonstrators didn't know. The demonstrators had obviously hoped to be handcuffed and dragged bleeding from the stage while the news photographers and TV cameras (which had appeared mysteriously out of the night) snapped their pictures. But none of this happened. Finally Mike agreed to let the leader speak for five minutes if he would then leave peacefully. Fortunately, his threats were captured on the still-running tape recorder.

"This house of slime, this house of profanity will never be allowed to exist. This is just the beginning of the JDL campaign to eradicate the bastard movement. We consider you whores and traitors to your people. This is just the beginning. The burning of this building will be the end."

The group then marched offstage, shaking their fists—but not before someone spit on me, the only *goy* on the platform.

The next morning the New York *Times* carried the story, along with the accusation from the leader that all those people at B'nai Yeshua had been paid $10 a person to love—for no one loves without being paid for it.

He was closer to the truth than he suspected.

It's the business of the church to love—even when you get spit on.

Ironically, one of the classic statements on love (even though the word is never mentioned) was written by the German pastor, Martin Niemoller, one of the outstanding Protestant scholars in Europe during World War II. In writing about the political and religious persecution of the Jews in Nazi Germany, Niemoller stated: "In Germany the Nazis came for the Communists, and I didn't speak up because I was not a Communist. Then they came for the Jews and I didn't speak up because I was not a Jew. Then they came for the Trade Unionists and I didn't speak up because I wasn't a Trade Unionist. Then they came for the Catholics and I was a Protestant so I didn't speak up. Then they came for me—but by that time there was no one to speak up for anyone."

We are not only our brother's keeper, we are our brother's lover—even when he spits on us.

Three weeks later I was speaking at Gerald Derstine's beautiful Christian Retreat in Bradenton, Florida. The second night I poked a little fun at some of Christendom's sacred cows—the idols we set up. After the service I was standing at the front of the auditorium shaking hands with a number of people who gathered around. There was a lot of love flowing when suddenly I was face to face with a stocky, serious-faced woman in her early 50s. Her graying hair was pulled back and tied tightly in a bun. She wore no makeup and her face was hard, her eyes flashing anger.

"You are a servant of the devil," she said loudly.

Suddenly everything was deathly still. She continued, "How dare you make fun of the cross around my neck and the dove on my license plate? Jesus died on this cross. God sent that dove to bring His Holy Spirit."

I should have kept my mouth shut. "Lady, Jesus didn't die on that cross. That cross is made of gold, and you bought it from some moneychanger in the temple."

It was then she spit on me. A great big spit which clung briefly to the lapel of my coat and then dribbled down toward my shoe.

"Why don't you give us the Word instead of all this garbage?" she sneered, and then stalked off in the direction of Gerald who was standing in the back of the auditorium. I hoped, for his sake, she was out of spit.

"Now what are you supposed to do?" a sympathetic woman asked as she handed me a kleenex.

"I'm supposed to wait until she stops croaking," I said seriously. "Then I'll go up and kiss her. Who knows, perhaps she'll turn into a princess."

Everyone laughed, and the fellowship was restored. But it's more than a laughing matter. The story of the handsome prince who came under the spell of the wicked witch and was turned into a frog—redeemable only through a kiss—is far more spiritual truth than a fairy tale. There are a lot of froggy people in this world, not a few of whom are in the church. The only way they can be transformed is for someone who has a lot to lose, like a Christian, to see the potential beneath their frogginess and kiss them into their inheritance.

But in kissing frogs, the Christian makes himself vulnerable. There is always the danger the frog will spit on you—or even worse. It may be the frog is not a handsome prince at all but just a frog keeping a tally sheet of suckers.

Yet we must keep on bending, stooping, kissing and hoping. Sometimes it's the frog himself who objects. "I'm poison; kiss me and you'll die too." Or perhaps he's a liberated frog who says, "I don't want to be a prince. I only want self-fulfillment as an amphibian." Other times the pressure comes from those around us who are too dignified to stoop and kiss and are threatened by our serving posture. But someone must run the risk, for there is no other way this ugly, froggy old earth will be redeemed.

Under the warts is the image of God. It has been covered by sin and hardened, often, by those who came in the name of the church with whips rather than the balm of Gilead. But the potential of kingship remains and can be released only through someone willing to bend, stoop and kiss.

Our life pattern is Jesus, who was the greatest frog kisser of all. He gave up His exalted place in heaven to walk among us as a servant, to wash dirty feet, receive our spit and our spears and in a final act of supreme grace to send His Holy Spirit to fill the very ones who rejected Him so they could carry on the work He began—kissing frogs.

The young JDL leader said it's unnatural to love. He's right. Only those whose lives are controlled by another Spirit will do such foolish things as turn the other cheek, walk the second mile, join an enemy in song (and teach him an extra stanza or two) and stoop to kiss frogs.

Why, one will hardly die for a righteous man—though perhaps for a good man one will dare even to die. But God shows his love for us in that while we were yet sinners [*while we were yet spitting on him*] Christ died for us (Romans 5:7–8, RSV).

That's the ultimate in kissing frogs.

Can men of God, despite pride and rigidity, do less?

There is so much we do not understand about the ways of God, especially why everything in the Kingdom seems so upside down to our way of thinking. Bruce Morgan is right when he says if we continued to live by the law which says an eye for an eye and a tooth for a tooth, we'd soon create a blind and toothless generation. God has a better way—the way of grace. Yet even this defies description and explanation—at least from man's point of view.

The prophet Habakkuk, hundreds of years before Christ, spent a good portion of his life trying to figure out why God allows people to be turned into frogs in the first place. Habakkuk's little book is composed of two long complaints and a sigh of resignation. Habakkuk didn't like the way God was running the universe, especially with the way He was dealing with His chosen people, Israel. It didn't seem right that God was going to destroy His own nation, even if they were wicked. Especially was Habakkuk upset that God was using a nation even more wicked than Judah to do His dirty work for Him. God answered Habakkuk's complaint with a simple statement of fact, saying in essence, "O man of this earth, you don't know what you're talking about. True, I am sending the Chaldeans to destroy the nation of Judah. But take comfort, for in turn the Chaldeans will be destroyed also."

That didn't seem to comfort the prophet very much. It was like saying, "Yes, that mob is going to burn your house, kill your wife and children and drag you off into slavery. But take heart, for in the long run they will be punished for their wicked deeds."

So Habakkuk complained again. He acknowledged the nation of Judah deserved to be punished, but he still didn't understand. A second time God answered his complaint with exactly the same answer He gave the first time. That should not surprise us, for God's answers are always constant. There is no turning with Him, no changes. His ways are absolute; it is man who must change—not God.

It was not until Habakkuk bent his knee before God in resignation, praying what Catherine Marshall calls the most powerful of all prayers, the prayer of relinquishment, that his complaints turned to a cry of victory. The heart of Habakkuk's book can be summed up in three progressive verses. He began with a statement of blind disgust:

> For the vision is yet for an appointed time . . . the just shall live by his faith (Habakkuk 2:3–4).

He moved to a revelation:

> For the earth shall be filled with the knowledge of the glory of the Lord, as the waters cover the sea (2:14).

And wound up with an exhortation of affirmation:

> But the Lord is in his holy temple: let all the earth keep silence before him (2:20).

He then closes his book with a mighty prayer of resignation which G. Campbell Morgan once called "the greatest and most priceless passage in the whole of poetic prophecy":

> Although the fig tree shall not blossom, neither shall fruit be in the vines; the labour of the olive shall fail, and the fields shall yield no

194

meat; the flock shall be cut off from the fold, and there shall be no herd in the stalls: Yet I will rejoice in the Lord, I will joy in the God of my salvation. The Lord God is my strength, and he will make my feet like hinds' feet, and he will make me to walk upon mine high places (3:17-19).

That's looking at frogs and seeing princes. But before the transformation can take place, there is an awful lot of suffering. Any theology which denies suffering as a reality is incomplete and deals only on a superficial level, for suffering is God's greatest tool to accomplish His will. That's the reason God used Chaldeans to bring havoc on His chosen race, why He allowed the Jews and Romans to team up and crucify His Son, why He lets His people get spit on. It's all part of the training course designed by the Father and implemented by the Holy Spirit to bring us to the place of conformity to God's Son, Jesus Christ.

A former church musician called from Houston, asking if I would see him if he flew to Melbourne. I have a soft spot in my heart for men of God who have, for whatever reason, dropped out of the ministry. Beneath the froggy exterior I keep seeing the heart of a prince yearning to return to the service of the King. This man, at one time had been well-known among evangelical Christians. But there had been problems. Years ago while he was living in Memphis he had an affair with a single girl. She bore an illegitimate son. He loved her deeply, but because of his ministry—and because he already had a wife—he chose not to live with her.

The other woman took her child and moved to Houston where she went into the real estate business. The evangelist, on the other hand, tried to continue with his ministry. But there was no anointing of God. Things were not going well in his own house, even though they had, by then, a little baby of their own. His wife learned about his affair and was making life miserable. Finally, in desperation, the man left his wife and son and moved to Houston to be with his mistress.

But things were no better. By that time the illegitimate son had grown up and left home. He was part of the drug culture and rebellious toward all authority. He did not know the man who had moved in with his mother was his real father and would not have cared had he known. The evangelist's wife, back in Tennessee, filed for divorce. She sold his beautiful grand piano and was threatening to get rid of all his other personal things. His state of misery finally became so acute that he called me from Houston, asking if he could fly over and talk.

I heard his sad story. The Chaldeans had stripped him clean The only point of contact left between him and God was his 11-year-old son back in Memphis, living with his wife. "I can walk away from my wife," he told me frankly. "I can walk away from my mistress. I can even walk away from God. But every time I put my head on my pillow, I think about that little curly-headed kid with the big glasses growing up back in Memphis without a daddy—and I can't stand it. I can't sleep. I can't eat. My heart is broken. All I can think about is that innocent child and all I have done to hurt him. Yet I cannot go back. My wife doesn't want me, and I don't want her. What can I do?"

He sat across from me, his head in his hands, his handsome face bathed in tears. Some say guilt is not of God. But guilt is of God if you're guilty. And this man was guilty. It was God who had brought him to this place of desperation.

"I have gone from preacher to preacher," he said. "They have listened to my story and every one of them has said, 'You need to become a Christian.'" He looked up at me. "But I am born again. There have been great moments in my life when I've loved God and tried to follow Him. I believe with all my heart I am a Christian. But all anyone can see is this horrible mess I am in. They see that I have walked away from my wife and child, that I am living with my mistress, that I have fathered a bastard, that I have left the church—and they say, 'Man, you need to accept Christ.'"

"Christians aren't immune from sin," I said frankly. "You're already a Christian. That's why you are so miserable. But an experience with Christ is not enough. You need the power of the Holy Spirit."

God doesn't say we move into sinless perfection the moment we are born again. True, our source of sin is cut off, but the human

196

nature remains, and we always live with the dregs. There is always the remnant of that old life, meaning we must constantly repent. I looked at the broken man in the chair. "It's not that you need a new salvation; you need to submit to the mighty hand of God that is at work in your life because you are a born-again person. How long can you rebel?"

I paused, then said matter-of-factly, "I will tell you the way out of your dilemma. All you have to do is to follow my advice, and your problem will be solved."

"Anything," he said with anxiety on his face. "I'll do anything just to be free."

"You must turn your back on both situations. You must turn your back on your mistress in Houston and never return to her. You must not even go back to pick up your belongings. Have her send them to you.

"Second, you must turn your back on your wife and your 11-year-old son. Give them up to God. Admit you have lost it all. Let your wife sell all your personal belongings. Let her go through with the divorce if that is what she wants. Relinquish all."

"But what will I do, then?" he asked.

"Oh, you'll stay right here. You can move in with some of our people, even with me if necessary, until you can find an apartment. Then you will get a job in this community. You will work with your hands at hard manual labor. You will be tightly surrounded by loving men and women who will help bring you to wholeness in this community setting. You are to remain here for one year. At the end of that time, all your problems will be solved, including the horrible situation between you and your young son."

"That's no answer," he said, his voice edged with anger.

"It's the only answer I have for you," I said gently.

"I thank you for your offer," he said in a stiff voice as he rose to his feet. "But you are asking the impossible."

"I don't think you understand what I'm offering," I said. "I am offering myself. I am opening my home and my life to take you in and steer you in the right direction—toward God."

"There must be an easier way," he said, starting to leave. "I'll just have to find it elsewhere."

"Listen to me," I said with as much sensitivity as I could. "If you do not obey willingly, then God will use force. He will do that because you are His child, because you are born again. He chastises those whom He loves. You think things are bad now; ask Him again and you'll get an even harder answer. Wait until your wife marries another man and your child is raised by someone who does not love him as a father—and all you can do about it is shiver in the night and weep. God loves you enough to rip your heart until you turn to Him."

Like the rich young ruler to whom Jesus said essentially the same thing, he turned away. The price was too great. And I could not go after him. Not that I did not want to, for I saw a beautiful prince beneath his froggy exterior—but I could only offer to kiss him. If he refused, as he did, there was nothing I could do. He walked out. I have not heard from him since.

In every man's life there are two gardens. One is like that garden from which man was exiled. It is the place where we once enjoyed all the beautiful things of God. There we felt alive. Creative. Filled with joy. In that garden, walking side by side with beautiful people, we felt fulfilled, exhilarated, satisfied. But we overstepped the invisible yet well-defined limitations. We tasted of forbidden fruit, feeling if fellowship was that good, how much better intimacy as well. Then, instead of repenting, we ran and hid—trying to justify our sin. So that Garden is now eternally closed. There stands at the gate an angel with a flaming sword, hiding the entrance behind his awfulness. Even the memories of those wonderful experiences are smudged and spoiled under the shame of our sin. To that garden there is no returning.

But in each man's life there is another garden—a little corner where precious things have been willfully buried. There is, on the back side of every lonely heart, a little private cemetery where we go, on occasion, to mourn and place flowers. Buried there are the things we have willfully—although reluctantly—banished from our lives. There, beneath the soil of obedience to God, lie buried priceless relationships, precious intimacies, loves dearer than life itself, things lawful yet not expedient. But in obedience we have put them aside. Using the spade of self-denial we have opened the ground to lay them tenderly beneath the sod. And although the grass has now covered the sites, the tombstones still recall the memories of deep earthly loves, the longings of our souls, even the dreams and desires of our hearts which we believed were given by God. Yet because of the time, or the tender circumstances, or the effect on gentle lambs, or simply the rightness of the act— we voluntarily turned our backs on the good in order to choose the best.

There is a difference between the two gardens. To the first we can never return. There we were discovered in our sin—and driven out. But we are given liberty to walk freely down the tender paths of the second garden, to listen to the echoes, to relive, if only in our hearts, the gentle moments of love and desire. For God is gracious to those who, as an act of obedience, bury the good beneath the soil of self-crucifixion—in order to await the resurrection of the best. For one day, when all the seeds of self are totally beneath the sod, there will come a cracking of the earth and a great resurrection of that which has been buried to His glory— rising in a glorified form.

Resurgam! I shall live again.

However, until that happens, the purposes of God may seem to be all darkness, rather than light.

Returning from a recent trip to the Sinai, our small group joined another tour group which had attended one of the World Conferences on the Holy Spirit sponsored by Logos International Fellowship. From Jerusalem we rode on huge tour buses to the Allenby Bridge across the Jordan River, then shifted to Arab buses to drive into Amman, Jordan, and on to the airport to catch our plane back to New York.

It was a strange transition, from our spartan and simple life in the desert to the bustling life of the tourist, riding in air-conditioned buses with people more concerned about their own personal needs than the needs of others. This was accented by the confusion at the Amman airport where we joined with almost 400 other people trying to force their way aboard a Royal Jordanian Airlines 747 jet. It was pandemonium. At the last moment the ticket agent for the airline had canceled all reserved seats and told the people they could sit anywhere they wanted. It was an every-man-for-himself situation as we tried to board the plane.

Nothing will bring out the carnal nature like a "you're-on-your-own" set of instructions. In particular, I was impressed with a middle-aged couple near us who had spent most of the day complaining that the meals were bad, the bus ride was bumpy, the tour guides discourteous and, in short, telling people they were disgusted and would never again come on such a tour. When the announcement was made that all seat assignments had been canceled and the people could sit wherever they wanted, the man grabbed his wife by her arm and with a curt, "Come on, Charlotte, let's go," started pushing his way through the crowd to the front of the line, determined to get the best seats themselves, regardless of who else got aboard.

Seeing their rude determination, many people simply stepped back and let them go ahead. All the glory of Israel and all the joy of the magnificent conference seemed to have been forgotten in the arrogance of this couple as they forced their way to the front of the line.

When the doors to the plane were finally opened, they went running down the aisle and picked the choice bulkhead seats so they could stretch their legs during the long overseas flight. As the other people boarded, they sat in their seats, looking straight ahead, a tiny smirk on their faces. If survival belonged to the fittest, they certainly qualified as fit for something.

The plane was almost full when I noticed my friend Dan Malachuk, who had sponsored the conference, helping his wife, Viola, up the stairs into the coach section. Viola had broken her foot in Israel and was hobbling painfully along, her leg encased in a huge plaster cast. All the good seats were gone, chosen long before by folks like the pushy couple who had rudely forced their way on first. Sensing that the Malachuks would have no place to sit, I got up from my seat in the rear of the plane and came forward to where the pushy couple were sitting.

"I hate to ask you to do this," I said, "but there is a lady with a broken foot coming aboard. She needs a seat where she can stretch her leg during the flight and prop it up."

I just stood there looking at the couple.

The man gave me an extremely mean look. "Are you suggesting we give them our seats?"

I just stood there, smiling. "There are a number of seats in the rear of the plane. You could be reasonably comfortable back there with the rest of us."

"You really mean it, don't you?" he sneered. "You have the gall to come up here and ask us to give up our good seats."

"Yes, sir," I said. "I really hate it. But this lady needs a place to prop her leg. Surely you could do that for the cause of Jesus."

"Well, I don't like it," he said. "I guess I don't have any choice. But this is the last time I'll ever come on any kind of trip with people like you."

Mumbling, grumbling, he got all his bags from under his seat and went back down the aisle to empty seats in the back. Viola had just arrived and tried to thank them, but they just brushed past her. She and Dan took their seats and with a moan of pain she stretched her leg so Dan could prop it up on her toilet case. I returned to my seat near my desert friends, feeling terrible.

Sitting down beside Mike Evans, who had been with me in the Sinai, I fidgeted. "Mike, I really feel bad about having to ask that couple to move. They've had such a hard time. Now they're back there cramped into seats not nearly as nice as the ones they had. I think I'll go back and try to comfort them."

Mike reached up and grabbed my arm. "God has been working on that couple ever since they've been on the tour," he said significantly. "Don't interrupt what the Holy Spirit is doing."

I sat back down in my seat. Mike was right. In my desire to be a peacemaker, I had let my soul begin to rule my spirit. Here was a couple, a man and wife, who someplace along the line had committed themselves to the lordship of Jesus Christ. Now God was using some extremely rough circumstances to smooth their sharp edges. It would be unwise for me to pour oil on water which God had troubled.

Just before we took off, someone in the first class section came back and arranged for the Malachuks to move to the front of the plane, where the seats were wider and there was plenty of

201

room to stretch out. When they did, the grumpy couple was able to return to their original seats at the bulkhead. But they remained angry all the way across the ocean. However, I agree with Mike that it was probably the most memorable plane ride they ever had, for the Holy Spirit was obviously at work in the lives of two Kingdom frogs.

Affliction, chastisement, hardship, suffering—all are God's means to bring us to the place of obedience, to bring us to the place of the Spirit-controlled life. Why be satisfied with a lily pad, when a throne awaits your call?

XII

Riding the Wind

As long as I can remember there has been locked in my heart the desire to do daring things, to risk my life, so to speak, in adventure. But fear had locked the door on my venturing spirit—fear, and self-imposed circumstances. The only times I dared step out were to do clandestine things which only temporarily satisfied that driving desire to achieve, create, risk, and dare. At the same time, though, I continued to yearn for a legitimate expression to that longing, some way to unlock the door of the cage of my soul so my spirit could soar like the eagle.

Some men find their outlet in the world of business—risking great sums of money for the thrill of gain. Others turn to athletics, disciplining their bodies so they may risk all on the high diving board, by pitting themselves against a brawny opponent or defying death by scaling some challenging mountain peak. Others satisfy their drive for adventure by defying the world to discover them as they move from one tryst to another, planning ingenious ways to meet their lover in a forlorn rendezvous. Most, however, are forced to satisfy their spirit of adventure vicariously. This accounts, in the main, for the tremendous popularity of adventure movies, spy novels, western sagas on television and even pornographic literature and films. All provide a measure of vicarious release to the chained spirit of adventure which beats its wings on the bars of the cages of the soul. Or, like Thurber's Walter Mitty, we develop our own secret life of fantasy. We lie awake at night imagining we are not really a middle-aged grocer, a computer technician or even the pastor of a church. Rather, putting aside the reality of a slumbering wife in our subdivision bedroom, we become, during those last moments of waking consciousness, a renowned brain surgeon, a dashing fighter pilot or a deep sea diver on a mission of mercy to rescue helpless sailors from a disabled submarine. However, by liberating our fantasies and imaginations, we only feed crumbs to the eagle of our spirit, rather than allowing him to do what he yearns to do—soar free on the thermal currents of God, venturing forth through the tough places.

In my own desperate attempts to free my spirit for that for which I had been born, I ran the gauntlet of all these escapes—and many more. In each of them I found a taste of reality, but it was never lasting—or satisfying. Like a runaway boy, drifting down a river on a raft, I began to catch a whiff of salt air and hear the roar of the surf. But I could in no way comprehend the immensity of what God had in store for me as I rounded the next bend and came face to face with who I was created to be.

Jesus said that when the Holy Spirit comes into our lives He will lead us to all truth. Receiving Him is the greatest of all adventures. He is the key which unlocks the door of our inner being and allows our own spirit, that part of us breathed into us by the Father, to soar free—liberated.

The baptism in the Holy Spirit, though glorious, is also fraught with danger and risk. No longer will we ever be satisfied to feed our own spirit crumbs of fantasy and imagination. Having tasted the reality of God, we will be compelled to move upward, escaping the bonds of our carnal nature and taking on, more and more, the adventurous, daring attributes of God's Son—who was the greatest explorer and adventurer of all. For those few who are willing to risk all, to venture out, to die to self, there are precious and unique blessings ahead which the less venturesome will never experience. Such blessings cannot be transmitted, only experienced; they are existential, not visionary; they cannot be given away, only enjoyed at the moment. Such experiences—and there will be innumerable ones for the Spirit-controlled individual—are like those fragile yet exquisite wild flowers sometimes found on the windswept pinnacle of the mountain. You stoop and examine, enjoy and are blessed by their symmetry, elegance and loveliness. How splendid is their form, how delicate their petals, how brilliant their color. The next day you return with a loved one, but the flowers are gone. They lasted but a day, and only the ones present at the hour they blossomed could experience and enjoy. They are God's gift to those who dare venture out.

I close this book by telling you three little stories which illustrate how the Holy Spirit has activated my own spirit of adventure. He has unlocked the cage of my soul and allowed the eagle to ride the winds to the tops of mountains where I have tasted nectar I once thought reserved for God alone. I no longer have to fantasize, to daydream at my desk or sit in the evening staring at the fire, imagining romantic things. Since that grand unlocking a dozen years ago, life has been one continuing adventure. Those close to me are aware of my occasional slips back into carnality. But despite this, I know something special has happened to me. And that's the reason I want to share these little stories, stories of times when the eagle of my spirit caught the upward surge of God's thermals and allowed me to brush my feathers across the face of God.

The first took place on one of my research trips into the Sinai. During our last night in the desert we pulled our vehicle into a hidden canyon next to a unique, sandswept grotto. Hollowed out of the side of the wadi, gouged by the fingers of the wind from thousands of years of shaping, was a natural chapel. That evening after supper, two of the men placed candles in some of the hundreds of little sockets which had been carved by the wind from the red sandstone sides of the open-topped cave, hollow sockets behind a breathtaking façade of red and purple stone. Then, sitting on the soft sand, we waited as the brief twilight turned into darkness. In the dancing shadows of the flickering candlelight which played across the sand and brushed the faces of the men sitting quietly around the grotto—we listened.

At first all we could hear was the gentle sound of the dying wind as it swished and moaned through the rocks. Then, as darkness enveloped us and the Sinai stars appeared overhead in all their brilliance, all we could hear was our own breathing, and the gentle beating of a dozen hearts beside us.

Someone quoted a passage from the Psalms:

Before the mountains were brought forth, or ever thou hadst formed the earth and the world, even from everlasting to everlasting, thou art God . . .

Someone else prayed a soft prayer of thanksgiving and praise Someone else began to sing:

Praise the name of Jesus,
  He's my Rock, He's my Fortress .

We joined in and then let our voices follow the focus of our hearts as our singing departed from the confines of structure and soared gently into the Spirit, listening, at the same time, as the angels of the Sinai—those special heavenly beings who live in that desolate section of the world—joined in. How seldom do they have a chance in that forsaken wilderness to blend their voices with those of the redeemed.

Then, as the evening grew quiet—with a stillness not equaled anyplace else on earth—one of the men, Derrel Emmerson, began to sing alone. I listened intently, for it was a new song. It was beautiful, a quiet chorus of praise which I assumed Derrel had often sung in his church back in the Washington, D.C., area. He sang three stanzas, repeating the chorus between each stanza. I wished I had brought my little tape recorder into the grotto so I could have captured the song. I made a mental note to ask him to sing it into my recorder the next day. I wanted to learn it so I could take it back and teach it to my friends in Florida.

The next morning as we were breaking camp to head northward, I took my little tape recorder out of my duffel bag, found Derrel where he was rolling up his sleeping bag and asked if he would repeat the song he sang last night.

"What song?" Derrel asked.

"The one you sang in the grotto," I answered. "That beautiful little chorus your folks must sing in your church."

Derrel grinned. "I don't remember it."

"I don't understand. You sang all three stanzas last night. I can almost remember it myself but not quite."

"I'm sorry," he laughed, returning to his packing in the sand. "But I was singing in the Spirit. It was all spontaneous."

"But it had perfect rhyme and meter. You repeated the chorus with each stanza."

"I know," he said. "But it was just one of those very special times. I sensed the presence of the angels around me, and suddenly I was singing. Perhaps it was only for their ears, since they don't have much company down here. Whatever, it was obviously not meant to be repeated—for I cannot remember a single line of the lyrics or melody."

There are special blessings, I've learned, awaiting those who venture out. Authored in eternity, they break through into time and space only as men move upward toward God. They are never to be repeated, never to be shared, never to be wrapped in a package to be given away. They are like the blessings of breath: inhaled deeply, disseminated into the system and never to be recovered in form, only in energy. Each step of the way He guides, leading us to new heights of adventure and experience. The way may seem dangerous as we turn loose of all the safety devices of the past and set our faces toward the things of the Spirit, but there is a glorious reward far more precious than the turquoise nuggets of the ancient mines which awaits those who dare run the risk of discovery.

The joy of adventure remains only as long as God controls. When man steps in with his reasons and fears to institutionalize and structure (or even record) that which is meant to flow free and unencumbered, life leaves. Yet it is this lack of institutionalizing which is the single factor preventing us from venturing out. How desperately the human soul wants to see a blueprint of the next step, to exert an element of control over what is about to happen. That is only our own humanity, which is afraid of the unknown, not that essence of God inside each of us. It is the essence of God which urges us to dare, to release our tow line to that mechanical device which has helped us break the elementary bonds of earth, and soar free on Zephyr's currents toward the dwelling place of the Most High.

After that final night in the wilderness, our small group of men packed our gear and boarded our open truck for the long ride back to Jerusalem. Driving eastward through the expanding valleys we hit the coastal road along the Gulf of Elat and drove north through the deep, geographical rift called the "Arabah" to the western coast of the Dead Sea. The west wind blowing off the Negev Desert was oven temperature, and by the time we reached the beautiful oasis at Ein Gedi we were almost parched.

Ein Gedi is a deep ravine almost two miles long. References to it appear throughout the Bible. It was here David encountered Saul and had the opportunity to slay him while he was alone in one of the numerous caves along the valley. Instead, he only cut a piece of cloth from Saul's garment and told his lieutenants that he could not "touch God's anointed." It was also here that David wrote some of his most beautiful psalms. The valley still abounds with wild life, mountain sheep, ibex and smaller rodents.

The Hebrew word "ein" means "spring." And at the top of the deep ravine is a magnificent waterfall, flowing from this huge spring. Below are a series of smaller waterfalls and deep pools of clear, running water. The stream eventually spills into the Dead Sea, 1,200 feet below sea level. While the rest of the men went ahead to the waterfall at the top of the ravine, three of us—Mike Evans, Derrel Emmerson and I—stopped to swim in a secluded pool formed from solid rock. I had been to the top before, and after the hot dusty ride climaxing two weeks in the desert, I was ready for a cool dip in pure water.

We stripped, laid our shorts and sandals on a high rock near the water and plunged into the icy pool. For days our skin had been parching in the sun, and the sensation of the cool water swirling around our bodies as we splashed and frolicked was delightful. In the shallow places we could rest on the cool rocks, letting the water caress our skin and enjoying the sun which filtered through the overhanging trees and danced like diamonds on the surface.

After long minutes of immersing our bodies in the water, we crawled up on a huge warm boulder. The other men in our group had scattered up and down the canyon. Yet we knew, all three of us in a corporate way, we were not alone in that quiet, secluded place. Others had been there before us: David the shepherd, the mighty warrior Joab, the prophet Samuel. Their spirits had left an indelible presence in the canyon. But it was not this "communion of the saints" which attracted us nor even again the presence of angels as much as our deep awareness of the presence of the Holy Spirit.

In an act of simple worship, the three of us stood, stark naked, our bare feet on the warm surface of the rock, and raised our hands toward heaven. The sun broke through the trees and bathed us in warmth, drying our wet bodies as we stood, voicing our praise to God in word and "spiritual song," singing in the spirit and shouting praises which echoed back and forth off the steep rock walls of the wadi. It was a special moment of high ecstasy, rapturous in nature, as we presented our bodies before Jehovah God.

Free from all inhibitions, released from embarrassment, liberated from the restraints of culture and clothes, I began to soar. Ecstasy, in this case, cannot be equated with the popular and cheapened sense of "hysteria" but goes far deeper to the historical, etymological sense of "ex-stasis"—that is, literally to "stand out from," to be freed from the perpetual dichotomy of most human activity until there is but one focus—God. *Ecstasy* is the accurate term for the intensity of consciousness that occurs in pure worship. It is far more than the Bacchic concept of "letting go"; it involves the total person—body, soul, and spirit—subconscious acting in unity with the conscious—intellect, emotion and spirit joining in one intense concentration on God. Not before, nor since, have I felt as totally immersed in the *ecstasy* of worship—soaring with the eagles.

The third and final adventure story I want to tell has to do with the lesson I learned from my father shortly after I returned from that particular trip to the Sinai. Watching my dad grow old was one of the great experiences of my life. My father was my hero. I admired everything he did. I admired the way he quoted long passages of Kipling, Longfellow and James Whitcomb Riley. When I was a child I respected him as a man of ethics and nobility, a churchman in the cultural sense of the word. Later, after he surrendered his life to Jesus Christ in his 60th year, I respected him even more as a committed Christian. I was impressed with his business ability. I honored his financial wisdom. But most of all, I respected him as a man. Although his world, during those last few years of his life, was confined to his wheelchair, his desk and his bed, nevertheless he remained a great adventurer. Always exploring. Always venturing out in his mind and spirit.

On his 80th birthday he began to grow a mustache. He had always been clean shaven, but the closer he grew to eternity, the more he let his inhibitions and traditions fall away.

"I've wanted to grow a mustache since I started shaving, 67 years ago," he said. "But it was never proper in my circles. Now I am putting away many of my proper things and becoming real."

He wore it for five years and shaved it off. "It's just not me," he said. "But I'm glad I did it just the same."

I loved him for it. And I loved him for the other areas of adventure I recognized in his life. We had always been a very "proper" family. But in his later years, Daddy finally found freedom to put his arms around women other than his beloved wife of more than 50 years. The older he grew, he told me, the more he realized he had confused impropriety with impurity. Life was too short not to enjoy all the beautiful things God had put around him.

When we prayed together, as we often did when I visited him, he would defy his old Methodist tradition and join in with a hearty "Amen!" or a sincere "Praise the Lord!" Sometimes he would sit in his wheelchair and raise his hands in worship as I read to him or as one of his women friends played the piano and sang. He was not ashamed when others saw him weep when he was moved emotionally. And he loved to take my mother's hand or kiss her in front of the children and grandchildren, something we had never seen him do in his younger years. Some may have equated his "freedom" with senility or old age; I attributed it to spiritual maturity.

Thus, as he approached the time of dying, I watched him closely.

Of all the things I wanted to learn from him, how to approach death was the most important. I have often contrasted my reaction to my father's preparation to die with that of the contemporary poet, Dylan Thomas. Thomas, writing on the death of his father, you remember, began his poem by saying:

> Do not go gentle into that good night,
> Old age should burn and rave at the close of day;
> Rage, rage against the dying of the light.

And the poem ends:

> And you, my father, there on the sad height,
> Curse, bless me now with your fierce tears, I pray.
> Do not go gentle into that good night.
> Rage rage against the dying of the light.

Of course it was the son writing, not the father. The father had to confront death and in some way accept it. But he did it battling against the insurgent spirit of the son, who, despite the piercing elegance of the poem, was still rebelling against a God who would take from him the man who meant most in his life.

On the other hand, I never, not once, had any desire to ask my father to linger or to plead with him to rage against his appointment with death. Indeed, I urged him to go gentle into that good night and to bless me, not with fierce tears, but to bless me with insights into eternity—and to communicate, as much as was humanly possible, all he learned as he walked through the valley of the shadow.

My father saw old age as the greatest of all the adventures of life. His ongoing prayer was that as his body wore out, he would remain alert in mind so he could savor and enjoy all that lay ahead. My father never drank alcohol—not a drop that I know of. Alcohol was a depressant, he said, and he wanted to remain alert with every cell of his body to experience all that God had for him as he ascended the heights. Nor did he need it, as some do, to free him from his inhibitions. In his later years he found the stimulant of the Holy Spirit was all that was necessary to give him the upsurge of vitality necessary to sense and enjoy the experiences of life.

Yet as I watched my father—moving rapidly toward eternity— become free, I realized how stiff and unyielding I remained in many areas of my life. Especially was this true in my expression of affection between us. Our family had never been overtly affectionate. We seldom hugged and almost never kissed—at least not when I was a boy. Occasionally my mother would kiss me, but I had never, to my knowledge, kissed my daddy. We men shook hands. Daddy taught us how to give a firm, manly handshake and how to look the other fellow straight in the eye while we were doing it. But as I watched him become free and felt my own love for him growing, I longed to express my affection in a more physical way. Yet every time I was with him and it came time to say good-by, instead of bending and kissing him as he sat in his wheelchair, I always stuck out my hand. Even the words "I love you" stuck in my throat. Like taking off my clothes at Ein Gedi, it was something I wanted to do—but was afraid to try.

Finally I could stand it no longer. My sophistication and my twisted concepts of masculinity were choking me to death. One Saturday afternoon I got in the car and made a special trip south along the Florida coast to my parents' home, 35 miles away. Walking into my dad's little study, I found him in his wheelchair, at work on his ledger.

"I have come for one purpose," I said. "I want to tell you something and then I want to do something."

He looked up, grinned, and said, "Fine."

Suddenly I felt like a fool. I was 46 years old—he was 86. But I had come this far and was not going to back out.

"I love you," I said, choking up.

"Is that what you came to tell me?" he asked gently, putting his pen on the desk beside his green ledger and resting his hands in his lap.

"Yes, sir," I said.

"You didn't have to come all the way down here to tell me that," he grinned. Then he added, "But I'm sure glad you did."

"I've wanted to voice the words with my lips for years," I said.

"I find it easy to write them on paper. And I know you have known. But it has been difficult for me to say it with my mouth. Perhaps," I added, "I needed to say it more for me than for you."

His face grew pensive, and he nodded slowly.

"There is something else," I said.

He did not look up from his place at the desk but continued to look straight ahead, nodding slowly.

I bent and kissed him, first on one cheek, then the other, then on top of his bald forehead.

He reached up, took my arms in his strong hands, and pulled me down to him so he could put his arms around my neck. For long moments we remained in that awkward position—me bending over his wheelchair, he with his arms around my neck, pulling my face up against his. Finally he released me, and I straightened up. There was a trace of tears in his eyes, and his lip quivered as he spoke.

"My father died when I was a young man back in Indiana," he said. "I left home shortly afterwards to go to college, teach school and finally go to France in World War I. After the war I moved to Florida. I never returned home except for occasional visits to see my mother.

"When my mother grew old, I invited her to come live with us." He paused, and his face broke into one of those knowing grins. "Guess what she said? She said, 'No, I'll stay right on here in Morristown in this house. But I love you for asking me to come live with you and even though I'll never do it, I hope you keep right on asking me up until the day I die.'"

Looking up at me, he added, his lip quivering again, "I know you love me. But I hope you keep right on telling me—up until the day I die."

Something broke loose in me that Saturday afternoon. Something which had been knotted up for years. Once again, as I had in the Sinai, I felt my spirit burst free. I left my parents' house in Vero Beach wanting to run home, leaping and dancing, rather than getting in the car and driving back up the coast. My wings, like the eagle's, were locked against the storm. I was soaring.

Dr. J. Wilbur Chapman is reported to have asked General William Booth, the founder of the Salvation Army, what was the secret of his success. Booth replied, "I will tell you the secret. God has had all there was of me."

I'm not there yet, but I'm a lot closer than I have ever been. That's why I have written this book. It's all tied in with my own purpose in life—my defined reason for existence. I wrote it to encourage you to release yourself to the control of the Holy Spirit, to dare to cross mine fields, to climb mountains, to explore caves, to hear the voice from behind the ranges. I have written to urge you to attempt the impossible, to run the risk of failure, to dare to praise, to dare to love, to dare to die to self. I have written in hopes you will become the person you are—which is the essence of salvation—and to know the joy, the thrill, of letting the Holy Spirit control your life as you soar like the eagle through the tough ventures of life.

A Way
through
the Wilderness

Jamie Buckingham

KINGSWAY PUBLICATIONS

EASTBOURNE

Dedicated to
all God's children
who are walking through
a dry and barren wilderness

"See, I am doing a new thing!
*   Now it springs up; do you not perceive it?*
I am making a way in the desert
*   and streams in the wasteland."*

(Isaiah 43:19, NIV)

In Appreciation:

My fellow sojourners who across the years have followed me on pilgrimages through the Sinai.

1976
Bruce Buckingham
Randy Ostrander

1978
Dallas Albritton
Bob Crumley
Derrel Emmerson
Mike Evans
Gib Jones
Bill Nelson
Angus Sargeant, M.D.**
George Sowerby
Hugh Welchel
Frank Whigham
Bob Wright
John Zentmeyer**

1979
Dick Blackwell
Dick Bolen
Wayne Buck
Stan Elrod***
Mickey Evans**
Jim Gills, M.D.
Charles Kopp
Dick Love
Willie Malone
Peter Marshall
Francis Nicholson
Angus Sargeant, M.D.**
John Sherrill
Steve Strang
John Zentmeyer**

1980
Mel Anderson
Steve Anderson
Jim Bauman
Gene Berrey
Stan Elrod***
Zane Elrod
Bill Ilnisky
Mike Karl
Joe Ed McGahey
Richard Payne
Alton Reeder, M.D.
Carl Wills
Cecil Wilson

1982
Peter Darg
Stan Elrod***
Mickey Evans**
Rick Foster
John French
David Hinders
Leonard LeSourd
Derald McDaniel
John Tripp
Jack Wells, M.D.

Guides
Ora Lipschitz
Norman Lytle
Shai Sofer
Amir Azia
Timi ben Yoseph

**Two-time sojourner
***Three-time sojourner

Contents

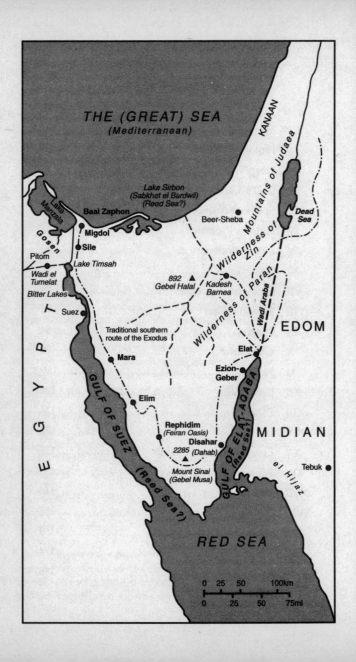

Introduction

In the Footsteps of Moses

Few places on earth are as remote, yet as evocative, as the "great and terrible wilderness" of the Sinai. The very name stirs childhood memories of stories emanating from that awesome and holy place.

Each time I have been there, though, trekking the burning sands and climbing the craggy mountains, I have become even more aware of the eternal nature of God. In this place are still found the principles that enable all God's children to make it through their own personal wildernesses.

The conflicts faced by those early Israelites—about 3,200 years ago, as they left Egypt for the freedom of a promised land—still beset us all. Fear. Uncertainty. Grief. Anger. Doubt. Discouragement. Temptation. These are the constant companions of all pilgrims. Those wandering ancients faced them all.

But though the problems linger with us, the solutions are equally apparent. I found my answers not only as I sojourned through the Sinai but as I struggled through my own personal wilderness.

Some years ago, as I emerged from the dark night of my own soul, when it seemed I had not only destroyed myself and my family but done damage to the Kingdom of God by my foolish actions, I determined to trace the physical path of

9

those early searchers of promise. My first trip to the Sinai was a terrifying experience. I spent the entire two weeks trying to adjust to the shock of desert living. But I was fascinated by the place and returned again and again.

During those subsequent trips, I discovered there is indeed a way through the wilderness. The path has been clearly marked by those who have gone before. Any man or woman who dares turn his back on whatever holds him in bondage can still find the Promised Land. The principles of deliverance are the same today as they were when Moses led the Exodus 3,200 years ago.

I stood on the banks of the *Yam-Suph*, the Sea of Reeds (mistakenly translated as the Red Sea, which I will explain later), marveling at the grace of God that opened the water before the children of Israel. I suffered from drinking the bitter waters at Marah, rested in the wonderful shade at Elim, climbed Mt. Tahuneh where Aaron and Hur held up the hands of Moses, and I stood on the summit of *Jebel Musa*—the Mountain of God—where God thundered His law and covenants for all history to hear and heed. I hungered at the Graves of Craving, wept in the awesome stillness of the desert nights, and laughed with my companions as we discovered hope and joy in unexpected places. In the end, I climbed Mt. Nebo and viewed, as did dying Moses, the lush green of the Promised Land on the other side of Jordan.

Through all this burning wilderness I found evidence of the presence of God. No longer does He traverse the desert in a pillar of cloud by day and a column of fire by night; instead He speaks in the still, small voice heard by Elijah in this same place. Thus the wilderness remains a place of purification and preparation—a place where a man can learn to distinguish between the clamoring voices of this world and the often quiet, gentle voice of God.

From the dawn of civilization the Sinai has been a place of conflict. This seemingly worthless piece of gritty land—looking on the map like a sharp wedge driven between Africa and Arab Asia—has been the most besieged territory in the world. At last count it had been the battleground for at least fifty invading armies since the time of recorded history. As a result, it has been occupied by some alien force ever since the Early

Bronze Age—five thousand years ago. It remains today as it was in the time of Moses, a giant and scorching crucible that has melted armies, destroyed kings, and burned from proud men both sin and selfishness until they have emerged pure and prepared for ministry.

The Sinai peninsula is an arid wilderness of mystic and ethereal beauty. Dunes and marshes line its northern coast along the Mediterranean Sea. A limestone plateau, called *el Thei*, with low hills ending in a sharp precipice that stretches nearly the entire width of the peninsula, fills the central portion of the triangle. It barely supports enough vegetation to feed the goats and sheep of the ever-wandering Bedouin tribes. In the south, rugged mountains lie between the Gulfs of Suez and Aqaba, forming rows of granite walls that change color with each passing hour.

Caravans of merchants have traversed the *Via Maris*—the "way of the sea"—along the Mediterranean to the north, bringing their wares across the golden crescent from Africa to Asia. This was known also as "the way of the Philistines" and has remained, to this day, a place where wars have been fought.

In the south, where the high mountains jut upward from the desert floor, divided only by the mysterious wadis or dried waterways that separate them, Moses first met God at a burning bush. He later returned with the entire nation of Israel as they fled from the bondage of Egypt and stopped at this same mountain to hear the thundering voice of God give the Ten Commandments, which have formed the basis of all law in the Western world.

Moses' journey began on the banks of the Nile in Egypt and ended on the lonely peak of Mt. Nebo in Jordan. On the map, the distance between these two places is not much greater than that between New York City and Washington, D.C. But the geography is dwarfed by the scope of events that took place here. It is, as another pilgrim once remarked, an exceedingly finite place for the infinite to have happened.

Most scholars say it was during the time of Rameses II, who reigned from 1304 to 1237 B.C., that the Exodus took place. Central to the story is a man called Moses. No man in history towers taller. Called *Moshe* in Hebrew, *Mosa* or *Musa* in Arabic, and *Moses* in English (by way of the Greek), his footsteps still go before all who walk through their own personal wilderness—making their way from the bondage of sin and traditionalism to the liberty and freedom offered by God.

Though the infant Moses was pulled from the bulrushes along the Nile by the daughter of Pharaoh, Moses likely kept in contact with his Hebrew family while growing up. His mother nursed him as a child, and two older siblings—Aaron and Miriam—would have been his early playmates. The Israelites had earlier—perhaps as much as 400 years earlier—migrated to Egypt from Canaan. Their champion in Egypt was the next-to-youngest child of Jacob, Joseph, who had been sold into slavery by his jealous brothers. Joseph had risen to second-in-command in Egypt and found a place of refuge for his family when they appeared needing food. In subsequent years, however, *"there arose up a new king over Egypt, which knew not Joseph,"* and Goshen, where the Israelites lived, became a house of bondage and slavery. For almost ten generations these once-proud people were slaves to the Egyptians, building their pyramids and making bricks for their houses.

Although Moses was raised in the palace of the Pharaoh, he never lost contact with his roots. The day came when he could no longer take the hypocrisy of pretending to be one man while really being another. Angered beyond control at the injustice being done his people, he killed one of the Egyptian overseers whom he had seen beating an Israelite slave. When his crime was discovered, this prince of Egypt was forced to flee into that void of wind, sand and rock shimmering in a blue haze to the east—the wilderness of Sinai.

Over the next forty years Moses went through a gradual transformation. He met and married a Bedouin shepherd girl, Zipporah, and moved in with her family headed by the Midianite priest, Jethro. In essence, he became a Bedouin shepherd, wandering with the other nomads tending sheep and goats. In this atmosphere he raised his two sons, Gershom and Eliezer. Also in this atmosphere he had deeply impressed upon his mind that there was but a single God, rather than the many gods worshiped in Egypt. Even though he had doubtless heard the story of the God with no name and no image from his own people in Egypt—a story that had been passed down by word of mouth around the late-night campfires—it was from Jethro, a distant relative of Abraham, that the concept became reality.

At the end of this forty-year period, Moses, now 80 years of age, heard a voice from God while tending Jethro's flocks near the base of Mt. Sinai. As far as we know, it was the first time in 400 years that the Lord had confronted one of His chosen people. Nor had any man ever been summoned to a more important task. "I am sending you to Pharaoh to bring my people the Israelites out of Egypt" (Exodus 3:10).

Thus, out of the burning desert emerged not a prince of Egypt but a prophet, returning to lead his people into a land unknown to any of them but promised of God. Reinforced with signs and miracles and awed by the determination of the man he had sent into exile so many years before, Pharaoh finally succumbed to the pressures of God. The children of Israel were released to find their way through the wilderness to the land of promise.

What follows is history: the opening of the sea to allow the Israelites to pass through, the miracle of water from the desert, manna every morning, and finally a great military victory on the eve of hearing God's voice from Mt. Sinai.

At Rephidim the Israelites were attacked by a desert people called the Amalekites. Moses climbed nearby Mt. Tahuneh with his brother Aaron and his brother-in-law Hur. As long as Moses stretched out his wooden staff over the valley below, the troops, under Joshua, advanced. When his arms grew tired and fell, the Amalekites advanced. To assure victory, Aaron and Hur had to hold up Moses' arms.

I climbed that mountain early one morning. At the urging of my friends, I stretched out my arm over the imposing valley below as the imaginary legions of Amalekites advanced and receded in my mind. After five minutes my arm and shoulder ached so much my arm began to drop. Two friends, laughing and calling me a poor leader, stepped in to hold up my drooping arm. Even then, as the heat of the day drained my energy, I realized I was no match for the man of God who had once stood at this same place interceding for his people. The cost of apostleship, I saw, was much greater than the accompanying glory.

Down the wadi from Rephidim the land opens into a great plain called *er Raha*, where the children of Israel encamped at the base of the Mountain of God. There, rising into the rich blue sky, is the magnificent three-columned granite apex of Mt. Sinai. Mt. Sinai is actually a massif of several mountains. The highest peak is *Jebel Katerina*, 8,651 feet, touched by *Ras Safsafa* and *Jebel Musa* (the Mountain of Moses), which soars to the height of 7,497 feet.

It is impossible to approach Mt. Sinai—much less climb to its awesome summit—without being overwhelmed by the glory and majesty of the huge mass of granite and gneiss rock. It glows a deep purple in the sunset and flashes red and gold in the light of dawn. When the noonday sun beats mercilessly on its barren sides, it turns almost white. Even when snow covers its peak in the winter, the awesomeness of its craggy nature still thunders from beneath the blanket of whiteness. It is one of the world's truly unique places. It was here that the entire mountain range thundered and quaked as God spoke to His people; and regardless of the fact that there are no holy places, only holy people, this place still bears, indelibly, the footprint of God.

From Mt. Sinai Moses turned north—an eleven-day journey—to the oasis of Kadesh-Barnea near the border of Canaan. But the Israelites balked at entering the Promised Land. As a result the entire nation was condemned to wander in the wilderness until a new generation whose moral fiber was uncorroded by slavery grew up to possess the land promised by God. Therefore, even though he had already spent forty years in the Sinai, Moses was forced to spend another forty years until this grumbling nation of Israelites was ready to follow God's command.

Somewhere near Kadesh-Barnea occurred the pivotal incident in the life of the old leader. In a final test, God asked him to speak to a rock and bring forth water. Instead, Moses reverted to a technique he had used many years before—and hit the rock with his staff. The toll of the wilderness had been too much. Bound by tradition, he was unable to obey. As a result, while Moses stayed behind on the lofty peak of Mt. Nebo, the new generation of Israelites finally crossed into the Promised Land under their new leader, Joshua.

According to an old Jewish tradition, God kissed His faithful servant as he died. And in the book of Jude, we read that while Satan contended for Moses' body, God sent the archangel Michael to stand guard. Deuteronomy records that the aged prophet was buried by God Himself and that *"no man knoweth of his sepulchre."*

The wilderness does not have to be a place of hopeless fear and utter despair. Despite the hard lessons learned, the taste of bitter water, the conflict with self, nature and desert enemies, it can be a place of tranquil beauty, perfect rest and warm fellowship with fellow pilgrims. To bypass the wilderness in our journey to the Promised Land is to bypass God. And what is the use of occupying a land of promise unless the God of promise goes with us?

In eulogizing the Irish poet William Butler Yeats, who often wrote from his own desert place, W. H. Auden wrote a poem that ends:

> Follow, poet, follow right
> To the bottom of the night,
> With your unconstraining voice
> Still persuade us to rejoice . . .
> In the deserts of the heart
> Let the healing fountain start.
> In the prison of his days
> Teach the free man how to praise.

This is the purpose of the wilderness experiences of life—to lead us to the place where the healing fountain starts.

Prologue

There is an ancient legend of an old Bedouin sheikh—the priestly patriarch or chief elder—of the Jebeliya tribe. His name was Sheikh Awad, and he lived in the high mountain region near the base of Mt. Sinai.

Early morning of the day he was to be officially set apart as the sheikh, an angel visited him.

"As the spiritual leader of this tribe of wandering nomads," the angel said, "you will need special wisdom."

The old man knelt in the sand and held his hands up in acknowledgment of his need.

"God is going to give you a special gift of discerning truth," the angel continued.

Suddenly the angel was gone. But when the wizened old man opened his hand, there was a small round stone in the palm—left, no doubt, by the angel. The stone had special mystical qualities that enabled the sheikh, when sitting in judgment over his people, always to know if a person was lying or telling the truth.

When Sheikh Awad died, his son inherited his father's position of spiritual leader of the Jebeliya tribe. He also inherited the stone, which he then had set in a ring.

At the tribal councils, which were held at the tomb of Sheikh Awad, the stone was always used to discern the truth. If a man was accused of lying, the Council of Elders would call all the men of the tribe together. The stone, now set in the ring, would be placed in a glass of water. After the man testified, he

16

would be required to drink of the glass three times. If he had lied, he would drop dead.

The elders often pointed to the many graves around the tomb of Sheikh Awad as solemn testimony of the ring's power.

One afternoon a small group of us paused at the tomb of Sheikh Awad on our journey inland across the wilderness toward Mt. Sinai. Entering the nearby *maqad*—the single-room stone shelter next to the whitewashed tomb—we sat on the sand floor as our guide told us, again, the story of Sheikh Awad and his mystical stone.

"Last year," our guide said, "I was here when the Council of Elders held court. For the first time I saw the stone. It is now in the belonging of the son of the son of Sheikh Awad."

He then related a fascinating story. A Bedouin man had been robbed of certain goods that he later found in the tent of another man. The accused man denied he had stolen the goods, saying he had bought them from a third man. The third man, however, when questioned, denied ever having had the goods.

Someone was lying.

The Council of Elders called the men of the tribe together. More than 600 men came on camels and by foot, gathering at the tomb of Sheikh Awad—where we were at that moment.

The son of the son of Sheikh Awad called the two accused men forward. Again both denied guilt. The sheikh then brought forth the ring and the glass of water. He dropped the ring into the glass and handed it to the first accused.

The man took three quick drinks—and with a smile turned and handed it to the second accused.

The man stood, staring into the glass. Then, without drinking, he handed the glass back to the son of the son of Sheikh Awad.

A great cry went up from all the men standing around the *maqad*. Guilt had been determined and the elders quickly ruled a fine plus return of the stolen goods. The mystical gift· from the angel had once again distinguished between truth and error.

When I began research on this book, I too asked for the gift of Sheikh Awad. I did not expect, nor desire, a stone. I asked for something far more meaningful to me—the internal gift of the Holy Spirit to enable me to discern truth from error and the ability to communicate that truth to my fellow pilgrims struggling through the wilderness places of life.

It is difficult, in the Sinai, to distinguish between legend and fact. How many Israelites made this journey? Did they travel through the deep wadis of the south, or across the sand by the Way of the Philistines to the north? Did Moses really strike a rock and bring forth water? And which mountain is really the mysterious Mt. Sinai—the Mountain of God?

Even though I have opinions, I have left the eternal debates of questions to scholars. For truth—the truth I wish to communicate in this book—is not relegated to historical places or even limited to whose interpretation of Scripture we accept. It is found, rather, in the still small voice that speaks to the hearts of men.

So, despite the diversities of opinion that surround the epic events of the Exodus, there are principles found in the Bible that, if applied to whatever wilderness you are passing through, will lead you from bondage to freedom, from darkness to light, out of the wilderness into God's land of eternal promise. For in its pages we will meet that perfect Guide who still says, "I am making a way in the desert."

What I share in this book is truth, the kind of truth that will set you free. Having said that, I do not hesitate to drink from the glass.

Jamie Buckingham
Melbourne, Florida

I

Hospitality

"And where is he?" [Jethro] asked his daughters. "Why did you leave him? Invite him to have something to eat."

(Exodus 2:20)

The first reaction to any wilderness is withdrawal. The pain of losing a loved one, the shock of losing a job, the deep disappointment of being betrayed by someone you love—all tend to drive us into deep withdrawal.

Invariably our first reaction is, "Leave me alone."

God understands this. He also understands our even greater need to be part of a family—to be touched by loving hands, held by loving arms. Thus, into every wilderness experience of ours, God sends special messengers to minister to us. To Jesus He sent angels. To Elijah He sent ravens. To Moses He sent an old Bedouin sheikh.

Jethro, with warm, simple hospitality, helped the former prince of Egypt emerge from his shell of grief and self-pity and enter a world of preparation, a world designed by God to train him for the time he would return to Egypt for a far greater purpose.

Moses, at age 40, had been second-in-command in the most powerful and academically advanced nation of history. As an infant, he had been rescued from the sword of Pharaoh and raised by Pharaoh's daughter as a prince. Trained in courtly manners and given the best education available, his foster mother looked for the day when Moses would replace her father on the throne of Egypt.

But God had other plans, plans that could come to pass only after the egotism of Egypt had been burned from His servant in the crucible of the wilderness.

It began, as most wilderness wanderings begin, with an act of sin. In the Egyptian province of Goshen, where the Hebrew slaves were toiling in the blistering sun making bricks in the stiff clay pits, Moses killed an Egyptian taskmaster who was whipping a defenseless Hebrew slave.

It was a chivalrous act, well-meant, springing largely from human sympathy. Ironically, it was one of the first genuinely unselfish things Moses had done. At the same time, it was an act of murder, and the consequences were swift and merciless.

In his own strength, Moses was not strong enough to lead. So, using the justice of the Egyptians, God did something that still mystifies mortal man: He began the process of spiritual education by thrusting Moses into the great and terrible wilderness of the Sinai. Here he learned to distinguish between passion and principle, between impulse and settled purpose. Only in the wilderness does one learn that mere need never constitutes a call. One learns to wait on the voice of God.

Formal education is only the beginning of spiritual preparation. At the age of 40, Moses entered God's graduate school. The next forty years were spent in the deprivation of the wilderness. These were years in which his rough edges were sanded smooth. The literal blast furnace of the Sinai refined the character of a man God was going to use. There he learned to pray and he learned the values of solitude. There, starting with a few sheep and goats, he learned the principles of leadership. But he did not have to struggle alone. God put a family around him—the family of Jethro—who taught him the ways of the desert people, the ways of hospitality.

Moses had been into the Sinai before, but always as a military commander, never as a solitary pilgrim. There is evidence he may have led at least one expedition as far south as Dophkah, where the remains of an ancient Egyptian temple still stand at the site of the turquoise mines near Serabit el Khadim. But viewing the desert from a pharaoh's chariot is much different from viewing it as a lonely sojourner in exile, plodding through the sand and clambering over the rocks: a man who had lost not only his country but his family as well.

Filled with despair and confusion, the once prince of Egypt staggered into the burning crucible of the wilderness.

Making his way across the peninsula to nowhere, he began his wanderings. Awed by the blood-red sky at dawn, the star-studded cover of the night canopy, by the gaunt face of a primeval crag, by the vast emptiness, by the seemingly end-less stretch of burning sand, he stumbled on until he came to an oasis. Exhausted, he drank from the pool of water, then fell into the shade and slept. He was awakened by human voices speaking the ancient language still spoken by the old Israel-ites in the slave quarters of Egypt.

Young maidens, Bedouin girls in their early and mid-teens, had come to water their father's flocks. Shepherds from other tribes were at the oasis also. Recognizing the girls as strangers in the area, they were driving them away. Still angry from everything that had happened to him, Moses emerged from the shadows to strike out at the shepherd bullies. His wooden staff swinging, he charged at them, prepared to do to them what he had done to the Egyptian taskmaster. They fled, and the shepherd girls, grateful, once again drove their flocks to the water at the pool.

Giggling and hiding behind their veils, they returned to the nearby tent of their father, the Bedouin sheikh called Jethro (also called Reuel) who had moved his tribe from the territory southeast of Aqaba to forage in the Sinai.

"Why did you leave him?" Jethro quizzed his daughters. "Invite him to have something to eat."

That night Moses sat in the tent of Jethro and ate his first wilderness meal. He was about to learn the first of many wilderness lessons.

Sitting in the tiny *succoth,* or thatched hut made of date palm leaves, Moses watched, fascinated, as Jethro's beautiful young daughter Zipporah ground grain brought with them from Midian. Two large round stones were placed on top of each other. The bottom stone had a small trough around the edge. The top stone had a wooden handle affixed to one side so it could be turned on an axle that joined both stones in the middle. The maiden slowly poured the grain through a hole in the top stone, at the same time turning the stone so that the grain was crushed between the stones. The flour was collected in the small trough at the edge.

When there was enough, Zipporah added water and salt to the flour, kneaded it into a dough ball about the size of a grapefruit, then patted it out into large flat cakes about an inch thick. Next Zipporah laid the cake—called *libre**—directly onto the glowing coals made from dried camel dung. Watching carefully to see it did not char, she then flipped it over so the baked side was on top. Scraping up sand and ashes, she covered the entire cake, coals and all.

In a few moments her mother arrived with a huge dish of boiled mutton and herbs that had been cooking in another booth. Zipporah then brushed the sand from the bread and, holding it between her hands, slapped it with both hands in a clapping motion, knocking off sand and char.

Jethro motioned for the family to be seated, crosslegged in a circle around the fire. Moses sat next to the sheikh as the honored guest. Before eating they prayed. It was a strange experience for Moses. There were no images, no idols, just the mention of an unknown God, "El."

"Who is this El?" Moses asked. "Is He like the sun god *Re*, the river god *Osiris*, or *Hathor* whom the Egyptians worship at Dophkah?"

"I have heard of these false gods," Jethro replied, tearing off a piece of bread and dipping it into the stew bowl. "El is higher than them all. There are no gods but Him. El is at the center of all being. He spoke in times past to our father Abraham. Your ancestor Jacob bought a parcel of land for one hundred pieces of silver at Shechem in Canaan and set up an altar to El, whom he called *El Elohe* or *El Elyon*, the Most High God."

"I have heard that story from my mother in Egypt, but none of my people know the name of that god. It has long been forgotten. They know Him only as the god with no name and no image—the god of Abraham, Isaac and Jacob."

Jethro smiled and nodded. "I, too, am a son of Abraham. My ancestor, Midian—the fourth son of Abraham by Mother

---

* This same bread, when cooked on a piece of metal laid over the coals, is called *fatir*. It is similar to the modern pita bread of the Middle East, though it is thinner and does not have a double crust, or pocket. It is often cooked over dried camel dung, small pellets about the size of charcoal briquets, which burn like charcoal.

Keturah—was sent away into the east country. Our people tell of a visit by El to Father Abraham when he was one hundred less one. El changed his name from Abram, exalted father, to Abraham, father of many. Abraham then called El by the name of *El Shaddai*—God Almighty. He and all the males in his household were circumcised as a sign of the covenant that is yet to be fulfilled."

Moses sat long into the night, listening to the fascinating stories of Jethro. It is easy to learn from a man of hospitality.

This unwritten code of hospitality is still practiced in the Sinai. It is a code that originated with Abraham, whom Jew and Moslem both call "Father of Hospitality." It was Abraham who first decreed that the essentials of life were never to be denied any wilderness pilgrim, be he friend or enemy.

In Genesis 18, Abraham was approached by three strangers as he camped at Mamre. Sitting at the entrance to his tent, the childless, discouraged old nomad, the first of the Bedouins, saw the men approaching across the desert. He quickly brought them water to drink, then provided the extra luxury of water to wash their feet. Finally he offered them the shade of his tree.

The tree, mentioned in Genesis 18:4 and later in verse 8, is known as an *eshel*, or tamarisk, tree. After the wayfarers had eaten and been refreshed, they blessed Abraham by announcing Sarah would have a child. The Jewish Talmud says Abraham then responded by saying, "Now bless him of whose bounty ye have eaten. Think not it is of mine ye have eaten. No, it is of Him who spoke and the world was created."

One of the old Talmudic sages explains that *eshel* actually means a hospice, and consists of the initial letters of the three words that indicated hospitality: *achila* (food), *shetiya* (drink) and *lina* (accommodation for the night).

After the treaty with Abimelech, the Philistine chieftain, Abraham planted a tamarisk *(eshel)* tree in Beersheba (Genesis 21:33) to remind all who passed that way of the bond of hospitality among desert people. Ever since, the wells, the fire and the shade have belonged to all mankind.

There is no greater pleasure for the Bedouin than that of offering hospitality. Welcoming travelers is at the core of desert culture and is performed even if it means sharing the last piece of bread.

One evening just at dusk, our small group of desert travelers pulled into a Bedouin camp that consisted of two tents and an old tin and cardboard shack. We had been traveling all day through the narrow wadis and across the burning sand trying to reach the Gulf of Suez in our two Land Rovers. At that point we hoped to pick up the path traveled by Moses, which would lead us eventually to Mt. Sinai itself.

As the sun settled in the west, we noticed black clouds building to the south over the high mountains. Gusts of wind brought the smell of rain. We had been sleeping out each night, spreading our sleeping bags under the stars since it seldom rains in the desert, nor is there any moisture from dew. Thus we had no shelter in case it did rain during the night.

As we drove into the Bedouin camp, the old patriarch came out of one of the tents to greet us. Instead of asking, "Where are you from?" or even, "What do you want?", he grinned, extended his hand to all and welcomed our group of twelve men with *"Ahlan Wa Sahlan"*—"You are part of the family."

That night we had no choice but to sleep in his tent. He insisted. It would have been a great insult to have refused him the privilege of giving us the finest he had to offer. In return, he and his family crowded into the tiny cardboard and tin shack. Fortunately it did not rain, for they would have been soaked. Yet it would have made no difference to them. To have entertained strangers was the highest honor that could have come their way. Although we were welcome to stay the accepted three and a half days, we left the next morning, our hearts warmed, our stomachs full of their food.

Every passerby is invited to stay and relax. He is then offered little cups of strong, bitter coffee—the Bedouin equivalent of a cocktail. He may also be handed a steaming hot glass of extra sweet tea, prized by the Bedouin as a source of quick energy. Honored guests are feted with the meat of a goat slaughtered especially for them. To the Bedouin, whose entire wealth is in his flock, this is indeed a sacrifice.

So strong is the code of hospitality that rejection of it is received as an insult. A Bedouin demonstrates his kindness by sharing the little he has. A well-known story tells of a Bedouin who slaughtered his famous stallion, the fastest horse in the desert, in order to serve his guests a meal. He preferred to part with his beloved mount rather than risk being called a miser who did not show proper hospitality.

Likewise, the tent of the Bedouin is looked upon as a place of refuge. The host, once he has accepted a guest, feels obligated to protect him at all costs—even at his own peril.

During the Turkish rule of the Sinai, two fugitives once took refuge in the tent of a great Bedouin sheikh just as they were about to be caught by pursuing soldiers. When the soldiers arrived, they demanded the chief hand over the culprits. The old chief, standing before his tent with rifle in hand, refused. One of the soldiers decided to enter the tent and arrest the wanted men. Instantly the Bedouin raised his rifle and fired a deafening shot. The soldiers turned back, only to discover the chief had not shot at them; he had shot and killed his favorite mare.

"Be careful," an old man standing near the tent said to the soldiers. "The chief has just killed what is most dear to his heart. He has nothing more to lose."

The Turkish soldiers understood and fled back into the desert.

It was this lesson of hospitality Moses learned from Jethro— the first of many lessons he was to learn from this wise old sheikh whom God had sent into his life as a professor of post-graduate studies.

I, too, have encountered such hospitality at the hands of the Bedouin. Late one afternoon, as the sun was sinking in the west, my Jewish guide and I were invited into the tent of an old Bedouin sheikh whom I had met on a previous journey into the Sinai. He insisted we join him for coffee and then stay for dinner, such as it was.

We protested, not wanting to impose on his meager supply of food. He grinned a toothless smile and said he had no choice but to be our host. Waving toward the darkening sky, he reminded us of an old Bedouin proverb: "As long as the evening star shines, I am bound by Allah to offer hospitality to my guests."

We entered his tent while his wife scampered off to fix a few things for supper. Motioning us to sit, he busied himself with a brass *finjan*, an ornate, narrow-necked coffeepot blackened on the bottom from years of use over an open fire. He introduced us to his family who joined us, sitting crosslegged on the sand in a semicircle around the small fire that burned in the entrance to his tent. While I tried to converse with our host in my broken Arabic, my guide pointed to my hat. I thought he was telling me I should remove it as a courtesy to the Bedouin tent. But when I took it off, my guide took it from me, rose and disappeared outside the tent.

A few minutes later he returned. My hat was filled with small round camel droppings. The guide, realizing that the old Bedouin was making coffee and would need more fuel, had gone outside and picked up a hatful of dried camel dung to be used as we might use charcoal for a fire. When our host saw the expression on my face—after all, it was my hat filled with camel dung!—he laughed so hard tears rolled down his wrinkled brown cheeks.

I eventually joined in the laughter, but only after thoroughly beating my hat on the ground to remove any trace of its recent cargo.

I watched as our host, clad in his *galabiya* (a sort of caftan), his head covered with a checkered *kafeyah*, mixed the ground coffee with a generous measure of cardamom seeds called *hell* in Arabic. Adding water, he placed the *finjan* directly on the glowing coals of the dung fire, which filled the tent with pleasant, spicy smoke. He then joined us in the circle, sitting crosslegged with his robe draped over his spread knees.

When the coffee began to bubble and steam, he reached down with his bare hands and lifted the brass *finjan* off the fire. Ceremoniously he poured coffee into tiny glass cups which were brown-stained inside from many such occasions. I glanced at my guide and he nodded discreetly. Custom demanded I drink it. Despite the filth in the bottom of the glass cups, I smiled at my host—and sipped. It was so bitter I had to work to keep from sputtering. But I drank it all. Slowly.

While all this was going on, a young Bedouin man, obviously a member of the household but without the open friendliness of the old sheikh, entered the tent. Seeing us, he stiffened. Without speaking or acknowledging our presence in any way, he quickly took a seat on the ground outside the circle near the back flap of the tent. Only after remaining there several minutes, listening intently to our conversation, did he finally join the circle. Smiling, nodding politely, he poured himself a cup of coffee from the pot which had been replaced on the coals, and later he joined us in the dinner of pita bread, goat's cheese and fried chickpeas that had been mashed into a paste to go on the bread.

Later my Jewish guide explained the Bedouin custom. The young man, he said, was examining us to determine if we were friend or enemy. Thus he did not join us in the circle to begin with but sat at the rear of the tent until it became clear to him we were trustworthy. Had he gotten up and left without joining the circle, that would have been a sign to the sheikh that we were not to be trusted—even though the hospitality code demanded we be fed just the same.

A similar procedure is used if a member of the tribe brings a guest to the guest tent or hut. If he sits down beside his guest, it is a sign the man is a friend. If he ushers the guest into the inner circle, however, and then sits down next to the wall of the tent, apart from his guest, it is a sign he has been coerced into bringing the guest. Even though the man is welcomed and fed, he is still suspect. One of the men in the tent will always keep his hand on the handle of his dagger, just in case the wolf sheds his sheepskin before the meal is over.

All this is done to preserve hospitality, yet to allow the tribespeople the opportunity of using discernment until they are certain whether the guest is friend or enemy. Thus, into this basic fabric of hospitality has been woven an ingenious thread of signs and signals—all part of the wilderness code of hospitality. Even though the desert abounds in brigands and thieves, human life is still sacred and cherished for all, if possible.

The code of hospitality recognizes that no man can exist alone in the wilderness. It is one of the deep truths learned in tough times. We are not only forced to lean on each other for help, but we are obligated to reach out to the stranger who knocks at our door.

It was this lesson Prince Moses learned from old Jethro. A well, which took a man many months to dig, is his. But the water belongs to all men. The unwritten law of the desert forbids a man putting a fence around a well or spring.

The same is true of shade. If a straggling pilgrim comes to your tree or tent, he is always welcome to sit and rest. To deny shade to a stranger, as the sun broils and the *sharav* or *hamsin* (hot wind off the desert) blows like the breath of a furnace, could mean quick death. Likewise, the warmth of an evening fire belongs to all who cross the wilderness. No man is left outside in the freezing winter elements but is always welcomed into the warm tent.

When a modern pilgrim crosses the Sinai wilderness and comes upon the tomb of a sheikh, its whitewashed dome visible for many miles, he will also find nearby a *maqad*, or hospice house. This one-room stone building with a sand floor is for hospitality. No one knows as the wilderness dweller does how important it is to have a place of refuge from the elements. Inside will be a fireblackened teakettle or *finjan*, several small pots and pans for cooking, some dried camel dung for a fire, perhaps some tea or ground coffee, herbs, a jug of water, some rice and maybe a store of flour to make pita. Those who eat and are refreshed are expected to return as soon as possible to replenish the pantry. If not, when the tribe gathers once a year at the tomb of the sheikh, they will replenish the supplies in the *maqad*.

As usual, all things are free.

Desert courtesy captures this truth: there are some things that belong to God, and thus belong to all people. It is the lesson of hospitality—the lesson of sharing.

It would have been natural for Moses to have withdrawn into a shell of self-pity when he left Egypt. But, as the psalmist reminds us, God sets the solitary in families (Psalm 68:6). Such families are not like prisons, with wardens constantly checking and requiring. Families are freeing institutions, opening the doors and windows of the jails into which we withdraw when we are alone.

To Moses God gave the family of Jethro. Intellectual reasoning, even preaching, were not enough to set Moses free from the bondage of grief and isolation. God knew Moses did not need preachments. He needed love. What he needed was what we all need—an arm around his shoulder, a soft bosom on which to lay his head, a good meal, fellowship in a family and a gentle voice saying, "I understand." Beyond that man cannot go, but God stands at the door beckoning.

In our wilderness wanderings we will eventually learn that. We will learn to diminish our preaching, refrain from advice and directions, and follow the example of Jethro: "Why did you leave him alone? Invite him to have something to eat."

Of such is the Kingdom of heaven. It is a free gift from the *maqad*, a gift we shall one day replenish when we pass this way again.

II

God's Call

. . . and he led the flock to the backside of the desert, and
came to the mountain of God. . . .   (Exodus 3:1, KJV)

There is a day in every life that comes unannounced, un-heralded. No trumpets sound, there are no lightning flash-es—but as we look back on it, we realize that day was the turning point of our life.

That special day for Moses began as all other days in the wilderness. For weeks the 80-year-old man had been moving his scraggly flock of sheep and goats through the deep wadis of the southern Sinai.

The rising sun climbed the back of the far-off peaks in Midian, mountains red and purple with shades of lavender and gray. Over there, beyond the deep waters of the Gulf of Aqaba, was the land of Esau. Esau, the man with the ginger-colored hair, who never fully inherited the birthright stolen by his brother, Jacob.

Moses awoke and stretched. Even at 80, he was in remark-able physical condition. The discipline of the desert and prop-er nutrition—both helped account for his excellent health. He had already outlived his debauched counterparts in long-forgotten Egypt.

Lying comfortably in the soft sand of the enclosed wadi, he watched his mixed flock of sheep and goats scattering out ahead of him, searching for grass. It was time, he thought, to find new pasture.

The sun rose higher, illuminating the huge mountain ahead of him. For two weeks he had been making his way inland from the coastal village of DiZhav through Wadi Nasb. It was a favorite grazing spot, for the winter floods washed grass seed from the high mountainsides down into the basin of the canyon, where it sprouted as fodder for his flocks. Each day he had climbed higher and higher into the mountain passes. This morning, as the sun reflected off the massive range ahead of him, he knew it was time to press on to greener pastures. He was particularly eager to push through the pass and emerge onto the high inland plain of *er Rakha*, where his flocks could feed for days.

As the sun continued its rise, an auroral orange filled the wadi, then flashed like a brilliant shard of flaming metal against the sides of the red mountain before him. Almost instantly the entire southern massif of the ancient, empty peninsula was bathed in the white heat of the next day.

Moses arose and, whistling for his flock, watched with satisfaction as they ran toward him, falling into line behind him as he moved forward toward the base of the towering granite mountain. All passage through the Sinai is done through the wadis—rough, circuitous saw cuts through the desert mountains. The wadis double as dried riverbeds and remain parched except for one or two days of those rare years when, in keeping with the antipodal extremes in the Sinai, they course with murderous, bubbling flashfloods that roll boulders, palm trees, entire Bedouin encampments toward the sea many miles beyond and below.

Shouldering his pack and checking to make certain his goatskin still contained water, Moses moved slowly westward, the sun at his back. As the wadi narrowed, its massive rock walls displayed the sharp, delicate and splintered violence that is common throughout the wilderness. The hills lie at broken angles to everything around them, sedimentary lines all turned sideways and pointing down toward the specific fault that twisted them.

Suddenly the sun crested the mountains behind him and the wadi was filled with searing heat. The goats, more agile than the sheep, were climbing the steep sides of the canyon. They avoided the bitter caper plants—known as hyssop—that grew in the cracks and crevices, but munched on other scarce vegetation. Moses, realizing the foolishness of remaining in the blistering sun, allowed his flock to graze as he stopped in the shade of an outcropping rock to watch. It was a day like so many other days over the last forty years.

The sun climbed quickly to its zenith, its scorching light illuminating every crack, every aperture of the landscape. The sheep and goats browsed as they had every other day, nibbling at the scant herbage. Nothing seemed to indicate this day was to be different from any of the other days.

Moses turned and looked to his left at the giant form of the triple-peaked mountain that arose abruptly from the wadi. In front of him, spread out like a huge flat dish, was the plain of *Er Rakha*. It had taken Moses all these years to get accustomed to the awful silence. Only vaguely could he recall the chirping of the crickets and katydids, the rumble of the bullfrogs and bellowing of the crocodiles in Egypt. Egypt had disappeared forever into the past. He thought of his older brother, Aaron, and Miriam, his sister. Were they still alive back in Egypt? Surely his mother and father had long since passed away. It made no difference. Now he had a new family: Zipporah, his wife, and his two sons, Gershom and Eliezer, now grown almost to manhood. Like his old father-in-law, Jethro, Moses had become a Bedouin. His life centered around the mundane—caring for his wife and children, tending his sheep and goats.

Moses leaned back against the rock and closed his eyes, holding his five-foot staff loosely. Jethro had told him tales of this place, of a mountain that roared, of the voice of the God Jethro called "El" that was sometimes heard in the absolute silence at the base of the mountain.

Through his closed eyelids, Moses was suddenly aware of another light, different from the sunlight. Gradually he opened his eyes and looked toward the base of the great mountain. A bush had burst into flames. This was not an uncommon sight during the heat of summer, as the dried bushes sometimes caught the isolated rays of the sun magnified through the quartz crystals lying randomly on the ground and burst into flames. Quartz crystals were common in this area of the Sinai, and Moses had often used them to refract the sun's rays to start his own fire of dried camel dung.

But there was something different about this fire. The

thornbush, which was green, was burning brightly—but it was not consumed. The fire itself seemed to be ethereal, ghostly.

There was a time in Moses' life many, many years before when he would not have had time to check out such a sight. In fact, he would have been so busy with his tasks in the Egyptian court, he probably would not have even noticed it. But the years in the wilderness had changed all that. Now there was time to smell the tiny wildflowers, to stop and talk to the small creatures of the desert, to fondle his sheep and goats, to carve figures from acacia wood or hew them from the easily shaped sandstone. It had taken years, but now Moses had slowed down enough from the maddening pace of life to have time to stop and listen.

"I will go over and see this strange sight—why the bush does not burn up," he mused.

From that moment, all his life was altered. The door, which had been closed so long it resembled the wall, suddenly opened. For as he approached the bush, a voice spoke, calling him by name: "Moses, Moses!"

That voice still speaks to wilderness wanderers. Though the day may seem to be a day like every other day, and the bush like all bushes, things are not always as they seem. Elizabeth Barrett Browning captured the concept:

> Earth's crammed with heaven,
> And every common bush afire with God;
> But only he who sees takes off his shoes. . . .

The tragedy of our wilderness experience is not that we have to go through grief and suffering, but that we often miss the blessings from burning bushes—the things through which God speaks. Through a letter from a friend, the words of a book, a long-forgotten song, the voice of a teacher, the beauty of a holy life, the innocence of a child, God still calls us by name and makes His eternal purpose known.

Even then, though we may see the miraculous and hear in the midst of it a voice calling our name, nothing is fulfilled until we respond. The Scriptures are full of stories of divine summonses, and of the men who responded—men like

Moses who had been prepared and were now ready to be used.

Learning to wait patiently, learning to do today what your hand finds to do, learning to hear the call of God when it comes, and to respond—that is what the wilderness is all about. Once a man submits his life to God's control, he voluntarily surrenders the right to determine or the power to vary the consequences of that decision. From that moment on, no situation can ever come into the life of the believer which has not first passed through the hands of God and thus has redeeming quality.

Our task, even though we may be wandering in some wilderness, is to remain ready. Our lamps should never be allowed to run low on oil, for who knows when a summons may come? Blessed is the free, unengaged spirit who has not encumbered himself with the things and cares of this world, who can at once put aside all he is doing to answer the call of God.

Many years later the prophet Isaiah would encourage a battered people to "wait upon the Lord." Waiting, Isaiah said, would bring renewed strength. While *wait* in the Hebrew has several connotations, the word used in Isaiah 40 means to be entwined about, to become part of. It is best illustrated by looking at a braided rope that is actually several strands woven together to become one large, strong strand. Though the smaller ropes are actually separate, they become one because they have been entwined and twisted together.

Moses had spent forty years waiting. But the waiting was not limited to the passing of time. It had to do with faithful service to Jethro—and the task before him. He had learned that service to God often means nothing more than doing with all his might what his hand found to do.

Waiting on the Lord, as one does in a wilderness experience, means we should become entwined with Him, braided into Him, as we become part of Him and He becomes part of us.

The burning bush gave direction to Moses' life—a life that for eighty years had been spent in preparation. He had been called by God, handed a commission, and sent forth to accomplish a task.

To all those wandering in the wilderness, let it be said: bushes still catch on fire and God still calls men by their names. But the call comes only to those who are busy with the smaller tasks already assigned.

III

Spiritual Authority

The Lord said to him, "What is that in your hand?" "A staff," he replied.

(Exodus 4:2)

When God needs a tool for His service, He usually looks for something common to use. He doesn't reach for a knife that is "factory-sharpened"; He prefers to hone His own edge out of rough metal.

The apostle Paul was the most unlikely man imaginable to carry the gospel to the Gentile world. He was not only a Jewish Pharisee; he was an ardent persecutor of Christians. But a touch from God changed all that on the road to Damascus.

Who would have thought the Messiah would have been heralded by a wild prophet who roamed the wilderness dressed in skins, eating locusts and wild honey? Or that the Messiah would have submitted to such a man for water baptism? Yet Jesus said of John the Baptist, "Among those born of women there is no one greater than John."

When Samuel went to the house of Jesse in search of God's choice for a king over Israel, he wound up anointing with oil the runt of the litter. All the other boys had kingly appearances, but the youngest son was ruddy, with red hair and freckles—a simple shepherd boy with slingshot and harp. Yet because of the touch of God, David was called "a man after God's own heart."

When God needed a man to defeat the Midianites, He turned to a confessed coward hiding behind the winepress. But the touch of God turned Gideon into a "mighty warrior." Rahab, a prostitute in Jericho, became the mother of all Israel. Out of her came the house of David, which eventually produced the Messiah.

Thus it is not unusual that God would choose a murderer who had just finished serving a forty-year prison term in the wilderness to lead His people from slavery into the Promised Land. Nor is it unusual that instead of putting a golden scepter into his hand, He transformed Moses' wooden shepherd's staff into the "rod of God."

The call of God at the burning bush was so radical, so unexpected, that Moses had difficulty comprehending. He did not doubt God, but he genuinely feared that when he tried to tell others, they would not believe.

It was then God asked that classic question: "What is that in your hand?"

"Only a walking staff," Moses replied.

Even the casual reader of the Bible can almost hear God chuckle. Chances are it was the same heavy wooden stick Moses had used to murder the Egyptian slavemaster. Later he had used it to thump the heads of the bully-shepherds harassing Jethro's daughters. But across the years, the five-foot staff had become not a weapon but a companion. It was hard to imagine Moses without his staff. Now God indicated it was to become something far more than a simple staff.

"Throw it on the ground," God told Moses.

Instantly it was transformed into a viper. Moses jumped back. But God, whose voice demanded absolute obedience, told Moses to pick it up by the tail. Instantly the snake was transformed back into a staff.

In Egypt the serpent occupied a central role in temple worship. When Moses, at God's command, picked up the serpent, it was a sign—not to others who might not believe, but to Moses himself. At the word of God, the serpent of Egypt would become a staff in the hand of Moses. All Moses had to do was to obey God at every turn. If he would do that, even when he was commanded to do the ridiculous or the dangerous, Pharaoh and the whole force of the Egyptian empire would be his to wield as easily as he wielded his staff.

Thus the shepherd's staff was transformed into a rod of spiritual authority, from that time on to be called the "rod of God." That "rod of God," in the hands of a man of God, would open seas, bring water from mountains and defeat the army of Amalek. Yet there was another lesson Moses forgot: in every rod there is a serpent. If authority is misused, the serpent strikes, and the bite is often deadly for the man holding the rod. Only once did Moses abuse his authority. As an old man he used his rod in anger—to strike a rock to bring forth water, rather than speak to it. God did not remove him from leadership, nor did He punish him, but Moses forfeited the right to enter the Promised Land. Such is the penalty of abusing God's power, for unto whom much is given, much is required.

The principle of the transformed staff, however, remains absolute. God is ever transforming the secular into the sacred, storing His heavenly treasure in earthen vessels, touching the common things and causing them to shine with His glory. A ram's horn, an ox goad, an earthen pitcher, a shepherd's sling, a lowly manger, five loaves and two fishes, an old rugged cross—God delights in using the foolish to confound the wise. A rod with God behind it is mightier than all the armies that ever marched—as Pharaoh was painfully to discover.

Forty years earlier Moses had not been ready. Then he thought he could correct all the injustice of Egypt—and the injustice of the desert—by using his rod as a weapon. Now that murderer's tool had been transformed, as had the murderer himself. It took the wilderness to purify, prepare and process the man of God. During that time, the stick in his hands lost its potency as a weapon and became a simple staff. He used it to climb the mountains, to beat the low brush in which the lambs were caught, to kill snakes, to chase off wolves and hyenas, to hold out over his sheep and count them as they came to the well to drink. Yet through all those forty years, God was forging a leader who did not need a sword to enforce authority.

Spiritual leaders are never elected; they are called by God. When God calls, He also equips, and makes the ministry fruitful. How can you tell if a man is a shepherd? Look behind him to see if there are sheep who know his voice and are following. The true shepherd has a flock. The rest are simply hirelings. His badge of authority may be a simple staff, but if he is called, that staff holds in it the awesome authority of God—an authority recognized by all.

In Moses' case, as with his ancestor Jacob, the symbol of authority was once a symbol of sin and selfishness. After his midnight encounter with an angel, Jacob forever walked with a limp, so others would know he had been touched by God. So Moses carried a blood-stained staff, now the symbol of moral purity and uprightness.

That, by the way, was the meaning of the second sign God gave Moses at the burning bush. God told Moses to put his hand into his robe. When he pulled it out, it was leprous—the symbol of sin. But when he put his hand back into the folds of his robe and withdrew it, it was cleansed. So God told Moses that never again would he have to hang his head in shame over past sin. As easily as God could change a serpent into a staff, so He could heal disease and forgive sin.

The fact that Moses' symbol of authority was a staff and not a scepter is significant. God did not appoint Moses king. He was to be an apostle, a spiritual father, a chief shepherd. That meant he would not use the kind of kingly authority that comes from perfect things—like scepters made of gold—but authority filtered from God through the commonplace.

The staff itself—bent, gnarled, chipped from many years of service—was a constant reminder to Moses of God's grace. No leader is perfect; so God takes the imperfect and through it accomplishes His perfect will. As one old Bible teacher used to say, "God can strike a lot of straight blows with a crooked stick."

The staff was an encumbrance as well. All the other leaders in Egypt carried swords or spears. But Moses was instructed to approach Pharaoh carrying his staff. He was to be deliberately conspicuous, out-of-place, so God's glory could be evident.

That is one of the prices of leadership. Moses could no longer act like a follower. He had been designated as a leader. As such, his behavior would always be different. The leader cannot enjoy the luxury of living like a follower. He cannot pretend he is not a leader. Leadership encumbers.

Moses realized this and did all he could to escape the call of God and the responsibilities of leadership. He argued with God: "Who am I, that I should go to Pharaoh?" Then he said he didn't know God's name, that the people wouldn't believe him without some kind of sign, and that he was not an eloquent speaker. Finally he wailed, "O Lord, please send someone else to do it" (Exodus 4:13).

God cut him short. "The Lord's anger burned against Moses." Moses had said too much. God had called and there was no escaping the call.

David knew how impossible it was to run away from God's call:

> Where can I go from your Spirit?
> Where can I flee from your presence?
> If I go up to the heavens, you are there;
> if I make my bed in the depths, you are
> there.
> If I rise on the wings of the dawn,
> if I settle on the far side of the sea,
> even there your hand will guide me,
> your right hand will hold me fast.
>
> (Psalm 139:7-10)

When Moses left the burning bush, he was no longer carrying a staff. He had in his hand the rod of God. Nor was he any longer a wanderer: he was a leader. It was time to return to Jethro, inform him that the God of no name and no image had appeared at the base of Mt. Sinai and commissioned him to a task. He was now a man under authority. He was a man of authority.

Often we shrink from the call of God, fearing it will deprive us of pleasure, cause us to be ridiculed, force us from the comforts of home into a rigorous life of discipline. As such, we often equate the call of God with going to our doom.

Yet for each of us, God has something far greater than living out our lives in the wilderness. In Moses' case, it was a life filled with the excitement of the extraordinary. There would be a great song of victory on the banks of the sea, an appointment with God on a mountaintop, being recognized as a worker of miracles and a healer of those bitten by serpents. He would receive a vision of glory, would be buried by the hand of an archangel, and would receive the supreme honor of standing with the Lord Jesus on the Mount of Transfiguration. Moses was called not to doom but to glory.

God honors simple things. He honors the man, the woman, who does what needs to be done, regardless of what it costs. He honors the person who, putting his hand to the plow, does not turn back. He honors the person who does today what his hand finds to do, and does it with all diligence.

The person constantly wishing for a better station in life seldom achieves. Somehow his big dream of the future often blocks a man from accomplishing the little things demanded by the present. But God never skips steps. He does not hopscotch through life, jumping over squares to miss the rock. He hits every step and brings us up through the ranks one grade at a time until we are ready to assume the task for which He has been preparing us all along.

"What is that in your hand?"

Something common, no doubt. Perhaps something stained with the sin of the past. But when God touches it, it becomes the symbol of authority.

> . . . There is hope for a tree:
>   If it is cut down, it will sprout again,
>   and its new shoots will not fail.
> Its roots may grow old in the ground
>   and its stump die in the soil,
> yet at the scent of water it will bud
>   and put forth shoots like a plant.

(Job 14:7-9)

IV

Hidden Promises

*When they came to Marah, they could not drink its water
because it was bitter.*   (Exodus 15:23)

God never brings a hindrance into our lives that He does not
intend to be used to open another door that would not have
opened otherwise.

When God spoke to Moses at the burning bush at the base
of Mt. Sinai, commissioning him to return to Egypt to lead the
Israelites out of bondage, He had a clear-cut plan. He said He
was concerned about the suffering of the Israelites. He said He
had come to rescue them and take them to a land of milk and
honey. He said He would not forsake them as they traveled
and would bring them to Mt. Sinai to worship Him (Exodus
3:7-12).

But such promises are hard to remember when you run out
of water in the desert.

Even Moses doubted in the beginning. Returning to Egypt,
he encountered great opposition, not only from the Egyptians
but from the Israelites he was trying to lead to freedom. In
Exodus 5:22 he cries out to God: "O Lord, why have you
brought trouble upon this people? Is this why you sent me?
Ever since I went to Pharaoh to speak in your name, he has
brought trouble upon this people, and you have not rescued
your people at all."

Later, however, encouraged by the miracles God had

worked through him—miracles that finally forced Pharaoh to release the Israelite slaves—Moses was reassured.

The next crisis of his leadership came at the edge of the Reed Sea. (The "Red Sea" of Exodus 13:18 is an incorrect translation of the Hebrew *Yam-Suph*, which means, literally, "Sea of Reeds.") This is probably located in the vicinity of the Bitter Lakes just north of the Gulf of Suez, an area about five miles wide and between ten and fifteen feet deep. Here, even though the Egyptian army was in hot pursuit and the impassable waters were before them, Moses was able to assure the people: "Do not be afraid. Stand firm and you will see the deliverance the Lord will bring you today. The Egyptians you see today you will never see again. The Lord will fight for you; you need only to be still" (Exodus 14:13-14). In short: "Don't just do something, stand there!"

Yet the deliverance of the children of Israel through the parting of the sea, and the subsequent destruction of the entire Egyptian army, was still not enough to convince the people that God's word to Moses at the burning bush was real. No sooner had they finished their celebration on the shores of the sea than they found themselves once again on the move. Instead of leading the people across the northern Sinai by the *Via Maris* —the "way of the sea" (a much shorter and easier way to cross the wilderness in order to get to Canaan)—Moses turned south along the eastern shore of the Gulf of Suez. It was a journey he had made many times. He was returning to Mt. Sinai so the promise of God could be fulfilled that the people would worship Him at the Mountain of God.

According to Exodus 12:37, there were 600,000 adult males and their families, plus the priestly tribe of Levi and the various camp followers—including some Egyptians who wanted to flee the nation. If this is a correct translation, it would mean the Exodus number could reach close to three million. However, the geographical logistics simply do not allow room to move that many people through the narrow wadis of the peninsula.

Other scholars point out that the Hebrew word *eleph*, which is usually translated *thousand*, can also be translated *family*. That would give a much more realistic figure. In other places in the Bible, the word *eleph* means "military units," meaning the exact number of people is unknown, but they were accompanied by at least 600 armed men, or armed squadrons.

When we get to the book of Numbers, however, we find there were 22,273 male babies born during the first year of the wanderings. Thus the actual number in the Exodus remains a mystery. Certainly it was far less than the traditional figure of millions, but probably more than 15,000, as some suspect.

Regardless of size, the fact of Moses' leadership remains indisputable, and for the most part the route is still rather clearly marked.

I have traveled that route, south along the shore to the Gulf of Suez through the scorching sands of the wilderness of Shur and Etham. My first trip to this region was in late spring, about the same time of year the Israelites passed that way. The sun was quickly dehydrating my body and parching my throat as I came against the problem that faces all desert travelers—lack of water.

Three days is the maximum time the human body can go without water in the desert. I thought of those Israelites so many years before. At least I had a canteen—and there was additional water on the desert vehicle that had gone on before. Those Israelites, however, had quickly run out of water after they left Egypt. Stretched to their absolute limit, the people were about to die when ahead they spotted the palm trees that marked the location of an oasis. Gasping, falling over each other, the cattle and flocks stampeding, they ran the last few feet toward the waters of Marah. There they fell on their faces beside the tepid pool.

Suddenly a great cry went up from the parched throats of the people kneeling beside the water. It was bitter. "Now," they cried, "we shall surely die of thirst!"

Moses was a seasoned guide. For forty years he had lived in that wilderness. He knew every watering place, every path through the wilderness. Surely he knew about the springs along the Gulf of Suez.

These springs are the same today as they were in Moses' time. When I reached Marah that hot afternoon, I found the same thing the Israelites discovered. The water of the springs, although clear and beautiful to look at, was laced with calcium and magnesium. This high mineral content makes the water so bitter it is almost impossible to drink.

Bending beside the spring, I ran my fingers through the water. It actually felt oily to the touch. All around the edge I could see the powdery white mineral residue where the rock sides of the spring touched the water.

"The Bedouins have a saying," my guide laughed. "'One spoonful and you go for a week.' In fact," he continued, "be careful not to lick your fingers now that you've put them into the water. The mineral is so potent your stomach will cramp in just a few minutes."

I quickly wiped my fingers on my shirt. Having experienced once before the awesome power of that bitter water in my intestines, I was not eager to replay the scene.

The actual location of Marah remains a mystery. Far to the south, near el Tur, is a place called "The Springs of Moses." This, according to the Arabs, is "Marah." There, in an old bathhouse, hot springs bubble from the ground into a covered pool. I have bathed in that water many times. It feels oily on the skin, and when it dries in the hot arid wind, it leaves a white powder all over your body. Despite the fact that there is bitter water at el Tur, however, it is far to the south of where the Israelites would have stopped after their first three days of travel from Egypt.

Most of the water along the Gulf of Suez is bad. On the other side of the peninsula, along the much deeper Gulf of Aqaba, the springs are usually sweet. But along the western side of the wilderness, near the relatively shallow Gulf of Suez, the water is filled with magnesium and other minerals. It is this combination of chemicals that constitutes the powerful laxative and causes intense and almost instant bowel problems.

The biblical account is stark and vivid. "For three days they traveled in the desert without finding water. When they came to Marah, they could not drink its water because it was bitter. [That is why the place is called Marah, which means 'bitter.'] So the people grumbled against Moses, saying, 'What are we to drink?'" (Exodus 15:22-24).

It was a desperate situation. All seemed destined to die.

Moses "cried unto the Lord." As an Egyptian he would have rebuked the people, demanding they drink. Or he might have threatened them. But his own wilderness time had changed his character. Full of patience, he turned instead to the One who had brought them to this place, to the One who hears every moan of agony from those He created. Surely God knew the water was bitter. Why then had He brought them this way?

God directed Moses to a nearby tree. Breaking the limbs to release the sap, he threw the wood into the water. The chemical reaction caused the minerals to precipitate to the bottom, leaving the water sweet to drink.

Beside each bitter Marah in the wilderness grows a tree that makes the water sweet. No wilderness pool is without such a tree. Poison and antidote, infection and cure, pain and relief, temptation and a way of escape—God always provides the sweet to remove the taste of the bitter. We do not always see it, but it is always there, if we are not too busy grumbling and complaining about the circumstances.

Yet somehow turning the water from bitter to sweet seemed to be God's second-best. Jesus, in the Garden of Gethsemane, had confessed He did not want to drink the "bitter cup," yet He surrendered to God's will. "Nevertheless," He prayed as He knelt in the dark night of His soul, "not my will but thine be done." By grumbling, the children of Israel had refused the bitter cup—and missed God's best purpose for their lives.

In Exodus 15:25, the historical account says the Lord was *testing* the people at Marah. In the Western concept, testing is for the purpose of ascertaining knowledge. It is used to determine how much one has learned. But the biblical concept of testing is not to ascertain knowledge; it is a method of teaching. When God "tests" His people, He is not doing so to find out whether they have learned their lesson and deserve a good grade. God's tests are learning experiences, designed by the Teacher to share knowledge, not to determine its presence or absence.

Thus, when God tested the people at Marah, He did it with a decree, not a questionnaire. He said, "If you listen carefully to the voice of the Lord your God and do what is right in his eyes, if you pay attention to his commands and keep all his decrees, I will not bring on you any of the diseases I brought on the Egyptians, for I am the Lord who heals you" (Exodus 15:26).

For almost half a millenium, God had been silent. Now He

had begun His progressive revelation of His nature and character to the people of earth. For the Jews, this would culminate with the giving of the law on Mt. Sinai. In the final analysis, God would fully reveal Himself through His Son, Jesus Christ. But it is significant to note that the first time God spoke to the people (He had spoken earlier to and through Moses), even before He thundered His law from Mt. Sinai, He revealed Himself as the Lord who heals sick bodies. Our God is a God who heals.

It is a marvelous promise that, like all God's promises, is conditional—found in the subjunctive mood and preceded by an *if*. The promise of the absence of disease is for those who (1) listen carefully to the voice of the Lord; (2) do what is right in His eyes; (3) pay attention to His commands; and (4) keep all His decrees. Only then does a man have the right to claim the promise of "none of these diseases."

An old Bible teacher used to remind his pupils that not only was the Lord interested in getting the people out of Egypt, He also wanted to get Egypt out of the people. That, perhaps, is at the heart of all wilderness experiences. In this case, the people had brought a lot of Egypt with them—internally. Egypt was a filthy nation. The entire nation had just undergone a siege of flies, locusts, dead frogs, boils and impure water. In the resulting plague, hundreds of thousands of Egyptian children had died. The Israelites, for the most part, had escaped the plagues. But they had still brought with them the contamination of Egypt. These included not only amoebic dysentery, but bilharzia, a weakening disease borne by snails in the slow-moving irrigation ditches of the Nile Valley (which still affects eighty percent of the peasants of Egypt). Now at Marah, the Lord spoke and told them He would not allow the Egyptian diseases to afflict them—if they but obeyed Him.

What did God want the Israelites to do? Obviously He wanted them to drink the water of Marah. But it was filled with magnesium. True, but even Moses could not have known about the medicinal qualities of calcium and magnesium. For one thing, magnesium is a powerful laxative. It was God's way of cleaning out their systems. Had they drunk the bitter water, and continued to drink it despite its effects on their intestines, their bodies would have ceased the purgative action and grown accustomed to the water. In the process, however, they would have expelled most of the amoeba, parasites and death-dealing germs they brought with them from Egypt.

There is another medicinal quality about the water of Marah. Calcium and magnesium form the basis of a drug called *dolomite*. Dolomite pills are used by professional athletes who perform in the sun. It is basically a muscle control drug to be used in extremely hot weather. Joggers, tennis players, those who exert themselves in hot weather often take dolomite to control muscle spasms. It is also used by patients with heart problems to control the heart muscle and keep it from going into fibrillation, which is the muscle beating out of control.

God had provided just the right medicine, not only to clean out the systems of the former slaves, but to prepare their bodies for the long and arduous journey through the desert. Thus their first stop in the wilderness journey was not a place of despair but a place where God had provided medicinal water.

We find later in the Exodus account that despite God's proclamation that "I am the God who heals thee," many of the people died of disease during the wilderness wanderings. Does that mean the promise of God was not valid? No, it simply points out the conditional nature of all God's promises. Often what seems foolish in our eyes is part of God's higher plan. Drinking the water of Marah did not make sense. But God had a plan far greater than man's desire to escape intestinal discomfort and a puckered mouth.

Over and over we are reminded that the reason for wilderness experiences is purification and preparation. The waters of Marah would have certainly brought almost instant purification. God was about to change the entire eating structure of the nation. No longer would they gorge themselves on shellfish, pork and the highly spiced foods of Egypt. To accomplish this change, God started with a purge, ridding them of all their perverse yearnings and desires. He was about to introduce them to their new dietary structure known ever since as "kosher." But the people rebelled at the first test. Thus the promise of a people without disease had to wait for a generation who listened carefully to the voice of the Lord and did not grumble at His commands.

The principle holds true even today. God wants us not only to live, but to live abundantly. His desire is for us to have long, productive and creative lives. So He continually leads us back to the waters of Marah where our crusty spirits may be broken—that the Spirit of God may enter.

V

Living Waters

*Then they came to Elim, where there were twelve springs and
seventy palm trees, and they camped there near the water.*

(Exodus 15:27)

Shortly after the Six-Day War in 1967, Dr. Yitzhak Gutterman, a well-known desert botanist, and a group of Israeli
researchers conducted a survey of the southern Sinai. While
passing through Ras G'ara, near the Gulf of Suez, they spotted some corpses blackened by the desert sun. They were the
remains of Egyptian soldiers who had retreated on foot from
Sharm el Sheikh at the southern tip of the Sinai and were
trying to reach their own lines. The unscarred bodies left no
doubt to Dr. Gutterman that the soldiers had not died of battle
wounds but from lack of water. Tragically, there was water less
than twenty yards from where the soldiers had fallen along
the sandy coast. But it was underground—and only a man
familiar with the wilderness would have known how to find
it.

Following that incident, Dr. Gutterman dedicated his life to
helping others find water in the desert.

Every wilderness wanderer knows that water is the source
of life. Without it, life in the desert is always on the brink of
death.

Desert plants are uniquely adapted to live with scarce water.
Their spiny leaves and tough surfaces mean less evaporation.
The acacia tree, that sturdy thorn tree that seems to grow in

50

the most desolate places, is capable of putting down roots
more than thirty feet to find water. Even the smaller plants,
such as the scuffy brown rotem bush, send out a huge root
system and draw water from deep in the earth. Often I have
dug around the base of a bush with green leaves and discovered water near the surface. I have also discovered the
secret of covering the branches of a rotem bush with a plastic
bag. In the cool of the evening this will produce enough water
in a few hours through condensation to keep a man alive.

Desert animals are also adapted to live without water. The
camel, which made its appearance in the Sinai about the time
of the Exodus, is especially adapted. Although the longest
documented trek of a camel between watering points is nearly
600 miles in 21 days, the Bedouin know it can go even longer if
necessary. Contrary to popular opinion, the camel does not
store water in its hump. Water is stored in the red corpuscles of
the bloodstream, which can expand to 240 times their original
volume when the camel drinks. After long periods without
water, the camel is capable of drinking over 400 pints of water
at one time, which is immediately distributed through the
entire body, restoring his water loss in just a few minutes.

Human beings do not fare as well in the desert. The Bedouin have learned the necessity of covering the entire body to
prevent an abnormal loss of water. Black robes, incidentally,
actually lower the skin temperature and prevent even more
evaporation. Often I have had to compel my companions to
drink from their canteens, even though they did not feel
thirsty; for on a hot day a person climbing in the desert can
lose more than four quarts of water in one hour. Even while
resting in the desert shade, the human body excretes more
than two quarts of water in an hour. Man in the desert is
always on the brink of death.

The children of Israel had never been thirsty before they
began their desert trek. Despite the fact that the water of Egypt
was polluted, there was always enough of it. The mighty Nile
never went dry.

The desert, though, was different. Here the sun drew moisture from their bodies at an incredible rate. Leaving Egypt in
the middle of the month of *Nissan,* which corresponds to the
first week of April, they encountered desert temperatures of

100 degrees F. By the middle of *Tammuz*, three months later, midday temperatures would soar past 120. Only the strong could survive.

Death by dehydration does not come rapidly. It creeps up on you. Even the seemingly natural sign of thirst is absent. I remember one evening when one of the men in a group I was escorting through the desert almost died of dehydration. Early that morning, before we left the safety of our vehicle for a steep mountain climb, I warned those in the small party of the dangers of dehydration. I told them to drink water from their canteens every half-hour, whether they were thirsty or not.

That night we camped in a box canyon. I noticed that one of the men, normally active and full of vitality, seemed sluggish and lethargic. His voice was slurred and he finally left the circle of men around the campfire, saying he was not hungry. In a few moments I heard him in the darkness, heaving with violent nausea.

While one of the men rolled out his sleeping bag on the sand, I questioned him about the day's activities. Had he been drinking water? No, he said, he didn't like water. He preferred coffee. Had he urinated during the day? Yes, but only once. What was the color of his urine? A dark brown, he confessed, almost like syrup. He was close to death.

We quickly tucked him into his sleeping bag to prevent any more moisture loss to the dry desert air. Then we began the slow process of replenishing the liquids in his body—liquids he insisted he did not want to drink. We started with salty soups. Then water. Within two hours he was feeling better. Before he went to sleep, the doctor in our group fixed a two-gallon container of medicated water, which he put beside the head of his sleeping bag.

"When I wake in the morning," he told my foolish friend, "I want that container empty. I will wake you every hour during the night and expect you to drink a quart at a time. If you don't, you may not wake at all when the sun rises."

It was ample motive to drink.

Similar problems face us as we move through our spiritual wilderness. Spiritual thirst, the need for living water, is the dominating factor in the lives of all human beings. It begins with a deep longing for something to satisfy inner cravings.

Although we realize that Jesus said the man who "hungers and thirsts after righteousness shall be filled," we are often shocked to find we are thirsting for the wrong things. We don't want righteousness; we prefer selfish gain and pleasure. The desire pursues us from Egypt and tracks us across the deserts of our lives, until we cry out as Paul did: "When I want to do good, evil is right there with me. . . . What a wretched man I am! Who will rescue me from this body of death?" (Romans 7:21-24).

In fact, it is these very cravings that cause many of us to behave in such a way that we are forced into the wilderness to begin with.

In his concept of the "God-shaped vacuum," St. Augustine once prayed, "Our hearts are restless until we find our rest in Thee." Thus, while it is thirst that drives us forward, we are never satisfied, no matter how much we drink, until we drink from the fountain of Living Water.

The children of Israel, with Marah behind them, staggered on through the desert sands along the Gulf of Suez. Their thirst had returned as the days grew longer and hotter. Slowly the great procession turned inland, following the directions of Moses who had been this way many times before. Ahead lay the huge red and brown mountains of the southern Sinai. With weary feet the Israelites climbed the gentle slopes of a sandy alluvial plain which fanned from a narrow wadi and emptied into the Gulf of Suez behind them. Climbing, slipping over pebbly ground, their lips parched, their bodies fatigued, they were close to death. Slowly the long procession funneled into the narrow wadi between two huge red mountain ranges and disappeared inland.

No one knows exactly where Elim is. Chances are it was in what is now Wadi Feiran, where still exists one of the most beautiful oases in the Middle East. It is described in Scriptures as a "place where there were twelve springs and seventy palm trees" (Exodus 15:27). It was here the Israelites camped and were refreshed.

There are three basic sources of water in the desert: cisterns, wells and springs. While Elim was an oasis with springs, the Bedouin also hew cisterns and dig wells. The cistern system is ingenious. Through a pattern of ditches and aqueducts, they channel water from the intermittent rains into the basins for storage. The huge cisterns at the mountain fortress of Masada near the Dead Sea held millions of gallons of water collected in this way, which could be dipped to the top by buckets. At best, though, this was but a temporary way to store water.

In most cases, water in the desert is obtained from wells.

It was said of Jacob that everywhere he went, he built an altar and dug a well. The problem, of course, was knowing where to dig.

To the Bedouin this is a simple matter. It is said that the desert sand is to the Bedouin what the morning newspaper is to the Englishman—only with fewer misprints. He knows not only how to track, but where to find water.

As I stood beside an old Bedouin man one afternoon, he showed me, by studying the landscape, where he should dig his well. The mountains in the southern Sinai are volcanic. At some time in the past, the long, deep veins between the igneous rocks were filled with volcanic magma—forced up from deep in the earth under great pressure. When the magma cooled, it produced dark, black seams that streak across the mountain ranges at right angles to the wadis.

"Look there," the old man said, pointing at the side of the mountain. I saw the dark seams—black with spots of green and copper. "We call them *dykes*."

I climbed up on the side of the ravine and could see this particular dyke extending across the desert for miles. It looked like the angry crayon mark of a small child as it contrasted against the light-colored granite and sandstone. To the side I noticed others only inches wide. This particular one was at least four feet wide. I knew it extended probably hundreds of feet into the earth.

Looking down on the old Bedouin, who was making a mark in the sand where his boys would come later to dig the well, I could see where the dyke intersected the floor of the wadi and disappeared into the ground. It then reappeared on the other side, snaking its way up the side of the cliff to continue its streak across the mountain range. That was evidence it had continued on under the sand bed of the wadi.

"When the wadi fills with water during the winter rain," the old man told me as we made our way back toward his tent, "much of the water soaks into the sandy bottom of the canyon. What is on the upstream side of the dyke forms an underground lake."

It was into this natural reservoir, trapped by the dam beneath the sand, he would dig his well. The presence of a date palm nearby was additional confirmation that there was water beneath the surface of the sand.

The digging would be tedious. It would take at least two men. One would dig with a shovel, shoring up the sides with rocks as he went down through the sand. The other would pull the excess sand to the surface in a bucket on a rope. I was glad the old Bedouin had not asked me to help. Going down thirty to sixty feet into a well was something I was quite content to let someone else do!

For the children of Israel, having to dig a well and then leave it behind was a wrenching process. To them God gave a magnificent promise, however, that one day He would bring them to a land with "wells you did not dig" (Deuteronomy 6:11).

One of the signs of entrance into the Promised Land is adequate spiritual nourishment. There may be giants and walled cities, but those who have entered the Promised Land will always be able to quench their spiritual thirst because of a covenant relationship with Christ. In the wilderness, however, one often has to dig his own wells.

It is not enough, in the desert, to depend on surface water—blessings that fall intermittently. Man needs a much deeper source of life than that brought by showers of blessings. He must have a source upon which he can draw when there has been no rain for years.

David wrote about the spiritual man who was "like a tree planted by streams of water, which yields its fruit in season" (Psalm 1:3). Interestingly, the Spanish Bible does not translate "streams" with the usual Spanish word *rio*. It uses the less common word *arroyo*. The river David was talking about was not a flowing stream but a dry gulch—a wadi. The spiritual man does not need constantly flowing water in order to prosper. He prospers even when the skies are cloudless and the land parched. He prospers because his roots, on the upstream side of the dyke, go deep into the sand and draw from the underground supply.

Cisterns are not adequate when the sun grows hot and there is no rain for years. Jeremiah warned the people of Israel about the danger of this. "My people have committed two sins," the Lord said through Jeremiah. "They have forsaken me, the spring of living water, and have dug their own cisterns, broken cisterns that cannot hold water" (Jeremiah 2:13).

Neither cisterns nor wells give a sure supply of water. Only the presence of a spring, where water flows freely of its own accord, affords certainty. Elim was such a place—with twelve springs surrounded by numerous date palms. This water was not collected by man's efforts, nor did it have to be drawn to the surface by man's efforts. It flowed freely for anyone who would come and drink.

Jesus was talking about this when He sat at Jacob's well in Samaria. In the story in John 4, He was sitting on the edge of a well when a Samaritan woman approached to draw water. In His conversation with her Jesus said, "Everyone who drinks this water will be thirsty again, but whoever drinks the water I give him will never thirst. Indeed, the water I give him will become in him a spring of water welling up to eternal life" (John 4:13-14).

The King James Version says, "A well of water springing up." But that is a poor translation. Jesus never talks about wells; He talks of springs. A well is something man has to dig. A spring is a gift from God. Religious people—Pharisees and others who feel they have to earn salvation—dig wells. The spring, like God's grace, bubbles up from underground of its own accord. You don't have to do anything to earn it. You don't have to labor for it. Like salvation, it is a free gift to all who stoop to drink.

At another time Jesus spoke more of this: "If a man is thirsty, let him come to me and drink. Whoever believes in me, as the Scripture has said, *streams* of living water will flow from within him" (John 7:37, italics added).

The writer says Jesus was speaking of the Holy Spirit who is never a cistern, never a well, but always a spring. He becomes a river flowing out of the heart of all those who come to Jesus and drink of Living Water.

The wilderness prepares us to become more than a vessel to hold water. In the wilderness we actually become a source of water for others.

For every Marah, there is an Elim just beyond. We are never bidden by God in our wilderness trek to continue to drink the bitter water. After the crucifixion comes the glorious resurrection. At Elim we rest. We encamp near the water. Here He makes His sheep lie down in green pastures and leads us beside the still waters. Here our soul is restored

What a God is ours! He drowns our foes in the sea and disciplines His children in the next breath. He leads us to the bitter waters of Marah, then urges us to move on to the cool shade of Elim. He thunders from the mountaintop but feeds His flock and gently leads those that are with young. In every desert there is an Elim. Here we pause, are refreshed, and move on to a land of streams and rivers.

VI

Discoveries

They left the Desert of Sin and camped at Dophkah.
(Numbers 33:12)

Every wilderness abounds with serendipities—accidental but wonderful discoveries. They come at least-expected times and in least-expected places, to encourage us in our trek through the tough times of life.

Who of us, struggling through some seeming desert waste or toiling up some peakless mountain, has not rounded a turn and come face-to-face with a marvelous little surprise—and from it drawn strength for the journey? No wilderness is without them.

I think of the time, shivering from the cold blast of winter that swirled off the side of Mt. Sinai with icy needles, I crawled into a deserted hermit's cave for warmth. There before me, as though some angel had seen me coming and laid it on an outcropping rock at the back of the cave, was a tattered Bible. It was open to the very passage in Isaiah from which this book takes its title: "I will even make a way in the wilderness, and rivers in the desert" (Isaiah 43:19, KJV). Those words not only warmed me that chilly afternoon, but sparked an idea that eventually became this book.

God has placed at select turns in our lives these unexpected, fascinating treasures to enrich our lives and give us hope that others have passed this way before us—and not only achieved victory but left behind a message of hope.

The Sinai is no exception, for it is a land of constant surprises, endless serendipities.

More than a thousand years before Moses slogged his way through his own personal wilderness, paying the penalty for his sin but being prepared for the history-changing situation that lay ahead, the Sinai was being occupied by a people who gave a name to the territory.

From the Chaldean city of Ur, the legendary home of the patriarch Abraham, came another man, Naram-Sin, the king of Akkad. Conquering the lands north of the Persian Gulf, he moved westward and occupied (according to a deciphered Assyrian fragment) a land he called Maganna ("the country of copper") and Milukkha ("the country of blue stone"). Blue stone, of course, is found in the vicinity of copper mines. It is called turquoise.

Naram-Sin headed a cult that worshiped the moon god Sin (pronounced *sign*, with no connection to the English word *sin*). They conquered and settled in the western portion of the wilderness peninsula along the Gulf of Suez. Across the years, their descendants were known by a variety of names. All of them, at one time or another, worshiped the moon god Sin. Thus the region along the Gulf of Suez became known as "the wilderness of Sin" and the entire peninsula was called Sin-ai.

Several hundred years after Naram-Sin settled in the Sinai, the family of Israel moved to Egypt to take up residence following a famine in Canaan. It was not long before their brother/benefactor Joseph died, and according to Exodus, "a new king, who did not know about Joseph, came to power in Egypt" (Exodus 1:8). He made slaves of the Israelites and put them to work at hard labor.

During this time, the Egyptians began expanding their borders and colonized the Sinai. They wanted to use the barren wasteland for two purposes—first, as a wall (or *shur*) to keep out invaders from the east. Second, they wanted to work the copper and turquoise mines that had been discovered originally by Naram-Sin. The greatest lode was found in the mountains that rise to the east of the Gulf of Suez, about halfway down the peninsula, at a place called Serabit el Khadim.

It was the vanquished children of Israel, of course, who were used as slaves to dig the mines in the sides of the high mountains. (Serabit el Khadim means "heights of the slave.")

For several hundred years the Egyptians carried on their lucrative mining operations at Serabit. This was interrupted when a group of Semitic people called Hyksos invaded Egypt through the Sinai and ruled the Nile Valley from about 1700 to 1580 B.C. During this time the Sinai mines at Serabit fell into disuse. After the Hyksos were driven from Egypt, however, the expeditions to the Sinai resumed, this time under military escort. A large garrison of Egyptian soldiers was stationed at Serabit to oversee the Israelite slaves.

Ironically, the Egyptians also worshiped, among other deities, a moon god called Thoth. The slaves were forced to build a temple at Serabit el Khadim to honor Thoth, who was represented on the walls as a baboon or ibis-headed figure. The primary deity of the temple, however, was the well-known Egyptian goddess of turquoise, Hathor. Hathor, who was also goddess of love, mirth and joy, was represented by a woman's body with the head of a cow.

A huge complex grew up around the Temple of Hathor, which included a courtyard, sanctuaries, purification baths, a sacrificial altar and a barracks area for the Egyptian soldiers who policed the slaves. Remains of the temple still stand on the top of the mountain at Serabit el Khadim, with numerous inscriptions in hieroglyphics—an unwieldy alphabet of picture-writing with more than 700 basic characters. This was augmented by some Egyptians who had also mastered the 300 Sumerian cuneiform symbols.

There is some evidence that Moses may have headed up an expedition of Egyptian soldiers or miners during the first forty years of his life, and perhaps he even visited Serabit el Khadim, which is also called Dophkah in the Bible. Later, when he led the children of Israel out of Egypt, he encamped at Dophkah. Sometime prior to the Exodus, however, the supply of copper and turquoise had been expended and the mines had been closed. The slaves were returned to Egypt to work in the clay pits.

To those Hebrews who had once slaved in those impossible conditions, who had seen their loved ones die in the mines from lack of water and exposure to the elements, who had been forced to help build the temple to the heathen gods and goddesses, it must have given great satisfaction to pass by on their way to the Promised Land—free.

Before the mines were closed, however, an extraordinary intellectual event occurred at Serabit. The Israelite slaves, although they spoke their original tongue—a crude type of Hebrew—had no written language. In fact, at that time, except for the Egyptian hieroglyphics, there were no written languages anywhere in the world, for no alphabet had yet been devised. While tradition credits the Phoenicians with the birth of the alphabet, later archaeological discoveries have revealed an amazing fact. Sometime between 1500 B.C. when the Egyptians reopened the mines and 1300 B.C. when the mines played out, these brilliant slaves did something no one else in the world had ever done: they developed an alphabet.

Sometimes the most creative things come out of wilderness experiences. This wilderness of hardship and slavery became the birthplace of our modern alphabet, the birthplace of writing as we know it today.

Conceivably it was the Levites who developed the alphabet. These priests, into whose hands had been entrusted the keeping of the memory of the God with no image and no name, the God of Abraham, Isaac and Jacob, were forced into slave labor in the sweltering turquoise mines of the desert. Yet there, in the most dismal conditions, they devised an alphabet. It was this same alphabet that another of their tribe, Moses, would use to write the first five books of the Bible, which included all the covenants, laws and ordinances of God.

This first alphabet, known as Proto-Canaanitic symbols, was a major departure from the hieroglyphics of the Egyptians. Instead of being merely pictures representing words, these were symbols representing basic consonantal sounds, from which an infinite variety of new words could be formed. This evolved into the Proto-Sinaitic alphabet, which formed the basis of the Phoenician alphabet, from which our own alphabet was derived.

It was also at Serabit el Khadim that I discovered my own serendipity.

A small group of us had climbed the 5,000-foot mountain to

view the caves and have a brief devotional service at the ruins of the temple to Hathor. The idea of worshiping the living Lord at the place where men once worshiped false gods was exciting.

But it was also sad. Wandering through the temple remains, I saw the place where sacrifices—perhaps human sacrifices—were offered to appease the heathen gods and goddesses. Higher up were the quarters where the sacred prostitutes satisfied the sexual appetites of heathen worshipers. No doubt these included Hebrew women forced into prostitution, especially the young teenage virgins brought from Egypt to satisfy the garrisoned soldiers.

I walked slowly through the ruins, my spirit hearing the cries that went up from those forced to profane the most sacred things of their lives. Was there no hope in this place? I groaned. Here on this isolated mountaintop, God's chosen people were treated worse than beasts of burden: abused, humiliated, used and finally killed.

I thought of the word God had given to Isaac: "Do not go down to Egypt; live in the land where I tell you to live. Stay in this land for a while, and I will be with you and will bless you. For to you and your descendants I will give all these lands and will confirm the oath I swore to your father Abraham" (Genesis 26:2-3).

But Isaac's grandchildren had sinned. Consumed with jealousy, they had sold their baby brother to slavetraders who had taken him to Egypt. As a result, the entire clan was eventually forced into Egypt also. The next ten generations suffered from the sins of their fathers.

Where were You, God? I questioned in my heart. *Where were You during all those years of hardship and deprivation?* There had been no spoken word from God for 400 years—from the time God spoke to Joseph until He spoke to Moses just a few miles from where I was standing. *Was it because these people had forgotten You? Had they turned their backs on You during this blackest time in their history?*

I wandered around the side of the mountain and there, on the path in front of me, like the dark eye sockets of a skull, was the entrance to the mines. I shuddered. What agony must have been suffered in those caverns! Old men, young boys, chained together as they dug in the sweltering heat, as their naked bodies shivered when the fierce winter winds swept across the mountaintops, covering their beards with ice. I looked out across the awesome landscape. How ironic—the place named for the moon goddess even looked like a moonscape. Was there no word from God ever heard during that horrible time?

My Jewish guide was motioning me to come forward. I stumbled along the narrow path on the side of the mountain and entered the farthest mine opening, a small, cavelike socket that dropped down through the red and brown rock into a huge open cavern.

The guide, a brilliant Jewish woman, was pointing. "There, on the ceiling and walls. Do you see it?"

The amber and red walls curved up to form a rock ceiling over our heads, barely giving us enough room to stand. Distinct on the walls were the ancient inscriptions—chisel marks where the Hebrew slaves had carved words using their newly developed alphabet.

I stood for a long time, looking. The characters were obviously a prototype of modern-day Hebrew. I could even recognize a few of the letters from my days in Hebrew classes in seminary. Archaeologists had long before determined its originality and authenticity. It was the oldest known inscription of the alphabet as we now know it.

I was standing at the birthplace of the alphabet.

"What does it say?" I asked my guide, perhaps the world's foremost authority on the Sinai.

She carefully pointed out inscription by inscription. "There are two messages," she said. "The first one contains practical instructions for the other miners. 'You shall give Abubu eight portions of. . . .'" The last words were obliterated.

I was stunned. It was one of the major purposes of all writing—to pass along practical instructions as an extension of the mind and voice. As it was now, so it was in the beginning.

"What about the other inscription?" I asked.

"It is a very simple message," she said. "Obviously written by one of the old Levi slaves. It says, 'God is eternal.'"

I stood for long moments staring at my serendipity. Here,

hundreds of years after God spoke His covenant to the father of these people, just a few miles from the spot where, many years later, He would thunder His laws and commands from Mt. Sinai, in the midst of the most miserable bondage the world has ever known—God had a man. He had revealed Himself, not to a pharaoh but to a humble slave miner who had left chiseled in stone the first words ever written—the eternal nature of God.

The turquoise of the Sinai was of poor quality. The Egyptians soon discovered that it faded and became worthless. All those years of digging in the earth left nothing to show except a brief message on the wall of a cave.

In every wilderness God has a witness.

VII

Changed Appetites

"If only we had meat to eat! . . . But now we have lost our appetite; we never see anything but this manna!"

(Numbers 11:4, 6)

The experienced desert traveler knows better than to spread his sleeping bag under a tree or near the base of a cliff. Spiders, scorpions, even snakes have been known to drop from the heights onto a sleeping man's face. The wise wanderer always sleeps in the open.

One of the men in our group, whom I'll call Hal, disregarded the warning. When we arrived at our camping place after dark, he was too weary from the day's journey to think of anything but rest. He unrolled his sleeping bag and placed it under the drooping boughs of a large tamarisk tree.

The next morning I wakened at dawn. Lying sleepily in my bag a few yards away from the tree, I heard Hal give a startled gasp. I sat up, saw he had camped under the tree, and immediately wondered if he had been bitten by a scorpion or snake. Then I heard our guide, a muscular Israeli soldier, laughing.

I scrambled out of my bag and ran toward the tree. Hal was prone in his bag, only his head poking out, his eyes darting in all directions. His sleeping bag was covered with dozens of white spots, each about the size of a half-dollar. I looked around and saw the same flaky wafers all over the ground near his head.

"What is it?" Hal asked, staring at the guide, who was standing over him chuckling.

"That's what it is," the guide answered with a wide grin.

"I said, 'What is it?'" Hal's fear had turned to irritation, for he sensed he was being mocked.

"That is what it is," the guide laughed. "It is called 'What is it?'" Then he motioned at the substance on the ground around the sleeping bag. "In Hebrew the word is *man hu*, which means 'What is it?' The Bedouin call it *mann*. Who knows, perhaps it is the manna of the Bible."

By that time the rest of the group had gathered and were picking up the little wafers, sticky and sweet, and tasting them. Of course the bottom side was covered with sand, and what had fallen on the sleeping bag had soaked in and hardened, leaving a real mess.

But at least it wasn't a scorpion or a snake.

In the southern Sinai from May to July, a tiny insect punctures the bark of the tamarisk tree, drinks the sap and exudes a clear liquid that solidifies as a sugary globule when it hits the ground. When the sun comes up, it melts quickly and disappears. The fact that it is called *man hu* or *mann* reminded us, indeed, of the manna of the Bible, which was described as "thin flakes like frost on the ground [which] appeared on the desert floor" when the dew disappeared in the morning. It was "white like coriander seed and tasted like wafers made with honey" (Exodus 16:14, 31).

Moses called it "bread" and told the people to gather it and eat it. It was God's provision since their food had run out. It would last them until they reached the Promised Land, just a few miles to the north. It could be ground in the mills or beaten in the mortars and boiled in pots or baked as cakes (Numbers 11:8). It was to be eaten the day it was gathered or it would spoil. Only on the day before the Sabbath could they gather enough for two days. It kept the Israelites alive—and healthy—for forty years in the wilderness.

Although it is an intriguing concept, I do not believe the present-day *mann* is actually the manna of the Bible, although it seems to be similar. The present *mann* is confined to the southern Sinai and found only in small quantities during the late spring months. The manna of the Bible fell abundantly throughout the year and was found as far north as Kadesh-Barnea, where the Israelites camped for 38 years during their wilderness trek. It was without doubt a miracle from God specifically for His chosen people.

Despite the fact it was "God's provision," it was anything but tasty. The Israelite women used great ingenuity to change its appearance—but manna every day was a radical change of diet to people who had grown accustomed to the spices and meats of Egypt.

The first encounter with manna came when the Israelites ran out of food after leaving Elim on their way to Mt. Sinai. There had been some more complaining in the camp. God seemed to understand and said to Moses, "I will rain down bread from heaven for you" (Exodus 16:4). It was another remarkable and miraculous evidence of a God who cared and was able to provide.

At the same time quail appeared, a special bonus of meat from the Lord. During the late spring—and this would have taken place in early July—huge flocks of quail often migrate from Africa over the Sinai on their flights north for the summer. It is not unusual to find them by the hundreds along the beaches, where they lie exhausted after their long overwater flight. Until restrictive laws were passed, the Bedouin often stretched low, long nets along the sand dunes near the shore to snare the weary, low-flying birds. But this time the quail came inland and literally fell at the feet of the Israelites, providing them with the best meal they had had since leaving Egypt.

While the quail did not reappear as a steady diet, the manna did. Every morning. Despite the fact it was God's divine provision, the Israelites soon grew tired of the same diet, and once again, after leaving Mt. Sinai on their way to Kadesh-Barnea, the grumbling resumed. This time God reacted sternly.

Moses had earlier warned the people about complaining. "You are not grumbling against us, but against the Lord," he told them point-blank (Exodus 16:8).

While they turned a deaf and rebellious ear to Moses' warning, God's reaction was unmistakably impressive. At a place called Kibroth-hattaavah—which means "graves of craving"—

quail appeared by the thousands. The people, instead of giving God praise, rushed out and stuffed themselves. This brought God's wrath upon them so that even while they were gorging themselves, many died.

Today, scattered throughout the Sinai, are strange, round, above-ground grave sites called *nawamis*. Archaeologists say these free-standing stone enclosures are the oldest existing above-ground structures in the world. Although they have long since been emptied by robbers and archaeologists, when first discovered they were filled with human bones. Tradition says they were the bones of the grumblers who were discontented with God's manna and lusted for the fleshpots of Egypt.

The tragedy of human history is that man never seems to learn from his mistakes, or the mistakes of those who have gone before him. The man who insists upon learning everything from personal experience will seldom make any progress. At worst, he will perish in the wilderness. The wise pilgrim builds on the past.

The human heart is the same in all generations, and Satan has no new tactics available. When the apostle Paul was writing to the church in Corinth of the events that happened to the children of Israel in the Sinai, he warned them not to repeat history. "God was not pleased with most of them," he wrote. "Their bodies were scattered over the desert" (I Corinthians 10:5).

Paul listed the things the Israelites did that displeased God: idolatry, pagan revelry, sexual immorality, presuming on God's goodness, and grumbling. "These things happened to them as examples and were written down as warnings for us. . . . So, if you think you are standing firm, be careful that you don't fall!" (I Corinthians 10:11-12).

It's significant that Paul lists grumbling as equal to pagan revelry, idolatry and sexual immorality. There is a school of thought that says it's all right to curse at God. "Get it off your chest," we are told. But such an attitude assumes God never responds to man's actions. The wilderness wanderings teach us otherwise. God has a keen ear. It is especially tuned to those caught in desert experiences, for God does not allow His children to experience the wilderness without purpose. Even the changing of our diet from meat to manna is part of God's greater plan for our lives.

God has a purpose for everything He does. There was purpose in the manna. At the bitter springs of Marah, He wanted to purge their systems. Next He purposed to change their diet. As at Marah, however, the people rebelled. They failed to see that God had a master plan, that nothing was left to chance. Had the Israelites stopped to think, they would have understood that God was pledged by the most solemn obligations to provide for them. They grumbled because they did not believe. Even as Jesus was unable to work miracles in Nazareth "because of their unbelief," so the Israelites missed God's blessing when they doubted and grumbled. For the sin of unbelief is the greatest of all sins. There is, of course, a difference between healthy dissatisfaction and grumbling. Grumbling against circumstances says, in essence, that God does not love us or He would not treat us this way.

Granted, manna was not what they ordered off God's menu. They wanted the food of Egypt. Yet God's ways are not our ways. His provision often looks superficial to the carnal mind. "If we're God's 'chosen people,' why do we have such a meager diet? We should eat like kings—like the pharaoh." It was the sin of presumption, for they felt they knew better than God what they should eat. They were too shortsighted to understand a God who insisted on closing the door to Egypt's food forever, and who was more interested in teaching them the discipline of obedience than in satisfying their carnal cravings.

Temptation, which in its basic form is always a desire to return to Egypt, demands a tempter—one who stimulates our minds away from God. The "tempters" in this case were those Egyptians who had been invited to join the Exodus when the Israelites fled Egypt. But they were not part of the covenant group. The Bible calls them "the rabble" or the "mixed multitude."

"The rabble with them began to crave other food, and again the Israelites started wailing and said, 'If only we had meat to eat! We remember the fish we ate in Egypt at no cost—also the cucumbers, melons, leeks, onions and garlic. But now we have lost our appetite; we never see anything but this man-na!'" (Numbers 11:4-6).

Many of the laws given from Mt. Sinai dealt with mixing with unbelievers. Especially was marriage with unbelievers condemned. Jesus later pointed out that no man can serve two masters, and Paul talked about those "enemies of the cross" whose "god is their stomach . . . their mind is on earthly things" (Philippians 3:18-19). The Lord commanded His people to come apart and be a "separate people"—not to mix with "the rabble." But not only did the Israelites mix with them in the wilderness; they *listened* to them. And many joined them in their grumbling. "The rabble" desired the safety of the fellowship but were constantly campaigning for the best of Egypt as well. They were convinced but not converted.

The problem with mixed multitudes is differing appetites. Appetites are determined largely by family background. The Egyptians yearned for leeks and garlic, meat and melons; while Moses, who had spent the last forty years in the wilderness, was profoundly grateful for the gift of manna. Now, as the desert heat burned mercilessly on these wanderers, they remembered the temporary relief of Egypt's cooling melons and cucumbers. Unfortunately, they forgot the lash of the taskmaster and the agony of slavery.

When Moses refused to listen to their grumbling and requests to turn back, they rebelled. It was, in essence, a counterrevolution—a common problem faced by all revolutionary leaders whose followers, after the first victories, often grow discouraged over the sparse diet and long trek before reaching "the Promised Land."

God prescribed a strict diet of manna along with restrictions for gathering and storing. It was more than many could take. It's not that they wanted to return to bondage; they just wanted a quick respite into the past—an overnight excursion, so to speak, back into sin.

But such excursions are always forbidden by God, for they bring with them a rekindling of old tastes for things not healthy. Manna was not tasty. But God was changing tastes. He was transforming a group of sloppy, undisciplined former slaves into an army. There is no place for gourmet menus in the wilderness. Here men exist on bare essentials—getting their minds off their bellies and onto God.

This was made clear to me on my first excursion into the Sinai. I had brought with me my teenage son, Bruce. Although he adapted well to the rigors of desert living, he was constantly wishing (out loud) for an ice-cold carbonated drink. Our guide was amused at this "American desire" and pointed out the danger of such a drink in the desert.

"It tickles the throat and fools you into thinking your thirst is quenched," he said. "In the desert you do not drink to satisfy your throat. You drink to replenish the liquid the sun sucks from the cells of your body. Thus you must learn to change your appetite. Instead of drinking to enjoy, you drink to live. It is far better to drink warm water that will go into your entire system than to satisfy the desire of your throat and run the risk of dehydration."

The same principle works in the spiritual area as well. The manna of God was to be only temporary. Just a few days ahead lay the Promised Land with milk, wine and honey. Only further disobedience caused God to have to keep the manna coming—for forty years.

The carnal appetite, which God was burning from them with His prescribed diet, is never satisfied. It is like the throat that has been tickled by carbonated soda water laced with sugar. It always yearns for more. It causes men to run after every new "prophet" who comes on the scene with a "new revelation" from God. It causes men to trade the written Word of God for the philosophy of man since it seems more palatable. It causes men to demand melons and meat while disdaining what God has placed before them.

But the only way to reach the Promised Land is by eating God's diet. Leeks, onions and garlic will not get you into Canaan, for that diet is always accompanied by the bondage of Egypt. In the wilderness we must make priority decisions. Are we willing to give up what satisfies the belly in order to have what satisfies the soul?

Those who ignore or refuse God's provision while lusting for the former things (which the Bible says must eventually be "put away") will soon perish and be buried in the sands of the wilderness—the very place where God's manna which they rejected so covered the earth.

Yet the others—those who accept God's meager diet on faith, believing God has a purpose for what He serves up— enter into a marvelous truth that lean diets are intended only for a season. To those who obey and do not grumble, there lies ahead a table in the wilderness. Here, then, is the truth: While we are in the wilderness, we are not of the wilderness. We are bound for a Promised Land.

VIII

Relationships

"It is an everlasting covenant of salt before the Lord for both you and your offspring."

(Numbers 18:19)

Those of us making our way through our personal wildernesses are forced, for the purpose of preservation, to huddle. At night when the rocks cool and the frigid winter wind whistles through the deep wadis, we gather in our tents to savor each other's warmth.

In the scorching heat of noonday, when the only shade is an overhanging rock, we build our booths of date palm branches to escape the deadly sun.

At the wells we huddle, sharing from the cups of our hands.

Those of us who have spent long periods in the Sinai realize quickly that there are few genuine habitable places in the wilderness. The wilderness is not a place to settle, only a place to pass through. But to live apart, even on a pilgrimage, invites death. Thus the wilderness forces us into relationships.

Often we are not aware of the intensity of these relationships until it is time to separate. Then, like children on the last night of a lengthy summer camp, or like soldiers gathering in the barracks the night before each returns to his home following the war, we grow nostalgic. After having been thrust together for the sake of survival, we often find we've done more than survive; we have begun to live.

73

I remember one of those "last nights" in particular. Our group of twelve men had gathered in a natural grotto, hewn by the hand of the wind over countless centuries. The sandstone walls of the cave provided scores of tiny alcoves where we placed candles. Then, settling on the soft white sand, we got quiet, praying, singing softly and simply sitting still. Our little "family," which had been together for two weeks, was at the end of the trail. The next day we would load up our Land Rover and head back along the Gulf of Aqaba, through Elat, northward through the Aravah to the Dead Sea, past Jericho and back to Jerusalem. There the "family" would dissolve, each of us flying back to wherever we came from to resume our busy schedules.

But while we had been in the Sinai we had grown close. We had entered into relationships. In this crucible, men who had been strangers had become friends for life, bound together by the commonness of our trek through tough times. Just having been there somehow made us brothers, pledged to a sacred fraternity of those who had also passed this way.

The wilderness breeds loyalty. It forces us into a camaraderie of deep covenant relationships.

In the Middle East, families still return for reunions at the time of harvest. Even though they no longer harvest the fields, they still remember the covenants of the past when it was necessary to work together or perish separately.

So it is with families who have been through hard times together, who have together suffered great losses. They are always closer than those children of opulence who have never had to struggle for food and shelter.

Thus it is not surprising that God chose the wilderness to reveal His covenant nature. Covenant in its purest form is a binding and solemn agreement between individuals who compact toward a common goal. It grows out of conflict and is always tested by suffering.

To Noah, staggered by the immensity of God's wrath, God covenanted: "I have set my rainbow in the clouds, and it will be the sign of the covenant" (Genesis 9:13).

To Abraham, wandering childless and without purpose in the desert, God covenanted: "This is my covenant with you: You will be the father of many nations" (Genesis 17:4).

Such were the covenants between God and man. But there were covenants between men of God as well. Of these, none is as strong and binding as the oldest of them all—the covenant of loyalty. It was birthed in the awesome grandeur of the desert between men to whom loyalty spelled the difference between life and death. It was called the Covenant of Salt.

There is no recorded time for its beginning. Indeed, it seems to be the oldest of all the covenants and was already in effect as a recognized pact when the children of Israel began their slow and torturous trek across the wilderness of the Sinai.

It is first mentioned in Numbers 18:19 as a sign to the priests in their offerings to the Lord. "Whatever is set aside from the holy offerings. . . . It is an everlasting covenant of salt before the Lord for both you and your offspring."

Later God told the Levites to season all grain offerings with salt. "Do not leave the salt of the covenant of your God out of your grain offerings; add salt to all your offerings" (Leviticus 2:13).

From the very earliest times salt was a symbol of the covenant.

To the Levites it was a sign of perpetual purity. But to the people it had a much broader meaning—a meaning preserved to this day among the people who live in the Sinai, those nomadic Bedouin whose history predates even the time of Moses.

The Bedouin have a lofty concept of the sanctity of women. Besides this, women play the role of shepherd. Since the flocks are the life sustenance of the tribe, and the shepherds are at the heart of the flock structure, it is necessary to protect the women. The law of the desert says if a man molests a woman, then the woman's husband or her brothers are free to go after the molester, track him down and kill him. Not only do they have jurisdiction over the life of the molester, but over the lives of his brothers as well, to prevent revenge. In the desert, a man is literally his brother's keeper, since his own life may depend on his brother's behavior.

As a result of this seemingly harsh but fair law, women go unmolested. They wear the traditional black dress with black facial veil that causes them to stand out against the white sand of the desert. No man can use the excuse of just "happening" upon a woman shepherd, for they can be spotted from a great distance. And the law of the desert says, "Stay clear."

Of course, this hampers the legitimate romantic inclinations of any man with honorable intentions. To approach a woman randomly, even for honorable reasons, is to invite trouble since she may accuse him of molesting her. Therefore, the Bedouin use an ancient but complicated procedure for romantic introduction.

The young man is never allowed to propose to a girl or, for that matter, even approach her outright. Rather, after watching her from afar as she tends her flock, the young man will wait until she has left the place where she watered her animals, and when night comes he will come to the well or spring. He will then put his footprint in the sand in a conspicuous place where she can see it the next day. When she returns to the watering spot, she sees his footprint. If she is interested in meeting him, she will place her footprint alongside his in the sand. Returning again after she has left, and seeing the two prints side-by-side in the sand, the young man knows the way is now open for the next step.

Even then he may not approach her. Nor does he even approach her father. Instead, he sends his brother or a friend to go and sit down and talk with the father. They will discuss many things, as Bedouin do. They will talk about the father's sheep and goats, about tribal situations, about relatives, about the weather. Finally the intermediary will get around to bringing up the subject of the father's daughter. After many compliments he will mention that his brother (or his friend) is interested in meeting the daughter and would like the father's permission. If the father indicates he approves of this relationship (rather than one he may have already picked out), he gives permission for the young man to come see him personally. Once done, he then gives permission to the young man to speak to his daughter.

After a period of time, if marriage is acceptable, the bridegroom brings many expensive gifts. The father of the bride then arranges a betrothal ceremony, which is as binding as marriage. This is followed, later on, by a three-day marriage ceremony accompanied by feasting and merriment, complete with camel races and festivities for family and friends who come from many miles.

Following the wedding, the bride returns to the tent of her mother and learns other things about married life. During this time, the groom will return to his place and make his winter tent, the heavy black tent of goat's hair and skins, to protect his bride from the harsh desert winters. When this task is completed, the groom places his tent near the tent of the bride's father and, in a final ceremony, comes to the family tent to claim his bride—a ceremony alluded to in the book of Revelation called "the marriage supper of the Lamb" when the Bridegroom (Christ) returns to claim His bride (the Church) who has been prepared "without spot or wrinkle."

An ancient Bedouin custom calls for the "circumcision" of infant girls to discourage indiscriminate sexual activity before marriage. This excising is done to prevent the sexual act from being pleasurable and thus to protect the girl's virginity—which is promised by the bride's father to the bridegroom as part of the marriage contract. (Only the Jebeliya tribe, located in the vicinity of St. Catherine's Monastery—who were once Christian but became Moslem—do not excise the baby girls.)

To determine the virgin state of the bride, the bridegroom places a white ceremonial sheet on the ground beneath the bride on her nuptial night. This sheet is then shown to the bride's father the next morning. The presence of a spot of blood is proof of virginity, and a sign the marriage covenant is valid. Its absence is valid reason for divorce. The bridegroom is then allowed to reclaim all the gifts that he gave the bride's father.

If the marriage is happily consummated, the young couple join the household of the bride's father and continue to tend the flocks of the father-in-law into the future.

During the process of the marriage ceremony, which is conducted by the tribal sheikh (priest, head elder), the covenant of salt takes place. Sometimes salt is sprinkled upon the joined hands of the bridal couple. Other times it is sprinkled on their heads.

Salt is a sign of precious and sacred covenant, for covenants are never entered into without a sign. Each time God entered into a covenant with man, there was a sign. With Noah, it was a rainbow in the sky. With Abraham, it was accompanied by circumcision. With Moses, it was the tablets of stone. Later, heaps of stones were often set up as memorials. The sacrificial offerings were a continuing sign of the covenant.

In Jesus' story of the return of the Prodigal Son, the killing of the fatted calf was more than a celebration: it was a sign of a covenant between father and son. When John the Baptist pointed to Jesus on the banks of the Jordan River and proclaimed, "Look, the Lamb of God, who takes away the sin of the world," he was referring to a new covenant—a sign fulfilled literally in the Eucharist when Jesus said, "This cup is the new covenant in my blood."

To the Bedouin, salt was (and is) of great value in the desert. In fact, the legend goes, in early times blocks of salt were part of the dowry of the young woman preparing for marriage—as valuable in the desert as gold on the stock market.

In common life, salt was a symbol of covenant relationships. Salt contained the power to strengthen food and preserve it from putrefaction and corruption. In the sacrifice this meant the unbending truthfulness and loyalty between God and man. Thus it was commanded that the Levites present salt in the grain offering and add it to all the other offerings as a sign of continued loyalty and purification.

It is stated that, in the time of David, his kingdom was established by a covenant of salt—a covenant that was for him and his descendants forever. "Ought ye not to know that the Lord God of Israel gave the kingdom over Israel to David for ever, even to him and to his sons by a covenant of salt?" (II Chronicles 13:5, KJV).

Salt represented covenant relationships. Even in the desert today when Arab men get together, they may express their loyalty and devotion to one another by saying, "There is salt between us."

When Jesus told His disciples, "Ye are the salt of the earth," He was speaking of this covenant of loyalty. Many of us have heard sermons on that passage from the Sermon on the Mount, pointing out how salt preserves, purifies, seasons, even creates thirst. All are true points. But they are merely incidental to the central theme of the biblical concept of salt, for salt represents covenant. It represents covenant between men, and between men and God.

Salt means loyalty. When Jesus emphasized the imperativeness of saltiness, He was referring to the necessity of walking out the covenant with God and with one another. Such covenants are forged and consummated in the crucible of wilderness experiences.

Covenant people are people who have come through the fire together. They are people loyal to one another. They are people who will die for each other. They are people who refuse to entertain malicious charges against each other. They are people who love one another, who serve one another, who do not need to swear to one another because their word is their bond. They are people of one family.

Shakespeare understood this when he had old Polonius advise Laertes in *Hamlet* with these words:

> Be thou familiar, but by no means vulgar.
> The friends thou hast, and their adoption
> tried,
> Grapple them to thy soul with hoops of steel;
> But do not dull thy palm with entertainment
> Of each new-hatched, unfledged comrade.

Covenant friends are friends tried in the wilderness. When one finds such a friend, he should be grappled to one's soul with hoops of steel.

Leonardo da Vinci caught this concept in his painting of the Last Supper. All the men sitting at the table with Jesus were men of loyalty—all save one. On the table in front of Judas was an upended salt shaker, its contents spilling onto the cloth. It was the perfect symbol of broken covenant.

We live in an age of easiness. We do our best to keep away from hardship. Even family discipline is legislated against by government bodies. Covenants no longer exist. Contracts are easily dissolved. Divorce is easier than marriage. Children are free to leave their parents. Parents desert children and brag about it. Churches, which are supposed to be spiritual families, often split over issues of ego. Arabs and Jews, coming from the same stock, attempt to eliminate each other from the earth.

Men and women who have walked through the wilderness together, on the other hand, form binding relationships that are never broken. Here covenants are formed. They are tested until proven secure.

Such loyalty forms a kind of cloth, tightly woven with threads of love and trust. This cloth covers each other's faults from the eyes of a cruel world. It bandages each other's wounds, and becomes a banner that leads us together toward a land of promise.

So it is with the covenant of salt—the perfect symbol of the wilderness compact. Salt is composed of two elements that, if taken separately, are poison: sodium and chlorine. Either will kill instantly. But mixed together, these two elements form an ingredient absolutely essential to life.

The wilderness experienced by itself kills. But the wilderness experienced with others brews a recipe of hardy nourishment.

Such is the covenant of salt.

IX

Pilgrims

In all the travels of the Israelites, whenever the cloud lifted from above the tabernacle, they would set out; but if the cloud did not lift, they did not set out—until the day it lifted.

(Exodus 40:36-37)

There are three kinds of people in the wilderness. The hermits move in from the outside, settle in caves and stay in one place until they die. The Bedouin are nomads, on the move but always in a circle. However, God never intends for His children to settle in the wilderness as hermits or nomads. We are thus to be the third breed of wilderness person—the pilgrim. Each wilderness experience becomes a pilgrimage—an experience in which we meet, know and follow God to His land of promise.

The process is simple, although often painful.

The chemist of the Holy Spirit takes the elements of our lives and drops them into the mortar of the wilderness setting. Then, using circumstances as a pestle, He crushes our natural elements until they come into union with each other. Pouring that fine dust into a crucible, He turns up the heat until all the impurities burst into tiny flames and disappear, leaving behind the purified self, perfectly integrated, ready for service—working all things together for good.

This is never a static process. It always involves change and progress from one stage to another. It can be done only on the move.

To some degree, all life on earth is a wilderness experience. As surely as sparks fly upward, Job pointed out, we are born into trouble. But the wilderness is a passage through trouble, not a place to stop and wallow in our adversity. As the old Negro spiritual says: "This world is not my home, I'm just a-passing through."

Every road sign on our trek through the wilderness of this mortal life points toward a glorious consummation of life eternal with God. We are not born to die; we are born to be reborn—and live forever. As we move toward that heavenly experience, which awaits all the saints, we pass through trouble, adversity, grief, pain and hardships—all wilderness experiences. But these deserts are not designed to choke the life from us; rather, they are designed to mold us and shape us into the image of Christ. We are not ever to allow ourselves to become desert settlers like the hermits of old, or even the Bedouin of today. We are pilgrims, "a-passing through."

God knew how easy it would be for these former slaves who had never been anywhere to settle for another Egypt. The first order of business, therefore, as a father keeps a freezing child walking to keep him alive, was to keep the children of Israel on the move. Stopping, especially if they stopped without purpose, would allow them to begin thinking of the fleshpots of Egypt, or to grow lazy and inert and settle for second-best, rather than move on to the Promised Land.

At Marah they stopped, grumbled and resigned themselves to die in the desert. At Sinai they stopped, grumbled and finally built a golden calf to occupy their time and worship. At Kadesh-Barnea, where they spent 38 years, they grew tired of manna, grumbled and cried out to return to Egypt. At Kadesh-Barnea they voted to settle in the desert rather than occupy the Promised Land. Every time they stopped, it seemed, they grew lethargic and dissatisfied.

To keep them up and moving, God placed a cloud over the tabernacle by day and a pillar of fire by night.

The cloud, which glowed with fire during the night, was placed over the tabernacle itself—the tent of meeting that contained the Ark of the Covenant. As long as the cloud was stationary, the people remained in that place. When the cloud moved, they folded their tents, dismantled the tabernacle, packed all their belongings and moved out under the cloud. According to the Book of Numbers, sometimes the cloud remained stationary only a few days at a time. Sometimes the cloud stayed only from evening till morning. At other times it remained over the tabernacle for months or a year at a time. But "at the Lord's command they encamped, and at the Lord's command they set out" (Numbers 9:23).

It is an ancient and valid military procedure to train men until they react to orders instinctively. The manual of arms, even though it is never used in war, is a training procedure, teaching soldiers to react to an order instinctively without arguing. A good soldier never asks why. He simply does his job, believing there is purpose behind the order which he does not understand, but which a superior military intellect does understand. As Tennyson had his Light Brigade say: "Ours not to question why, ours but to do and die. . . ."

But there was an even greater purpose in keeping the Hebrews moving. God wanted them to keep their eyes on Him. Hermits—those who live in caves and spend their lives contemplating—tend to become self-conscious rather than others-conscious. But the purpose of any wilderness is to force us to get our eyes off ourselves, off our problems, off the circumstances—to enter into family relationships where God is Father. The placement of the cloud demanded this. It covered the entire nation of people. If the children of Israel were ever to leave this "great and terrible wilderness," it would have to be under God's direction and protection, and as a group.

Every morning, therefore, they were forced to leave their tents and look up to see if the cloud had moved. Even after they reached Kadesh-Barnea, the cloud remained. On occasion it moved just slightly, perhaps just over the next sand dune. Since the Israelites were placed in position around the tabernacle, with each tribe occupying a certain sector, any movement of the tabernacle meant the entire camp had to move. Therefore, whether they moved ten miles or only 200 yards, it still meant pulling up all the tent pegs, folding their tents, and moving to another location.

Dissatisfaction with God's plan was invariably accompanied by grumbling. Time after time God demanded that the children of Israel stop their grumbling and fasten their eyes on Him, rather than look always at the less-than-perfect circumstances. In fact, it seems God deliberately allowed some of these adverse circumstances just so the children of Israel would be forced to look to Him—or perish.

Perhaps the most dramatic event occurred after the Israelites left Kadesh-Barnea and were marching slowly toward Edom on their way to Canaan. Once again the people grew impatient with God. "They spoke against God and against Moses, and said, 'Why have you brought us up out of Egypt to die in the desert? There is no bread! There is no water! And we detest this miserable food!'" (Numbers 21:5).

It was a complaint God had heard many times from these people. To teach them a lesson, "the Lord sent venomous snakes among them; they bit the people and many Israelites died" (verse 6).

Immediately the people repented and came crying to Moses, saying, "We sinned when we spoke against the Lord and against you. Pray that the Lord will take the snakes away from us" (verse 7).

But instead of removing the snakes, God taught them a lesson. He taught them to look to Him, rather than at the circumstances. The Lord told Moses to make a bronze snake and put it on a pole. "Anyone who is bitten can look at it and live," God said (verse 8).

Twelve hundred years later Jesus, speaking to an expert in Jewish history, reminded him of this experience. He had just told Nicodemus that natural birth does not qualify a man to enter the Kingdom of heaven; he needs to be born again of the Spirit. When Nicodemus questioned him, Jesus said, "Just as Moses lifted up the snake in the desert, so the Son of Man must be lifted up, that everyone who believes in him may have eternal life" (John 3:14-15).

In both instances God was saying, "It is not enough to lean to your own understanding. Life is found only when you trust Me to direct your paths."

The poison vipers still live in the desert. One afternoon a small group of us were driving through a mile-wide wadi south of Mt. Sinai when our six-wheel-drive truck hit a rock and destroyed a tire. It was the fourth tire we had destroyed in two days. It was going to take several hours for our driver to pull the tire from the rim, patch the tube and replace the tire.

While this was going on, four of us headed for the only shade within a mile—a spiny acacia tree growing in the middle of the wadi. I was standing next to one of the men under the tree when I looked down. There, half-buried in the sand at the base of the tree, only inches from my friend's open-toed sandal, was a deadly carpet viper, coiled to strike.

I silently motioned the other men to step back. With my hand on my friend's shoulder, I directed his eyes to his feet. We had been warned of the carpet viper. This one, gray and green in color, had already raised its head—beady eyes staring, forked tongue darting in and out. Belonging to the cobra family, its venom attacks the central nervous system, bringing agonizing death in less than ten minutes.

Gradually we moved backwards, away from the swaying head of the three-foot snake. Once at a safe distance, we found large stones and killed the snake. "You are very fortunate," our guide said solemnly. "Only God could have saved you had you been bitten."

It was that concept that the Lord was trying to implant in the hearts of the Israelites. Much earlier He had said, "I am the Lord who heals you." Thirty-eight years later, He demonstrated that truth when He told the people to look to Him when they were bitten. It was a lesson all pilgrims must learn—or die.

The only time a wilderness experience becomes a tragedy is when we fail to understand that the purpose of adversity is to force us to look to God. The wilderness is a school. While there are those who seem to be professional students—always sitting at a desk like overgrown oafs, finding it safer to attend school than earn a living—God's purpose for us is to graduate and become self-supporting.

When we understand we are enrolled in "the school of the wilderness" for a season only, and shall eventually "pass through to the other side," we cannot only exist, we can even enjoy the passage. But if we grow discouraged, if we grow spiritually lazy and linger behind, if we get our eyes off the goal of the Promised Land and become enamored of the wilderness itself, we will surely die.

The true pilgrim never stops to build monuments in the wilderness. At best, he may leave road signs pointing the way for the next group of pilgrims. But if he remains behind when the cloud moves, he will never have the desire or initiative to catch up.

The mark of identity of the Israelites was not their common slavehood of the past. The mark of identity was the fact they were all pilgrims, under the leadership of God who was "on the move."

"Unless you go with us . . . what will distinguish your people from all the other people on the face of the earth?" Moses asked God. They were pilgrims, moving through the wilderness, led by God.

It is interesting that today's archaeologists have been unable to discover a single shred of archaeological evidence in the Sinai to substantiate the Exodus. There are records on stone or buried in the ground of all the people who lived in the Sinai, before and after the Exodus. The Amalekites, the Hyksos, the Egyptians, the Nabateans—all left their marks. Archaeologists digging in the sand have been able to identify civilizations dating all the way back to the Early Bronze Age five thousand years ago. In fact, traces of Early Bronze Age domestic ruins and pottery shards at Wadi esh Sheikh in south-central Sinai indicate a large settlement there.

But there is absolutely no record of the Israelites. There are no rock carvings, no signs of permanent buildings, not even any pottery shards. The reason? The Israelites were a people on the move. Pilgrims. As the Jews today, they were a neat people. They did not leave their garbage behind. They were a busy people with no time to stop and chip graffiti on the walls of canyons. Despite their grumblings and complainings, they had a goal. They were a people under leadership, moving from slavery to freedom. Thus it is silent proof of the authenticity of the biblical account that no archaeological evidence has been found—for pilgrims seldom leave anything behind.

Following the cloud meant the Israelites had to keep their lives simple. They could not become too comfortable because any day they could awake and find the cloud had moved over the next sand dune, down the wadi, to the next mountaintop. How easy it is to miss God's direction by investing too much in material things, by giving too much emphasis to our earthly place. Leaving it, then, becomes a wrenching experience. Nothing is as sad as the man who has heard the call of God, but could not go because he has pledged his soul to the finance company.

Peter Marshall put it well in one of his famous prayers before the U.S. Senate:

> Forbid it, Lord, that our roots become too firmly attached to this earth, that we should fall in love with things. Help us to understand that the pilgrimage of this life is but an introduction, a preface, a training school for what is to come. . . .

Life is designed by God as a pilgrimage composed of many wildernesses. God is forever saying to all of us, Travel light. Do not stop to build monuments. Do not overload yourself with sentimental memorabilia that ties the heartstrings to things of the past. Do not stake out sections of land as "sacred" and declare you can never leave them behind. If you have precious belongings, send them ahead. For as Jesus said, "Where your treasure is, there is your heart also."

I still shudder when I recall the half-sneer, half-laugh from the Jewish archaeologist when I asked about Jewish shrines. "We Jews do not build shrines," she said. "Only Christians stop to do that. We worship a God who is on the move."

It is significant to note that the Jews never returned to build a shrine on Mt. Sinai, nor on the banks of the Sea of Reeds. Their allegiance was to a God symbolized by the mobile tabernacle and the Ark of the Covenant that preceded the column as it moved.

It is one of the important lessons of the desert: Keep moving! The pilgrim who pauses too long in any one place dies. Even the Bedouin, who seem bound like Prometheus to the rock of their wilderness wanderings, realize they must keep on the move. The Bedouin, though, are not pilgrims. They are nomads, wandering with the seasons in circles, with no Promised Land to beckon them onward. They are the prototype of spiritual squatters who camp smugly at certain points of tradition or doctrine—while the wind of God's Spirit blows past.

This is the story of the hermits who fled to the Sinai during the fourth and fifth centuries. Monks, recluses, they moved out of the mainstream of life—and never returned. Mistakenly they thought the cloud had come to rest over them, permanently.

During the years following the reign of the Roman emperor Constantine, who made Christianity acceptable (indeed, in many instances, made it mandatory), the Sinai became a haven for men looking for inner peace. From the naked hills of the Judean desert down through the Negev to the southern tip of the Sinai Peninsula, one still finds hermits' caves wherever there is spring water.

The word *hermit* came from the Greek word for desert, *eremia*. The desert and hermitry were inseparable in the Byzantine mind. For the hermit, God could be found only in the cruelest extremes. They abandoned their pagan world to seek, according to Catholic scholar Thomas Merton, salvation. They regarded society as a shipwreck from which each single individual had to swim for his life. Their only escape was the desert in which the impurities and dross of society could be burned and purged from their minds and hearts and bodies.

Some of them lived out their lives in total silence, even clipping their tongues so they could not speak even if tempted. Chains, near-starvation, self-flagellation and long exposure to unbearable elements were the usual course of life for these strange men who, fleeing this world, settled in a wilderness that God had long since left behind.

Their pilgrimage, as they saw it, was inner. They came to stay in order to take an inward journey to personal salvation. But in the process they stagnated. Instead of becoming servants, they became dependent upon others more practical and utilitarian to serve them. Eventually—like the Dead Sea which receives but never gives—some became mad parasites and died. And while a few did indeed come face-to-face with God, most hermits remain tragic examples in history of pilgrims who viewed the cloud as stationary.

We must learn a lesson from the hermits, though it be a negative one. Man is never called to enter a wilderness to find God, which is the essence of religion. Rather, when circumstances force us into a wilderness, we should have faith to believe God will take the initiative and reveal Himself to us in His time and place. Our responsibility is to respond, and stay under the cloud as it moves to God's destined purpose for our lives.

To view the wilderness as an end—a place of abiding, rather than a place through which one passes on his way to a land of promise—is the greatest of tragedies. Since God never intended that His children enter a wilderness and remain, each wilderness experience should be accompanied by a sense of nagging dissatisfaction, a deep longing for the Promised Land to come. Pilgrims should be careful not to try to escape the suffering God places on His children, until the object of that suffering is complete. At the same time, they should arise every morning and look upward—expecting, yea *knowing*, that one day the cloud will move.

Depression, discouragement, unhappiness, feelings of unworthiness—all these are moods of the wilderness. But the promise of God is far greater and can be experienced long before one actually emerges from the wilderness. Therefore, it is not unusual to hear, even from wilderness beds, songs in the night.

Even though the reed is bruised He will not break it off. Even though the wick is only smoldering He will not snuff it out. While each desert is a place of burning, the promise of God remains: "When you walk through the fire, you will not be burned; the flames will not set you ablaze" (Isaiah 43:2).

X

Obedience

"Strike the rock, and water will come out of it for the people to drink."

(Exodus 17:6)

Few desert experiences are as welcome—or as terrifying—as rain. Especially is this true in the high mountain regions of the Sinai.

Average rainfall in the southern Sinai is less than three inches per year. There are no rivers, no lakes, no forests, no meadows—just bare rock, boulders and sand, with only a few plants adapted to these harsh conditions. Rain rarely falls, but when it does, it is torrential. In fact, the desert may go for years without any rain, then have it all fall at one time.

My first encounter with rain in the Sinai was an awesome experience. Our small group had made camp early in a narrow part of Wadi Nasb. It was an ideal place to spend the night. The almost sheer granite walls of the canyon extended upward from the soft white sand of the wadi floor. The narrow, twisting pass provided a sense of ultimate privacy as we unloaded our sleeping gear from the truck and set up the butane tanks so we could heat water for our evening meal.

All day long we had noticed a rare buildup of clouds to the southwest, over the St. Catherine range near Mt. Sinai. The clouds were miles away, however, and we did not expect it would rain on us during the night—although there was a strong possibility it had been raining in the high mountains.

I had gone up the wadi several hundred yards to find an "alone place" to spread my sleeping bag for the night when I noticed the sand under my feet was moist. I had been in this area a number of times and knew there were no springs. Why then this moisture, when overhead it was clear?

Instead of unrolling my sleeping bag, I returned to the truck and told our guide what I had discovered.

"It's time to move to higher ground," he said. "This wadi may be getting ready to fill up with water."

We quickly called the men together, reloaded the truck and headed back down the wadi. By the time we reached a wider place where we could pull the truck onto a high plateau, the water was already beginning to flow down this ancient waterway. The rain in the high mountains, although miles from where we were, had cascaded off the sides of the granite mountains in great sheets. Like waterfalls, it had flooded the narrow wadis. Growing in size, the raging river was surging toward the sea through the waterways that empty in this region near Dahab. This has happened for centuries, causing a huge alluvial plain that fans out from the coast into the Gulf of Aqaba.

From our new high perch we watched the wadi, where only minutes before we had been spreading our sleeping bags, become a raging, torrential river. The muddy water came pouring out of the mouth of the wadi in an awesome eruption. Within minutes it was no longer a trickling stream, but a mighty cataract almost twelve feet deep, sweeping along everything that lay in its path. Trees were uprooted and huge boulders tumbled along as wood chips in the current. I sat watching, amazed, fascinated at the power of the eruption.

The year before a similar flood had swept down out of the high mountains toward the south, roaring through the wadis and erupting at Sharm el Sheikh, filling the hotel up to the second floor with water and sand before emptying into the Red Sea. That particular flood had swept away two Bedouin villages, killing three children. On another occasion, just a few months prior, a similar flashflood had poured out of the Negev Desert near Ein Gedi, washing away the main highway from Jericho to Eilat and sweeping a pickup truck with three teenagers into the Dead Sea, where all perished.

Sitting on my rocky perch high above the raging torrent, I gave thanks we had not been caught in that narrow wadi at night, resting in our sleeping bags when the water from the high mountains surged through. Then we waited for the water to go down, which took about an hour, and then made our way to another area where we spent the night on dry sand. The next morning, after the sun was up and the desert exposed to the heat and wind, the ground was once again parched and dry. We continued our way up Wadi Nasb to our destination.

During these occasional flashfloods an extraordinary event may take place. As the wall of water rages through the wadis, sometimes as deep as thirty feet, it exerts great force on the walls of the canyons. At the places where igneous and sedimentary rocks come together in the sides of the mountains, the water occasionally hollows out great fissures inside the mountains. These hollow mountains become literal reservoirs, holding sometimes thousands of gallons, forced into them by the floods.

After the flood has passed, the water begins to seep from its mountain reservoir. Calcium deposits quickly form around the opening, sealing off the water in the rock. When the winter snows melt, this moisture percolates into the ground and replenishes these reservoirs. Sometimes this water will be absorbed into the ground and reappear farther down the wadi as a spring. At other times it remains trapped in the rock.

I have watched a Bedouin shepherd, in an action called a *t'mile*, take his heavy staff and, by striking the rock at exactly the right point, break loose the blockage, allowing the water to gush forth. It was this action Moses took when faced with another water emergency.

Continuing their trek inland toward the high mountains, the Israelites noticed how the scenery began to change. The burning sand gave way to massive granite mountains. These were crossed by numerous dykes, flows of magma that had forced their way up along fissures in the rocks from earlier volcanic action. The colors changed, too, from gray and yellow sand to the mixture of rock displays in various shades of red, pink, black and purple, crossed by the dykes with streaks of dark green, black and crimson. There was no vegetation, no skin to cover this skeleton of the countryside. The people walked silently as their leader marched through the narrow canyons and around steep bends where minute by minute the scenery changed before their eyes, forbidding and breathtaking.

To each of the Israelites the mountains had a different meaning. To some they looked like the work of a master mason; to others like a host of bowed and petrified giants. Still others felt they were looking at a battlefield abandoned by giants who had been hurling great stones at each other. Whatever the feeling, each one sensed he was entering an area that was sacred, holy, set apart.

Before them, in the distant southeast, they could catch glimpses of the sun reflecting off the towering peak of Mt. Sinai. To get there, they would have to go through Watia Pass, a deep cleft in a peculiar wall-like body of granite that looked like the work of a sword-wielding giant who had slashed the landscape in frustrated anger. Beyond the pass the landscape changed, the mountains becoming even wilder, higher and more barren. How could they survive? Where, here in these high, desolate mountains, could they find water?

Therefore, despite feelings of awe, the grumbling began once again. "The whole Israelite community set out from the Desert of Sin, traveling from place to place as the Lord commanded. They camped at Rephidim, but there was no water for the people to drink. So they quarreled with Moses and said, 'Give us water to drink'" (Exodus 17:1-2).

Moses rebuked the people, saying they were doubting God's ability to take care of them. But thirst drives people into panic. As they murmured at the springs of Marah, so they did at Rephidim. "Why did you bring us up out of Egypt to make us and our children and livestock die of thirst?" (Exodus 17:3).

Exasperated, Moses cried out to God for help. Then, deep in his spirit, he remembered this place. The presence of the dykes, the mixture of sandstone and granite—surely there would be a water reservoir behind one of these rock walls.

Moving ahead of the people with some of the older tribal leaders, he walked slowly up the wadi, gently tapping the rock walls with his staff. Suddenly there was a soft spot. Commanding the people to fetch their water containers, he drew back his staff and with a mighty blow smashed his heavy rod into the calcium deposit on the side of the mountain.

Instantly it broke, and water gushed forth.

It was really not necessary, for just a mile or so beyond that place lay the richest, lushest oasis in the Sinai. Moses could have commanded the people to stop their murmuring, put them in a forced march, and reached the oasis in Wadi Feiran within the hour. But God wanted to reveal His miraculous power through Moses. Even though the *t'mile* was something Moses had done before at different places in the Sinai, this was a new occurrence for the Israelites. The people were on the verge of losing respect for their leader. On the morrow, another event (which will be covered in the next chapter) was to take place, one that would change the course of their lives, and the direction of their leader's life as well. Therefore, even though God could have directed Moses to keep moving to the natural springs just ahead, He chose instead to let Moses get the glory in the eyes of the people by striking the rock.

It would be another forty years before Moses was faced with a similar challenge. It happened in the vicinity of Kadesh-Barnea about the time the wilderness wanderings were over. The exact time and place remain unknown. Preparation was almost complete for them to move northward to possess the land. Once again, though, the Israelites were without water.

As he had done years before near Rephidim, Moses approached the Lord. "Take the staff, and you and your brother Aaron gather the assembly together. Speak to that rock before their eyes and it will pour out its water. You will bring water out of the rock for the community so they and their livestock can drink" (Numbers 20:8).

But a subtle change had taken place in Moses over the years. Earlier in his life he had been a man who listened keenly and adjusted immediately. He had been a man of daring, venturesome faith. But Moses had grown old. His ways were set. He no longer welcomed change but resisted it by fleeing to the safe harbor of tradition. He was like Tevye in Sholem Aleichem's *Fiddler on the Roof.* "How do we keep our balance?" the old Jew asked. "I can tell you in one word: tradition. . . .

Without our traditions our lives would be as shaky as a fiddler on the roof."

Moses was no longer willing to dance to God's tune. The roof was too steep. The danger of falling too great. He had slipped into a trap many wilderness pilgrims mire in—the trap of tradition. He failed to remember how many tombstones dotted the desert with the epitaph *We've Never Done It This Way Before.*

True, there is protection in tradition. It eliminates unnecessary risk; it prevents our making the same mistake twice. Tradition takes the fiddler from the roof and places him on solid ground—perhaps even locks him in the basement of the church. But there is a vast difference between learning from history and becoming a slave to dead tradition. There is safety in tradition, but it often keeps one from hearing the voice of God. Equally tragic, tradition may bind the one who does hear that voice.

Moses was no longer a new wineskin. He had become old. His wineskin was dry and cracked. His spirit, although still faithful to God, had lost its elasticity. He no longer had the willingness to expand. It was easier to do it as he had done it in the past—successfully, I may add—than to venture out and attempt something new, even though God had commanded it.

Thus, instead of speaking to the rock as God had commanded, Moses reverted to a time-tested procedure. He struck the rock in a *t'mile* as he had done so many years before at Rephidim. Not only that, but he struck it with bitterness and arrogance. "Listen, you rebels," he shouted, "must we bring you water out of this rock?" (Numbers 20:10).

Water came forth, of course. Humanistic knowledge, too, produces results. But even though Moses brought forth water, he did it in his own strength. Many years later, as the Jews were rebuilding the Temple under Zerubbabel, God again spoke of this single aspect of His character: He demands absolute obedience by leaders, and He will not share the glory with any man. The work of the Lord must not be done by human cunning or strength. "'Not by might nor by power, but by my Spirit,' says the Lord Almighty" (Zechariah 4:6).

Therefore, even though Moses got results—and the people

were pleased—another truth was evident: *God is not as interested in ends as He is in means.* In fact, how we do a thing seems more important to God than whether we succeed. The means are not only more important than the end; the means are an end themselves. It was a truth Jesus also taught: God does not require men to succeed, He just requires them to be faithful.

Earlier, at Rephidim, God had pushed Moses to front stage. He wanted the people to hear him, to respect him, to follow him. But this was a new generation. These young men and women were learning there was more to being under authority than following a powerful, knowledgeable, charismatic leader who knew how to get water out of a rock. They were learning to hear the voice of God for themselves. And that is always done best by following the example of their leader—a leader who had just proved himself unable.

It is a sad commentary on many of us. We begin so well and finish so poorly—not because we sin but because we get careless, because we lose that fine edge of faith, because we find it easier to drive in the ruts than to strike out over new territory.

Moses was like the Jewish driver of our desert vehicle who refused to leave the ruts in one of the wide wadis. I had asked him to pull out of the ruts made by a previous truck many months before so we could explore an abandoned turquoise mine.

"Too dangerous," he grunted. He then went on to explain how the Egyptians had placed explosive landmines in this particular wadi during the Six-Day War. They had then fled, but before the Israelis could clear the mines, a flashflood had roared through the wadi, scattering the mines for miles down the old riverbed. The only safe place to drive was in the ruts. In fact, the driver told me, just a few months before an Israeli colonel had been killed when his jeep ran over one of those old landmines and it exploded.

I understood his point. But staying in the ruts would mean we could never explore the unknown. "Just walk lightly," he said, slouching down in his seat and pulling his cap over his eyes for a nap. "I'll be waiting here—if you get back."

We did get back, our pockets full of bright green and aqua turquoise nuggets. The driver examined our treasures, then reminded us it was "Tradition!" that had kept the Jews alive all these centuries. "But," he chuckled, "we don't have any turquoise either."

Ruts are safe and comfortable. But the primary lesson of the wilderness is to bring us to the place where we can hear God and walk in His ways—even when He says to get out of the ruts.

Moses had lost his willingness to change. It was a sad day, for that meant he was disqualified to lead the young Israelites into Canaan. But the nation of Israel needed a leader who could obey orders. At the *Yam Suph*, Moses held out his rod and the wind blew back the water. But soon, in just a few months, this new generation would be approaching another watery barrier. The Jordan would be at flood stage. And instead of placing a man at the edge of the water, God had a deeper intention for this emerging nation. God wanted them to exhibit faith. They were to march into the water as it swirled around their feet. Only then would the water recede—not at the voice of a leader, but at the faith of men of God marching forward into a new world. If Moses could not obey God at the rock at Kadesh-Barnea, what would he do at the Jordan? Or, even more critical, how would he respond to the illogical instructions at the seige of Jericho? The wilderness lessons are stark.

What worked yesterday is not sufficient for today.

God's word yesterday must be adjusted by God's word today.

To be tyrannized by the past is the worst of all tyrannies.

The rut of tradition is but one step removed from a grave in the wilderness.

God's word to His pilgrims is fresh every morning. It is a lamp to our feet and a light to our path. Even though it may run counter to our traditions, or seem foolish at times, the man who trusts in Him will never be embarrassed or defeated.

> I will instruct you and teach you in the way
>   you should go;
> I will counsel you and watch over you.
> Do not be like the horse or the mule,
>   which have no understanding

but must be controlled by bit and bridle
   or they will not come to you.
Many are the woes of the wicked,
   but the Lord's unfailing love
   surrounds the man who trusts in him.

                    (Psalm 32:8-10)

XI

Faith

Moses built an altar and called it The Lord is my Banner. He said, "For hands were lifted up to the throne of the Lord."
(Exodus 17:15-16)

As the Israelites moved deeper into the Sinai, the faith of Moses was evidenced again and again. But no place was it enunciated more clearly than when the Israelites arrived at Rephidim and were attacked by the fierce army of Amalek.

I have walked that same path toward Wadi Feiran where we find ancient Rephidim. The Israelites were weary from their journey, and the older and more infirm were straggling behind as the slow-moving procession made its tedious climb upward through Wadi Feiran toward the high mountain area. A little over halfway between Suez and Mt. Sinai, near the base of Jebel Serabal, is the most beautiful oasis in the Sinai. A number of springs feed an underground river that flows on a rock base just beneath the surface of the shallow sand. Thousands of date palms fill the narrow wadi, which changes suddenly from dry desert to lush oasis at the elevation of 1,500 feet above sea level.

Although the high walls of the wadi seem to shut off the outside world, because of the presence of abundant water there is also abundant life. Camping there at night, I am always aware of the abundance of animal life. Jackals howl at night, and on several occasions, having spent the night on the sand near the base of an overhanging cliff, I have awakened to find leopard tracks near my sleeping bag. Here the voice of the bulbul is heard. But the sound most precious to the weary pilgrim overrides all others—the constant trickle of water.

This beautiful oasis extends for miles through Wadi Feiran. Groves of palms, tamarisks and olive trees provide shade and food. Bundles of luscious grapes dangle from green vineyards. Orange and grapefruit trees, planted by the Bedouin, provide fresh juice. As the wadi narrows at Rephidim, the mountains on both sides grow taller and the walls of the wadi steeper. They form a tumbled mass of color and shape. White boulders, walls of pink porphyry provide clefts from which herbs and flowers seem to spring. Towering red mountains contrast with the deep green of the waving palms. All provide a place of tranquillity and rest.

Wadi Feiran is now the home of many Bedouin who have gathered around the abundant water supply. But in Moses' time it was the dwelling place of the fierce Amalekites—the cave-dwellers.

According to Genesis 36:12, Amalek was a grandchild of Esau—Jacob's brother. But while Moses seems to have inherited Jacob's character (remember Jacob's name was later changed to *Israel*, which means "one who wrestled with God and lost"), the Amalekites remained, as their ancient forefather Esau, angry. These children of Esau have continued in their hatred against Israel whom they feel cheated them of their birthright. The confrontation between these two distant cousins at Rephidim marked perhaps the first conflict in history between Arab and Jew.

In Deuteronomy Moses reminded the Israelites just how treacherous these ancient terrorists were. "When you were weary and worn out, they met you on your journey and cut off all who were lagging behind; they had no fear of God" (Deuteronomy 25:18).

It was a wicked deed, slaughtering the old people and the children, the pregnant women and the sick who could not move quite as fast as the rest of the procession. Attacking at night as the straggling band of Jews made their way wearily toward the springs ahead, the Amalekites hit and ran. They knew nothing of the hospitality of their Bedouin cousins who offered food, water and shade to these pilgrims. They instead represented the enemies of God. As Moses said, "They had no fear of God."

There are, I believe, two kinds of people on earth. There are those who wrestle with God hoping to lose. Although some may say they always want to do the will of God, all mankind is still struggling with Him. The first group, however, honors Him in the struggle and does not want to bring harm to His cause or His people. Then there are those who are the "enemies of God." Their sole purpose is the elimination of all who call upon the name of Jehovah.

The Amalekites were such a people. They represented, however, more than a warring tribe composed of the descendants of Amalek. They represented that entire breed of people who are enemies of God and enemies of God's people. Like the serpent that strikes anything close by, the Amalekites did not need to be provoked to attack. The mere presence of God's people near their lair was all the justification they needed to kill. They had no regard for the sanctity of human life, no morals, no sense of ethics. Their sole purpose was to drive the Israelites into the sea. They were, to a real degree, the forerunners of all those nations in the Middle East who even today maintain an identical purpose.

The prophet Balaam described the Amalekites as "the first fruits of the heathen," or the beginning of all those races of people hostile toward the people of God. The contest between Amalek and the Israelites, therefore, takes on an ominous overtone when viewed as the foreshadow of the conflicts to follow, for the battle at Rephidim was the first attack of the kingdoms of this world against the Kingdom of God.

Moses understood this. He realized this battle represented a spiritual attack against the Kingdom of God. Thus he wisely chose to fight the battle both in "the heavenlies" and on earth.

Up until this point in history, Moses had been both leader and overseer, pastor and apostle, prophet and priest. At Rephidim his role as leader began to change. He was now 81 years old and, although still healthy and strong, realized the call on his life had broadened from that of being a line officer to that of a field general. From this point on, Moses gradually emerged not as the physical leader of Israel but as their spiritual overseer. It is the growth many wilderness leaders experience: from father to grandfather, from president to chairman of the board, from pastor to apostle.

The overseer is not only a man who discerns spirits; he is a man of spiritual discernment. As overseer, Moses was now leading not by might nor by power but by God's Spirit. It was a radical change from the man who started out by swinging his staff at the heads of those who opposed him. Now, though, he had a vision not just for a single battle but for the entire Kingdom.

The true overseer has the qualities attributed to the sons of Issachar in I Chronicles 12:32. It was said they "understood the times and knew what Israel should do." Moses had become that kind of man. While his young captain, Joshua, was in the valley with his sword, Moses was on the mountaintop with his rod stretched heavenward. He knew the battle was more than a military skirmish; it involved, at its heart, spiritual warfare.

Pastors may have insight, but the apostle has oversight. The apostle knows the direction the body should go and has a vision for the entire work. In the valley below, his "point man," Joshua, was leading the troops in victorious warfare. But General Moses had withdrawn, not for the sake of safety but in order to do the more important work—interceding and giving overall direction.

As the Israelites progressed in their own spiritual trek, drawing closer to the purposes of God, God did not always fight for them as He had done at the crossing of the sea. Now Israel was forced to fight also. Later, in the Promised Land, they would discover that although God promised them all the land where they set their feet, that land was invariably occupied by some enemy. No amount of "speaking a word of faith" would cause the enemy to flee. They had to physically force the enemy from the land. It was this combination of faith and works that brought them into final victory, both at Rephidim and in Canaan.

It was this lesson Moses wanted to teach his followers. Therefore, he turned the actual fighting over to a younger man, Hoshea, a prince of the tribe of Ephraim, whose name was changed to Joshua—"Jehovah is help."

It was an odd assortment of strategies: Joshua fighting with the sword while the overseer climbed the mountain with his two old companions—Aaron, his brother, and Hur, whom historian Josephus says was the husband of Moses' older sister, Miriam.

Even though Mt. Tahuneh, which Moses climbed, is only 750 feet above the valley floor, it is an arduous climb. I made that climb early one morning with a group of companions. The path was poorly marked, and very shortly our group was spread out over the precipitous face of the mountain like a flock of scattered mountain goats.

At one point I found myself in the middle of an ancient rockslide. I had no choice but to keep going, despite the cries from others to turn back. I realized I had to keep moving upward or be caught in a deluge of loose stones. Halfway up the steep ascent the slide began to move. Every place I put my feet, every place I put my hands, the rocks moved under me. It was an eerie feeling, and I was grateful for the shouts of encouragement from my friends, above and below, as I inched my way to safety and finally made it to the top. I thought of those three old men, climbing no doubt in the pre-dawn darkness to escape detection by the Amalekites who lived in the numerous caves, and I wondered how they had made it.

At the top, as the sun rose in the east over the blue range of the Sinai mountains, Moses took his place over the two armies now facing each other in the valley far below. As long as Moses held up his rod over the valley, the battle went in favor of the Israelites. When his hands dropped, the Amalekites surged ahead. Realizing what was at stake, Aaron and Hur moved a stone under Moses so he could sit down, then held his hands aloft until the sun set over Mt. Serabal in the southwest and the Amalekites were thoroughly defeated.

It is a thrilling story, and the lessons to be learned are of exceptional value to those of us on our own trek through the wilderness.

Primary is the absolute need for intercessory prayer when we come face-to-face with unconquerable enemies. While the battle in the valley is very real, the ultimate battle is always fought in the realm of the heavenlies. By holding up his hands, Moses was signifying he was in harmony with God—which is the essence of faith.

To the casual observer, it seemed Captain Joshua was winning a military battle. But a true analysis shows there was more taking place than the natural eye could see. The real battle was in the heavenlies as the angels of God battled the angels of darkness—a battle that is won only when the people of God join forces with the angels.

Over and over in the Scripture we see what happens when men, even two or three, come together in harmony with God. In the Upper Room 120 men and women were "all together in one place." As soon as they came into harmony with God's purpose, the Holy Spirit came as a mighty wind and filled the whole house where they were sitting. When a father came to Jesus on behalf of his dying daughter and linked his faith with the faith of Jesus, the daughter, who had actually died, came back to life. When Simon Peter withdrew to a bedroom and stood over the corpse of a dead child, singing the same song God was singing, the child breathed again.

It is this principle of faith that demands a father give "spiritual covering" to his family. When the father is not in his rightful place, the battle goes against them. But when the father occupies his place between God and the enemy, holding up his hands in intercession for his wife, his sons and daughters, his grandchildren—the battle in the valley below goes in favor of God's people.

Miracles always accompany faith. Faith allows God to flow unrestricted through a human instrument, as breath blows through a trumpet or flute, bringing God's music to earth. Rephidim, therefore, presents a beautiful picture of three old men in prayer, two holding up the hands of the third, turning the tide of battle for those below.

In earlier days Moses would never have thought of winning a battle except by using his staff to crack the head of an enemy soldier. But such victories, he now realized, often end in personal defeat, or at best are limited to skirmishes won but battles lost. In this case God said the victory won at Rephidim was complete. He told Moses to "write this on a scroll as something to be remembered and make sure that Joshua hears it, because I will completely erase the memory of the Amalekites from under heaven" (Exodus 17:14).

Later Moses did tell Joshua, "When the Lord your God

gives you rest from all the enemies around you in the land he
is giving you to possess as an inheritance, you shall blot out
the memory of Amalek from under heaven. Do not forget!"
(Deuteronomy 25:19).

It was a needed admonition, for the enemies of God did not
disappear at Rephidim. In fact, the "Amalekites" kept reap-
pearing throughout Israeli history. Joshua had additional battles with them in Canaan. King Saul fought them. David had
to fight them. Yet from the time of the battle at Rephidim there
is no mention ever made of the name Amalek in non-biblical
history. Even in biblical history they are referred to only by the
name *shusa*. (In Hebrew, *shosehu* means "plundered.") But it is
good to know that despite the constant reappearance in history of the enemies of God, they are a defeated people.

There is a final lesson, equally important, to be learned at
Rephidim. The rod that Moses held up was the banner of God.
It was the symbol of recognition that while man does the
work, God gets the glory. After the battle was over and the
Amalekites had been defeated, Moses took stones and built
an altar on top of Mt. Tahuneh to perpetuate the event. He
called the altar *Jehovahnissi*, "the Lord is my banner." He gave
God the glory.

Whether it is modern political Israel or those who have been
grafted into the branch and make up the Church, the people
of God must continue to fight. But the victory is God's, and
only as the people give God the glory is the victory guaranteed. The people of God have the rod of almighty power in
Jesus Christ. As long as that rod is lifted toward heaven,
whether it be over a field of snakes or over the warring hordes
of the enemies of God, the victory is assured. When God is
given the glory, the blessings secured by His covenant promise are always in force, even for those of us trekking through
our own Rephidims on the way to the Promised Land.

XII

Leadership

"What is this you are doing for the people? Why do you sit alone as judge . . . ?"

(Exodus 18:14)

No burden is so heavy as the burden of leadership. I have been intrigued, therefore, to discover that one of the purposes of the wilderness is to teach us how to lead others. Indeed, Jesus said the heart of His ministry was to enlist men to become "fishers of men."

At the end of His earthly life, Jesus called His disciples around Him and said, "Therefore go and make disciples of all nations . . . teaching them to obey everything I have commanded you" (Matthew 28:19-20). Earlier, when these same men were together, Jesus told them: "As the Father has sent me, I am sending you." Then, breathing on them, He had said, "Receive the Holy Spirit" (John 20:21-22). His last words to Simon Peter came in the form of a commission to lead others: "Feed my lambs. . . . Take care of my sheep. . . . Feed my sheep" (John 21:15-17).

Like many great leaders, the character of Moses was a long time in formation. His great leadership was not due to some rare combination of personal gifts; rather, it was a gift from God developed and improved during his forty-year matriculation at Wilderness University.

Moses was a man like all of us, with flaws that veined the pure marble of his character, with a horrendous temper that sometimes overshadowed his fabled meekness, and a stubborn will that was in constant conflict with his deep compassion and unselfishness. Like all of us, he was a man constantly wrestling with God—but always with the purpose of losing the match.

The character of the leader, however, is as dear to God as the work he is doing; and God spares no pains to complete the design to which He has set His hand. It is not surprising, therefore, that at the moment of Moses' greatest triumphs, God sent a man to speak a word of correction, and to change his way of ministry so radically that the entire structure of the Kingdom of God on earth was to be altered.

Few men can stand great or continued success. It is relatively easy to walk as a broken man, realizing that we are nothing and that God alone is worthy to be praised. But to receive the praise and accolades of others, to be looked upon as a "great man," as a "giant of the faith"—that is the path that causes the step of even the strongest to falter.

It is easier to be abased than to abound, to be empty than to be full, to rise from failure than to walk in success. Even though we continue to pray, and to utter the words "I give God the glory," how subtle the heart is turned until the time comes when we could well say with mad Nebuchadnezzar, "Is not this the great Babylon I have built as the royal residence, by my mighty power and for the glory of my majesty?" (Daniel 4:30).

But whenever this happens, when the heart of the leader is filled with pride and a feeling of self-accomplishment, there comes an end to his usefulness. God will not share His glory with anyone else. It is His solemn decree that no flesh shall glory in His presence.

This is why so many of God's servants, men who once led other men in remarkable ways, are laid aside. As long as they were weak, they were strong, but once they became strong in themselves, and began to listen to the praise of others, they became useless to God.

Tragic is the fall of any man; but especially tragic is the fall of a leader. Years spent in preparation, tears spent weeping at the feet of God, generations spent struggling through the wilderness—all lost and left behind when a man grows strong in himself and begins to imagine that what he has accomplished has been by his own strength, rather than by the grace of God. Such men may continue to preach, but their words no longer stir the dry bones with the breath of God. Such men are Samsons, going forth but not realizing the Lord has departed from them. They are like fishermen who think their loaded nets are due to their own expertise, instead of being the gift of the One who gathered the fish on that particular side of the boat.

Moses was in danger of such a fall. Everything had gone his way from the time he first accosted Pharaoh in his palace. For almost a year his life had been an uninterrupted stream of success. He had brought the world's proudest ruler to his knees. The elders of the ancient nation of Israel revered him. After all, God had chosen him to lead the world's greatest Exodus. His success was evidenced in the parted sea, the drowned army, the song of victory, the fall of the manna, the knowledge of the wilderness, the water from the rock, and then his latest victory over the Amalekites when all he did was climb the mountain and hold out his rod. No wonder the people flocked to him night and day as a man of superb wisdom and unlimited knowledge! All these things combined to place him in an unparalleled position of absolute authority and glory.

What an awesome position! What a frightening position! How easy it is, even in the wilderness, to imagine you have now learned all there is to learn and that the exaltation now coming your way is justified—indeed, deserved.

Therefore God, who was not ready for Moses to join the list of proud but useless ministers who sadden history's scroll, sent into his life a wise but humble man to puncture his balloon of ego. To whom could Moses submit? There was only one man who could be classified as his peer—or, even stronger, his superior. And God sent that man to Moses within days following the defeat of the Amalekites. He was Jethro, Moses' old mentor—and incidentally, his father-in-law—the only elder he had ever known.

The aged priest of Midian had been kept fully informed of the progress of his son-in-law, probably from the time Moses left Jethro, his wife, Zipporah, and his two sons to fulfill his promise to God to bring the Israelites back to Mt. Sinai. When the word came that Moses and his kinsmen had left Rephidim and were marching through the Naqb el Hawa—the "valley of the wind"—Jethro knew it was time to join him. Gathering his family about him, including Zipporah and the two sons who had been entrusted to his care, he traveled overland to meet Moses on the great plain that stretched forth from the base of Sinai—er Rakha.

After the customary salutations, the sharing of hospitality and the proper introductions, Moses and Jethro spent the night talking. Zipporah would have been scurrying around the tent, fixing food, making sure her husband was comfortable. Sitting crosslegged in Bedouin fashion, Moses told Jethro all God had done. Jethro listened intently and responded: "Praise be to the Lord . . . who rescued the people from the hand of the Egyptians. Now I know that the Lord is greater than all other gods, for he did this to those who had treated Israel arrogantly" (Exodus 18:10-11).

There followed first a time of worship, then a time of celebration. The family was once again united.

The next day the cloud that had been leading the Israelites through the deep wadis was stationary. Instead of moving, it hovered over the camp as though moored by an invisible cable. Moses took the opportunity to hold court, for he filled not only the role of senator and president, but chief justice as well. In fact, he also served as chief of police, county commissioner and head of the water and sewer division. He was also in charge of planning and zoning, the department of transportation, the department of agriculture, and was chief of veterinary medicine. But on this day an incident took place that was destined to change the course of governmental history, not only for the nation of Israel but for the entire world.

"The next day Moses took his seat to serve as judge for the people, and they stood around him from morning till evening" (Exodus 18:13).

It was Moses' time to shine in the presence of his old father-in-law. The last time Jethro had seen him, Moses was nothing more than an old shepherd heading out alone across the wilderness to rejoin his kinsmen in Egypt. Now he had returned as a great charismatic leader, revered, respected, leading an entire nation on a supernatural pilgrimage to a Promised Land. This was Moses' chance to invite his old teacher to come and see—to feel proud that his son-in-law had done so well in such a short period of time.

But Jethro's reaction was nothing short of startling. That night, as they sat again in their tent, Moses waited for Jethro's approval. Instead, the wizened old Bedouin, sitting crosslegged on the sand, looked across the fire and asked, "What is this you are doing for the people? . . . What you are doing is not good. You and these people who come to you will only wear yourselves out. The work is too heavy for you; you cannot handle it alone" (Exodus 18:14, 17-18).

Moses sat silently. How desperately he wanted Jethro's approval! Yet deep inside he sensed God was speaking. It was time to listen, not to grow defensive or to pout. He knew that the primary reason they were in the wilderness was to hear the voice of God. Why should he be exempt from teaching? If God was a God of change, as he had been teaching his followers, then it stood to reason there would be times when the leader himself would have to change.

Now was such a time. As he had for many years, Moses leaned forward to hear what his old teacher, the only father he had ever known, had to say.

"Listen now to me and I will give you some advice," Jethro began, "and may God be with you." Then he quickly outlined the five basic ingredients of spiritual leadership—things Moses needed to incorporate into his life if he were to minister effectively and not in his own strength.

1. You must be a priest—the people's representative before God.
2. You must be a teacher, teaching them the decrees and laws.
3. You must be an example, showing them the way to live and the duties they are to perform.
4. You must be an administrator, selecting capable men from all the people and appointing them as officials over thousands, hundreds, fifties and tens.
5. You must be a judge, having them bring the difficult cases to you but letting them decide the simple cases for themselves.

"If you do this and God so commands," Jethro finished, "you will be able to stand the strain, and all these people will go home satisfied" (cf. Exodus 18:19-26).

When God speaks through a man, the wise man of God will recognize the voice. Moses knew the wisdom coming from Jethro was the wisdom of God. He acted on the advice, and immediately established other men in the body to share in the leadership. Even though he would still be recognized as the head, others would share in the ministry—and God would get the glory.

It is never God's will for a man of God to burn himself out, even in service for God. God does not want us to overtax our machinery. It is man who drives slaves with a whip. God is never in a hurry. He causes clouds to pause, commands a Sabbath rest, and smiles when His servants slow down and relax. God realizes the weight of the burden of leadership. Therefore He has designed a plan that, if worked correctly, will provide not only rest for the leader but satisfaction for all the others called into service.

The wise leader knows it is much better to teach a man how to fish than to give him a fish, much better to enlist an army than to fight the enemy singlehandedly.

Many years later, the apostle Paul would take this same principle and apply it to the Church. He would point out there is a difference between the role of pastor and the role of apostle. He would tell the churches of the foolishness of expecting one man to be all things—preacher, spiritual overseer, evangelist, teacher and pastor. Each office is different, he said in Ephesians 4, and should be filled by different men. This way no single man is faced with the danger of taking the glory for himself, or of working himself into a premature grave and leaving the sheep shepherdless.

Long after Jethro had returned to Midian, Moses, who no longer seemed to need to be all things to all people, again divided the leadership responsibilities, backing off even further from the one-man rule.

Despite the fact that his pastors were functioning well in their jobs over the people, he still felt the burden of responsibility. He needed men, not only to perform the pastoral, administrative and judicial duties, but men who would stand with him as elders, to bear the burden of the entire body.

This time there was no Jethro to advise him. But this time none was needed. Moses had learned the lesson of shared responsibility—of multiple leadership. He realized the job was too big for him and he approached God, admitting the burden of spiritual responsibility was too heavy for one man to carry.

God told him to call out from the people seventy men who were already serving in some phase of leadership, older men who had proven themselves as leaders and officials. While these men had been active in the governmental activities of the nation, God was now going to set them apart as spiritual elders to share the burden with Moses. "I will take of the Spirit that is on you," He told Moses, "and put the Spirit on them. They will help you carry the burden of the people so that you will not have to carry it alone" (Numbers 11:17).

Still later, shortly before he died, Moses took a final step in sharing the leadership. He set apart Joshua as an apostle. "So the Lord said to Moses, 'Take Joshua son of Nun, a man in whom is the spirit, and lay your hand on him. . . . Give him some of your authority so the whole Israelite community will obey him'" (Numbers 27:18, 20).

The principle of leadership, as learned in the crucible of the wilderness, is the principle of change. God has no static government, nor does He allow men enough knowledge to form a static theology. The moment that happens, the moment we declare we know the full purpose of God in government or theology, that is the moment we discover the cloud has moved and we are no longer under it.

Jesus likened the Kingdom of God to new wine—always expanding, growing, changing. To pour such into a traditional, dried wineskin would be a disaster. Only as the wineskin remains flexible, He said, elastic and willing to change shape and size, can the Kingdom be contained.

Such is the danger of static leadership. Leaders are always expendable. The moment the leader feels he is necessary to God, he becomes useless to the people. Theology, too, must remain flexible, for men are always receiving new illumination on old truth which, if valid, must be applied to the lives of growing men.

Our concepts of God, therefore, must be always changing, ever growing. The true leader realizes he does not have a corner on truth but must lead with an open ear, not by some creed chiseled in stone but by listening to the ever-speaking voice of God. Books on theology, which are the manuals leaders must use, should always close with a semicolon, leaving space for new understanding as it comes in our wilderness journey.

The wilderness does not make leaders; it simply reveals them. Then, if they are wise, they will get on with the business of raising up other leaders—so the Kingdom may grow and God may get the glory.

XIII

Patience

Listen to the path; it is wiser than he who travels it.
—Bedouin proverb

In certain sections of the Sinai, the Bedouin gather honey from the date palms called *devash*. I've watched the women take the honey, complete with its comb, and place it in cloth sacks made of loosely woven material. This is suspended from the branch of a tree and allowed to drip slowly into containers placed below. It takes a long time, sometimes days, for the honey to ooze out of the comb and drip through the straining cloth into the urns.

Once I asked if I could hasten the process by squeezing the bag. The old woman shook her finger in my face, and from behind the black veil that covered her mouth told me that to squeeze the sack would streak the honey, making it less valuable.

There are certain wilderness lessons that cannot be learned in the rush of life, in the excitement of Egypt. These can be learned only in the slow process of trudging. Here, as we walk doggedly—sometimes blindly—through our personal wilderness, the dripping action takes place: for lessons are learned, not in rapid squeezing but in the perspective of time. In the wilderness the honeycomb of our reactions and incompleteness is left in the bag. Only what is pure oozes through to be collected in the urn.

My visits to St. Catherine's Monastery near the base of Mt.

Sinai always brought this to mind. The monastery is one of the most interesting places in the world. In the fourth century, Emperor Constantine and his mother, Empress Helena, embraced Christianity. In 327 A.D. the elderly Empress Helena undertook a pilgrimage to the Sinai. Near the base of Jebel Musa, she found a small community of hermits who pointed out what looked like a raspberry bush and told her it was the original burning bush. Helena ordered a small chapel to be built around the bush and dedicated it to the holy virgin. The chapel became the center of Christian activity in the high mountain region.

Two hundred years later, in 527 A.D., the small chapel was enlarged by Emperor Justinian into a formidable monastery, a fortress to protect the hermits from marauding bands of robbers. Sometime after that it was rededicated to St. Catherine, the virgin martyr of fourth-century Alexandria. It has been inhabited by monks and pilgrims for more than sixteen centuries, making it one of the oldest continuously occupied buildings in the world.

Nestled against the base of Jebel Safsafa, one of the towering red granite peaks of the Mt. Sinai cluster, the monastery is literally squeezed into a narrow wadi that immediately fans out to er Rakha, the wide plain where the Israelites camped while Moses was on the mountain. It has withstood the Islamic invasion of the seventh century, flashfloods, earthquakes and bands of marauding nomadic tribes for sixteen centuries. During this time it has housed a small group of Greek Orthodox monks whose sole task is to maintain the monastery.

Secluded in their utter remoteness, St. Catherine's monks have been known to let whole eras go by without notice. A visitor in 1946 was astonished to learn the monks had not heard of World War II and that some were unaware of World War I. They spend their time tending the ancient library, one of the oldest and richest in the world, constantly repairing the crumbling walls and walkways, and caring for the precious icons and the gold and silver ornaments that decorate the elegant chapel.

Since the Six-Day War in 1967, however, the outside world has forced itself on the abbey. An airport was built nearby. A paved road now runs through Wadi Feiran from the Gulf of Suez to the entrance of the monastery. Over the last years, before the Sinai was handed back to Egypt in 1982 (a decision that does not seem to affect the operation of the ancient monastery in the least), as many as 100,000 tourists a year descended on the black-frocked monks to disturb their tranquillity and gawk at the ancient artifacts and ornate chapel.

Although I much prefer the solitude of the desert to the bustling activity of the monastery and the somber attitudes of the monks, my visits to Jebel Musa have always led me back to St. Catherine's for brief visits. The water is the best in the Sinai; a visit to the charnal house where the bones of all the deceased monks lie exposed in bins awaiting the final resurrection is interesting; and occasionally one of the usually preoccupied fifteen monks will take time from his polishing and dusting to smile and pose for pictures.

After days of trekking through the desert with a small group of dusty pilgrims—cooking our own food in the open, camping out at night, climbing mountains and drawing water from the wells—we would finally arrive at the entrance to the ancient monastery.

Sometimes we would descend upon the fortress-looking building from the high mountain path, having spent the night on Mt. Sinai. Other times we would make our approach from the plain of er Rakha, either on foot or by camelback.

Each time, however, as I led my dusty, unshaved desert pilgrims into the monastery compound, I have been struck by the contrast we made to the groups of tourists who had flown in to the nearby airport or traveled overland by bus from Elat or Cairo.

These gawkers, dressed in their city clothes with necks hung with cameras, had only hours before left the comfort of their air-conditioned hotel rooms in a modern city. After a quick look at the monastery (some might stay long enough to climb Jebel Musa by the stone stairs, spending ten minutes on the summit taking more pictures), the tourists would hurry back to the airport or to their air-conditioned buses. Returning home, they would show their slides and proclaim themselves experts on the Sinai. After all, they had seen the mountain, talked to an old Bedouin (and perhaps, after paying him a dollar, mounted up on his camel for more pictures), and listened to the memorized lecture droned by some guide who knew better than to answer questions. The more venturesome might even have spent the night at one of the dormitory rooms at the monastery, but none would have dared enter the surrounding desert. They were all in too much of a hurry.

But a quick visit to the desert does no more make one an expert on the wilderness than a visit to a history class makes one an archaeologist.

Some things cannot be learned on the run. They must be learned slowly, as honey drips through the muslin delaine. They must be walked out through the experience of time. It is difficult to hear God on the run. Elijah discovered this truth many years after Moses learned the same thing. Not until the prophet got quiet and waited in the high oasis on the mountain was he able to hear.

So it is with all impatient men, for God is not seen by those in rapid transit. Isaiah heard only after he pulled aside from the throng of worshipers in the Temple and sat quietly in the presence of God. David heard Him on the hillside tending his lambs, alone with harp and flute. Jesus heard best when He withdrew from the mobs—even from His disciples—and took time to spend the night praying on some mountain, or kneeling alone in a garden. John the apostle, with nothing but the time of exile on his hands, heard Him as he waited patiently on the isle of Patmos.

The soft occasions, the quick squeezings of the bag, do not bring out the deepest of man. Only as he sinks his roots into the hard, rocky soil of the wilderness, only as he waits patiently for his bush to burn, only as he withdraws for his own forty days and forty nights of waiting, does he find his Source. The trouble, it seems, is that God is not in a hurry, and I am.

One of the great virtues learned in the wilderness is patience. In the desert you forget calendars. You leave your watch behind, for it is useless. You go to bed at sunset and rise at dawn. Meals are scheduled by body needs, not to satisfy clocks and appointments. In the desert, one learns to wait.

How programmed we are to produce! Goal-oriented, production-conscious, we have been trained to close each day with a question: How much did I produce today? Did I meet my quota? Everything is geared to what the production control people call "the bottom line"—which is preceded invariably by a dollar sign. It is a mentality developed by a materialistic society that places the prime emphasis on doing rather than being.

But in the wilderness, you learn patience. Here you have time—lots of it. There is time to grow still. Time to pull aside and look at a bush burn. Time to sit with friends and talk. Time to pray. Time to explore. Time to rest. Time to walk long distances without the anxiety of having to be back to meet a schedule. In the desert you rediscover the precious commodity of time. As faith has been boxed in by religious rites, so has time been relegated by our hurry-up society into a framework of calendars and clocks. Only in the wilderness do you discover how precious it is to have enough time to do what you want.

Perhaps it is best described in the desert term for time—the number *forty.* Over and over we find the term in our Bibles. Noah was in the ark forty days and forty nights. Moses was forty years old when he was exiled to the Sinai. He remained another forty years. He was on Mt. Sinai forty days and nights—two times. The twelve spies scouted out the land of Canaan for forty days. The children of Israel wandered for forty years. Elijah's journey into the wilderness lasted forty days. Jonah warned Ninevah they had forty days to repent. Jesus fasted in the wilderness forty days and nights, and when He appeared to His disciples following His resurrection, He was present forty days.

In many instances the term *forty* means a time of cleansing and preparation. But the term also appears in other contexts in the desert, especially in the Bedouin culture. There is a Moslem legend that 40,000 prophets have arisen out of Sinai since the beginning of time. Bedouin call the cold winter *el-arbiniyah,* the forty days. They also speak of a remedy for sickness called *el-arbain,* which is a mixture of forty plant species mixed with olive oil and butter. Forty days is the appointed time for mourning. The quail-hunting season lasts forty days. Flies pester the sheep and goats for forty days at the beginning of summer and forty days at the end of summer. If you are forty paces from the home of a man who gives you shelter, you are in a "safe zone" and cannot be attacked by a pursuing army.

What does the term *forty* really mean? Although the true meaning has been lost across the centuries, in nearly all cases it stems from the root meaning of *a long time*.

In the case of Moses' lifespan, and the time spent in the wilderness by the children of Israel, it is probably a literal term. In other instances, it is a general term that means simply "a long time." Even so, it must be remembered that forty is not a natural number, like the lunar or menstrual periods of thirty days. It is a supernatural number signifying preparation for importance. To that degree, it is not what happens during the "forty" days or years that is revelatory, but what takes place when the cycle is over—immediately afterwards. For Jesus, it was the beginning of His earthly ministry. The same holds true in the case of Moses—and most certainly with the corporate body of Israel. For all of them, the wilderness was not the real world; it was a place through which they passed—patiently—to be prepared for what lay ahead.

God may be found in the wilderness. But the entire scale of time and place in the wilderness is "utterly other," apart from time and space as we know it in our rapid-transit society.

In my times in the desert I have become aware of its agelessness and vastness. Each time I have entered the Sinai I have purposefully taken off my watch and left my appointment calendar behind. Here it makes no difference how old I am, what the date is, or whether it is 9:00 a.m. or noon. I have learned to get up with the dawn and crawl into my sleeping bag when the sun sets.

When I asked a Bedouin how long it would take to move his sheep to another pasture, he shrugged and replied, "Not long." When I asked what time tea would be served in his tent he said, "When the water boils." I still remember the smiles the Bedouin men gave me when, after eating a leisurely meal around their campfire at night, I asked when we as their guests should go to bed. "When you get sleepy," they laughed.

Each answer was given with a shrug—and a grin. In other words, Why be in such a hurry? You have plenty of time. Perhaps forty years.

So I have learned from these citizens of the desert, just as I have learned from the trees and plants. Desert trees do not bloom on command. The date palm, for instance, produces its fruit in its season. Then it waits patiently as the next crop is prepared. No amount of commands to "Hurry up!" will make it produce faster. It waits on God's time.

The psalmist said the blessed man is "like a tree planted by streams of water, which yields its fruit in season and whose leaf does not wither" (Psalm 1:3).

My times in the wilderness have taught me that God does not expect fruit every day—even the fruit of the Spirit. In fact, there have been times, after times of exasperation, when my only response to the situation is to mutter, "Damn!" That is different from grumbling. It is simply a commentary on how I felt.

God did not condemn Moses when he smashed the tablets of the Law in his thunderous reaction to finding the golden calf at the base of the mountain. He recognized there were limits to each man's ability to control his emotions. God had plenty of time, so He adjusted His schedule to allow another forty days and nights so Moses could cleanse his soul and once again hear God speak.

There are seasons when the man of God flourishes spiritually. Then there are times when the leaves of our life fall, the fruit disappears, and for all appearances our tree is lifeless. But each tree has a season, and in the proper season the fruit reappears.

I have walked through the agriculture experimentation stations in Israel where these industrious people have developed trees that produce fruit all year long. These trees have fruit and blossoms on their branches at the same time. But the fruit is never as tasty as that which comes from the tree that produces only once a year, then waits patiently for the next crop to mature.

The psalmist equates the "blessed man" with a tree "planted by streams of water." It is a strange simile when you consider the wilderness, for there are no such rivers in the desert. The best you can find is a dry riverbed, a wadi, which is filled with water only on occasion.

The difference is profound. Any tree can produce when

planted on the shores of a sparkling river. But in the wilderness, where there are no rivers, the fruit trees need to find nourishment in another way. The beautiful date palm, for instance, which produces the most delicious of all desert fruit, finds water by sending its roots into the underground reservoirs. It does not depend on showers of blessings to keep it producing, but draws its strength from the hidden nourishment found deep in the soil of the wilderness.

This is the lesson of the desert. When your branches are barren, when all your buds have dried up, when your leaves droop in discouragement—remember your roots. Remember that just beneath the sand there are underground reservoirs where the water is pure. Relax. Take your time. And know that in your season, you shall bear fruit again.

XIV

Intercession

"But now, please forgive their sin—but if not, then blot me out of the book you have written."

(Exodus 32:32)

The ascent to Mt. Sinai is one of the most torturous, yet one of the most exhilarating experiences known to humankind.

Leaving Rephidim, I have often had to decide which of the two approaches to the Mountain of God I would take. The first is called "The Pilgrim's Path" of Naqb el Hawa—the valley of the wind. It is the traditional footpath that ends at the plain of er Rakha—the place of rest. The path is too narrow and precipitous for the vast hordes of Israelites to have traveled. Although I love to walk the seven miles or so from the tomb of Sheikh Awad to the plain of er Rakha, I suspect the children of Israel must have come east from Rephidim through Wadi esh Sheikh, then turned south past what is now the tomb of Sheikh Nabi Salh to approach the mountain.

Wadi esh Sheikh is the longest, widest and most continuous of the wadis in southern Sinai. On either side the Israelites saw the precipitous mountains rearing their inaccessible ramparts of red sandstone and variegated granite. Ibex, the long-horned mountain goat with antlers curling backwards in a great circle, peered down on them from lofty positions. Gazelle skipped across the open valley before them, darting quickly into the shadows. From the caves the huge spotted leopards growled and slunk backwards into the darkness. The wadis opening on the sides appeared as majestic corridors of a vast temple, with the pillar of cloud ushering them from the narthex of Rephidim through the sanctuary of Wadi esh Sheikh to the high altar of Mt. Sinai.

From either approach you suddenly enter, without warning, the perfectly level plain of er Rakha. Two miles long and a half-mile wide, it is dotted with broom bushes and small rocks. The mountains that gather around this plain have sloping sides and form a natural amphitheatre. Only on the southern end does the terrain change. There, jutting out of the sand of the desert and towering up into the azure blue sky, is the massive stone Mountain of God. Deeply cleft with fissures, and torn as though it has struggled to push its way up from the desert floor, it is a mountain touched by the hand of God and burned with fire.

Here, in this awesome wilderness sanctuary, the pilgrims were to receive new revelation concerning the character of God. All they knew of Him up until this time was He was a God of no name and no image who talked with Moses. Now they were to discover new and startling aspects of His nature.

When God established His covenant with Abraham, He revealed Himself as *El Shaddai*, a term meaning simply "God Almighty." At the burning bush, He told Moses He was not only El Shaddai, the God of Abraham, Isaac and Jacob; He went ahead to say He was *ehyeh asher ehyeh*—"I am that I am." At this point, God declared He was more than the essence of being, which is the root of the verb *I am.* He said He was the cause of being—underived existence coupled with an independent and uncontrolled will.

On Mt. Tahuneh Moses went a step further and called Him Jehovah-nissi—"The Lord is my banner." On Mt. Sinai, however, God came to Moses and called Himself by a far more personal name. The true pronunciation has long since been lost, but it is represented by the four Hebrew letters *YHWH*. It was lost because the Jews—except for the high priest—have scrupulously avoided ever mentioning it aloud. Instead, when they used it they always substituted another Hebrew word—Adonai. (According to Jewish tradition, *YHWH* was pronounced but once a year by the high priest on the Day of Atonement when he entered the Holy of Holies.)

Thus the name of God was not only kept at arm's length; it

was never to be looked upon, much less spoken, so sacred was it. When the Scriptures were written, there was need to call God *something*, so the writers added vowel points (which had not been used in the original writing since the old alphabet was only consonants) and *YHWH* became *Yahweh*. This was translated out in the later renderings as Jehovah—the self-existent God. This name, Yahweh or Jehovah, has its roots in *ehyeh*—underived existence.

During the march from Egypt to Mt. Sinai, God spoke basically to Moses. Only on rare occasions, such as at the springs of Marah, did the people hear His voice. The rest of the time He was reflected in the pillar of cloud by day and the column of fire at night—the God of no name and no image.

The revelation of the law on Mt. Sinai had a great impact, since now the God of history, the God of underived existence, made Himself known. Bit by bit, in a process known as progressive revelation, God revealed Himself—first to Moses and then to the people.

In the biblical account of the meetings between God and Moses on Mt. Sinai, a marvelous progression of familiarity begins to take place. It begins with the formal statement in Exodus 19:3: "Then Moses went up to God, and the Lord called to him from the mountain. . . ."

Following this, Moses descended to the plain to report to the people. Twice more he ascended the mountain, each time coming back to warn the people of God's holiness.

On the third day, the mountain began to rumble. It was covered with a dark cloud with lightning flashes and the pealing sound of angelic trumpet blasts. With the people standing in awe around the base of the mountain, having consecrated themselves and having been warned not to touch the sides of the mountain until they heard the long blast from the shofar—the ram's horn—they waited in awed silence as Moses once again ascended the mountain and disappeared into the dark cloud.

But it was not yet time to receive the commandments. Instead God, in a revelation of love and caution, told Moses to descend once again and make sure the people understood the nature of His holiness—how they would be destroyed if they disobeyed.

It is not clear whether Moses climbed to the peak of the

mountain, which extends almost 4,500 feet above the plain. But for the 80-year-old man it was a powerful effort. Once more the weary Moses descended, warned the people, then for the fourth time ascended again, this time taking his brother Aaron with him.

While Aaron listened in stunned silence, God spoke the words of the Ten Commandments and certain other ordinances. God again told Moses of the Promised Land and His desire for the people to move with dispatch and possess it. If they would obey Him, He said, they would not be sick, nor would the pregnant women miscarry their babies despite the hardships of the journey. He would send hornets to drive out the enemy as the Israelites approached the Promised Land. (This promise came true when the Israelites many years later marched against the Jebusites in Transjordan. At that time swarms of hornets routed the enemy, making their defeat certain.) It was a wonderful revelation of a loving and gracious God who promised to care for and protect His people as long as they obeyed Him.

Moses returned to the people and told them all God had said. Relieved and excited, they responded with one voice: "Everything the Lord has said we will do" (Exodus 24:3).

Moses then took the rest of the day to write down all the Lord had spoken. Early the next morning he built an altar at the foot of the mountain and prepared the people to receive the covenants of God. Then, for the fifth time, he climbed back up the mountain. Once again Aaron, the elders, and a few others went with him. Partway up, they came to a small oasis—a natural amphitheatre—called a *farsh*. They paused and suddenly God appeared. The entire peak of the mountain, which can be seen clearly from the farsh, became as sapphire, so powerful was His presence and so great His glory.

God called to Moses out of His glory, telling him to climb even higher. From the elders he chose only Joshua to accompany him, sending Aaron and Hur back down to watch over the people who waited below. Leaving Joshua partway up the trail to the summit, he climbed on to the peak alone. There he received not only the Ten Commandments, written on tablets of stone by the finger of God, but specific instructions on the erection of the tabernacle.

Descending the mountain with Joshua, he discovered the people had forgotten all their vows to be faithful. They had taken their golden rings and bracelets, melted them down and molded a golden calf—similar to the Egyptian Apis-bull that had been worshiped by Pharaoh.

To exalt the bull and give it divine status was a relapse into the Egyptian religion. Moses was outraged by the backsliding of his people who just days before had vowed, "Everything the Lord has said we will do." Raising the stone tablets over his head, he smashed them to the ground. It was a symbol that the covenant was declared null and void, for until the people actually received the tablets, the covenant was not in force. He blamed Aaron for the calf, who offered one of the most feeble excuses recorded in the Bible. "I don't know what happened," Aaron lamented. "All we did was throw the gold into the fire and out came this calf."

Realizing that Aaron was not capable of leading, that he had let the people run wild and could not control them, Moses called the people together and said, "Whoever is for the Lord, come to me."

His own tribe, the Levites, gathered around him. Moses then gave them a terrible command to take swords and kill all those who had led the rebellion. Even though the scene sounds grisly, God meant what He said when He warned the people that He was a holy God, that His commands were not to be taken lightly. That day more than 3,000 Israelites were slaughtered—and the revolution was put quickly to a finish.

The following day, his anger abated, Moses said to the people: "You have committed a great sin. But now I will go up to the Lord; perhaps I can make atonement for your sin" (Exodus 32:30).

What happened on the mountain that last trip has no comparison in history save what happened many years later at Calvary. Confessing the sin of his people, Moses took the place of the lonely advocate between God and the people. He was convinced of God's justice and did not see how God could go back on His solemn threat to destroy the nation. Yet if that judgment were to be averted, it must be in consequence of an atonement. The only thing he could offer was himself. Yet, he wondered, was even that enough?

Someplace along the line, during his conversations with

God, he had come to understand God was not only a God of justice; He was a God of mercy. And even though words like *lovingkindness* and *our Father* were yet to be defined, Moses had learned through his wilderness wanderings that only by suffering could one redeem another. It was the law of substitution. In deep pathos, therefore, the prince and leader of the nation fell on his face before God and proposed that he, the chosen servant, should be weighed in the scale against the people, and that God should accept his blood as a ransom for their life.

"Oh, what a great sin these people have committed! They have made themselves gods of gold. But now, please forgive their sin—" His words faltered. He could speak no more, as this supreme gesture on his part was choked by a paroxysm of grief, a sob of irrepressible emotion.

Finally, the words came forth: " . . . But if not, then blot me out of the book you have written" (Exodus 32:31-32).

Years later Jesus would remind His followers that this concept of self-sacrifice reflects the very heart of God's purpose for the world. "Greater love has no one than this, that one lay down his life for his friends" (John 15:13).

Moses had learned the ultimate lesson of the wilderness—that the love of God will cause us to give ourselves fully and completely for others.

Of course, the offer was rejected. No one but Messiah can atone for the sins of others. Yet because of the offer, God spared the people. It would be up to the Son of God to pay the price of "sins committed beforehand [which had gone] unpunished" (Romans 3:25).

Once more Moses remained on the mountain forty days. It was his last visit to Mt. Sinai. Returning to the people the final time, he carried with him two more tablets of stone. Where the first ones had been written by the finger of God, these had been laboriously chipped out by Moses' own hand. The covenant was complete. The people had been saved. Now it was time to head north toward Kadesh-Barnea, and the final siege of Canaan under the banner of God.

XV

Living Commandments

"If you make an altar of stones for me, do not build it with dressed stones, for you will defile it if you use a tool on it."
(Exodus 20:25)

It seems strange that God would give commandments knowing the people could not keep them.

The first high priest, Aaron, broke the second commandment even before the tablets of stone were handed over to the people. Moses broke the third when he misused the name of God by striking the rock after the Lord told him to speak to it only. Every one of the Ten Commandments was broken by the people before they got away from Mt. Sinai—and they have continued to be broken to this day.

If the Ten Commandments were impossible to keep, then why were they given? They were given to reveal the nature of God. For God is far more interested in a people who want to establish a relationship with Him than in a people who keep all the rules but never learn to abide in His presence.

In the wilderness one quickly realizes there are certain rules that, if flaunted, bring death. To drink poisoned water means death. To put your hand into the hole of a carpet viper or cobra means death. To wade in the shallow water off the coast of Aqaba and step on a stone fish means death. To eat the flesh of pork, which is often filled with trichinae, could mean death.

Even more important than the rules, however, is the relationship. The man who does no more than keep the rules dies.

But the man who sees the law, any law, as a means to know God, comes into a relationship that brings him into life.

Thus, even though the poisonous carpet vipers and black mambas that bit the Israelites in the wilderness meant death, when they looked upward to God (symbolized by the brazen serpent raised on a staff) they found life.

No sooner had God given His Ten Commandments to Moses than He began sharing some specific ordinances—rules for behavior dealing with the interpretation of the Commandments. One of the first of these had to do with the construction of altars.

"If you make an altar of stones for me," God told Moses, "do not build it with dressed [cut or hewn] stones, for you will defile it if you use a tool on it" (Exodus 20:25).

For ten generations the Israelites had been chiseling stones—stones to be used in the altars, idols and tombs of Egypt. The pyramids, those sacred tombs of the Egyptian pharaohs, were made of hewn stone. The Hebrew slaves had spent their last years in Egypt making bricks, shaped to fit into place in man's altars to false gods.

Now God was revealing a new concept. Jehovah, unlike all the Egyptian gods, did not need shaped stones. He did not need man's efforts for acceptable worship. He preferred the natural things—altars made of naturally shaped stones that had never been touched by hammer or chisel.

There is a sameness about bricks which is common to people in bondage and slavery. Bricks and hewn stones are made to conform. There is never any variation allowed. All are made to fit exactly into a designated place, with little or no irregularity or originality allowed or needed.

Slavery always produces bricks. Whether it is in the tone of the voice, the cut of the hair or clothes, the vocabulary one uses—you can always tell a person who is in bondage because he sounds and looks just like everyone else. Uniqueness is quenched. Individuality is not allowed. Genuine creativity is limited to products that look like those produced yesterday, and like those produced by everyone else.

Earlier Moses complained to God that instead of a disciplined army, he was being forced to lead a nation of uncut stones. Not a single one of them seemed to "fit." On a number of occasions Moses was tempted to chip them to shape, to make them conform to the image he felt they should take. Each time God said, "Hands off! I will do it. It is My job to conform each man to the shape I want him to take. I am the Master Builder who fits each stone into his place."

Each group of men I have taken with me into the Sinai has been composed of such "uncut stones"—strongly individualistic men who in most cases had never met each other until we set out for the wilderness. Despite every well-intentioned promise to "walk peaceably" with each other during the two-week trek through the wilderness, by the fourth or fifth day the veneers would begin to wear off. On several occasions the situations became downright explosive.

Stuck for 1,400 miles on a six-wheel-drive truck bouncing along through the wadis between mountains on trails that no ordinary vehicle could traverse, miles from any semblance of civilization, we discovered something quickly: we had to get along with the group despite our individuality. To leave the group would mean death in the desert. To expel one of the men from the group, no matter how badly he was behaving, would mean sending him to his death.

I remember one trip on which a conflict began to develop between two of the strongest-willed men—one a physician who is a marathon runner, and the other a jut-jawed, highly opinionated minister.

Tension had been building because the minister was free with his opinions about some of the men who were not measuring up spiritually. Most of the men had backed away from this "uncut stone," concluding the desert was no place to confront a prophet.

The physician, although easygoing in attitude, was intensely disciplined. Up each morning before the rest of us were out of our sleeping bags, he would run eight to ten miles across the desert sand before the sun got too hot. Then came the day when he told our guide he would run on ahead of the truck while the rest of us swam in an oasis near what was then the Egyptian border.

By the time the truck finally caught up with him ten miles later, several of the men in the group were worried. He had not taken a canteen and was running without the protection of a shirt—which is sheer folly in the desert. When we finally caught up with him, running happily along the Gulf of Suez in Egyptian territory, even I was relieved.

When the doctor climbed into the truck, however, the minister exploded in a fury of condemnation. What right did he have, the minister wanted to know, to leave the group in such a dangerous locale? In addition, the minister thought running was an unhealthy obsession, and he proceeded to tell him so in pointed terms.

The air was tense. I sensed a confrontation brewing between these two rough stones—a confrontation that could be painful to all of us since we were all thrust together in this venture.

That night around the campfire, several of the men told the minister he had lacked tact in his remarks on the truck. That led to a rehash of what had happened. The doctor apologized for scaring everyone, but said his running had merely become part of his lifestyle; it wasn't an obsession.

Unfortunately, this didn't satisfy the minister who, true to his prophetic calling, wanted to point out a few other faults he had noticed. The group took this for a few minutes and finally the doctor, in a straightforward manner, looked across the campfire at the minister.

"I am not nearly as concerned for you as I am for your wife. She must have to go through hell living with you."

It was like pouring gunpowder on a smoldering fire. Not since Moses cursed the followers of Korah had the desert heard such a reaction as we experienced that night around the campfire.

Finally one of the men told the minister that he had no right to dish out criticism unless he could also take it. He pointed out that the minister had just reacted in a way he had said was wrong for others.

The confrontation between the two was a watershed for our trip. The minister was more subdued during the rest of the time in the desert. The doctor was more careful to stay with the group. And the fact that the group had participated in that open confrontation brought everyone closer. Instead of being just a group of American men on a trip to the Sinai, we became a body of believers—uncut stones fitted together by the hand of God to form an altar pleasing to Him.

It was this same wilderness lesson Moses finally learned, and eventually taught to his followers. God does not want us all to look alike, behave alike, even believe alike. But He does want us to get along together without trying to fashion ourselves in the image of others, or trying to force others into our own image.

Shortly after the people left Mt. Sinai on their way north to Kadesh-Barnea, Moses called seventy men out of the tribes and ordained them as spiritual elders over the entire nation. The ordination service was held in the outer court of the tabernacle, but two men for some unknown reason missed the service. Eldad and Medad remained in the camping area. When the Spirit of God fell on the other 68 men, however, and they began to prophesy, the same phenomenon happened to Eldad and Medad on the other side of the campground.

A young man came running to Moses: "Eldad and Medad are prophesying in the camp."

Immediately Joshua, a bit jealous that the rules were being bent, objected. And Moses replied sternly, "Are you jealous for my sake? I wish that all the Lord's people were prophets and that the Lord would put His Spirit on them!" (Numbers 11:26-29).

Eldad and Medad were uncut stones, and Moses knew better than to try to hew them into his (or Joshua's) image. If God wanted to use them even though they did not fit the mold, that was God's business, not his.

It is this individualistic nature that has kept God's word alive and burning in the hearts of men across the centuries. Men such as Theodor Herzl, Eliezer Ben Yehuda and David Ben Gurion kept the dream of the Jewish nation alive in the hearts of men, even though they were viewed by most around them as uncut stones. Others, often cast as misfits in society— men such as John Hus, Martin Luther, John Wesley, and a host of contemporary uncut stones—have been instrumental in spreading the gospel of the Kingdom, despite their strange ways and sometimes odd behavior. Surely it is this concept the Lord wants kept alive in all of us!

I have in the front of my Bible a note I scribbled to myself a number of years ago that reminds me of God's purpose in my own life. It says simply, "Jamie, don't let the world—or the institutional church—fashion you into its mold."

The Lord reveals to those who walk through tough times that true worship of Him is never relegated to the places of hewn stone. Much later Jesus mentioned this same principle when He spoke to a Samaritan woman drawing water from Jacob's well near the little town of Sychar. "Our fathers worshiped on this mountain," she said, pointing to the top of nearby Mt. Gerazim, "but you Jews claim that the place where we must worship is in Jerusalem."

Jesus answered prophetically when He said, "A time is coming and has now come when the true worshipers will worship the Father in spirit and truth, for they are the kind of worshipers the Father seeks. God is spirit, and his worshipers must worship in spirit and in truth" (John 4:19-24).

The wilderness teaches us that God is not so interested in rules as He is in relationships. It is true that God puts conditions on His beloved and limitations on His children. But as we walk with Him through the wilderness, we gradually get our eyes off His rules and onto His face.

The Israelites had been in slavery for ten generations. Now they were free, but in their newfound freedom they became freewheeling. They said, "We can do anything we want." God therefore put severe restrictions on them—not to destroy their creativity, but to channel it into productive areas. Very patiently, very gently, He brought them to Himself. He showed them that in order to have complete freedom they had to be a people under authority, for true happiness comes only when we are in submission to God, and to one another.

Later in God's history, we find the Law was not meant to be an end, but a means to a greater end. The Ten Commandments, although they are not to be flaunted, were given primarily to reveal the character and nature of God. If all we do is try to keep the rules, we will ever be in slavery. But if we use the rules to move in closer to God, then we discover the laws are not chains that hold us down but guideposts that describe the character of a God who wants to reveal Himself to us.

The problem is not whether we work on the Sabbath, but

rather, What kind of God is He? What is He like? Why does He tell us to rest?

God is like our father, so we honor our father and mother.

God gives us life, so we do not murder.

God owns all things, so we do not steal.

God hallows marriage, so we do not commit adultery.

That is the purpose of the commandments—to reveal God. It is not doing what He says that brings life; it is abiding in His presence that keeps us alive.

God told Moses, therefore, "Build Me altars of unshaped stones. Each worshiper is precious to Me, regardless of shape or color. I love them, sharp edges and all, and can use them to build a Kingdom, if you let Me do the fitting."

"As you come to him," Peter said centuries later, "the living Stone—rejected by men but chosen by God and precious to him—you also, like living stones, are being built into a spiritual house to be a holy priesthood, offering spiritual sacrifices acceptable to God through Jesus Christ" (I Peter 2:4-5).

"The power of sin is the law," the apostle Paul said, referring to man's tendency to force everything into a mold. "But thanks be to God! He gives us the victory through our Lord Jesus Christ" (I Corinthians 15:56-57).

XVI

Silence

*"When my glory passes by, I will put you in a cleft in the rock
and cover you with my hand."*

(Exodus 33:22)

The most awesome aspect of the desert, perhaps the most
terrifying aspect, is its total silence.

No place on earth is as silent as the Sinai. To those of us
surrounded by noise, who have grown accustomed to the
"madding crowd," the silence of the desert quickly becomes a
fearsome thing.

For most people, silence creates a nervousness, an anxiety
that forces us to seek noise; and if we do not find it, to create it.
To some, silence becomes a gaping abyss that swallows us up,
forcing us to turn inward to the even more awesome wilderness of self-understanding and self-revelation. To others, silence is the playground of our demons, which we keep fenced
in only by our much talking and much activity. To grow silent
opens the gates. Thus we fear the silence and go to great
lengths to escape it.

We live in a society tormented by words, both spoken and
written. The resulting inward noise remains, echoing through
the chambers of our minds long after the shouting and whis-
pering have ceased. Words form the floors, walls and ceilings
of our thoughts. Indeed, we cannot think without them. They
come at us from electronic boxes, from signboards, from the
printed page, from jangling telephones, from pulpits, bump-

er stickers and magazines. They form the houses of our existence.

One writer relates that driving through a large city he suddenly had the strange sensation of driving through a huge dictionary. Everywhere he looked there were words saying, "Use me, take me, buy me, drink me, eat me, smell me, touch me, kiss me, sleep with me." These words have nested like parasites in every nook and cranny of our existence. They suck the life from us while deceiving us into believing we cannot live without them. To think conceptually, without letting our minds form the ideas into paragraphs and sentences, is an art lost to the Western world.

To soothe these words, we accompany them with music. If we are not singing them, we use music to back them up, to make them more palatable to our jangled spirits. Prayers in church are accompanied by background music. Soap is sold with a tune. Armies march to the sound of fife and drum. Drama on television and the screen always seems incomplete without the ever-present background of strings, brass and woodwinds. The dentist pulls our teeth to Muzak. We buy our clothing to the soft sound of violins and harps. We take our seats on the airlines to the accompaniment of melodies piped in through the "sound system." We have wedding music, funeral dirges, lullabies and music for every season. It is a marvelous world of harmonic sound—all composed to fill the silence we so fear.

Even without our words and music, there is still noise. The clanking of machinery, the whir of gadgets, the roar of the wind, the crashing of the surf, the buzz of insects day and night. There are street noises, factory noises, swamp and forest noises. There is the cawing of crows and the mooing of cows, the swish of wind through the grass, the crackling of the fire, the splashing of rain, the creaking of the floor, the sighs of lovers and the patter of tiny feet. All the world is full of sound.

But the desert is silent. Here there are no insects, no chirping katydids, no croaking frogs. Even the wind is silent as it blows noiselessly across the barren sand. The silence is so loud it is frightening. Yet it is here, in the silence, that God speaks loudest.

Elijah experienced this during his stay on Mt. Sinai. Having fled for his life, he arrived exhausted and despondent. Collapsing near a spring in a high mountain oasis halfway up the steep ascent to the summit, the troubled prophet had to wait until the wind, earthquake and fire of his inner man was quieted before he was able to hear the still, small voice of God.

Vivid in my memory is a chilly November night spent at the base of Mt. Sinai. Although I had spent many nights in the desert, this was my first time to sleep at the base of the Mountain of God at the 4,000-foot level. That night, although the temperature dropped below freezing, I lay on my back in my sleeping bag, my hands folded beneath my head to cushion it from the pebbly rocks, and stared upward at the unbelievable canopy of stars overhead. The outline of Jebel Musa—Mt. Moses—was an awesome granite shadow against the glistening black of the sky with its billions of flashing pinpoints of yellow and green. It was cold—and silent. I remembered something an old monk had written, hundreds of years before, of his first experience in the Sinai: "It is the silence that speaks the loudest."

That night, looking up into the magnificent display of God's creation in the heavens, a cosmorama that yet defies description, I, too, experienced the silence of Moses and Elijah—an outer silence that only accented the noise within. It started when I heard, for the first time in my life, my own heart pumping blood through my veins. Turning my head, I could hear the bones of my neck rasping together. But it was the deeper noise that caused the ultimate distraction. The moans of things left behind. The clatter of anxiety for things to come. The ping of guilt. The rumble of fears. The sigh of memories. The tearing sound of homesickness. That night, at the base of the holy mountain, I understood why God had to keep Moses alone for forty days and nights before Moses could hear Him speak. For God speaks in silence, and silence is hard to come by.

Earlier, when Moses made his descent from the mountain, his arrival in the camp of the Israelites was heralded by discordant sound. The people had in his absence created a golden calf to fill the void. The noise was the sound of their idol worship.

When Moses returned to the Mountain of God, after having

destroyed the golden calf and smashed the covenant stones, he had to wait another forty days and nights before he could once again hear God. His spirit, too, had been polluted by the clashing of ideas, his silence broken by the sounds of sin. To enter into that place of holiness where God abides—the place of absolute silence—once again he had to allow his spirit to be purged of sound. For the inner man is constantly tormented by noise.

"Be still before the Lord," Zechariah warned all mankind, ". . . because he has roused himself from his holy dwelling" (Zechariah 2:13).

"Be silent before the Sovereign Lord," echoed Zephaniah (Zephaniah 1:7).

It is silence that gives meaning to the Word of God. Someone has said the Bible is the Word of God rather than the words of God. This is so, for in grasping the Word we begin to hear His words, spoken in the silence of our own hearts.

The desert fathers, those early hermits who fled to the Sinai in the third and fourth centuries to seek personal salvation, were in reality trying to escape from the noise of the world. Although they eventually died away—for their purpose of living was all inward with little understanding of the need to share—they did leave one valid contribution. They taught us the value of silence. Somehow they believed they could best find God in silence—and knew of no place more silent than the Sinai.

There is a delightful story about one of those early hermit leaders who had moved to the desert in the third century. His name was Abbot Macarius. When he had finished blessing his small group of desert dwellers, he said to them, "Brethren, flee." One of the men, puzzled, asked, "How can we fly further than this, seeing we are here in the desert?" Macarius looked at him. Placing his finger on his mouth, he said, "Flee from this." It was his personal vow of silence. He then turned, entered his small cell carved from the rock and shut the door. It was his way of saying what the prophet had said long before him: "The Lord is in his holy temple; let all the earth be silent before him" (Habakkuk 2:20).

"I have often repented of having spoken," Abbot Arsenius said, "but never of having remained silent."

It was this same concept that motivated Benedict, the father of monastic life. He put great emphasis on silence as a way of life, believing that only when the human heart was stilled could the still, small voice be heard. Benedict went on to warn his followers against not only evil talk, but against all talk. Speaking when one should remain silent could quickly lead one away from God and into the path of calling attention to self. Like the desert fathers, he believed that "every conversation tended to interest them in this world, to make them less of strangers and more of citizens."

St. John of the Cross used to refer to the times when his "house was all stilled." During this process, the emotional, psychological, physical, even spiritual dwellers all sat down and grew quiet. All distractions ceased and God finally spoke.

The Way of Silence is foreign to those of us who work with words, whose lives are spent communicating on a horizontal level. Yet Moses discovered that when he was silent vertically, he was then able to speak before the people. It's sad, but what many speakers hope to be their finest hour—ministering to the multitudes—is often the time of greatest emptiness for speaker as well as listener. Yet when we wait silently before God, we often come away refreshed, the fire of our inner man refueled, able to say in few words what would have ordinarily taken hours.

One of these early hermits, Abbot Agatho, carried a stone in his mouth for three years until he learned to be silent. A modern mystic, Henri Nouwen, writes: "As soon as we begin to take hold of each other by our words, and use words to defend ourselves or offend others, the world no longer speaks of silence. But when the word calls for the healing and restoring stillness of its own silence, few words are needed and much can be said without much being spoken."

Silence is often equated—or at least linked in our minds—with darkness. Yet men of wisdom have learned, as Moses did on Mt. Sinai, that God dwells in the darkness. When God called Moses to the summit of the mountain to receive the Law, the entire mountain was covered with a thick cloud. As Moses ascended, he disappeared from sight to the people watching from below. The cloud grew darker until he was in total darkness. Yet here he found God. This was later confirmed by the shepherd king, David, who discovered that even the darkness is not dark to God. Indeed, "the night will shine like the day, for darkness is as light to you" (Psalm 139:12).

Perhaps this cannot be fully understood unless you, too, have walked in the darkness of the wilderness. Surely this is one of the great purposes of our wilderness experience, to teach us the value of total silence—to train us to listen to the still, small voice of God and to feel His presence in the darkness. Here in the wilderness, we discover that even the valley of the shadow of death holds no fear, "for thou art with me."

One afternoon I inquired of that lovable old Dutch saint Corrie ten Boom about the silence and the darkness of God. Years before, when she was 50 years of age, she had been forced into a Nazi concentration camp. There her old father and dear sister died horrible deaths. Yet out of that wilderness she learned the truth of Psalm 91:1: "He that dwelleth in the secret place of the most High shall abide under the shadow of the Almighty" (KJV).

She was 80 when I talked to her. "Even though we are to walk in the light with our brothers and sisters," she told me, "there comes a time, as you draw close to God, that you are consumed with darkness. This is true when you are abiding in the shadow. The closer you get to God, the less you understand Him. In the darkness of His presence, under the shadow of the Almighty, we learn to believe."

It is the difference between sight and faith. Sight—knowledge—is the breeding ground for noise and words. Faith, however, calls for silence. There we do not speak. This is the reason many men of faith are men of few words. What they have experienced defies description. It must be experienced, lived, not communicated.

Faith, we are often told, is not taught; it is caught.

In the thirty-third chapter of Exodus, there is a marvelous parenthetical story that describes the lesson Moses learned on Mt. Sinai. After descending from the mountain of darkness, and before the tabernacle became the official "tent of meeting" where man and God had their conversations, Moses had his own little place of silence. It was a small tent that he pitched outside the camp, some distance away from the mob of Israelites with all their noise. It was his version of what Jesus was later to describe as a "prayer closet." To Moses, it was his own "tent of meeting." When Moses would go outside the camp and enter this little tent, the pillar of cloud would come down and stay at the entrance. There, in total silence, the Lord spoke to Moses. It was their way of recreating the experience on Mt. Sinai.

"Whenever the people saw the pillar of cloud standing at the entrance to the tent, they all stood and worshiped, each at the entrance to his [own] tent." Then, when all the camp grew silent, "the Lord would speak to Moses face to face, as a man speaks with his friend" (Exodus 33:7-11).

It was during one of these long, solitary sessions that God told Moses, "My Presence will go with you, and I will give you rest" (Exodus 33:14).

Moses could contain himself no longer. Racing from the tent, he clambered up the side of the huge mountain that towered over the Israelites as they camped on the er Rakha plain at the base of Mt. Sinai. Panting more from exhilaration than exhaustion, he finally reached the top. There, standing far above all earthly sound where even the wind blowing in mighty gusts was freezingly silent, Moses lifted his voice and cried out to God: "Now show me your glory!"

The biblical description of this encounter between God and His servant is as electrifying as the static electricity that often sparks around the top of Mt. Sinai. I remember one cold winter morning, having ascended to the summit of that same mountain, standing with three companions and suddenly realizing that every hair on our bodies was standing straight out. When we reached out to touch each other, sparks jumped from our fingertips. Even our clothes seemed lifted away from our skin, so powerful was the electrical charge between the low-hanging clouds and the great granite and flint mountain.

It must have been that way when Moses, his heart aflame with a fire that threatened to consume him unless God responded, cried out to his Lord.

Perhaps it was this consuming passion that impressed God. Perhaps it was the fact that Moses had removed himself from the people and, in silence, wanted to see the face of God for no other reason than to see the face of God. Whatever the reason,

God's response was one of total elation. It was as if He Himself had thrown all caution to the winds as He answered: "I will cause all my goodness to pass in front of you, and I will proclaim my name, the Lord, in your presence."

Then, realizing He was about to offer something to Moses that would literally consume him, which no man could comprehend, He backed off. "But," He said, "you cannot see my face, for no one may see me and live."

He then directed Moses to a place on the mountain. "There is a place near me where you may stand on a rock. When my glory passes by, I will put you in a cleft in the rock and cover you with my hand until I have passed by. Then I will remove my hand and you will see my back; but my face must not be seen" (cf. Exodus 33:12-23).

It was as close as any man in history would come to seeing the face of God, until God's Son, Jesus the Messiah, would appear to reveal Jehovah in all His glory. Of Jesus, the apostle Paul said, "For God was pleased to have all his fullness dwell in him," and, "For in Christ all the fullness of the Deity lives in bodily form" (Colossians 1:19; 2:9).

Moses returned from his encounter with God a man of few words. Yet something had happened inside him. His face literally glowed with the glory of God—a shine that was so great he had to actually wear a veil to keep from being conspicuous. The words he did speak, however, were words of great power.

Words rooted in the soil of God are words that have emerged from the silence and lead us back into that silence.

Silence, we have been told, is emptiness. But in our walk through the wilderness, as we close our door on the shouts of men, the clashing of ideas, the clamor of things, even the music of praise, we find that silence is not emptiness, but Fullness and Presence. Here we get a glimpse of the great mystery of God—the mystery of God's own speaking.

Out of the silence and darkness of the past, God spoke the Word and through this Word created heaven and earth. As it was in the past, so it shall be in the future. For when the final seal—the seventh seal—was broken in John's revelation of things to come, "there was silence in heaven for about half an hour." Only when that silence was complete, and God's awesome mystery fully comprehended, was the angel allowed to approach the golden altar before the throne with the spoken prayers of the saints. Only after the silence were the seven angels allowed, one at a time, to put the trumpets to their lips to sound the blast that heralded the advent of the establishment of God's eternal Kingdom. Words may be the instruments of this present world, but silence is the mystery of the future world, and heralds the presence of God (cf. Revelation 8).

Hours before sunrise, after that awesome, silent experience at the base of Mt. Sinai, our small group of men arose to begin the three-hour climb to the summit. Our desire was to climb the mountain the way God had told Moses to do it. "Be ready in the morning, and then come up on Mount Sinai. Present yourself to me there on top of the mountain" (Exodus 34:2).

It was 3 a.m., and in order to reach the top by dawn, we had to climb in the dark. The night before, I had arranged for a young Bedouin boy, no more than twelve years old, who knew the path, to guide us up in the pre-dawn hours.

We began our climb in the chilly darkness. Feeling our way over the rocks, we finally reached the ancient camel path to the summit. The stars were brilliant, and I soon realized, as my eyes adjusted to the dim light, that there was enough light for the climb if we moved slowly, deliberately toward the peak—still another 3,500 feet above us.

All the men had flashlights. They crowded close together, on each other's heels, as they stumbled upwards. Falling over rocks, bumping their shins, they called out to each other words of caution.

Something was wrong. Mt. Sinai should be climbed as Moses climbed it, in silence. I stopped our young guide and called the men around me on the path.

"Put your flashlights away," I said. "Now stand still for a few moments. You'll find you will soon develop a night sight that will allow you to see in the darkness with the aid of the stars."

Then I asked them to space themselves several hundred feet apart and begin the ascent again, one at a time, in total silence. "For most of you, this will be your only opportunity to climb the Mountain of God. Do not spoil the moment by talking about inane things. Be silent. Let God speak to you as you climb."

So we did, each man climbing at his own speed up the steep path. As our eyes grew accustomed to the starlight, the rocks and mountains began to take shape around us. We could see the steep precipices beside the trail, falling off hundreds of feet into the valleys below. But there was ample light to see the entire panorama of the Sinai as it spread out before us with each ascending step. High above us, its craggy peak rearing in awesome grandeur against the starlit sky, was the summit of Mt. Sinai. In the silence God began to speak to my heart, just as He has to all men who dare the risky walk of faith.

In the thin cold air I walked silently, the only noise the crunch of my feet on the rocks. With each step in the darkness, it seemed His Spirit touched another tender area of my life, bringing revelation and healing. My heart was consumed with joy. I paused, listening in the silence, looking out over the dark mountaintops of the entire southern peninsula. Moses had stood here, hearing this same voice, looking forward to the perfect revelation of God through His Son which I now looked back upon. I could almost feel the glory of God in the moment. I breathed deeply. Silently. And moved on up the path.

I was far ahead of the group, and at one place I rounded a dark bend in the trail and could see, stretched out below me on the winding path, the dim figures of the twelve men, fellow pilgrims, spaced along the trail far below. Then I saw something else. The last two men had grown discouraged. They had turned on their flashlights and were climbing by artificial light. Unlike the rest of us, their sight was limited to the small circle of light in front of them. They could not see what I saw— the heavens, the majestic mountain peaks, the saw-toothed ranges stretching out toward the eastern sky that was now turning a pale rose against the black, heralding the coming of the sun. All they could see was that small circle of yellow light in front of them. The others, although they were walking in darkness, could see the entire landscape, even though on occasion they stumbled over the small rocks before them.

I was sad. The two men with flashlights would reach the summit and enjoy the sunrise along with the rest of us. But they were missing the greater glory that came by climbing by starlight. With their conversation, although muted and whispered, they were drowning out the voice of God that spoke to all the others in a profound and personal way.

There is a time, it seems, in our walk through the wilderness, that we must risk walking in darkness and silence. It is at this time we must take our understanding and comprehension of things as they seem, fold it into our backpack and walk with only the hand of God guiding us.

That is the lesson of the silence in the wilderness.

XVII

Solitude

*Then Moses entered the cloud as he went on up the mountain.
And he stayed on the mountain forty days and forty nights.*
(Exodus 24:18)

There are times when a man needs his family and his
friends around him—to comfort him, affirm him, correct him
or heal him. But there are other times when each of us needs to
be alone, totally withdrawn from all human voice or presence,
separated from the world in solitude with God.

Whereas silence is passive, solitude is an act of seeking and
finding that place of aloneness. Deep inside, all of us seem to
know intuitively that until we withdraw from all we consider
necessary to our comfort, we will not come face-to-face with
God. It is that nagging truth that keeps driving me back into
the desert. It is that same truth that has sustained me as I have
walked through my own inner wilderness.

Only in times and places of solitude do men have genuine
confrontation. Jacob was a family man, surrounded by wives,
concubines, children, kinsmen, handmaids, warriors and
workers. But there came a time in his life when he realized he
could no longer hide from himself. Sending everyone ahead,
he knelt one night beside the Brook Jabbok and entered into
solitude. There ensued that night a great battle as Jacob
wrestled with a heavenly being. As dawn approached and it
was evident Jacob's stubbornness had not yielded, the angel
started to leave. But Jacob, realizing he was fighting against

146

something he desperately needed, cried out, "I will not let you go unless you bless me" (Genesis 32:26).

The blessing came in the form of a hip deformity. From that time on, Isaac's younger son walked with a limp. But his life, as well as his name, was changed. No longer was he called *Jacob*, the manipulator. Now he was called *Israel*—one who wrestled with God, and lost.

When our wrestling is alone, as with Jacob at the Brook Jabbok, we come to understand the real battles we face are not with others, but with self—and with God. Only then do we understand that the purpose of the wilderness is not to break us, but to soften us so we may be molded into the image of God's Son. For God does not want broken men, only men who are yielded.

For this reason, however, we fear solitude even as we fear silence. As soon as we are alone, without people to talk to, books to read, TV to watch or phone calls to make, an inner chaos opens in us, threatening to swallow us like ships caught in a giant whirlpool. Thus we do everything we can to keep from having to be alone. We create activity involving others, we spend long nights in bars, we latch onto unhealthy relationships or create situations that demand others come to us. We feign need or sickness or, using some kind of twisted reverse psychology, stalk away from people hoping someone will come running after us. "Do not leave me alone!" is the cry of every lonely heart. And "solitary confinement" is considered the worst of all punishments man can mete to man.

Yet Moses, Elijah, David and Jesus—and millions of others who have walked through the wilderness—discovered that solitude is not a curse but a blessing. It is not something to be feared but a treat to be desired.

Over and over we read that Moses went alone—into the desert, up a mountain, into his little "tent of meeting"—and there he met God. In solitude we become present to ourselves. There we can live, as Anne Morrow Lindbergh says, "like a child or a saint in the immediacy of here and now." In solitude every act is a desert oasis, standing apart from the burning sand of our pilgrimage. Cleared from the encumbrances of time and space, we relish each sense. Here in this wonderful oasis, we are free to drink the water, rest in the shade, taste the delicacy of each fruit and reflect on the meaning of God and self. Solitude does not pull us away from our fellow human beings, but instead makes real fellowship possible in the right time and the right place.

Thomas Merton, who spent the last years of his life as a hermit, said his contemplative solitude brought him into intimate contact with others. In his diary he wrote: "It is in deep solitude that I find the gentleness with which I can truly love my brothers. The more solitary I am, the more affection I have for them. It is pure affection and filled with reverence for the solitude of others."

Merton, of course, was right. It needs to be mentioned, however, that while solitude brings us into encounter with God, the lack of conflict with brothers and sisters, the absence of "rubbing," often presents a false image of true love—a love without confrontation.

Solitude, however, does not separate us from those we truly love, but brings us instead into deep communion with them—even though we may not see them for long periods of time. It teaches us to respect the solitude of others. We do not go crashing in every time we see someone alone, feeling we must provide company, for we realize that to do so might interrupt the deepest communion one can have—communion with God and with self.

Yet the mere thought of having to spend time alone is terrifying to most of us. To be sent into a wilderness is bad enough, but to be sent alone is more than we can bear. We seem to realize that when we are alone, we are forced to face ourselves—and to face God. We use outer distractions, therefore, to shield ourselves from the interior noises, and from the awesome voice of God. Thus it is not surprising most of us do not like to be alone, or when we are alone, fill the time with mind-occupying activities. The confrontation with our inner conflicts is too painful to endure.

Jesus, however, told us: "When you pray, go into your room, close the door and pray to your Father, who is unseen" (Matthew 6:6).

This concept of the "prayer closet" is the thing that keeps many of us from praying at all, or at least limits our prayers to those we utter in public. For we know that entering a private room and shutting the door does not mean we leave all our doubts, fears, guilts, memories, angers and insecurities behind. Indeed, it means we often bring them with us into our prayer closet where, since they have no room to swirl around us, they come crashing down on top of us, forcing us to face them.

It is for precisely this reason Jesus said we should often pray alone. How else can we get honest with ourselves? How else can we hear the voice of God?

Although the desert fathers were men of solitude, they were also hermits, and as a result became parasites upon others who had to feed and protect them. This is the primary reason they died out. There was no sustained effort at reproduction. Thus, while their experiences teach us much of the value of silence and solitude, only a few of the desert fathers are worthy to be singled out as models for others making their way through the wilderness.

One of these was Abbot Anthony. After working as a poor laborer in Egypt in the middle of the third century, Anthony withdrew into the desert, where he lived for twenty years in complete solitude. During that time his worldly shell was cracked and the abyss of iniquity opened to him. But because of his unconditional surrender to Jesus Christ, he emerged from the desert a changed man.

The fact that he emerged qualifies him as a model. Most hermits entered the desert to remain the rest of their lives. But Anthony felt the lessons learned in solitude should be shared with others. This made him a pilgrim as well as a hermit. Even though he returned to his hermitage in his old age, he first shared with others all he learned from his prior walk with God. During this time people flocked to him, recognizing spiritual wholeness and the ability to minister healing, comfort and direction for other sincere seekers. All this came as a result of his solitude. Returning to his cave in the Sinai, Anthony died in the year 356 A.D. at the age of 106.

The story of Anthony shows that solitude can become the crucible in which genuine transformation can take place. Moses had no time for God as long as he was active in the courts of Pharaoh in Egypt. Only when he was thrust into the furnace of the wilderness did he learn to listen. Alone, he discovered what his heart had so long been searching for in various companionships. He discovered God.

There are three basic things that keep us from solitude: insecurity, greed and anger. Like spiritual handcuffs, these forces manacle us to the presence of other people, preventing us from drawing aside long enough to face ourselves, or to come face-to-face with God.

Insecurity stems from not knowing who we are in Jesus Christ. Our poor self-image is fortified by the fear our sin will always dominate our lives. We refuse to believe the Word of God, which states clearly our position as sons and daughters of God. Since no one wants to continually face a sinner, we keep others around us so we can point out their sins and not have to face ourselves in solitude.

Our insecurity demands continual affirmation. Who am I? I am one who needs to be liked, needs to be praised, needs to be admired, needs to be touched. Or perhaps I need to be hated, need to be rejected, need to be held up as a poor example. Always there is fear lurking that we are failures, that if the onion of our life is peeled away, the inner core will be empty. So we refuse to get alone, afraid we might meet ourselves and not like who we meet.

Greed and anger are the sour fruit of our dependencies upon people, rather than our dependency upon God. Anger is that bitter response to the experience of being deprived of something. Depending always upon what others think of us, we react with anger when someone criticizes us. Likewise, if our dependency is on what we have rather than who we are, then when we cannot acquire what we want, greed takes over and we demand more. Insecurity, anger and greed are evil deputies chaining us to depend upon others for our identity, rather than allowing us the privilege of slipping away alone into the presence of God.

But when we enter the furnace of solitude, all that is burned from us. Without solitude, we remain victims of a society that forces us to look to others for meaning. Jesus entered the furnace of solitude immediately following His baptism. He was "led by the Spirit into the desert to be tempted by the devil" (Matthew 4:1). Like Moses, He was alone in that desert place for forty days and nights. In His case, His aloneness brought Him face-to-face, not with His Father but with His archenemy, the devil.

Three times He was tempted in the areas of Everyman's compulsions: insecurity, greed and anger. He was offered the kingdoms of this world; He was tempted to test God; He was tempted to turn stones into bread. In each case, Jesus answered out of personal security and a solid self-image. He knew who He was. When the lengthy time of solitude was over, He emerged "in the power of the Spirit" ready to begin His ministry of miracles.

Jesus, like Moses, found solitude to be a place of great struggle and great encounter. It was the place of struggle against the lies and accusations of false identity, and it brought an encounter with a holy God who loved Him enough not to make the way easy.

This struggle is often called the *agonia*. This is the classic struggle that every man must undergo to realize his full potential. It encompasses this eternal question: What is God trying to do in and through me by way of suffering?

In the New Testament, we find Jesus took this suffering and conquered it for us—not to prevent us from experiencing our own *agonia*, but as we carry our cross with Jesus to experience what Paul described as "the fellowship of sharing in his sufferings" (Philippians 3:10). It is this suffering that allows us to "attain to the resurrection from the dead" (Philippians 3:11), rising with Him to the full and perfect life He offers. As Augustine reminded us, "God's glory is man fully alive."

St. John of the Cross, the ancient mystic, described the *agonia* as "the dark night of the soul." Such suffering is not endured in the presence of others—only in solitude. It is in solitude we experience "the fellowship of sharing in his sufferings." If we attempt to do this in a group, then our fellowship invariably becomes horizontal rather than vertical, and we are able to rise only to the level of the group, not to the resurrection of Christ.

Yet it is this process of suffering alone, in solitude, that purifies us and produces fullness in our spirits accompanied by divine union between God and man. The dark night of solitude brings us to a hush, a stillness that enables the Holy Spirit to work His inner transformation. Like the oyster, which reacts to the grain of irritating sand by covering it with a hard substance, so the fellowship of sharing Christ's sufferings produces in us a pearl of great price, even though it may be evidenced only when men see us walking with a limp.

In our relationships with others, therefore, we must be careful not to remove a suffering God has placed on a man until the object of that suffering is complete—else we may deprive him of the pearl being formed in his soul.

In solitude the outer shell is pulled away and the true man emerges. Yet it is this true man most of us fear. We fear he may be another Moses, destined to spend his life in the wilderness—and we quickly force him back into the shell lest he grab us by the hand and take us with him. When we are alone, therefore, instead of facing the true man, we send in our servants of imagination and fantasy to clothe him in outlandish costumes. We send him out on imaginary journeys to exotic places, always to return and tickle our fancy with his exploits.

We picture him, not at all as he is but as we imagine him to be: wealthy, powerful, feared; or perhaps ugly, poor and dying. Seldom, if ever, do we allow him to emerge as the pearl he really is—a man of God fashioned by our own suffering and empowered by Christ to resurrection life. Therefore we often spend (or rather waste) our precious moments of solitude struggling with a never-ending effort to convince ourselves of our unrighteousness (or of our virtue), without daring to face ourselves—and God—naked and unadorned.

Looking at Moses, however, alone in his little tent of meeting, camping out on the Mountain of God, herding his sheep and goats through the empty wadis of the desert, we discover that it was this literal solitude that brought him face-to-face with the living God. Solitude is thus the place of purification and transformation, the place of struggle and encounter. It is the place where God remodels us in His own image and frees us from the images of self we all bring with us when we enter the wilderness.

While solitude should become a way of life, it should not lead to the extreme of constant aloneness. That was the mistake of the hermits. God wants us in families. He commands we should not forsake assembling ourselves together. Solitude, rather, is a matter of the heart—an inner disposition that allows us to enter our "prayer closet" at any moment, whether we are among others or not. It is Paul's concept of being in a state of constant prayer. It does not mean we must chase everyone from our lives or enter our cell and close the door forever. It does mean we will practice discipline as Jesus did when He, on regular occasions, stole away from His disciples and got alone with God.

Every pilgrim needs, as Moses did, a little "tent of meeting" where he can shut out all the world and commune with his Father "as a man speaks with his friend." But while the times of physical aloneness are desirable—even necessary—those who learn the real lesson of solitude realize it is found in the peaceful hearts of those who have entered into rest.

There is a vast difference, of course, between solitude and loneliness. While loneliness is inner emptiness, solitude is inner fulfillment. As loneliness is not healed by companionship, however, neither does solitude become beneficial simply because one is alone. The lonely person has no inner time or inner rest to wait and listen. He wants answers to his overpowering questions, solutions to his constant problems. But in true solitude, we learn we can be alone and not lonely. In solitude we come face-to-face with the One who satisfies all our needs. It's not that He necessarily answers all our questions or solves all our problems. But when we are alone with Him, they just don't seem important anymore.

So we enter solitude, as Moses entered the darkness of the Mountain of God, with no other motive than to be alone with the Father. We do not enter in order to return and share what we have learned. If we do this, we will spend our solitude time taking notes on how to apply truth to the lives of others. No, we enter solitude as an end in itself, not a means to the end of sharing.

We enter solitude to seek the face of God, to commune with Him as friend to friend, to let Him speak to us about the deep things in our hearts, and with an utter contentment to remain in solitude forever if He so wills. It is only then God sends us back down the mountain to the people below who are struggling with the concepts of community, to teach them that only

as we come into His presence do we understand the true
meaning of living in the presence of others.

XVIII

On Eagles' Wings

"You yourselves have seen what I did to Egypt, and how I carried you on eagles' wings and brought you to myself."

(Exodus 19:4)

Some years ago Episcopal Bishop James Pike, at that time an elderly man, ventured with his wife into the rugged Judean wilderness—a desert not unlike areas of the southern Sinai. Separated from his wife, he wandered hopelessly lost for several days. His body was found at the bottom of a wadi where he had stumbled, fallen and died.

To be lost in the desert without a guide means almost certain death. The guide not only shows us the way, but knows where we can find food, water and shade. Anyone who ventures into the wilderness needs a guide—one who has been this way before.

Moses was such a guide for the children of Israel. For forty years he had lived in the wilderness of Sinai. He knew every wadi, every spring, every well. He knew which canyons had no outlet. He knew the caves of the enemy Amalekites. He knew the ways of the Bedouin. Without him, the Exodus would never have taken place.

The Israelites were a nation of slaves when they left Egypt. For almost four centuries they had been taking orders from slavemasters. They were tenderfeet when it came to the rugged kind of survival procedures necessary to stay alive on their own. Even though they grumbled and complained about their guide, they knew they could not survive without him.

Moses, on the other hand, was aware of his own shortcomings. He knew his knowledge was limited, and that he would need help himself. Such was the case as the children of Israel turned north from Mt. Sinai and headed toward the Promised Land. Although Moses knew the paths of the Sinai, he also knew he would soon run out of knowledge as they made their way north into the Negev Desert. It was then that an interesting occurrence took place.

Jethro, Moses' father-in-law, had visited him shortly before he reached Mt. Sinai. He had come to return Moses' wife, Zipporah, to her husband. He doubtless stayed with the Israelites while they were camped at er Rakha near the base of the mountain. He listened with approval as Moses put his advice into effect, dividing the governmental duties among other leaders. Then, as the cloud began to move once again and the Israelites started northward toward Kadesh-Barnea, Jethro and his sons bade Moses farewell. It was time to return to their flocks in Midian.

At this point Moses realized he was about to enter unknown territory. He assumed the cloud would pause for only a short time at Kadesh-Barnea, and then the Israelites would move through the Negev Desert into Canaan. Moses had never been that far north before. He needed expert help. He needed a guide.

He turned to Hobab, his brother-in-law who was an expert guide and tracker, and asked him to leave his father and travel with the Israelites as their scout. At first Hobab refused. He realized the children of Israel were on the move and to move with them would mean he could not return to Midian. But Moses persisted. "Please do not leave us. You know where we should camp in the desert, and you can be our eyes. If you come with us, we will share with you whatever good things the Lord gives us" (Numbers 10:29-32).

It was a marvelous offer, to include a foreigner in the inheritance. It is similar to the implied offer Naomi later made to her Moabitess daughter-in-law Ruth, who had begged, "Where you go I will go, and where you stay I will stay. Your people will be my people and your God my God. Where you die I will die, and there I will be buried" (Ruth 1:16-17).

Hobab consented, and he joined his family with Moses and the children of Israel. Later in the book of Judges and in I Samuel, we find reference to Hobab and his family as ones who inherited a permanent dwelling in the Promised Land (cf. Judges 1:16; I Samuel 15:6, 27:10, 30:29).

It was an interesting commentary on Moses' leadership. Although the pillar of cloud was the real guide of Israel during their journey northward, yet Hobab's local knowledge was of great use in locating the springs and places of pasture. He became "the eyes" of Moses, as he used his vast knowledge of the terrain for the glory of God.

While the leader is always dependent upon God's guidance in his trek across the wilderness, there is also the need of human assistance—spiritual directors, so to speak. The people followed Moses, but Moses leaned heavily upon Hobab who, although he appears as a minor character in the vast drama of the Exodus, was nevertheless as indispensable to the great hero as those unknown Indian scouts who helped the American pioneers with their wagon trains as they crossed the uncharted wilderness of the Wild West. Moses depended upon the best means that human skill and knowledge could suggest, yet he followed the overall guidance of the Lord.

At the same time, unlike the wagonmasters of the West, Moses' one consuming passion was not so much to reach the Promised Land but to teach the people to depend upon God as he depended upon Him. Moses knew the time was coming when he would die. He wanted the people to know how to use every spiritual resource at their disposal as they moved forward—including how to rely upon human resources such as men like Hobab, whom God would send along to help them. A "super-spiritual" leader might have refused the help of Hobab, saying he needed nothing but the pillar of cloud. But Moses was wise to the ways of the wilderness—and the ways of God. He recognized that even those things that seem natural and humanistic can be tools placed in the hands of a leader by God Himself to make the task easier.

This was the reason Moses turned southeast along the Gulf

of Suez when he left Egypt. The most direct route from Egypt to Canaan was across the northern Sinai—the *Via Maris*, sometimes known as "the way of the Philistines." As modern archaeologists have confirmed, however, there were numerous Egyptian military garrisons stationed throughout the areas of the north along the sea—as well as the fierce Philistines or desert barbarians. "Lest the people repent when they see war, and return to Egypt," Moses led them south toward Mt. Sinai. He knew that during the intervening months, before they finally reached Canaan, he would need to show them how to meet and know the Chief Guide—the Spirit of God who had spoken to him from the burning bush.

Before turning south, Moses paused on the shore of the sea and sang a ballad, recalling all the events connected with the escape from Egypt.

> "I will sing to the Lord,
>   for he is highly exalted.
> The horse and its rider
>   he has hurled into the sea."

(Exodus 15:1)

At the close of the song, his older sister, Miriam, picked up her tambourine and led the women of Israel in a dance of victory as they sang the refrain on the beach.

At the end of his life, Moses sang a second ballad. This one was much longer and more involved. Unlike the first song, it was not accompanied by dancing. In it, Moses emphasized that even though he had been the leader of Israel, it was God who had been their guide. Sensing he was about to die, he exhorted the people to "forget not" the Lord who had led them. In the ballad he compared the nation of Israel to a man lost in the wilderness without a guide.

> "In a desert land he found him,
>   in a barren and howling waste.
> He shielded him and cared for him;
>   he guarded him as the apple of his eye,
> like an eagle that stirs up its nest
>   and hovers over its young,

that spreads its wings to catch them
and carries them on its pinions.
The Lord alone led him;
no foreign god was with him."
(Deuteronomy 32:10-12)

Moses' reference to the eagle was in obedience to the first words God had spoken to him 39 years before as he stood on the summit of Mt. Sinai. "This is what you are to say to the house of Jacob and what you are to tell the people of Israel: 'You yourselves have seen what I did to Egypt, and how I carried you on eagles' wings and brought you to myself'" (Exodus 19:3-4).

Now, at the end of his life, Moses reminded his forgetful flock of the certainty of God's guidance. He warned them not to put their trust in man, but in God alone. All these years in the desert had been for one reason alone—to teach them how to follow God's guidance.

The eagle literally "rides the winds" of the desert, soaring high above the storms with effortless control. The Hebrew word for wind is *ruach*. It describes the harsh *sharav* that howls out of the west and, whipping across the hot sand, roars through the deep wadis. It is often accompanied by flashing lightning and rumbling thunder. *Ruach* speaks of the hot air thermals that boil up from the blistering sand, causing twisting tornados and destructive hail. Yet upon such a wind the eagle soars, high above the desert, until peace is restored.

Veterans of the desert have seen the mother eagle carrying her young as God described it to Moses. This magnificent bird builds her nest on the face of the cliff. The nest is never completely at the top where it might be violated by preying creatures, but it hangs at a precarious spot on the side of the precipice.

The nest is large, constructed of branches laced together with the skill of a crocheted blanket. The mother then lines it with her own feathers to make it soft. Finally she lays her eggs.

Once the eggs are hatched, the mother eagle begins the seemingly endless chore of supplying food for the hungry eaglets. They grow at an amazing rate. Then one day a traumatic event takes place. The mother eagle comes to the nest, not to feed her babies but to push them out. Using her great head, she shoves one bird at a time to the edge of the nest. Suddenly, with wildly flapping wings and tiny shrieks, the eaglet is hurtling down the face of the cliff to the floor of the wadi far below.

Just before he hits the earth, the mother eagle swoops down and under him. By instinct, he clutches at the feathers on her back. With tiny talons he holds on for dear life as she flies upward and returns him to the nest. Then, just as quickly, she repeats the process. Over and over it is down with each eaglet, until the time comes when they no longer need her. They have learned to fly on their own.

Such is the task of the true guide—not just to take us by the hand and lead us, but to teach us how to find the way for ourselves.

Late one afternoon, as our small group was making its way up the long traditional Pilgrim's Path—the Naqb el Hawa—to er Rakha, the huge plain that stretches out at the base of Mt. Sinai, we paused to make camp. Before us, rising abruptly and starkly from the plain, was the dramatic apex of the Mountain of God. Catching the setting sun with hues of pink and purple, it was a breathtaking sight to see.

None of the twelve men in the group talked much as we approached the base of the mountain. Before long each of us had separated to find our own quiet place. I climbed onto a huge boulder, still warm from the day's blistering heat, and stretched out on my back.

The sun, a scarlet fireball, was slowly sinking behind the rugged mountains of the southern peninsula. No human sounds interrupted. There was no movement but soft wind, no sound but the awesome sound of silence. The sky stretched out above me in a thin, washed blue, the air as buoyant as a cleansing stream. To the east, the evening star appeared as the sun slid lower behind the surrounding mountains, throwing its slanting light and shadow across the deepening purple landscape. New colors were teased out of the stones: tans, grays, browns, streaks of iron red, copper green mixed with ancient hues of bronze and rust.

I let my eyes wander to the peaks of the towering mountains around me—gaunt, treeless, now caught in the descending shadows as the sun dropped below their jagged reaches. Sunsets in the Sinai are not reflected in the sky, but on the earth. The first touch of evening's chill reminded me it would soon become too uncomfortable to remain on my stone pedestal, apart from my companions. I was grateful, I realized, for our guide, who had brought us to this beautiful place.

There drifted through my mind, on a gentle current, a verse from the Psalms: "I lift up my eyes to the hills—where does my help come from? My help comes from the Lord, the Maker of heaven and earth. He will not let your foot slip—he who watches over you will not slumber. . . . The Lord is your shade at your right hand; the sun will not harm you by day, nor the moon by night" (Psalm 121:1-6).

I thought of Moses—and of all the other Moseses I have known—who have trekked the lonely wilderness of the soul and returned to lead others to the land of promise. I thought, too, of the unknown Hobabs, who have led the leaders. Each of us, leader or follower, has had such a person in our life, a spiritual guide who has shown us the way.

God, I thought, is no longer preparing a dwelling place for His people. Now He is preparing a people for His dwelling place. In the wilderness, He purifies and cleanses—and provides a guide to take us through.

As I slid off my rock to join my friends at the campfire who were sitting down to a small dinner eaten from mess kits, I thought of an inscription I once read on a rock in Wadi Taba, just south of the modern city of Elat, only a few miles from the place where the children of Israel finished their journey out of the wilderness to enter the Promised Land. It could very well have been the place where Moses sang his final song.

The inscription was carved by an ancient guide who had led his pilgrims across the burning wilderness to their destination near the Gulf of Aqaba. It says:

I am the guide who not only knows the way, but knows the wells.

The true guide knows both—the path and the place of provision.

There is an ancient legend that originated in the desert, although it has long since been modernized. It is the story of an old desert traveler who looked back on his life in a dream. In the dream, he saw his footprints as he walked across the sandy wilderness of life. As he retraced his steps, he saw for the first time that he had been accompanied by a guide, for there were two sets of tracks. The second set belonged to the Lord, who had walked with him throughout his life.

But there were places in his life, difficult places he could recognize, where the second set of footprints disappeared. Recognizing these places in life as the places where he had experienced his deepest adversity—places of grief, despair and hopelessness—he cried out to the Lord.

"Why," he questioned, "did You leave me to walk alone during those times? It was then I needed You most."

"You don't understand, My child," the Lord replied gently. "I did not leave you in the difficult times. The reason you see only one set of footprints is that during those times I was carrying you."

"You have seen how I carried you on eagles' wings and brought you to myself."

XIX

Covenant Love

And they said to each other, "We should choose a leader and go back to Egypt."

(Numbers 14:4)

It is never God's intention to keep His children in the wilderness any longer than necessary. It took only eleven days for the Israelites to march from Sinai to Kadesh-Barnea. Here God intended the people to regroup after their forced march, feed their flocks, then go in and take the land He had promised them.

But history records they grew fainthearted at the last minute. Fearful they could not do what God commanded, they backed down. Surely it was the greatest disappointment in the life of Moses.

It never entered Moses' mind that the Israelites would do anything other than complete the march from Egypt to Sinai, receive the Law, and then follow God straight into the Promised Land. The idea that he would have to spend an additional forty years in the wilderness—having already served his time of preparation—was foreign to him. No doubt he was already planning the conquest of the new homeland and visualizing how the government of God would be established.

But something happened after they reached Kadesh-Barnea, that sparse oasis in the northern Sinai that was within literal sight of the Promised Land. Pausing there to regroup his forces, Moses was approached by a delegation from the people who said, "Don't you think it would be a good idea to send spies into the land before we move across the border?"

This was not part of God's original plan. God intended for the people to march forward, under the cloud of His anointing, and possess the land. They had already come more than 400 miles in fifteen months. Surely they had learned by now that God was faithful and could be trusted; that if He asked them to do anything, He would also provide the means to accomplish the task.

But instead of moving out with the morning's light to take the land, the people hesitated. It was the first step toward unbelief. Even though God seemed to permit the episode of sending out spies, the proposal did not originate with Him. Forty years later, when Moses was recounting all that took place, he reminded the people: "Then all of you came to me and said, 'Let us send men ahead to spy out the land for us and bring back a report . . .'" (Deuteronomy 1:22).

As in the case when the Israelites later demanded a king, God gave them what they asked for. Instead of acting in faith and believing God, they acted cautiously, fearing there might be giants in the land, walled cities and obstacles too great for them to overcome. Sure enough, there were. They received what they confessed, and their negative faith brought about their downfall.

Had not God promised them the land? Had He not proved faithful at every turn of their journey? Could they not trust His decision to go in at once and possess the land? Had He not said He would fight their battles for them? Why, then, this need to spy out the land? All they had to do was go up and possess the land. The command was simple: "See, the Lord your God has given you the land. Go up and take possession of it as the Lord, the God of your fathers, told you. Do not be afraid; do not be discouraged" (Deuteronomy 1:21).

Faith marches ahead when God speaks. But the Israelites "were not able to enter, because of their unbelief" (Hebrews 3:19).

It was spoken first in the murmur of caution from the people. Moses, unfortunately, listened. Instead of hearing faith, he heard unbelief.

Twelve spies were chosen, one from each tribe. Of these we

know the names of only two—Caleb, who "wholly followed the Lord," and Joshua, the "minister of Moses," whose name Moses had formerly changed from Hoshea (help) to Joshua (Jehovah is help).

The spies left the camp of Israel "at the time of the first ripe grapes"; that is, about the end of July. Skirting the army of the Canaanites who were encamped on the plain to the west of Kadesh, they entered the land and went all the way to the northern boundary of present-day Israel. Returning south, they passed through Hebron and the Valley of Eschol and explored the route that led into the Negev Desert by the western edge of the mountains. In one of these extensive valleys, they cut a gigantic cluster of grapes that was so heavy it took two men to carry it, slung on a staff over their shoulders. They also gathered pomegranates and figs and, after forty days' absence, reappeared in the camp of the Israelites at Kadesh-Barnea.

Despite their safe return, and the huge bounty they brought with them, only Joshua and Caleb gave a good report. The majority of the spies were negative. "[The land] does flow with milk and honey! Here is its fruit. But the people who live there are powerful, and the cities are fortified and very large. We even saw descendants of Anak [giants] there" (Numbers 13:27-28).

Caleb raised his voice. "We should go up and take possession of the land, for we can certainly do it."

But the other spies argued. "We can't attack those people; they are stronger than we are." Throughout the evening they went through the camp, poisoning the minds of the people, spreading fear and unbelief.

"The land we explored devours those living in it. . . ."

"All the people are of great size. . . ."

"We saw giants there. . . ."

"We seemed like grasshoppers in our own eyes, and we looked the same to them" (cf. Numbers 13:30-33).

People always love to hear a negative report, for the human heart loves to be deceived, loves to rebel against God. It is the nature of man to be fearful and to disobey God. Thus, when some voice of seeming authority speaks, or writes, the human heart listens.

The ten spies looked at the obstacles through the eyes of grasshoppers, but Joshua and Caleb looked at the difficulties through the eyes of God. The people, however, sided with the negative report. The obstacles were too many, the menaces too great. But in their decision, they made a fatal mistake. Unbelief never sees beyond the difficulties. It is always looking at walled cities and giants rather than at God. Faith looks at God; unbelief looks at the obstacles. Although faith never minimizes the dangers or the difficulties, it counts on God to overcome these things. The people, however, looked inward at themselves and saw themselves as grasshoppers. They tried to imagine how they looked through the eyes of the enemy and saw more grasshoppers. They failed to do the one thing Joshua and Caleb did—look at God.

That night, after the spies made their rounds through the camp distributing their poisonous reports, the people began to use worldly logic and reason. They said to one another, in effect: "We've made a mistake. If we stay here, our wives and children will be taken as plunder. It would be better for us to return to Egypt. We should choose a leader and go back to Egypt" (cf. Numbers 14:2-4).

It was the bitterest hour in Moses' life. After delivering them from the horrible slavery of Egypt, leading them supernaturally through the sea, seeing that all their needs were met, introducing them to the God of heaven and earth, interceding for them at Mt. Sinai when God would have destroyed the entire nation—indeed, offering his own life in exchange for theirs—and now bringing them to the very borders of the Promised Land, they had turned upon him.

Once before they had proposed to elect another leader to take them back to Egypt. But that was while Moses was away. This time the proposal was made to his face. It was as though a petition had been drawn up on his own parchment and placed on the pulpit as he stood to preach. The people whom he loved dearer than his own life, whose very existence was due to his intercession, had forgotten all he had done and were now declaring him an unfaithful leader. If he would not go with them back to Egypt, they would leave him alone in the desert with that small group who felt the same way he did.

The rejection was too much for Moses. He and Aaron, his

brother, fell on their faces before the entire assembly, too stunned to talk. Only Joshua and Caleb, still filled with faith and confidence, were able to speak. In anguish they tore their clothes and cried out, "Do not rebel against the Lord. Do not be afraid of the land. It will not devour us, we will devour it. The Lord is with us. Do not be afraid" (cf Numbers 14:9).

Their resistance only made the people angrier. They picked up stones, prepared to rush the four men and stone them to death, when suddenly a tremendous light appeared over the tabernacle. God, whose presence had been only a shadow in the cloud over the camp, suddenly appeared visibly in a brilliant burst of His *shekinah* glory. The people were paralyzed over the appearance of Jehovah as His angry voice rumbled from the midst of the light of His glory: "How long will these people treat me with contempt? How long will they refuse to believe in me, in spite of all the miraculous signs I have performed among them?" (Numbers 14:11).

Then, speaking directly to Moses in a voice loud enough for the entire nation to hear, God said He was going to wipe them all out with a plague. He was going to destroy them, every last one of them, and start again with only Moses, Joshua and Caleb and their families.

There are certain times in every man's life when he makes decisions that change the entire course of his destiny. These are "hinge moments" on which swings the future. This was such a time in the life of Moses. God was offering him the inheritance He had promised earlier to Abraham. No longer would Moses have to contend with the fainthearted, the unfaithful, the grumblers, the unbelievers. In a single moment God would wipe out the entire nation of unbelievers and start afresh with Moses and those faithful men who stood with him.

"Accept it," said the spirit of self. "You've gone the second mile. You've turned the other cheek. This opportunity will never come again. Take your rest and enjoy all that is due you."

"No," said Moses' nobler self. "At stake is far more than my own self. As much as I yearn to rest, to no longer have to fight with these squabbling people, to become a second Abraham, I cannot do it. I have made vows to these people, and even if they do not want my love, I have no choice but to love them. If they cannot inherit the land, then I cannot do it either. Such is the price of covenant love."

Just ahead, only a few miles to the north, were the mountains of the Promised Land—a land flowing with milk and honey. It was all his, with God's blessing. He was within a day's march of paradise. It was the fruition of his life. All he had to do was turn his back on those who were refusing his love and move ahead. He glanced up at the mob surrounding him, some still holding the stones they would have used to kill him. There they were, standing like marble statues, immobilized by the mighty presence of the glory of God, their expressions frozen on their faces, unable to speak or move.

Were they worth giving up all he had earned over these forty years in the wilderness? Were they worth dying for? Across the years perhaps there echoed a word that would one day redeem not just the nation of Israel but the entire earth: "But God demonstrates his own love for us in this: While we were yet sinners, Christ died for us" (Romans 5:8).

"I cannot accept the offer," Moses whispered into the dust where he lay on his face before God. "I cannot go over and possess the land because they cannot go with me."

He knew, the moment he uttered the statement, what God's verdict would be: "Turn back tomorrow and set out toward the desert." In his spirit he knew his decision would mean he would never see the Promised Land. But he had no choice, if he were to remain true to his character. He could not take the rest he longed for at the expense of the people to whom he had committed himself, even though they had disowned him. So he turned away from the open gate to paradise and chose to suffer with the people in their affliction, rather than enjoy the pleasures of Canaan without them. It was a rugged path he chose to walk, a path that would mean another forty years in the wilderness and a lonely death on Mt. Nebo, still just out of reach of the Promised Land. But it was a decision that saved the nation of Israel and softened God's heart so that despite His heavy judgment, a remnant was saved to go in at a later time to take what God had promised.

In the last stanza of "The Road Not Taken," Robert Frost

poetically captures this human experience common to many
of us walking through the wilderness:

> I shall be telling this with a sigh
> Somewhere ages and ages hence:
> Two roads diverged in a wood, and I—
> I took the one less traveled by,
> and that has made all the difference.

So Moses chose the road of covenant love, the lonely road.
In doing so he chose the road that God's Son, many years later,
would walk also—a road that, despite the pain of having to see
His servant suffer in behalf of His people, brought immense
pleasure to God.

God's judgment of Israel was devastating. "I have forgiven
them, as you asked," He told Moses. "Nevertheless, as surely
as I live and as surely as the glory of the Lord fills the whole
earth, not one of the men who saw my glory and the miraculous signs I performed in Egypt and in the desert but who
disobeyed me and tested me ten times—not one of them will
ever see the land I promised on oath to their forefathers. No
one who has treated me with contempt will ever see it. . . . In
this desert your bodies will fall—every one of you twenty
years old or more. . . . As for your children that you said
would be taken as plunder, I will bring them in to enjoy the
land you have rejected. . . . For forty years—one year for each
of the forty days you explored the land—you will suffer for
your sins and know what it is like to have me against you"
(Numbers 14:20-23, 29-34).

The inheritance was lost. What was theirs yesterday was
today taken away, all because of their unbelief, their unwilling-
ness to trust God.

Then the most amazing thing took place. The Israelites, in
an incredible bit of twisted spirituality, reasoned that the way
to undo their fate was to do the opposite of what they had
done the day before. If God was going to punish them (already the ten faithless spies who had spread their poison
report through the camp had died overnight of a horrible
disease for not possessing the land), then surely the way to

gain God's favor was to reverse their decision and set out the next morning to take the land.

Vainly Moses tried to stop them. He pointed out that God's decision was final. Not only that, the Ark of the Covenant would not be going with them; it would stay with him. But the people reasoned that all they had to do to reverse God's decision was to reverse their actions of the day before. They failed to understand what Job said sometime later: God requires repentance not only of what we have done, but of who we are. In this case, their sin against God was not their failure to possess the land. Their sin lay in rebellion against God and against God's leader—Moses. By their determination to go up the next day to possess the land, they were simply exhibiting how deep their sin was, for again they were refusing to submit to God's will and once again choosing another captain to lead them.

The wrong of rebellion and unbelief is not righted by attempting the exact opposite. It is still the same spirit which prompted the one that influences the other. Obedience that is not of simple faith is of self-confidence and therefore merely another kind of unbelief. It is not jutted-jaw determination that conquers the enemy; it is the presence of the Lord.

"Do not go up, because the Lord is not with you," Moses warned them. "Because you have turned away from the Lord, he will not be with you and you will fall by the sword" (Numbers 14:42-43).

But they did not heed Moses and added the sin of presumption to their disobedience. They presumed to go into battle without the presence of the Lord, when they should have been content to bow their knee, take their medicine, and give humble thanks that God even spared their lives. The result was disastrous. Moses recounted the episode in Deuteronomy 1:43-44: "In your arrogance you marched up into the hill country. The Amorites who lived in those hills came out against you; they chased you like a swarm of bees and beat you down from Seir all the way to Hormah."

As a result of his decision to remain with his people, a decision of covenant love, Moses spent another forty years in the wilderness. But unselfishness always brings its own reward—both on the person and on those he chooses to bless.

Although Moses never became a second Abraham, no man in history so typified the Son of God as this old leader—"Just as the Son of Man did not come to be served, but to serve, and to give his life as a ransom for many" (Matthew 20:28).

At the end of his second forty years, the Lord spoke again to Moses. "You have made your way around this hill country long enough; now turn north" (Deuteronomy 2:3). Even then the way was tough. They had to retrace their steps south all the way to Elat to escape war with the king of Edom. Then there were battles with the Amorites as they came north through what is now the nation of Jordan. There was an encounter with Balak, king of Moab, and a strange experience with a prophet named Balaam. There were final battles with warring tribes from Transjordan; but by that time the new generation of young Israelis had become an efficient, disciplined army. No longer were they a bunch of straggling, grumbling, ragtag slaves. They were, under Joshua, a fearsome military machine, ready to capture the walled cities of Canaan.

Moses gave his young charges final instructions. "When you cross the Jordan into Canaan, drive out all the inhabitants of the land before you. Destroy all their carved images. . . . Take possession of the land and settle in it. . . . Distribute it according to your ancestral tribes" (Numbers 33:51-54). He then appointed one leader for each tribe, designated the boundaries of the new land, and turned his back on the Promised Land.

It is not Mt. Sinai, with its rumblings and thunders, that frightens us. It is the silence and loneliness of Mt. Nebo—the fear of being left behind. That is the reason we build around ourselves elaborate structures, why we title ourselves with names of importance and standing, why we rush to join organizations. It is bad enough to be forced into a desert where the sun bleaches, where the hot wind dries, where the burning sand purges us of all our old ways; but to be left alone, to be left behind, is more than we can stand.

Yet all roads home lead through the wilderness. Here God allows the circumstances to strip us of all our nice things, to reduce us to primitive states. Here we discover the meaninglessness of material possessions and make preparation for the final day when our bodies, which we hold so precious, shall be reduced to ashes that the spirit may be liberated to glory.

As the Israelites, their wilderness lessons learned, moved toward the east bank of the Jordan, Moses slowly climbed nearby Mt. Nebo, which gave him an overview of the entire western scene from the Dead Sea to the Mediterranean. Beyond Jordan lay the lush, green Jericho valley close by the sparkling waters of the Dead Sea. High above Jericho, catching the rays of the setting sun, were the golden hills where one day David would build a new Tabernacle, where one day a cross would be raised, where one day the King of Glory would appear.

He stood there alone, his white beard blowing in the gentle wind, the gnarled and scarred rod of God in his hand. He had been left behind, this old man, as the new generation moved forward to possess the land. Aaron and Miriam had been buried in the wilderness. Zipporah was buried beside them. His sons had taken their place in the emerging nation. He stood alone—with God.

To some the scene is sad, but I prefer to believe Moses had transcended the need to occupy Canaan. It was no longer important, this world of rocks and sand. His long walk with God since that time he whispered his vow of covenant love had convinced him the things of this earth were nothing compared to what is most permanent and satisfying. True rest, he had learned, is never found in material things—even in a land of promise—but only in an abiding relationship with the heavenly Father.

I believe Moses was able to look ahead across the years, and see that the tiny strip of land far below, framed by the Jordan on the east, the sea on the west and the Sinai to the south, would always be a place of war and conflict. The descendants of Abraham, divided into factions, would continue their battle for possession of the land. But for Moses, the land was no longer important. The disappointment of Kadesh-Barnea was far behind. He would let those willing to fight for an earthly home go across Jordan. But he would stay behind, for he had found something far more satisfying than a land of promise.

After eighty years in the wilderness, he no longer needed an earthly house; his heart was content with the courts of God.

So out of the disappointments of Kadesh-Barnea emerged a man with another vision, laying hold of that which the moth of change and the rust of time could not destroy or corrupt. And on Nebo's lofty peak, as far below the new breed of Israelis moved in to possess the land, the old warrior turned his back and, with the arm of God around his shoulder, entered into the joy of his Lord.

XX

Spiritual Setbacks

*[Elijah] traveled forty days and forty nights until he reached
Horeb, the mountain of God. There he went into a cave and spent
the night.*

(I Kings 19:8-9)

More than halfway up Mt. Sinai there is a large green
hollow at the very center of the mountain. The Bedouin call
such a high mountain hollow a *farsh*—a mountain oasis. This
one, majestic in its suddenness to the climber, is known as
Farsh Eliahu, "Elijah's Farsh." From here, for the first time,
the climber can see the actual peak of Jebel Musa—the Mountain of God.

One never encounters the farsh expectedly. Although I
have climbed the mountain many times, I am always surprised by its appearance on the path. There are five paths to
the summit from the bottom of the mountain. All end at the
farsh, and from this point on there is but one trail to the peak.

The first time I climbed Mt. Sinai, I ascended from the back
side, climbing by starlight in the darkness of early morning.
Walking along that narrow canyon in the moments just before
dawn, a flush of red light beginning to filter through the valley
below, suddenly I was walking into a world of deep rose color,
warm and welcoming. Extending above me were the sheer red
granite cliffs on the eastern side of Mt. Sinai.

Where just moments before all was in deep purple shadow,
now the rose hue of dawn reflected off the towering cliff,

filling the deep ravine below with incredible colors that flowed across the saw-toothed ridges like a liquid rainbow. At my feet, the steep precipice fell away almost a thousand feet, straight down to the craggy rocks below. Ahead of me was a narrow cut through the rock—a vertical ravine with high black walls on either side.

I entered and thought of the valley of the shadow of death. Then the warm rose of the dawn filtered into the cut with me. The light intensified as I rounded a bend in the narrow path—so narrow I could reach out with either hand and touch the sides of the canyon. Beneath my feet the coarse sand crunched, and suddenly a deep flush of red and gold suffused everything—the walls, the floor of the canyon, myself. Squeezing through the tiny opening at the other end, I walked into a burst of brilliant gold light as the rays of the dawn sun filled the area before me. There, laid out before my feet, was the farsh—its tall green trees, called cypress trees, standing in cool and refreshing contrast to the brilliant gold light reflecting off the sides of the mountain.

At other times I have come up the front face of the mountain from St. Catherine's Monastery in the valley below. More than 3,200 steps have been hewn from the side of the mountain by zealous and dedicated monks in the early years of the last millennium.

There was a monk in the sixth century by the name of Stephanos, who spent his lifetime building and guarding a stone arch over the path at a spot just before the trail breaks into Farsh Eliahu, halfway to the top. After he finished the gate, he sat beside it in the shade, taking confessions from ascending pilgrims. His task was to discern the purpose of pilgrims who wanted to ascend Mt. Sinai. Those he found spiritually unworthy were sent back down the mountain, for, he felt, only those who were pure of heart could ascend the Mountain of God. Those who were impure, he believed, would be killed by the confrontation. The archway, known as St. Stephen's Gate, is still there—the entrance, so to speak, to the farsh.

There is, in every wilderness, a quiet farsh—a place of life-changing encounter. It is always a serendipity, a marvelous, sudden and unexpected discovery. One moment you are toiling upward, driven by forces you don't understand. The next moment you emerge into a beautiful "place of quiet rest, near to the heart of God." While high above on the isolated peaks the wind howls, in the farsh there is only a gentle breeze, cool shade and still water. Here the pastures are green, the table is set before you, and you find a cup overflowing with the goodness and mercy of God.

It was at this farsh, seated on an overhanging rock that extended over the floor of the eastern valley thousands of feet below, that I began asking that question which plagues all spiritual men. I had spent the night under that huge cypress tree, waking at various times and seeing its awesome silhouette against the starlit sky. Before sunrise, just as the first hues of gray began turning to rose, I had crawled from my sleeping bag, pulled on an extra sweater and climbed up on a rocky overhang where I could see the dawn reflected against the peak of the Mountain of God.

Why, I pondered, do those of us who live in the Promised Land keep finding ourselves back in the wilderness?

Surely, it seems, having once tasted of the blessings of God, there should be no desire, no need, ever to return to wilderness wanderings. Is not our ultimate goal to enter Canaan? Once there, then, why do we continually find ourselves back in the desert—wandering, thirsting, discouraged and sometimes without hope?

As gradually as the dawning of the sun that October morning, I began to fathom the answers to these perplexing questions.

Part of the confusion may stem from our misunderstanding of the nature of the Promised Land. The wilderness, in many aspects, was an easier place to live than the Promised Land. Granted, it was a place of wandering, a place of hard teaching, a place of painful purification. But it was also a place of provision and protection. There was free food every morning. There was protection from the vipers. God was visible throughout the day and night in the pillar of cloud and the pillar of fire. There was never any doubt about which direction to move. Concerning their entire forty-year trek, God reminded the Israelites, "Your clothes did not wear out, nor did the sandals on your feet" (Deuteronomy 29:5).

Yet when the wilderness training was over and the people of God entered the Promised Land, everything changed.

What was it that was actually promised in this Promised Land? It was "a land with large, flourishing cities you did not build, houses filled with all kinds of good things you did not provide, wells you did not dig, and vineyards and olive groves you did not plant . . ." (Deuteronomy 6:10-11).

Nothing was handed them on a silver platter, however. While God did promise Joshua, who led the Israelites across the Jordan River into Canaan, "I will give you every place where you set your foot . . . I will never leave you nor forsake you," He was not talking about nirvana, which is the popular view of what the Promised Land should be. Nirvana is a Buddhist concept of a state of perfect blessedness achieved by the extinction of individuality, by the extinction of all desires and passions and by the absorption of the soul into the supreme spirit. Nirvana is eternal blah-ness.

God's plan for His people in the Promised Land is far greater than the extinction of all desires. In the Promised Land, desire and passion are heightened. Granted, that necessitates self-control. But God never takes away our desires and passions. Instead, He heightens them. Then He focuses them to be used and enjoyed inside the framework He has designed. Sexual pleasure is designed for culmination in marriage. The desire and consumption of fine food and wine is to be enjoyed inside the framework of temperance and self-control. In the wilderness every step was directed by the finger of God; but in the Promised Land, while men and women are free from the bondage of legalistic law, they are now governed by laws written on the heart. Such laws, I might add, demand far more discipline than those chiseled in stone.

Even though God promised Joshua all the land where he set his foot, it was still up to the people actually to "possess" the land. That was accomplished not by sitting and waiting, but by aggressive military campaigns. In the Promised Land the opposition was fierce. The cities (which had been promised the Israelites) were walled and occupied by giants. The fields (which had been prepared) not only had to be tilled, planted, weeded and harvested, but the farmers constantly had to fight off invading bands of marauders who waited until the crops were ready and then swept down to plunder and steal.

It is not easy, living in the Promised Land. In fact, to some degree it is simpler and easier to live in the wilderness—an argument brought up many times by those who wanted to return to the bondage of Egypt, and again by those who voted at Kadesh-Barnea not to go in and occupy the land.

Thus the question "Why do the people of God constantly find themselves returning to the wilderness?" needs to be examined closely. Perhaps the place of adversity is not the wilderness at all. Perhaps one has grown so accustomed to God's provision for wilderness people, he does not recognize that the hardships being encountered are unique to those who live in the Promised Land.

Despair, temptation, discouragement, conflict—these are not just wilderness situations. They are situations faced by those in the Promised Land as well. Training and growth continue even after we enter the Promised Land—and perhaps in heaven as well. Only in the Far Eastern concept of nirvana do conflicts cease and the individual is absorbed into the whole. The promise of Jehovah through His Son Jesus Christ is much, much greater than the promise of Buddha.

In God's Promised Land, even though there is conflict and pain, struggle and despair, it is for the purpose of growth and change. Instead of absorbing our spirits into His Spirit, He heightens our individuality by placing His Spirit within each of us. Thus we begin to experience the ultimate of being—individuality. With individuality comes the anxiety of having to make decisions and the pain of suffering the consequence of wrong decisions. God never intended man to become senseless. Rather, He intends us to use all our senses, to become in the highest degree sensual people. Such is the promise of the Promised Land.

Since there are moments when even Promised Land people flee (or are thrust back) into the wilderness, let's look at some examples.

The apostle John, after outliving all the rest of the original apostles who were martyred, spent the last years of his life exiled in the wilderness, alone on the isle of Patmos. What a horrible place to end his life on earth for the one whom Jesus loved! Yet here John received the final revelation of God. In his private wilderness he met God anew. Here he saw a "new heaven and a new earth . . . the Holy City, the new Jerusalem, coming down out of heaven from God, prepared as a bride beautifully dressed for her husband." Here he heard a voice from the throne of God saying, "Now the dwelling of God is with men, and he will live with them. . . . There will be no more death or mourning or crying or pain, for the old order of things has passed away" (Revelation 21:1-4).

John, in his wilderness, saw as no man has seen, beyond the Promised Land metaphor to Ultimate Reality. He saw, not shadows on the back of a cave, as the Greek philosopher Plato described, but the Reality of Light streaming from the throne.

The apostle Paul, fresh from his encounter with the living Christ on the road to Damascus and still enjoying the first blush of the walk in the Spirit, was suddenly dismissed from the church. Let down in a basket over the city wall, he was sent into the Arabian desert on a three-year sojourn. There, during those silent years, he was taught by God's Spirit in the heart of a spiritual and physical wilderness.

Yet on his return he was judged by his fellow Christians to be immature and unfit for the ministry. Once again he was forced out of the church. It was the ultimate in rejection for the former Pharisee. His wilderness continued for eleven years, until God spoke to Barnabas and told him to go to Tarsus and fetch Paul to help with the ministry in Antioch. The wilderness was over, but the persecution never ceased, even though Paul was in his "Promised Land."

Jesus, Luke tells us, fresh from His baptism experience in the Jordan River, was "led by the Spirit into the desert." There, for forty days, He fasted and was submitted to great temptations by the devil.

Surely all these men—even the Son of God Himself—must have asked why. Why, after experiencing the taste of the Promised Land, am I once again in the wilderness?

We can only speculate on the answer—for seldom has God revealed the full answer to the question *Why?*

Far more important than *Why?* is the question *What?* That was the question God asked the prophet Elijah following his two-day run into the Negev Desert. Elijah was fresh from his amazing victory at Mt. Carmel where God had answered his prayer and caused even the heathen to cry out, "The Lord, He is God!" Then, hearing the threat of Queen Jezebel to have him publicly executed, Elijah's mood swung from elation to despair. He fled south.

Arriving at Beersheba on the southern border of Israel, he discovered a city filled with idolatrous shrines and a people committed to heathen licentiousness. He knew such a place would not tolerate the presence of Jehovah's prophet, fresh from the execution of the priests of Baal. So, leaving his servant behind, he ran farther south into the Negev, across the wilderness of el Thei until he came to a place of exhaustion.

How does one describe this wilderness place where the prophet Elijah finally dropped, moaning and gasping under a rotem bush? "I have had enough, Lord," he vomited out. "Take my life; I am no better than my ancestors." Then he collapsed under the scrub bush—known characteristically as a broom tree—and fell into an exhausted sleep.

When he awoke, he discovered hot bread and a jar of water—left, perhaps, by some angel. It was then God asked His question—the one that still echoes across the desert to all of us feeling angry or sorry for ourselves in our wilderness situation: "Man of God, what are you doing here?" Frightened, unable to answer, Elijah scrambled from his hiding place and traveled south another forty days on foot until he came to the "mountain of God"—that magnetic place that had drawn Moses from the flocks of Jethro to hear a voice speaking from a burning bush. Now this prophet, coming not from the bondage of Egypt but fresh from having seen the hand of God in the land of promise, began his arduous ascent up the craggy sides of the awesome mountain.

And so Elijah, confused and weary, suddenly crested that point in his climb just above the spot where St. Stephen's Gate now arches over the stone path, and emerged abruptly into the farsh. It was in this spot that the man of God had a life-changing encounter with the God of man.

While the peak of Mt. Sinai is the soul of the mountain, Elijah's Farsh is the heart. Here in this magnificent place, still 1,500 feet below the summit, all the weariness and turmoil of those ascending the mountain disappears. The farsh is closed around with peaks, as though the mountain is purposely protecting its secret from the outside world. It is encountered as one usually encounters God—suddenly. One moment you are arduously toiling, step by agonizing step up the steep ascent of Sinai. Then, suddenly and without warning, you crest at a level point in the rough path and emerge into this beautiful high oasis.

The modern pilgrim who dares ascend Mt. Sinai and stops at this farsh sees before him a tiny white chapel and a stone grotto dug into the side of the mountain. In the middle of the patch of bright green grass is a well, and beside the well stands one of the world's most famous trees. It is a gigantic evergreen, known as a cypress tree. Its grace and height demand instant attention. The tree seems to have grown in spurts across the years. Each time it seems to have put forth more greenery. The trunk emerges from the green clusters, bare and devoid of life, to the next level where foliage again appears. It is as though there are three trees in one—a trinity of trees, so to speak. Next to it is a smaller cypress tree, surrounded by other smaller cypress trees and a still smaller crabapple tree.

The mountains rise up steeply in all directions. Although hermits once lived here, the area is now grazed daily by a flock of black goats herded by a sturdy Bedouin girl shepherd.

That chilly October morning, seated high on my rocky promontory overlooking both the eastern valley thousands of feet below as well as the farsh, I watched my companions crawl from their sleeping bags to begin the day. The three camels, which had carried our camping gear up the steep trail, had risen from their odd squatting positions where they spent the night and were grazing on the patches of green grass behind a low stone wall.

How deeply I am attracted to this quiet, awesome place, I thought. The words of Kebel's description came to mind:

> On Horeb, with Elijah let us lie,
> Where all around, on mountain, sand, and
> sky
> God's chariot-wheels have left distinctest
> trace.

There is a whole new world to be encountered in the farsh. It is a secret garden in the midst of the wilderness, a place of greenery, of smooth rock faces, of chapels and hermit's caves, a place of wonderful memory and rich tradition where cool water springs forth, green grass covers the harsh brown of the high desert floor, and from which point one can see the holiest of places—the summit of the Mountain of God.

For some the farsh is but a place of rest and refreshment before they resume the arduous climb to the peak. For others, like Elijah, it is a place where one can receive profound revelation and a quiet word to return to the land of promise. In the farsh God speaks not in the wind, earthquake and fire that echoes from the summit, but in the still, small voice of the heart.

In that place you are able to pause and realize that the wilderness is not always harsh and cruel. It can be soothing, a place of retreat and peaceful rest apart from the turmoil of those pushing upward in their own strength.

There is an ancient Bedouin legend: "Behind the el Thei is the desert of the lost." El Thei is that vast desert of powdery dunes that stretches along the northern half of the peninsula. The desert people, the nomadic Bedouin, fear it as a place of desolation. They prefer the rugged mountains and deep wadis of the southern Sinai.

Elijah had crossed el Thei on his flight to the Mountain of God. Now, resting in the farsh, he heard God telling him to return. The true wanderers, those who dwell in the wilderness, would never respond to such a voice. They fear el Thei and the desert of the lost. But to a man like Elijah, who had left the land of promise on his personal pilgrimage into the wilderness, the command to return to Canaan was welcome. Unlike the Bedouin who have no direction, no goal, who still simply wander through the wilderness, Elijah knew what lay beyond el Thei—not a desert of the lost but the land of promise. Refreshed and strengthened by his encounter with God, he returned once again to the conflict, walking strong in the strength of the Lord.

So we return to the original question God asked of Elijah: "Man of God, what are you doing here?"

God did not ask, "Why are you in the wilderness?" Indeed,

that is the question man asks so unceasingly of God. Rather, God asked, "Now that you are here, what are you going to do about it?"

It is this question that still confronts all of us who flee or are forced back into the wilderness from the safety of our Promised Land. Exhausted and weary, we finally get quiet enough in our flight to rest at the farsh. Again the question sounds: What are you doing when things go against you, when the Jezebels of this world threaten to destroy you? What are you doing when there is no money in your house; when a loved one dies; when the doctor says, "No hope"; when some trusted friend lets you down?

It is at this time that the man of God, the woman of God, should pause to regroup. Here are a few suggestions—things to do while resting at the farsh.

1. *Remember your past.* The farsh is a good place to stop and remember. An old saint once said, "When I grow weary of well-doing, when my faith sags and my spiritual heart faints, I remember. I go back to my former life before I became captive to God. I take a long walk up and down the street of my sinfulness. When I return, I am so full of thanksgiving to the God who saved me, so full of the mercy and grace of God, that my heart is once again singing and my feet dancing with joy."

2. *Reassess your position.* The farsh is a place to take spiritual inventory. It is a time to say with David: "Search me, O God, and know my heart; test me and know my anxious thoughts. See if there is any offensive way in me, and lead me in the way everlasting" (Psalm 139:23-24).

It is at the farsh that one begins to determine exactly who is behind the adversity. Is it God or Satan? The man of God, pausing even in exhaustion, will eventually hear the still, small voice reminding him of the everlasting love of God. He will also realize that when God puts His finger on something wrong in a man's life, it is because He loves him.

King Solomon warned his children: "My son, do not despise the Lord's discipline and do not resent his rebuke, because the Lord disciplines those he loves, as a father the son he delights in" (Proverbs 3:11-12).

On the other hand, Solomon said, "Stern discipline awaits him who leaves the path; he who hates correction will die" (Proverbs 15:10).

James told his readers, many of whom were suffering untold hardships, to "consider it pure joy" when they faced adversity, for they were learning perseverance. That perseverance, he told them, would bring them to spiritual maturity and completeness.

God always first warns His children in private. Only if they do not repent does He apply the rod in public.

3. *Recognize your friends.* How easy it is, when fleeing, to think yourself friendless. Once before Elijah had been alone in the wilderness. That time he was brooding over the sins of the nation at the Brook Kerith in the wilderness east of the Jordan River. While he was there, ravens—wild scavenger birds considered a national nuisance—brought him both bread and meat.

Now, again, we find Elijah exhausted in the desert. This time, however, he is running away. Fear controls him, and he is fleeing in panic.

Alone, fearful, desperate for help, he succumbs under a broom tree. While he is sleeping, someone stops by with a jug of water. Building a small fire of camel dung, this unknown "angel" bakes pita bread and leaves it for the prophet that he may eat and drink when he awakes.

God has His servants everywhere—in the most unlikely forms.

The wilderness is always a place of loneliness, while the Promised Land is a place of fellowship. The New Testament describes the church as a *koinonia*, a community, a fellowship. This same church is described as a family, with brothers and sisters.

That is why God never intends for His servants to remain in the wilderness. Even the lovely farsh is but a place to pause and be refreshed in order to return to the rigors and struggle of the Promised Land. In the farsh, God gently reminded Elijah he was part of a great family—with 7,000 brothers and sisters who had not bowed the knee to Baal.

The strategy of the devil is to keep people separated from

one another in a hell of isolation and independence, relating their lives to each other only superficially. While we are called on by God to sharpen our individualism, that is never to be done independently from other members of the family of God.

That's what the Promised Land is all about—individuals bound together. But it often takes a trip back into the wilderness in order to appreciate all that means.

In the third century Cyprian, who later became Bishop of Carthage and was martyred for his faith, wrote a letter from his own spiritual farsh. It was addressed to his old friend Donatus, explaining what had happened to him.

> This seems a cheerful world, Donatus, when I view it from this fair garden, under the shadow of these vines. But if I climbed to some great mountain and looked out over the wide lands, you know very well what I would see: brigands on the high roads; pirates on the seas; in the amphitheatres men murdered to please the applauding crowds; under all roofs misery and selfishness. It is really a bad world, Donatus, an incredibly bad world.
>
> Yet, in the midst of it, I have found a quiet and holy people. They have discovered a joy which is a thousand times better than any pleasure of this sinful life. They are despised and persecuted, but they care not. They have overcome the world. These people, Donatus, are the Christians, and I am one of them.

In every wilderness there is a farsh—a quiet place where one may hear God, receive fresh revelation, be refreshed and strengthened in order to return to the work in the Promised Land. It is there the true man of God, the true woman of God, is able to pray with the old French mystic: "Make me thy captive, Lord; then I shall be free."

Epilogue

On all my research trips into the Sinai, traveling each time with a small group of men, the last night in the desert has always been the most significant. It would be this time, usually camped in the sandstone regions north and east of Mt. Sinai, that we would sit around a campfire and reminisce over the events of our time together, expressing our camaraderie and experiencing the sadness that always comes when a beautiful event is ending.

It was on one of those last nights that the meaning of the "Law" and the nature of the "Law-giver"—which is what Sinai is all about—became evident to me.

Like the other groups in years past, this particular group of thirteen men had never met one another prior to our gathering in New York to fly to Israel. On that evening, however, nearly three weeks before, we had prayed together in a secluded part of the airport waiting area, asking God to let us, for the next several weeks, become "the church in the Sinai."

None of us fully understood what that meant, but we all sensed it meant we would do more than climb mountains and camp out in the desert. We sensed it would mean entering into a relationship with each other, a relationship of love and honesty. What we did not anticipate was the pain we would experience as we arrived at that place of transparency.

Our two Israeli guides, both tough young soldiers who loved the Sinai, became part of our experiment. Although they were much younger than the men on the trip, they immediately became part of our "church." Interestingly enough, although this group of American business and professional men—doctors, engineers, lawyers and one minister—were all accustomed to giving orders, they all readily submitted to the authority of our Jewish guides.

Early in the trip, as we left Israel to make our way into the Sinai, our guides outlined some basic principles. One of these mandates was: "We don't take anything into the desert and leave it there." That meant all trash, even orange peelings, would be collected and returned to Israel. The Jews were determined to leave the desert in its original, unspoiled state.

The other mandate was: "We don't take anything out of the desert which we find there."

This was hard on several of the men who had come with anticipation of adding to their rock collections. As an exception to this rule, the guides agreed that if we checked with them first they might allow us to remove a piece of turquoise or perhaps one of the beautiful crystals that are sometimes found in the vicinity of St. Catherine's Monastery.

The next-to-last night we camped on the southern seashore along the Gulf of Aqaba near the Jewish community of Ofira. We spent the night on the beach. That evening, as the tide ebbed, several of us walked out on top of the coral reef that was now exposed. We had our flashlights, examining the beautiful shells and creatures left in the little tidal pools.

When we returned to our camp to make ready for bed, the Methodist minister who was in our group pulled me aside. "I feel ill," he said, holding his chest. "Before we go to sleep would you gather the 'church' and pray for me?"

We did just that. I asked the minister to sit on a rock in the middle of a small circle while the other men stood around touching him gently with their hands in a time of prayer. Our two Israeli guides, although they did not participate, watched respectfully from a distance as the church met in prayer.

The next night was our last night in the Sinai. Instead of going inland we had driven north along the coast to camp again on the beach, this time near Nuweiba. Again we built a campfire on the beach. This time we sat and shared all the things we had experienced together—not knowing that the experience we were about to have would give new meaning to our spiritual understanding of life and relationships.

As we finished our time of sharing and were separating to go to our sleeping bags, which were spread up and down the beach, the minister again pulled me aside. "My sickness is much worse," he said.

I looked at him. He was in obvious pain. "Have you talked to our doctor?" I asked.

"I don't need a doctor. I need a priest."

"I don't understand," I replied.

"I am sick because I have sinned. Our guide told us not to take anything out of the desert. Last night on the beach I found a beautiful seashell—a big one the size of a man's head. I stuffed it into my duffle bag. The moment I did I began having chest pains. They have gotten much worse, and I'm afraid I'll die here in the desert if I do not make things right with God."

"Why don't you just throw the shell back into the sea?"

"That won't do any good. I deliberately broke one of the laws. I've got to go to our guide and confess. I want you to go with me."

I dreaded the confrontation. We had been hoping to impress our guides by our Christian character; now the minister in our group had sinned and needed to make confession. I kept remembering the story of Joshua and Achan in the Bible. God had told the troops of Joshua that when they conquered the city of Jericho they were not to take any loot. But a man by the name of Achan had disobeyed God. He had stolen gold and silver items from the captured city. As a result, the next time the Israelites went into battle at Ai, they were defeated. Joshua discovered Achan's sin and had him stoned to death. Only then were the Israelites victorious in battle.

I went with the minister while he talked to the guide who was in charge. He also handed over the purloined seashell—a beautiful pronged shell of many colors. The guide was polite, and even listened to the minister's story of Joshua and Achan, although I suspected he didn't know who either man was. When it was all over the muscular young man, sitting on the stump of a palm tree near the back of our truck, said, "It seems to me you need to tell this story to your church."

I looked at the minister. He swallowed hard but nodded in agreement.

A few minutes later I had rounded up the men and we were back at the campfire.

I related all that had happened. Then I pointed to the minister who was sitting, head down, as part of the circle of men around the fire. "What should the church do with a man like this? He is a thief who has broken covenant with the church. He has been rebellious against authority. He has lied and tried to get away with his sin. Now, however, he has come and confessed. What should the church do with him?"

No one spoke. As I looked around the ring of men—desert comrades seated on the sand with the reflection of the small campfire flickering on their faces—I saw every man had his head bowed in shame.

"Since no one has an answer, I'll ask our Jewish guide what he thinks we should do with this thief who has broken the command of the most high God."

I turned to our two guides and singled out the one to whom the minister had confessed. "Amir, what should the church do with this thief who has stolen this seashell?"

Sensing the seriousness of the situation, the young Israeli stood to his feet. "It seems you have several options. For one, you could ask him to do penance."

"That is the Catholic position," I said.

"Or you could cast him out of the camp."

"That is the evangelical position."

"But it seems you can't do anything unless you know his heart. Did he really mean it when he repented and gave the shell back?"

I saw all the heads in the group come up from their chin-to-chest position. They began to nod in agreement. Yes, if the law is not judged by the condition of the heart, then it is nothing more than a rule to be kept rather than a guide to be lived.

"That settles it," I said. "We all agree our brother has genuinely repented. He says the pains in his chest have disappeared—indicating God's touch on his life. That closes the matter."

"Not quite." It was the medical doctor in our group who had spoken.

"What do you mean?"

"Well, I've got a seashell in my bag also."

Another man raised his hand sheepishly. "I don't have any seashells, but I have a bunch of rocks I've been collecting."

We went around the circle of men. Everyone in the group had stolen something out of the desert. They had squirreled the rocks and shells away in their bags, stuffed them into their extra shoes with the hope of smuggling them past our guides and taking them back home as souvenirs. The entire church was a den of thieves.

As we discussed it we found there was some confusion about the guidelines. One of the guides had said it was all right to take a few small stones or shells. The other had said flatly, "Take nothing unless you check with me." The church had received conflicting direction from two authorities. The men were not thieves. They just didn't understand the law.

I couldn't help but smile. On the final night of our pilgrimage, the Church of the Sinai had been born.

Then another interesting thing happened: human nature took over. Instead of dealing with what our Jewish guide had called "the matter of the heart," someone said, "Why don't we bring all the shells and rocks out and lay them here on the sand? Then we can measure them. We'll keep the little ones and leave the big ones in the desert."

The other men agreed enthusiastically. "That will settle the matter," one man, an attorney, said. "We can tell what is right and wrong by the size of the shells."

The shift of spiritual direction was terrifying. One moment we were a body of men, confused over direction but willing to judge only on the condition of a man's heart; the next we were a group of legalists ready to draw up rules and regulations and judge sin by the size of the seashell.

"What is a big shell and what is a little shell?" I asked.

The men looked at me. They hadn't thought of that. We had no absolute standard; and size, like sin, is often relative.

"We'll have to draw a line someplace," one of the men said. "Why don't we say anything over one inch in diameter is to be left behind?"

I looked over at our two Jewish guides. They were grinning. It was Amir who finally spoke, laughing: "Now you sound like my ancestors. It's not enough for God to give a law that speaks to the heart; you have to write a Talmud to explain the law. Why don't you go all the way and set up a Sanhedrin to decide which shells are big and which are little?"

Even though the campfire was dying, it was easy to see that every man's face had turned red. What had started as a matter of the heart had quickly become legalistic and mechanical. Rather than looking on the inward parts, we were looking on the size of the seashells. We finally decided the matter was too weighty for us to determine. By common consent we resolved that each man would have to decide for himself, and leave the final judgment in the hands of God.

I suspect if mankind is going to survive, it will not be because we have gotten rid of the fellows who have stolen the big shells while keeping the fellows who have stolen only little shells. Nor are we going to survive by expanding on God's law (which is written on the hearts of His children) and setting up even more rules of things we can and cannot do.

We will not survive because we believe the same way, nor because we behave the same way. We will survive as God's people only as we are filled with God's Spirit, looking upon each man's heart as God looks.

That is the lesson of the wilderness.

That is the purpose of the law.

That is the heart of God.

Classics from Arthur Wallis

by Arthur Wallis

The complete text of three bestselling titles from
Arthur Wallis.

- *Living God's Way* provides a course specially
  designed to disciple new Christians. With a clear
  and straightforward approach it covers the Bible's
  basic teaching so that the new Christian can gain a
  thorough and practical understanding of Christian
  commitment.

- *Going on God's Way* is designed to help you ensure
  that spiritual growth is a reality in your life and
  your church. Practical, relevant and biblical, it is
  ideal for individual or group use.

- *Into Battle* shows how victory over the enemy can
  become an increasing reality in every part of our
  lives – starting with repentance from sin, faith in
  the saving power of God and then baptism in water
  and the Holy Spirit.

K **Kingsway Publications**

Classics On Prayer

The complete text of three bestselling titles on Prayer.

- *Learning the Joy of Prayer* At a crucial stage in Larry Lea's life, when he felt discouraged, he was drawn again to that most familiar of prayers, 'the Lord's Prayer'. So began an exciting journey of discovery that turned his prayer life from drudgery to delight.

- *Pray in the Spirit* Arthur Wallis concentrates on the ministry of the Holy Spirit in relation to prayer, and investigates the full meaning of the apostle's injunction to 'pray in the Spirit'.

- *Praying Together* This personal and practical manual will spur you on to action, so that prayer with your partner becomes a living reality, not a hopeless ideal.

K
Kingsway Publications